# FODOR'S
# CIVIL WAR
# SITES

**FODOR'S MODERN GUIDES**

are compiled, researched, and edited by an
international team of travel writers, field
correspondents, and editors. The series was founded
by Eugene Fodor.

OFFICES
New York & London

Editor: ROBERT C. FISHER. Area Editors: VICTOR BLOCK, DEAN
BOSWELL, CAROLYN CARTER, BETTY ELLISON, JUSTIN L. FAHERTY,
AL FIEGEL, BERN KEATING, GLORIA HAYES KRAMER, CAROLYN R.
LANGDON, FLORENCE LEMKOWITZ, KAREN LINGO, CHARLES C.
PHILLIPS, JOHN PHILLIPS, PARKE ROUSE JR., KATHERINE D.
WALKER. Editorial Contributors: CASTLEWOOD. Editorial Associate:
LARRY NEVILLE. Drawings: DAVID CANRIGHT, SANDRA LANG. City
Plans and Area Maps: DYNO LOWENSTEIN.

# FODOR'S

# CIVIL WAR SITES

DAVID McKAY COMPANY, INC.
New York

AREA GUIDES:

EUROPE
AUSTRALIA, NEW ZEALAND
   AND THE SOUTH PACIFIC
CANADA
CARIBBEAN AND
   BAHAMAS
CENTRAL AMERICA
EASTERN EUROPE
INDIA AND NEPAL

JAPAN AND KOREA
MEXICO
NORTH AFRICA
PEOPLES REPUBLIC
   OF CHINA
SCANDINAVIA
SOUTH AMERICA
SOUTHEAST ASIA
SOVIET UNION
U.S.A. (1 vol.)

COUNTRY GUIDES

AUSTRIA
BELGIUM AND
   LUXEMBOURG
BERMUDA
BRAZIL
CZECHOSLOVAKIA
EGYPT
FRANCE
GERMANY
GREAT BRITAIN
GREECE
HOLLAND
HUNGARY

IRAN
IRELAND
ISRAEL
ITALY
JORDAN AND THE
   HOLY LAND
MOROCCO
PORTUGAL
SPAIN
SWITZERLAND
TUNISIA
TURKEY
YUGOSLAVIA

BUDGET GUIDES:

EUROPE ON A BUDGET
BUDGET TRAVEL IN AMERICA
BUDGET BRITAIN
BUDGET CARIBBEAN

BUDGET FRANCE
BUDGET GERMANY
BUDGET MEXICO

USA REGIONAL GUIDES:

FAR WEST
HAWAII
MID-ATLANTIC
MIDWEST

NEW ENGLAND
ROCKIES AND PLAINS
SOUTH
SOUTHWEST

USA STATE GUIDES:

CALIFORNIA               FLORIDA                    NEW YORK

USA SPECIAL INTEREST GUIDES:

CIVIL WAR SITES
INDIAN AMERICA
OLD SOUTH
OLD WEST

ONLY-IN-AMERICA
   VACATION GUIDE
OUTDOORS AMERICA
SEASIDE AMERICA
SUNBELT LEISURE GUIDE

SPECIAL INTEREST GUIDES (INTERNATIONAL):

ANIMAL PARKS OF AFRICA          RAILWAYS OF THE WORLD
WORLDWIDE ADVENTURE GUIDE

CITY GUIDES:

LONDON                    PARIS                      PEKING

MANUFACTURED IN THE UNITED STATES OF AMERICA

10 9 8 7 6 5 4 3 2 1

# CONTENTS

## FACTS AT YOUR FINGERTIPS

When to Go 1; What Will It Cost? 2; Planning Your Trip 2; Packing 3; Hints to the Motorist 4; Trailer Tips 5; Dixieland Trail 5; Camping Out 6; Pets 7; Tipping 7; Hotels and Motels 8; Dining Out 10; Hints to Handicapped Travelers 11; Tourist Information 12; Suggested Reading 12
*Map of History of the Civil War* 14

v

## FACTS AT YOUR FINGERTIPS

 **WHEN TO GO.** There really is no "best" time to visit the southeastern part of the U.S. Any time will do, for temperatures rarely drop below the 40s in winter or climb above the mid-80s in summer. Those who are uncomfortable in hot weather, however, may prefer to visit this region between late September and early June. Humidity may be high in the river valleys and in the low-lying areas along the coast; some cities, such as New Orleans, are notorious for combining the disadvantages of both, and in July and August they are truly steamy.

Spring is spectacular in the mid-Atlantic region, with millions of blossoms bursting forth everywhere. Cherry blossoms, azaleas, dogwood, camellias and apple blossoms follow each other through April and May. Summer can be enjoyable if you do as the local people do and slow down. It is in this region that you will first notice a very different pace to life from what you found in the north. The south really begins in Virginia, and you will sense its different rhythm and flavor from Washington onward.

The southwest has wide variations in temperature in all seasons. In general there is plenty of sunshine and low humidity except along the Gulf Coast. Air conditioning is almost universal throughout the hotter parts of the region. The biggest tourist season is late December through April, with February and March the peak months. Average temperatures in the winter months range from the mid-50s in the south to the 40s in the north. Summer highs are around 90 in the north to around 100 in the south (in June, July and August). However, anywhere away from the coastal plains the summer nights can be chilly.

**WHAT WILL IT COST?** A couple can travel in the United States for about $61 a day (not counting gasoline or other transportation costs), as shown by the table below.

Off-season travel is one way to cut expenses (for example, Miami Beach and other beach resorts frequently have accommodations available in summer for one-third the winter costs). Bargain accommodations can be found in most southern towns at family-style YMCAs and YWCAs, and there are still some of the old-style tourist homes in the South. Some 250 colleges in 41 states also offer dormitory rooms to tourists at rates of $2–$10 per night, with meals 60¢–$3.50 in the school cafeteria or coffee shop. You can get a list of these schools by writing to Teachers Travel Service, P.O. Box 7006, Berkeley, Cal. 94707, and enclosing $3.

Another way to cut down on the cost of your trip, and often increase the fun, is to look for resorts which haven't been "discovered" yet—prices are bound to be lower and facilities much less crowded.

Typical Expenses for Two

| | | |
|---|---:|---|
| Room at *moderate* hotel or motel | $25.00 | (plus tax) |
| Breakfast (including tip) | 5.00 | |
| Lunch at *Inexpensive* restaurant (including tip) | 5.00 | |
| Dinner and tip at *moderate* restaurant | 15.00 | |
| Sightseeing bus tour | 6.00 | |
| An evening drink | 3.00 | |
| Admission to museum or historic site | 2.00 | |
| | $61.00 | |

If you are budgeting your trip, don't forget to set aside a realistic amount for the possible rental of sports equipment (perhaps including a boat or canoe), entrance fees to amusement and historical sites, etc. Allow for tolls for bridges and super-highways (this can be a major item), extra film for cameras, and souvenirs.

After lodging, your next biggest expense will be food, and here you can make very substantial economies if you are willing to get along with only one meal a day (or less) in a restaurant. Plan to eat simply, and to picnic. It will save you time and money, and it will help you to enjoy your trip more. That beautiful scenery does not have to whiz by at 55 miles per hour. Many states have picnic and rest areas, often well-equipped and in scenic spots, even on highways and thruways, so finding a pleasant place to stop is usually not difficult. Before you leave home put together a picnic kit.

Sturdy plastic plates and cups are cheaper in the long run than throw-away paper ones; and the same goes for permanent metal flatware rather than the throw-away plastic kind. Pack a small electric pot and two thermoses, one for water and one for milk, tea, or coffee. In other words, one hot, and one cold. If you go by car, take along a small cooler. Bread, milk, cold cereal, jam, tea or instant coffee, fresh vegetables that need no cooking (such as lettuce, cucumbers, carrots, tomatoes, and mushrooms), cold cuts, cheese, nuts, raisins, eggs (hard boil them in the electric pot in your room the night before)—with only things like these you can eat conveniently, cheaply, and well.

**PLANNING YOUR TRIP.** When your itinerary is set and you know where and when you'll be traveling in the South, hotel reservations and ticket reservations, if you're not driving, must be attended to. A travel agent can be enormously helpful if you don't want to bother with these details yourself. His services, incidentally, won't cost you anything—except for any additional expenses such as telegrams, telephone calls, etc.—since his fee is paid by the hotel or carrier he books for you. And if you prefer to keep your own planning to a minimum by taking your vacation on a package tour, a travel agent will be able to explain fully all conditions, as well as "travel now, pay later" possibilities.

If you're driving, let the whole family in on the fun of discussing and mapping your route, or ask your automobile club to do this for you—and if you aren't a member of one, this is the time to join. Not only can the club help with routings, it can be invaluable in providing emergency service on the road. If you're planning your own route, be sure to get up-to-date road maps. (New highways and thruways are appearing and old ones being extended at an unbelievably rapid rate!) Most states will be happy to furnish current road maps which show points of interest such as historical sites, state and national parks, etc. Write the Tourist Information Department, State Capitol Building, in the capital city of each state you plan to visit. City chambers of commerce are additional sources of information.

Don't neglect at-home plans while you're away. Pets can be boarded out; newspaper and milk deliveries suspended; mail held temporarily by the post office or delivered to a neighbor; and police and fire departments notified when you are leaving and when you expect to return. And it's a good idea to arrange for your lawn to be mowed regularly while you're away. A further safeguard is to give a friend or neighbor your itinerary, car license number and a key to your home in case of an emergency while you're away.

An important aspect of trip planning is insurance, and before leaving you should be sure that all policies—auto, fire and homeowner's—are up to date. Some companies also have trip policies, and this can be an excellent investment if you meet with misfortune on the road. And, of course, the bulk of your funds for the trip itself should be converted to traveler's checks, since this is the safest way to carry money.

Don't forget to include in your budget a realistic amount for such things as rental of sports equipment, entrance fees, tolls for bridges and superhighways, extra film and souvenirs.

A delightful way to cut expenses is to plan some picnic meals. This not only saves time, but will get you out into that gorgeous scenery you would otherwise see only through the car window. Most southern states have picnic and rest areas even along major highways, and many of them are surprisingly well-equipped, some with outdoor grills and restroom facilities. With a little extra planning (pick up your lunch at a take-out restaurant at breakfast) and a Thermos or two in the car, you're all set for a stop that will send you on your way refreshed as well as full.

A plug-in water heater and a jar of instant coffee will not only save you time, but will pinch pennies as well. Fruit and rolls or pastries, bought the night before, plus your own coffee makes a relaxed, inexpensive motel-room breakfast that gets you off and away before traffic builds up.

 **PACKING.** *What to take, what to wear.* Make a packing list for each member of the family. Then check off items as you pack them. It will save time, reduce confusion. Time savers to carry along include extra photo film (plenty), suntan lotion, insect repellent, sufficient toothpaste, soap, etc. Always carry an extra pair of glasses, including sunglasses, particularly if they're prescription ones. A travel iron is always a good tote-along, as are some transparent plastic film bags (small and large) for wet suits, socks, etc. They are also excellent for packing shoes, cosmetics, and other easily damaged items. If you fly, remember that despite signs to the contrary airport security X-ray machines do in fact damage your films in about 17 percent of the cases. Have them inspected separately or pack them in special protective bags. Fun extras to carry include binoculars, a compass, and a magnifying glass—to read fine-print maps.

All members of the family should have sturdy shoes with nonslip soles. Keep them handy in the back of the car. You never know when you may want to stop and clamber along a rocky trail to some site. Carry the family rain gear in a separate bag, in the back of the car (so no one will have to get out and hunt for it in a downpour en route).

Women will probably want to stick to one or two basic colors for their holiday wardrobes, so that they can manage with one set of accessories. If possible, include one knit or jersey dress or a pants suit. For dress-up evenings, take along a few "basic" dresses you can vary with a simple change of accessories. That way you can dress up or down to suit the occasion.

Be sure to check what temperatures will be like along the route. Traveling in mountains can mean cool evenings, even in summer—and so can traveling through the desert. An extra sweater is always a safe thing to pack, even if just to protect you from the air conditioning.

Men will probably want a jacket along for dining out, and a dress shirt and tie for the most formal occasions. Turtlenecks are now accepted almost everywhere and are a comfortable accessory. Don't forget extra slacks.

Planning a lot of sun time? Don't forget something sufficiently cover-up to wear over swim suit en route to the pool, beach, or lakefront, and for those first few days when you're getting reacquainted with sun on tender skin.

One tip for frequent motel stops along the road is to pack two suitcases— one for the final destination, and the other with items for overnight stops; pajamas, shaving gear, cosmetics, toothbrushes, fresh shirt or dress. Put the overnight luggage into the trunk last, so it can be pulled out first on overnight stops. A safety hint: Don't string your suits and dresses on hangers along a chain or rod stretched across the back seat. This obstructs vision and can cause accidents.

 **HINTS TO THE MOTORIST.** Even before the advent of superhighways, roads in the South were built for high-speed driving. Today, with four- and six-lane Interstate networks covering the entire region, you will be able to cover long distances easily, and the long stretches of straightaway are varied with gradual curves, some stretching for half a mile or more.

Highway hypnosis is a distinct hazard on main highways and it comes from steady driving on roads which stretch for miles, without a break, at a set speed. Its principal symptoms are drowsiness and an inability to concentrate. If you become aware of either of these, stop immediately for a cup of coffee or tea, get out and take a brief walk, stop for a brief nap in the car, and when you resume driving, try varying your speed from time to time. Speed limits throughout the South never exceed 55 miles an hour to conform to gas conservation laws, but a short stretch of slower driving will keep you more alert and give you a chance to see more of the country.

If you should have car trouble, pull off the highway, raise the car hood, tie something white (a handkerchief, scarf, etc.) to the door handle on the driver's side, sit inside and wait for help. Limited-access highways are usually patrolled day and night by state highway officers, and even on country lanes, other drivers will be attracted to your car and someone will stop. Women drivers should be especially careful if stalled at night. They should stay inside the car with the doors locked until very sure that anyone who offers assistance is really a good Samaritan! Telephones along major highways are more frequent nowadays, and if you are a member of AAA, you can call the nearest garage listed in its directory. Even if you are not a member, the telephone operator will be able to connect you with a local garage.

All roads are well-engineered in the South, and even in the mountainous regions, you'll find them constructed for the average driver—well-graded, usually wide enough to allow passing and generally conducive to safe driving. Be certain to obey the posted speed limits, particularly on curves, be very careful about passing and use your engine in second or low gear on long descents to save your brakes.

If you will be pulling a trailer, check with your auto club, the police or the state motor vehicle department about special rules and safety regulations, some of which change frequently. Generally, speed limits are lower, there are prohibitions against parking on expressways and freeways, and some tunnels bar trailers equipped with propane gas for cooking.

Your driving vacation will be more enjoyable if you budget your time just as you do your money. On the open road, you'll be able to cover 250 miles a day comfortably, but in congested areas, you'll be wise to set a limit of 200 miles. After all, you want to arrive at each destination ready to *enjoy* sightseeing, so forget about the exhausting, big-push kind of driving and take time for occasional stops along the way.

 **TRAILER TIPS.** If you plan to pull a *trailer*—boat or house—on your holiday trip, and have never before done so, don't just hook up and set out. You need a whole new set of driving skills-starting, stopping, cornering, passing, *being* passed, and, most tricky of all, backing. Reading about it will help a little, but not much. Try to practice in an open field, but if this is not possible, take your maiden trip in light traffic. A few useful hints: In starting and stopping, do everything more slowly and gradually than you would normally; in cornering, swing wider than usual since the trailer won't follow exactly the rear wheels of the towing car. Too sharp a right turn will put your trailer wheels over the curb. Too sharp a left turn will squash a car waiting to let you make the turn. In passing, remember you're longer than usual. Allow more safe distance ahead to pull back into the right lane. A slight bit of extra steering will help if you're *being* passed by a large truck or bus. In these situations, the trailer is inclined to sway from air currents. Don't make it worse by slowing down. It's better to speed up slightly. In backing, the basic technique is to turn the steering wheel opposite to the way you would want the car to go if you were driving it alone. From there on, it's practice, practice, practice. Most states have special safety regulations for trailers, and these change frequently. If you plan to operate your trailer in several states, check with your motor club, the police, or the state motor vehicle department about the rules. Also talk it over with the dealer from whom you buy or lease your trailer. Generally, speed limits for cars hauling trailers are lower, parking of trailers (and automobiles) is prohibited on expressways and freeways, and tunnels often bar trailers equipped with cooking units which use propane gas.

 **DIXIELAND TRAIL.** You will encounter some of the South's finest vacation areas if you follow the Dixieland Trail through the land of Daniel Boone and Pogo, Civil War battlegrounds and Cherokee Indian reservations, TVA and the atomic world of tomorrow. The 2,200-mile trail through Georgia, Kentucky, North Carolina, South Carolina and Tennessee will not only take you to existing and developing vacation resorts, but will also lead you directly into the Old South's past. To do the entire length of the Trail justice, you should allow no less than three weeks, but an even better plan is to choose one portion and explore it thoroughly.

You might join the Trail at the *Cumberland Gap* on the Kentucky-Tennessee-Virginia border. Here you can stand on the high overlook through which Daniel Boone led the first settlers across the Wilderness Road in 1775. Moving into Kentucky, you will reach *Pine Mountain State Park* and perhaps stop for a performance of the outdoor drama, *Book of Job.* Go through *Barbourville,* where the *Daniel Boone Festival* is held in October, to *Cumberland Falls State Park,* then through *Lexington,* center of bluegrass and thoroughbreds, where horse lovers will want to visit some of the larger stables. Next comes *Frankfort,* where Daniel Boone and his wife are buried, then *Louisville,* home of the *Kentucky Derby.*

From here, the Trail swings south to the *Abraham Lincoln Birthplace National Historic Park* at *Hodgenville* and the *Mammoth Cave National Park.* The vast 170,000-acre peninsula between the new *Barkley Lake* and *Kentucky Lake* comes next; it is developing into a major national recreation area. The 2,300-mile shoreline of Kentucky Lake (largest of the 30 reservoirs in the Tennessee Valley Authority network) is bordered by four state parks and over 100 boat docks.

From *Paris Landing State Park,* a resort on the Tennessee side of the lake, you can take time for a short trip to *Memphis* or stay on the Trail to *Jackson,* where railroad buffs will be entranced by the *Casey Jones Museum.* From there to *Nashville* and a view of frontier elegance at Andrew Jackson's home, the *Hermitage* or a night of country music at *Grand Ole Opry.* Then drive through rich farm country around Shelbyville to *Chattanooga* and the breathtaking summit of *Lookout Mountain.*

The Trail enters Georgia here and major stops along the way are *Atlanta, Warm Springs* (and Franklin D. Roosevelt's *Little White House),* perhaps a stop at *Plains* or a sidetrip to the *Okefenokee Wildlife Refuge.*

The main Trail leads on to the famed *Sea Islands* coastal resort and continues up the coast into South Carolina's romantic Old South port of *Charleston.* For the remainder of the drive up South Carolina's coast, you'll be in real plantation country, for here are the rice plantations of the low country. At North Carolina's border, the Trail heads inland to *Pinehurst* and *Southern Pines,* where you'll want to have your golf clubs along.

Then comes *Durham,* home of Duke University, *Winston-Salem,* with its *old Moravian settlement,* and eventually the *Blue Ridge Parkway.* Look for *Southern Highland Crafts Guild* signs along the parkway for unforgettable handicrafts. The Trail continues west through the *Cherokee Indian Reservation,* the *Great Smoky Mountains National Park,* and across the Alleghenies to *Knoxville,* winding up at TVA's *Norris Dam and Lake* and the *American Museum of Atomic Energy* at Oak Ridge.

This is only a sample of what you'll find along the Dixieland Trail, and there are other state "trails" which will let you follow the history of each. You will, of course, find your own detours for not-to-be-missed side trips.

**CAMPING OUT.** Camping facilities have become an established part of the vacation scene all across the country, and the South is no exception. Private camping areas and trailer parks and public campgrounds in national parks, forests and state parks are to be found throughout the region. Facilities vary, of course, and each state chapter in this book will outline regulations and charges.

For hardier types, there are pack trips in the southern states. Organizations like the *Appalachian Mountain Club* and *American Youth Hostels* can furnish information on huts, hostels, trails, maps, guides and special tours. Some southern rivers are especially good for canoe trips and the Inland Waterway acts as an alternate highway for those with their own boats.

If camping per se is not your thing, there are farm vacations available in the South which are especially appealing to families with children. Some are really deluxe and even have a swimming pool, while others are simplicity itself and give you a firsthand glimpse of rural life in its most elementary terms.

**Useful addresses:** *National Parks Service,* U.S. Dept. of the Interior, Washington, D.C. 20025; *National Forest Service,* U.S. Dept. of Agriculture, Washington, D.C. 20025; *State Parks Dept.,* State Office Building, in any state in which you are interested. *The National Campers & Hikers Assoc.,* Box 451, Orange, N.J., 07051, *American Camping Assoc., Inc.,* Bradford Woods, Martinsville, Ind., *Camping Council,* 17 E 48th St., New York, N.Y. 10017, *Appalachian Mountain Club,* 5 Joy St., Boston, Mass. 02108, and *American Youth Hostels,* National Campus, Delaplane, Va. 22025, all can furnish helpful information.

**PETS.** Traveling by car with your pet dog or cat? More and more motels accept them but be sure to check before you register. Some turn them down, some want to look first, some offer special facilities. If it's a first-time trip for your pet, accustom it to car travel by short trips in your neighborhood. And when you're packing, include its favorite food, bowls, and toys. Discourage your dog from riding with its head out the window. Wind and dust particles can permanently damage its eyes. Don't leave your pet in a parked car on a hot day while you dawdle over lunch. Keep his bowl handy for water during stops for gas; gasoline attendants are usually very cooperative about this.

**TIPPING.** Tipping is supposed to be a personal thing, your way of expressing your appreciation of someone who has taken pleasure and pride in giving you attentive, efficient, and personal service. Because standards of personal service in the United States are highly uneven, you should, when you get genuinely good service, feel secure in rewarding it, and when you feel that the service you got was slovenly, indifferent, or surly, don't hesitate to show this by the size, or withholding, of your tip. Remember that in many places the help are paid very little and depend on tips for the better part of their income. This is supposed to give them incentive to serve you well. These days, the going rate on *restaurant* service is 15% on the amount *before* taxes. Tipping at counters is not universal, but many people leave $0.25 on anything up to $1, and 10% on anything over that. For *bellboys,* 25¢ per bag is usual. However, if you load him down with all manner of bags, hatboxes, cameras, coats, etc., you might consider giving an extra quarter or two. In many places the help rely on tips for a goodly portion of their income. For one-night stays in most *hotels* and *motels* you leave nothing. If you stay longer, at the end of your stay leave the maid $1–$1.25 per day, or $5 per person per week for multiple occupancy. If you are staying at an *American Plan* hostelry (meals included) $1.50 per day per person for the waiter or waitress is considered sufficient, and is left at the end of your stay. However, if you have been surrounded by an army of servants (one bringing relishes, another rolls, etc.), add a few extra dollars and give the lump sum to the captain or *maître d'hôtel* when you leave, asking him to allocate it.

For the many other services you may encounter in a big hotel or resort, figure roughly as follows: doorman, 25¢ for taxi handling, 50¢ for help with baggage; bellhop, 25¢ per bag, more if you load him down with extras;

parking attendant, 50¢; bartender, 15%; room service, 10-15% of that bill; laundry or valet service, 15% pool attendant, 50¢ per day; snackbar waiter at pool, beach, or golf club, 50¢ per person for food and 15% of the beverage check; locker attendant, 50¢ per person per day, or $2.50 per week; golf caddies, $1–2 per bag, or 15% of the greens fee for an 18-hole course, or $3 on a free course; barbers, 50¢; shoeshine attendants, 25¢; hairdressers, $1; manicurists, 50¢.

*Transportation:* Give 25¢ cents for any taxi under $1 and 15% for any above; however, drivers in New York, Las Vegas, and other major resorts *expect* 20%. Limousine service, 20%. Car rental agencies, nothing. Bus porters are tipped 25¢ per bag, drivers nothing. On charters and package tours, conductors and drivers usually get $5–$10 per day from the group as a whole, but be sure to ask whether this has already been figured into the package cost. On short local sightseeing runs, the driver-guide may get 25¢ per person, more if you think he has been especially helpful or personable. Airport bus drivers, nothing. Redcaps, in resort areas, 35¢ per suitcase, elsewhere, 25¢. Tipping at curbside check-in is unofficial, but same as above. On the plane, no tipping.

Railroads suggest you leave 10–15% per meal for dining car waiters, but the steward who seats you is not tipped. Sleeping-car porters get about $1 per person per night. The 25¢ or 35¢ you pay a railway station baggage porter is not a tip but the set fee that he must hand in at the end of the day along with the ticket stubs he has used. Therefore his tip is anything you give him above that, 25–50¢ per bag, depending on how heavy your luggage is.

 **HOTELS AND MOTELS.** In this book, hotel listings are limited as much as possible to those with Civil War or an Old South significance or flavor. These appear in capital letters in the listings. Where there are no such establishments we have listed some of the major chain hotels. Price categories are explained in each of the individual chapters.

By all means, try not to take pot luck for lodgings. Looking for a place to stay is time-consuming and may end with your being unhappy with the accommodations you find. If you should be without reservations, begin looking early in the afternoon, and if you find you won't reach a motel or hotel in which you have reservations before 5 or 6 P.M., be sure to call the desk clerk and let him know of your late arrival.

If your itinerary includes a stay at a popular resort at the height of the season, reserve well in advance and include a deposit. Most large cities serve as headquarters for conventions and other large gatherings, so you will be well advised to make advance reservations there, also.

Include a deposit for all places except motels (and for motels if they request one). Many chain or associated motels and hotels will make advance reservations for you at affiliated hostelries along your route.

A number of hotels and motels have one-day laundry and dry-cleaning services, and many motels have coin laundries. Most motels, but not all, have telephones in the room. If you want to be sure of room service, however, better stay at a hotel. Many motels have swimming pools, and even beachfront hotels frequently have a pool. Even some motels in the hearts of large cities have pools. An advantage at motels is the free parking. There's seldom a charge for parking at country and resort hotels.

*Hotel and motel chains.* In addition to the hundreds of excellent independent motels and hotels throughout the country, there are also many that belong to national or regional chains. A major advantage of the chains, to many travelers, is the ease of making reservations en route, or at one fell swoop in advance. If you are a guest at a member hotel or motel, the management will be delighted to secure you a sure booking at one of its affiliated hotels for the coming evening. Chains also usually have toll-free WATS (800) lines to assist you in making reservations on your own. This, of course, saves you time, worry and money. In some chains, you have the added advantage of knowing what the standards are all the way. The insistence on uniform standards of comfort, cleanliness and amenities is more common in motel than in hotel chains. (Easy to understand when you realize that most hotel chains are formed by simply buying up older, established hotels, while most motel chains have control of their units from start to finish.) This is not meant to denigrate the hotel chains; after all, individuality can be one of the great charms of a hotel. Some travelers, however, prefer independent motels and hotels because they are more likely to reflect the genuine character of the surrounding area.

## HOTEL AND MOTEL CATEGORIES

Hotels and motels in this guidebook are divided into five categories, arranged primarily by price, but also take into consideration the degree of comfort you can expect to enjoy, the amount of service you can anticipate, and the atmosphere which will surround you in the establishment of your choice. Failure to include certain establishments in our lists does not mean they are not worthwhile—they were omitted only for lack of space.

Although the names of the various hotel and motel categories are standard, *the prices listed under each category may vary from area to area*. This variance is meant to reflect local price standards, and take into account the fact that what might be considered a moderate price in a large urban area might be quite expensive in a rural region. *In every case, however, the dollar ranges for each category are clearly stated before each listing of establishments*.

**Super Deluxe:** In addition to offering all the amenities discussed under the deluxe category (below), the super deluxe hotel has a special atmosphere of glamor, good taste, and dignity. Its story will inevitably be full of many historical anecdotes, and it will probably be a favored meeting spot of local society, as well as world-famed personalities. In short, super deluxe means the tops.

**Deluxe:** We suggest that the minimum facilities must include bath and shower in all rooms, valet and laundry service, available suites, a well-appointed restaurant and a bar (local law permitting), room service, TV and telephone in room, air conditioning and heat (locale not precluding), pleasing decor, and an atmosphere of luxury, calm and elegance. There should be ample and personalized service. In a deluxe motel, there may be less service rendered by employees and more by machine or automation (such as refrigerators and ice-making machines in your room), but there should be a minimum of do-it-yourself in a truly deluxe establishment.

**Expensive:** All rooms must have bath or shower, valet and laundry service, restaurant and bar (local law permitting), limited room service, TV and telephone in room, heat and air conditioning (locale not precluding), pleasing decor. Hotels and motels in this category are frequently designed for commercial travelers or for families in a hurry and are somewhat impersonal in terms of service. As for motels in this category, valet and laundry service will probably be lacking; the units will be outstanding primarily for their convenient location and functional character, not for their attractive or comfortable qualities.

**Moderate:** Each room should have an attached bath or shower, restaurant or coffee shop, TV available, telephone in room, heat and air conditioning (locale not precluding), relatively convenient location, clean and comfortable rooms and public rooms. Motels in this category may not have attached bath or shower, may not have a restaurant or coffee shop (though one is usually nearby), and, of course, may have no public rooms to speak of.

**Inexpensive:** nearby bath or shower, telephone available, and clean rooms are the minimum.

Budget: In the last few years, the soaring prices of hotel and motel accommodations have given rise to a number of chains of budget motels. A few of these are nationwide, most of them are still regional. However, as their prices, in mid-1978 average $12.50 for a single and $15 for a double, their advantage over ordinary hotels and motels is obvious. Grouped by region, they are as follows. (The addresses and phone numbers of the central offices which supply free directories are given with the first listings.)

Nationwide: *Budget Host Inns,* Box 26092, Fort Worth, Texas 76116, (817) 732-2388; *Friendship Inns International,* 739 South 4th West, Salt Lake City, Utah 84101, (801) 532-1800.

 **DINING OUT.** Restaurants, too, are listed in this book according to their relation to the Civil War, the Old South, or even the Old West. Some have been in business many years, handing down favorite recipes that hark back to antebellum days. Some recreate the older atmosphere, and others simply reflect it in their decor. Price categories are spelled out in each chapter.

It is wise to make reservations in advance for evening meals. Hotel dining rooms have set dining hours, but most motels are more flexible and provide some sort of meal during most of the day.

Remember, when traveling in the South, that some restaurants, particularly in major cities, are a little fussy about dress, especially at night. Pants and pant suits are acceptable for women almost everywhere, but they should not be too casual. A tie and jacket are generally required for men, although more and more places allow turtlenecks. Shorts are almost always frowned upon for both men and women.

Standards of dress are becoming more relaxed, so a neatly dressed customer will usually experience no problem. If in doubt about accepted dress at a particular establishment, call ahead.

Roadside stands, turnpike restaurants and cafeterias have no fixed standards of dress.

If you're traveling with children, you may want to find out if a restaurant has a children's menu and commensurate prices (many do).

When figuring the tip on your check, base it on the total charges for the meal, not on the grand total, if that total includes a sales tax. Don't tip on tax.

The restaurants mentioned in this volume which are located in large metropolitan areas are categorized by type of cuisine: French, Chinese, Armenian, etc. with restaurants of a general nature listed as American-International. Restaurants in less populous areas are divided into price categories as follows: *Super Deluxe, Deluxe, Expensive, Moderate,* and *Inexpensive.* As a general rule, expect restaurants in metropolitan areas to be higher in price, but many restaurants that feature foreign cuisine are surprisingly inexpensive. Limitations of space make it impossible to include every establishment, so we have listed those which we recommend as the best within each price range.

## RESTAURANT CATEGORIES

Although the names of the various restaurant categories are standard throughout this series, the prices listed under each category may vary from area to area. This variation is meant to reflect local price standards, and take into account the fact that what might be considered a *moderate* price in a large urban area might be quite *expensive* in a rural region. In every case, however, the dollar ranges for each category are clearly stated before each listing of establishments.

*Super Deluxe:* This category will probably be pertinent to only one or two metropolitan areas. It indicates a lavishly decorated, outstanding restaurant, which now and then may delight in the fear it inspires. Frequently over-priced and over-rated, it will charge the customer at least $12 for soup, entree, and dessert. The average price for the same is apt to be closer to $16, although some will run much higher than this. As in all our other categories, this price range does not include cocktails, wines, cover or table charges, tip, or extravagant house specialties. The price range here indicates a typical roastbeef (prime ribs) dinner. The restaurant in this category must have a superb wine list, excellent service, immaculate kitchen, and a large, well-trained staff.

*Deluxe:* Many a fine restaurant around the country falls into this category. It will have its own well-deserved reputation for excellence, perhaps a house specialty or two for which it is famous, and an atmosphere of elegance or unique decor. It will have a good wine list where the law permits, and will be considered the best in town by the inhabitants. It will have a clean kitchen and attentive staff.

*Expensive:* In addition to the expected dishes, it will offer one or two house specialties, wine list and cocktails (where law permits), air conditioning (unless locale makes it unnecessary), a general reputation for very good food and an adequate staff, an elegant decor and appropriately dressed clientele.

*Moderate:* Cocktails and/or beer where the law permits, air conditioning (locale not precluding), clean kitchen, adequate staff, better-than-average service. General reputation for good, wholesome food.

*Inexpensive:* The bargain place in town, it is clean, even if plain. It will have air conditioning (when necessary), tables (not a counter), clean kitchen, and attempt to provide adequate service.

 **HINTS TO HANDICAPPED TRAVELERS.** One of the newest, and largest, groups to enter the travel scene is the handicapped, literally millions of people who are in fact physically able to travel and who do so enthusiastically when they know that they can move about in safety and comfort. Generally their tours parallel those of the non-handicapped traveller, but at a more leisurely pace, and with the logistics carefully checked out in advance. Important sources of information in this field are: 1) the book, *Access to the World: A Travel Guide for the Handicapped,* by Louise Weiss, published by Chatham Square Press, Inc., 401 Broadway, New York, N.Y. 10013. This book covers travel by air, ship, train, bus, car, and recreational vehicle; hotels and motels; travel agents and tour operators; destinations; access guides; health and medical problems; and travel organizations. 2) the *Travel Information Center,* Moss Rehabilitation Hospital, 12th Street and Tabor Road, Philadelphia, Penn. 19141. 3) *Easter Seal Society for Crippled Children and Adults,* Director of Education and Information Service, 2023 West Ogden Avenue, Chicago, Illinois 60612. Many of the country's national parks have special facilities for the handicapped. These are described in *National Park Guide for the Handicapped,* available from the U.S. Government Printing Office, Washington, DC 20402. TWA publishes a free 12-page pamphlet entitled *Consumer Information and Air Travel for the Handicapped* to explain available special arrangements and how to get them. Two other publications which give valuable information about motels, hotels, and restaurants (rating them, telling about steps, table heights, door widths, etc.) are *Where Turning Wheels Stop,* published by Paralyzed Veterans of America, 3636 16th St., N.W., Washington, D.C. 20010, and *The Wheelchair Traveler,* 22480 Cass Ave., Woodland Hills, Calif. 91364.

 **TOURIST INFORMATION.** *District of Columbia:* Washington Area Convention and Visitors Bureau, Board of Trade Bldg., 1129 20th St. NW, Washington, DC 20036.

*Maryland:* Maryland Office of Tourist Development, 1748 Forest Drive, Annapolis 21401.

*Pennsylvania:* Pennsylvania Bureau of Travel Development, Pennsylvania Department of Commerce, 206 South Office Bldg., Harrisburg 17120.

*Virginia:* Virginia State Travel Service, 6 North 6th St., Richmond 23219.

*West Virginia:* West Virginia Economic Development Division, Travel Development, Building 6, Room B-504, Charleston 25305.

*Alabama:* Alabama Bureau of Publicity and Information, Rm. 403, State Highway Bldg., Montgomery 36130.

*Florida:* Florida Division of Tourism, 107 W. Gaines St., Tallahassee 32304.

*Georgia:* Georgia Tourist Division, Georgia Bureau of Industry and Trade, PO Box 1776, Atlanta 30301.

*Louisiana:* Louisiana Office of Tourism, PO Box 44291, Baton Rouge 70804.

*Kentucky:* Kentucky Travel Promotion, Capitol Annex, Frankfort 40601.

*Mississippi:* Mississippi Tourism Dept., PO Box 849, Jackson 39205.

*North Carolina:* North Carolina Travel & Tourism Division, PO Box 25249, Raleigh 27611.

*South Carolina:* South Carolina Division of Tourism, Suite 113, Edgar A. Brown Bldg., 1205 Pendleton St., Columbia 29201.

*Tennessee:* Tennessee Department of Tourist Development, 505 Fesslers Lane, Nashville 37210

*Arkansas:* Arkansas Division of Tourism, 149 State Capitol, Little Rock 72201.

*Kansas:* Kansas Department of Economic Development, 503 Kansas Ave., Topeka 66603.

*Missouri:* Missouri Division of Tourism, PO Box 1055, Jefferson City, 65101.

*New Mexico:* New Mexico Tourist Division, Bataan Memorial Bldg., Santa Fe 87503.

*Oklahoma:* Oklahoma Division of Tourist Promotion, 500 Will Rogers Bldg., Oklahoma City 73105.

*Texas:* Texas Tourist Development Agency, Box 12008, Capitol Station, Austin 78711.

 **SUGGESTED READING.** No war in history has generated more books than America's Civil War, and it is impossible here to do more than indicate a few that may be considered classic.

The late Bruce Catton wrote numerous historical studies, including *A Stillness at Appomattox, This Hallowed Ground,* and his trilogy written for the Civil War Centennial: *The Coming Fury, Terrible Swift Sword,* and *Never Call Retreat.* He was also the author of three biographical volumes on U. S. Grant and provided the narrative for the American Heritage *Pictorial History of the Civil War.*

Another standard work is Allan Nevins' 8-volume *The Ordeal of the Union.*

Catton and Nevins are probably the best guides for those who have not previously done much reading on the subject.

For the buff, there are more books than anyone could read in one lifetime: books on battles, books on generals, books on the causes of the war, first-person accounts from the *Memoirs of U. S. Grant* to diaries of ordinary soldiers on both sides. The *Civil War Times Illustrated,* published by Historical Times, Inc., 206 Hanover St., Gettysburg, Pa., reviews new contributions to the literature as they appear, in addition to carrying specialized articles and advertisements; it is recommended to Civil War afficionados. Subscriptions are $12 per year (10 issues).

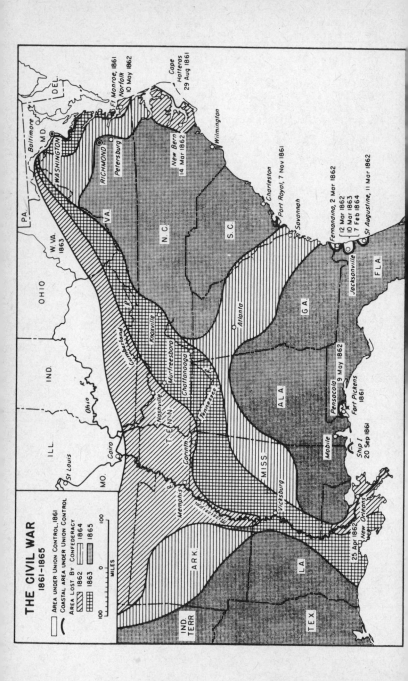

THE CIVIL WAR
1861-1865

Area under Union Control, 1861

Coastal area under Union Control.

AREA LOST BY CONFEDERACY
1862  1864
1863  1865

MILES
100    0    100

# ALABAMA

## Capital of the Confederacy

### by
### CALEB PIRTLE AND KAREN LINGO

*Caleb Pirtle was until recently the Travel Editor of* Southern Living
Magazine, *and has become one of the South's most eloquent and
amusing spokesmen. He lived in Birmingham, Alabama for five
years. Ms. Lingo, now Travel Editor of* Southern Living, *is a native
of Mulga, Alabama and is an active member of the Society of
American Travel Writers.*

Beneath the veneer of her hills and valleys, small towns and large
cities, Alabama bears the scars of a battle still referred to as "The
War." Like hard-won medals, they are preserved and displayed with
pride, and with a touch of sadness.

For Alabama is the birthplace of the Confederacy. It was in
Montgomery, on February 4, 1861, that leaders from six states in the
lower South met to form a new nation. For a little over three
months, until the capital was moved to Richmond, the Confederate
States of America operated from the heart of Alabama.

Jefferson Davis, elected president of the Confederacy, traveled to
Montgomery to pick up the reins of his new nation. And on
February 18, 1861, he marched down Dexter Avenue to the cadence
of a new tune—one called "Dixie." He was inaugurated on the front
portico of the state capitol. A bronze star marks that spot, where the
destinies of two nations and so many thousands of men were flung so
agonizingly into the maelstrom of civil war.

It was in Montgomery, too, that a telegraph operator sat and tapped out the order to fire on Fort Sumter. Exactly four years later to the day, on April 12, 1864, Montgomery, the Cradle of the Confederacy, surrendered without a fight.

Ironically, the architecture of the capitol itself was inspired by the one in Washington, D.C., the one that governed a nation at war with itself. Within that building the state's rich, historical background has been caught by an artist's brush in great, colorful murals.

Across the street is Jefferson Davis' home, poignantly referred to as the White House of the Confederacy. The dwelling resembles a giant dollhouse, its rooms lavishly furnished with velvet sofas, crystal chandeliers, oriental rugs and personal belongings of the Davis family.

In a sense, it's symbolic of the aristocratic hope and opulence of a region that—before a decade had ended—lay shattered and in rags.

For Union forces, before the war ceased, also got around to calling Montgomery home. In fact the Teague House, at High and South Perry Street, was used by Northern General J. H. Wilson during those days of conflict. Today it houses the State Chamber of Commerce. St. John's Episcopal Church, too, is a reminder of that era. Jefferson Davis attended services in the chapel. A bronze plaque marks the family pew.

The Murphy House, built before 1860, is a three-story Greek Revival building with white columns that now houses offices of the Waterworks Board. The Seibel-Ball-Lanier Home is an imposing Colonial house on a spacious landscaped lawn that contains carved marble mantels, ornate Regency mirror frames, and heirlooms. Also restored and opened to the public in Montgomery is the Ordeman-Shaw House.

Northerners, it seems, are often amused at Montgomery's inability to forget the War Between the States and the strategic role it played in that tragedy. But, it's usually pointed out, men here are as genuinely proud of their family's fight for independence as the Bostonians are of theirs against the British.

For the hostilities reached out and touched so much of Alabama.

## Marion

During the War Between the States, a Marion teacher, Nicola Marshall, created both the uniform and the flag for the Southern Confederacy. The pride of the town today is Marion Institute and its cadet corps. It, too, has been around long enough to have filled an important niche in Alabama's history, having been established 29 years before the fall of Fort Sumter.

Selma sits perched high atop the Alabama River. It was lovely. It was vulnerable. But it was also one of the most important manufacturing cities in the Confederacy, with an estimated 10,000 workmen producing virtually every material of war, including the Confederate ironclad *Tennessee*. So Selma became the target for frequent bombardment during the Civil War. It suffered immense destruction. But it's still lovely, proudly showing off a restored riverfront and Sturdivant Hall, built in 1853. The home has a neo-classic air about it. And very few ever bother to remember the name of its builder. But they all quickly point out that he was a relative of Robert E. Lee.

Decatur went through several years finding out that it was situated in a strategically important place. The town was the scene of so many Civil War battles that when peace was finally declared at Appomattox all but five buildings had been devastated and left in rubble.

Just south of Decatur, Hurricane Creek Gorge (now a privately owned park), a rugged slash of rock and timber, slices back into the foothills of the Appalachian Mountains, virtually lost in a thick umbrella of mountain laurel, hickory, and pine. Deep within that canyon, Confederate General Nathan Bedford Forrest hid away to await a Federal force led by Col. Abel D. Streight.

Only six miles away, Forrest and Streight would fight the battle of Day's Gap. Three times that small Rebel cavalry unit attacked, hoping to split Col. Streight's army and leave them stranded along the timbered ridges. Three times Forrest failed. And the Union troops marched away to destroy the railroad at Rome, Georgia.

While Forrest was challenging Col. Streight, a rural postman from Gadsden, John H. Wisdom, made a ride reminiscent of the one made by Paul Revere in another century and another war. He pushed his mounts for 67 miles and eight hours, from Gadsden to Rome, Georgia, to warn the people that the Yankees were coming. It gave the city enough time to prepare its defenses.

### "Damn the Torpedoes . . ."

It was on the waters of Mobile Bay that the most dramatic act of Alabama's participation in the Civil War took place. The scene was Fort Morgan, on the day Admiral David Farragut battled his way into Mobile Bay. He watched in anger as the vanguard of his fleet, the *Tecumseh,* pitched violently in those summer waters. The ironclad had been leading Farragut's armada of 17 ships against Fort Morgan when it suddenly slammed into a Confederate underwater mine, known during those latter days of the Civil War as a torpedo.

Farragut felt helpless. He had a huge fleet with 700 guns trained on the ramparts of Fort Morgan, but now he was forced to stand and watch the flailing *Tecumseh* take one last gulp of water and plunge into the depths of the bay. With a crew of 105 men aboard, it had sunk within 30 seconds after striking the mine. There had been no hope of rescue.

The Union admiral turned sharply on the decks of the *Hartford* and shouted:

"Damn the torpedoes. Full speed ahead."

The Northern troops attacked from land, while Farragut and his 16 ships launched a withering bombardment from the sea. The Confederate fortress was strong, but food and ammunition are both quick to run dry. Supplies were cut off by the Union blockade. And 18 days later the soldiers of Fort Morgan surrendered.

Inside the grand old fort today you can wind in and out of the
brick magazines, climb up and down the steep stone steps—one still
bloodstained from the wound of a Confederate defender—and walk
through the seemingly endless arches of the ramparts overlooking
the Gulf of Mexico. A large museum, modeled after the old Citadel
destroyed in the battle, holds thousands of relics and rare articles of
war.

Perhaps the story of Fort Morgan is best told in its International
Cemetery. It is dedicated "to the Dead of Five Nations, Seven
Decisive Battles, and Four Centuries of American History."

Not far away is Fort Gaines and its Confederate museum. It clings
to the beaches of Dauphin Island, still maintaining many gun
emplacements, as well as the anchor and chain from the *Hartford*.

Nearby on Dauphin Island is Olde Fort Alabama Relic Museum.
It displays fascinating exhibits of Indian and Civil War relics, along
with the finest archeological artifacts found anywhere on the Gulf
Coast.

### Tombigbee and Birmingham

Fort Tombigbee changed hands many times while watching over
the mighty Tombigbee River. During the War Between the States,
General Forrest located a "surveillance post" at the fort's site. Six
Confederates were stationed there with orders to watch for Union
troops and delay them with two small cannon if they advanced up
the Tombigbee River.

In the Birmingham area there is Arlington, an eight-room, two-
story dwelling fashioned in 1842 by William S. Mudd. Trees were cut
down on the property and hewn into lumber for the home's building
material. And nails, beams, and bricks were all hand-made by local
slaves. Arlington is surrounded by six landscaped acres, and its
rooms are amply furnished by original 19th-century furniture,
bringing together designs from France, Great Britain and America.
Arlington, in fact, graced the countryside for 30 years before anyone
ever decided there should even be a Birmingham.

The home now houses a Confederate museum. That's no surprise.
For during the closing months of the War Between the States,
Arlington was commandeered by Union General James H. Wilson.
From that house, he issued orders to burn the University of
Alabama at Tuscaloosa, to destroy the iron furnaces at nearby
Oxmoor and Irondale, and to eliminate the Confederate arsenal at
Selma.

It is because Arlington served as Wilson's home that it stands
unmarred by war today. Yet Wilson overlooked his greatest adver-
sary. For while he lived in Arlington, a Confederate spy named
Mary Gordon Duffee remained hidden in the great home's attic.

## PRACTICAL INFORMATION FOR ALABAMA

**FACTS AND FIGURES.** In Choctaw Indian, *Alabama* means "vegetarian-gatherers" or "thicket-clearers." The state boasts two nicknames: the Cotton State and the Yellowhammer State. Yellowhammer is also the state bird; camellia its flower; southern pine, its tree. Alabama's motto: *Audemus jura nostra defendere* ("We dare defend our rights"). "Alabama" is the state song.

Montgomery, the Confederacy's first capital, is the state capital. State population: approximately 3,500,000.

**HOW TO GET THERE.** *By air:* Birmingham may be reached on direct flights of Allegheny, Braniff, Delta, Eastern, Southern and United; Huntsville-Decatur on Eastern, Southern and United; Mobile on Eastern, National and Southern; Montgomery on Delta, Eastern and Southern; Anniston, Dothan, Gadsden and Tuscaloosa on Southern.

*By car:* I-59 runs from Chattanooga, Tenn., to Birmingham, Tuscaloosa; I-20 from Atlanta, Georgia, to Anniston and Birmingham; I-65 from Tenn. passes through Decatur, Cullman, Birmingham and Montgomery and terminates in Mobile; I-85 comes from Atlanta, via LaGrange, Georgia, to Auburn and Montgomery; I-10 from New Orleans to Biloxi, Miss., Mobile and Pensacola and Jacksonville, Florida.

*By bus:* Greyhound and Trailways have good service. In addition ABC Coach Lines, Central Texas Bus Lines, Inc., Great Southern Coaches, Inc., Gulf Transport Co., Illini-Swallow Lines, Inc., Indiana Motor Bus Co., Ingram Bus Lines, Inc., Jefferson Lines, Inc., Oklahoma Transportation Co., Short Way Lines and Southeastern Stages, Inc. come into the state.

*By train:* Amtrak trains go into Birmingham and Montgomery; Southern Railways go into Birmingham, Anniston, Eutaw, Livingston and Tuscaloosa.

**HOW TO GET AROUND.** *By air:* Local flights are provided by Southern, Al Air, South Central Air Transport (SCAT).

*By car:* I-65 goes from the Tenn. state line to Mobile; US-80 crosses the state from the Georgia State line to the Mississippi state line; US 43 from the Tenn. state line through Florence, Tuscaloosa to Mobile.

*Car rentals:* Hertz, Avis, National, Econo-Car, Budget Rent-A-Car and Dixie Drive-It-Yourself, Thrifty, Sears, and American International.

*By bus:* Greyhound and Trailways operate.

*By train:* Louisville & Nashville, Southern Railway System, Western Railway of Alabama, Central of Georgia, Gulf Mobile & Ohio and Atlantic Coast Line.

**TOURIST INFORMATION SERVICES.** There are numerous sources of tourist information in Alabama. Among them are: Alabama Bureau of Publicity and Information, State Highway Bldg., Montgomery 36104; Alabama State Parks, State Administrative Bldg., Montgomery 36104; Alabama Travel Council, 660 Adams Ave., Montgomery 36104; Forest Supervisor, U.S. Forest Service, P.O. Box 40, Montgomery for detailed information on recreational facilities in national forests. Alabama Department of Conservation and Natural Resources, Information and

Education Section, 64 N. Union St., Montgomery 36104, for fishing, hunting and camping. All local Chambers of Commerce. Alabama Mountain Lakes Association, P.O. Box 2222, Decatur 36501; DeKalb County Tourist Association, P.O. Box 316, Fort Payne 35967; Greater Birmingham Convention & Visitors Bureau, Suite 940, First Alabama Bank Bldg., Birmingham 35203; Gulf Shores Tourist Association, P.O. Drawer 457, Gulf Shores 36542; Mobile Tourist Information Center, Mobile Chamber of Commerce, P.O. Box 2187, Mobile 36601; Tallacoosa Highland Lakes Association, Rte. 1, P.O. Box 128, Sterrett 35147; Historic Chattahoochee Commission, P.O. Bo. 33, Eufaula 36027; NASA's Visitor Information Center, Alabama Space and Rocket Center, Alabama Highway 20 W, Huntsville 35807.

 **SEASONAL EVENTS.** Because of its warmer climate, Alabama features outdoor events throughout the year. Some highlights are:

*March. Mobile:* Tour of historic buildings. *Selma:* Historic Selma Pilgrimage.

*April. Eufaula:* Antebellum home pilgrimage. *Tuscaloosa:* Heritage Week Open House (mid-Apr.).

*May. Ft. Payne:* Tours of homes (3rd weekend).

*September. Loachapoka:* Annual Historical Fair. *Athens:* Tennessee Valley Old Time Fiddlers Convention.

*October. Huntsville:* Cotton Harvest. *Jacksonville:* Tour of Historic Homes and Churches. *Selma:* Riverfront Market Day.

*November. Demopolis:* Candlelight Tour of Gaineswood.

*December. Mobile:* Candlelight Christmas at Oakleigh. *Florence:* Open House at Pope's Tavern. *Birmingham:* Christmas at Arlington. *Bessemer:* Historic tour of McAdary, Sadler, and Owens houses.

On the first Mon. of every month you can witness "Barter Day" on Court House Sq. in *Scottsboro.*

 **STATE PARKS.** Alabama has 24 state parks: *Blue Springs; Buck's Pocket; Camden; Cheaha,* (highest point in Alabama); *Chewacla; De Soto, Little River Canyon* is the deepest gorge east of the Rockies, also has *De Soto Falls; Fort Morgan; Gulf; Joe Wheeler; Lake Guntersville; Monte Sano, Mound; Oak Mountain, Wind Creek; Bladon Springs; Chattahoochee; Chickasaw; Florala; Lake Lurleen; Lakepoint Resort; Paul M. Grist; Rickwood Caverns;* and *Tannehill.* There is camping and swimming at *Cheaha.* In addition *Gulf, Joe Wheeler* and *Lake Guntersville* also offer boating and fishing. Camping, water sports, Sun. open-air worship services at *Wind Creek.*

Family camping is possible in 13 of the parks. All provide picnic areas. Fishing tackle and rental boats are available from concessionaires at several parks.

In addition, Alabama has 22 managed, public fishing lakes under the administration of the Department of Conservation. These lakes range in size from 32 to 250 acres. There's a daily fee of $1 per fisherman.

Anglers are required to have fishing licenses for Alabama waters. A seven-day, nonresident license costs $2. A nonresident annual license costs $5.

 **CAMPING OUT.** Camping facilities for both those who enjoy living under canvas, and those who tow trailers are available in Alabama. There are 12 state parks: *Blue Springs,* 6 miles E of Clio; *Buck's Pocket,* 2 miles N of Groveoak; *Camden,* 6 miles NE of Camden; *Cheaha,* 17 miles N of

Lineville; *DeSoto,* 8 miles NE of Fort Payne; *Gulf,* 10 miles S of Foley; *Lake Guntersville,* 6 miles NE of Guntersville; *Lakepoint Resort,* 7 miles NE of Eufaula; *Lake Lurleen,* 12 miles NW of Tuscaloosa; *Oak Mountain,* 15 miles S of Birmingham; *Joe Wheeler,* 15 miles W of Athens; and *Wind Creek,* 7 miles SE of Alexander City.

The number of campsites with hookups range from 50 at *Blue Springs* to 468 at *Gulf State.* Family cottages are available at *Cheaha, DeSoto, Gulf, Joe Wheeler, Lake Guntersville, Oak Mountain, Camden, Chewacla,* and *Monte Sano* state parks.

There's a charge of $4 for tents and $4.50 for trailers, except at *Wind Creek,* where the fee is $1 less. Maximum occupancy is 8 persons per site. Two-week limit on stays.

*Brushy Lake,* 16 mi. S of Moulton, has 10 tent and camping sites; *Corinth Recreation Area* (open 4/1 to 10/31), 4 mi. E of Double Springs, 64; *Lake Chinnabee,* 10 mi. S of Oxford, 14; *Taska,* 2 mi. E of Tuskegee, 6 for tents only; *Open Pond,* 11 mi. SW of Andalucia, 20; *Payne Lake,* 24 mi. W of Centreville, 46; *Pine Glen,* 2-1/2 mi. W of Heflin, 13; *Coleman Lake* (open 5/1 to 10/31), 8 mi. No of Heflin, 40. Fee is $1 per day.

**TRAILER TIPS.** Alabama's trailer laws are similar to those of other states. Maximum over-all length of trailer and car is 50 feet. For 24-hour travel, widths are limited to 8 feet. Trailers up to 12 feet wide and 12½ feet high can be moved on the highways between sunrise and sunset.

Trailer camping facilities are found in state parks and in the national forests. In addition, there are a number of private trailer parks.

*KOA* has trailer facilities on *Lake Eufaula* ($5 per night for two, 75¢ ea. additional person, $1 electric hookup); *Montgomery* ($4 per vehicle plus 50¢ sewer hookup); $6 for two, $1 each additional person. *Mobile,* two locations (at junction of I–10 and US 90, $6.50 for two, $1 each additional person), (26 miles E of Mobile off I–10, $7 for two, $1 each additional person); *Valley Head,* adjacent to Sequoyah Caverns. ($5 per night for two, 75¢ ea. additional person; $4 maximum, a/c or electric heat 50¢ per day extra); *Jemison* ($5 for two, 50¢ each additional person, a/c or electric heat $1 extra); *Pell City* ($5.50 for two, 50¢ each additional person, a/c or electric heat $1 extra).

**MUSEUMS AND GALLERIES.** *Birmingham: Arlington Antebellum Home and Civil War Museum.* 331 Cotton Ave. SW. Built 1822. Gift shop. *Gulf Shores: Fort Morgan Museum. Tuskegee: Tuskegee George Washington Carver Museum,* on campus of Tuskegee Institute, houses the offices, laboratories, and collections of George Washington Carver. In 1896 he began experiments here with peanuts and sweet potatoes. Also features the story of Negro history and an Art Gallery. Free.

**Special Interest:** *Dauphin Island: Fort Gaines Confederate Museum, Fort McClellan: Edith Nourse Rogers Museum,* U.S. Women's Army Corps Center, Permanent and temporary military exhibits.

**Other:** *Old Tavern* in Tuscaloosa, a restored stagecoach stop in Alabama's old capital.

**HISTORIC SITES.** Famous battles of the Civil War are commemorated in many historic sites. *Bessemer: Tannehill State Park,* site of Confederate ironworks. At *Dauphin Island,* south of Mobile, *Fort Gaines* stands at the entrance to Mobile Bay, near the scene of 1864 Battle of Mobile Bay during which Admiral Farragut defeated Confederates. *Confederate Museum.* *Florence: Pope's Tavern,* old stagecoach stop that served as a hospital for both Confederate and Union soldiers. *Hillsboro: Wheeler Home,* residence of Confederate Gen. Joe Wheeler.

*Gulf Shores: Fort Morgan,* twin fort defending the entrance to Mobile Bay, captured by Union forces during Mobile Bay campaign. *Civil War Museum.* Free. *Mobile: Oakleigh Home,* 350 Oakleigh Pl *Monterey Home,* 1553 Monterey Place. *Montgomery: First White House of Confederacy,* Washington & Union Sts., displays personal furnishings of Jefferson Davis and his family, preserved since their brief residency there over 100 years ago. *Capitol Bldg.* Free. *Ordeman-Shaw Complex. Teague House* (State Chamber of Commerce Bldg.) Closed holidays. Free. Other homes of historical and artistic value include: *Arlington,* at Birmingham; *Gaineswood* and *Bluff Hall,* at Demopolis; *Magnolia Grove,* at Greensboro; *Sturdivant Hall* in Selma; and *The Gorgas House* in Tuscaloosa.

**TOURS.** The *Gray Line Tours,* part of a nation-wide system, offers a variety of package tours to Mobile's historic points of interest and famous gardens. Office located at 3 N. Royal.

**DRINKING LAWS.** Liquor is sold by the drink in licensed hotels, restaurants, and clubs in the state. It is sold in miniatures (1/10 pint bottles) and 1½ pints in restaurants and cocktail lounges, which also sell beer. Beer is sold for both on- and off-premises consumption. Liquor is also sold in state stores. No Sun. sales. Minimum age limit: 19 years. The state has some "dry" counties, but most of the metropolitan areas are "wet."

**HOTELS AND MOTELS.** Most of the motels and hotels in Alabama, especially those along the Gulf Coast, boast swimming pools and various other forms of indoor and outdoor recreational facilities. Listings are in order of price categories, i.e., *Expensive:* $22-$32; *Moderate:* $16-22; *Inexpensive:* $10-16. For a more complete explanation of hotel and motel categories see *Facts at Your Fingertips* at the front of this volume.

## ALBERTVILLE

**Kings Inn Motor Hotel.** *Inexpensive.* Pool, restaurant.

## ALEXANDER CITY

**Bob White Motel.** *Inexpensive.* Small. Pool. Pets accepted. Restaurant nr.

**Horseshoe Bend.** *Inexpensive.* On 280 Bypass, 1½ mi. SW. Comfortable, attractive rooms. Pool. Pets allowed. Cafe, bar. Tennis.

## ANNISTON

**Holiday Inn.** *Moderate.* Pool. Airport courtesy car. Restaurant. Pets accepted.

**Ramada Inn.** *Moderate.* Airport courtesy car. Well operated. Pool, color TV. Pets allowed.

**Anniston TraveLodge.** *Inexpensive.* af19Nice 2-story facility. Restaurant. Coff makers in rms. Pool. Some pets.

**Days Inn.** *Inexpensive.* One of fine chain. Pool, play area, gift shop, gas station. Tasty World restaurant. Pets.

**Downtowner.** *Inexpensive.* Appealing. Cafe, bar, pool. Airport courtesy car.

**Motel Van Thomas.** *Inexpensive.* Pleasant rooms. Pool. Pets accepted.

## AUBURN

**Jovonn Inn.** *Moderate.* Large. TV. Pool. Cafe, bar. Airport service. Pets allowed.

**Heart of Auburn Motel.** *Inexpensive.* A medium-size motel near the University. Attractively furnished; restaurant and room service. Pool. Pets allowed.

**Holiday Inn.** *Inexpensive.* Some studios. Pool. Airport courtesy car. Pets allowed.

## BIRMINGHAM

**Hyatt House.** *Expensive.* 901 21st St. N. Their Hugo's is one of the city's finest restaurants. Lounge.

**Kahler Plaza.** *Expensive.* 808 20th St. S. Fine restaurant, outstanding lounge for dancing.

**Sheraton Mountain Brook.** *Expensive.* Restaurant. Swimming pool. Lounge with live entertainment.

**Birmingham Airport Motel.** *Moderate.* Opposite air terminal. A large 3-story sound-proof motel with connecting units and day rates available. Restaurant, grille, cocktail lounge. Heated pool. Free parking for guests.

**Downtowner Motor Inn.** *Moderate.* 2224 5th Ave. N. A multi-level large member of chain. Restaurant, bar, entertainment, dancing. Some studio rooms. Heated pool. Free parking.

**Hilton Inn.** *Moderate.* 260 Goodwin Crest Dr. Restaurant, lounge with outstanding view of downtown. Airport courtesy car.

**Holiday Inn.** *Moderate.* Six locations. All have restaurant, pools, and allow pets. **Downtown:** 1313 3rd Ave. N. Entertainment. **East:** 7941 Crestwood Blvd.; **South:** 1548 Montgomery Hwy. Nicely located. Entertainment, dancing. Coffee in rms. **West:** 1098 9th Ave. 14 mi. SW on Rte. 11. **Civic Center:** 2230 10th Ave. N. Pool (heated). **Airport:** 5000 10 Ave. N.

**Jovonn Inn.** *Moderate.* Five miles N on Highway 31 N. Pool, restaurant. Lounge with live entertainment.

**Quality Inn.** *Moderate.* I–65 S at Oxmoor Rd. exit. Heated pool, coffee shop, lounge with entertainment.

**Ramada Inn.** *Moderate.* Three locations. All have TV, pool, cafe, bar, some pets. **South:** 1535 Montgomery Hwy. Pleasant locations and rooms. **Airport:** 5216 Airport Hwy. **West:** 12 mi. SW on Rte. 11 at junction of I–20 and I–59.

**Sheraton Motor Inn.** *Moderate.* 300 N. 10th St. Large. Restaurant, entertainment, dancing. Pool. Free parking.

**TraveLodge Civic Center.** *Moderate.* 1808 8th Ave. N. Appealing decor. Restaurant, bar.

**Birmingham TraveLodge.** *Inexpensive.* 821 S. 20th. Heated pool. Cafeteria nr.

**Motel Birmingham.** *Inexpensive.* 7905 Crestwood Blvd. Pleasant rooms; some family units and efficiencies. Coffee makers in rms. Restaurant nr. Pool.

**Passport Inn.** *Inexpensive.* Swimming pool. Restaurant. Adjacent to University of Alabama (Birmingham campus) and Medical Center.

**Primeway Inns.** *Inexpensive.* I–65 S at Oxmoor Rd. W. exit. Pool, restaurant, lounge. One of chain.

**St. Francis Hotel Courts.** *Inexpensive.* 1930 29th Ave. S. Large one- & two-level operation with choice of accommodations. Good restaurant in and nr. Bar. Pool. Pets allowed.

### BOAZ

**Holiday Inn.** *Moderate.* Pleasant accommodations. Heated pool. Pets allowed.

### CULLMAN

**Holiday Inn.** *Moderate.* Indoor pool (heated). Free airport transportation. Pets allowed.

**Anderson Motel.** *Inexpensive.* Medium-sized, with family units. Color TV, telephones. Restaurant. Pool and play area.

### DAUPHIN ISLAND

**Holiday Inn.** *Expensive.* Beachfront. Nice decor. Some rooms with balcony or terrace. Pool. Pets permitted. Seasonal rates.

### DECATUR

**Decatur Inn.** *Inexpensive.* Very attractive rooms. Restaurant. Huge pool. Pets permitted. Airport courtesy car.

**Holiday Inn.** *Inexpensive.* Two floors. Some studios. Restaurant. Pets allowed.

**Motel 6.** *Inexpensive.* Multi-storied. Nice. Pool (heated). Restaurant nr.

**Ramada Inn.** *Inexpensive.* Pleasant rooms. Airport courtesy car. Pool, pets.

**Red Carpet Inn.** *Inexpensive.* Heated pool. Restaurant. Pets accepted.

## DOTHAN

**Olympia Spa and Country Club.** *Moderate.* US 231 S. Restaurant. Golf.

**Quality Inn Carousel.** *Moderate.* 3591 Ross Clark Circle. Pleasant. Some studios. Restaurant, bar. Pool.

**Ramada Inn.** *Moderate.* 3001 Ross Clark Circle SW. Airport courtesy car. Very nice rooms, some studios. Restaurant, bar. Heated pool.

**Sheraton Motor Inn.** *Moderate.* 2195 Ross Clark Circle SE. All rooms with color TV. Dining room, lounge. Pool.

**Heart of Dothan.** *Inexpensive.* 314 N. Foster St.

**Holiday Inn.** *Inexpensive.* Ross Clark Circle SW. Free airport transportation. Appealing rooms. Pool. Pets permitted.

**Motel Leon.** *Inexpensive.* 1621 E. Main St. Restaurant.

## EUFAULA

**Holiday Inn.** *Moderate.* Restaurant. Pool. Airport courtesy car. Pets allowed.

**Lake Eufaula Motor Lodge.** *Inexpensive.* Coffee in room.

## FLORENCE

**Howard Johnson's Motor Lodge.** *Moderate.* Very nice. Restaurant, room service. Pool. Airport courtesy car.

**Florence TraveLodge.** *Inexpensive.* Attractive units. Air conditioning. TV, restaurant, heated pool. Wheelchair ramps.

**Motel 6.** *Inexpensive.* Multi-storied. Cafeteria adj. Heated pool.

## FLORENCE–MUSCLE SHOALS

**Holiday Inn.** *Moderate.* Airport courtesy car. Color TV. Restaurant. Huge pool. Pets permitted.

## FORT PAYNE

**Best Western Motel.** *Inexpensive.* Restaurant, pool. Airport courtesy car.

**Holiday Inn.** *Inexpensive.* Good accommodations. Restaurant. Pool. Airport courtesy car.

## GADSDEN

**Ramada Inn.** *Moderate.* Large. TV, pool, playground, cafe, bar, entertainment. Pets allowed.

**Downtown Motor Hotel.** *Inexpensive.* Restaurant, pool.

**Holiday Inn.** *Inexpensive.* Airport courtesy bus. Restaurant, pool, pets allowed.

## GREENVILLE

**Holiday Inn.** *Moderate.* Well managed; appealing rooms. Restaurant. Pool. Pets accepted.

## GULF SHORES

**Hardwick Apts. & Motel.** *Expensive.* Kitchen apts., by day or week. Pool, private beach, balconies. Small pets allowed.

**Holiday Inn.** *Moderate.* Located on Gulf. Restaurant, lounge.

**Sea Horse Resort.** *Moderate.* Modern, small resort motel has furnished efficiencies and 3-room cottages. Restaurant nr. Some coffee makers in room. Gulf beach and fishing. Pets allowed.

**Young's by the Sea.** *Moderate.* On Gulf with private beach and fishing pier. Efficiency apts. and cottages available.

## GUNTERSVILLE

**Holiday Lodge.** *Moderate.* Small motel near golf course. Pool.

**Lake Guntersville State Resort Park.** *Moderate.* Restaurant. Golf, beach, camping, tennis, cabins.

**Val-Monte Motor Hotel.** *Moderate.* 3½ mi. S, 1 mi. E off US 431. A medium-size resort motel. Large rooms and living-bedroom suites, efficiencies, kitchenettes. Restaurant, room service. Pools, playground, lawn games, putting green, 18-hole golf course; 9-hole, par-3 course lighted for night play; yacht basin, fishing, waterskiing. Seasonal rates.

## HUNTSVILLE

**Skycenter Hotel.** *Expensive.* At airport. Large, attractive. Some studios. Restaurant, entertainment, dancing. Golf, heated pool. Free parking.

**Carriage Inn.** *Moderate.* 3811 University Dr. Very appealing rooms, some with balcony. Restaurant, entertainment, dancing. Airport courtesy car. Pool. Pets allowed.

**Hilton Inn.** *Moderate.* Pool, dining room, cafe, bar, entertainment, airport service.

**Holiday Inn.** *Moderate.* 3810 University Dr. Airport courtesy car, restaurant, pool. Pets allowed.

**Ramada Inn.** *Moderate.* 3502 Memorial Pkwy. S. Appealing rooms, restaurant, pool.

**Sheraton Motor Inn.** *Moderate.* 4404 University Dr. Large and comfortable. Specialty restaurant, entertainment, dancing, pool.

**Howard Johnson's.** *Inexpensive.* 2524 Memorial Pkwy. N. Some private patios, balconies. Restaurant. Pool. Pets allowed.

**King's Inn Motor Hotel.** *Inexpensive.* 1220 N. Memorial Pkwy. Large, attractive motel. Restaurant, room service. Pool.

**Sands Motor Hotel.** *Inexpensive.* 2700 Memorial Pkwy. Multi-storied. Large, tastefully decorated motel. Restaurant, room service. Heated pool.

**Tourway Inn.** *Inexpensive.* 1304 Memorial Pkwy. N. Nice rooms; some studios. Coffee makers in rooms. Pool.

## JASPER

**Holiday Inn.** *Moderate.* Nice. Some suites; restaurant, pool. Pets allowed.

## MOBILE

**ADMIRAL SEMMES HOTEL AND MOTOR HOTEL.** *Expensive.* 250 & 251 Government St. Large, nicely decorated downtown operation. Some suites. Restaurant, room service, bar. Heated pool.

**MALAGA INN.** *Expensive.* 359 Church St. Excellent restaurant, pool. In restored buildings with a courtyard.

**Ramada Inn.** *Expensive.* Two locations: 1705 Dauphin Island Pkwy., and Airport Blvd. Large member of this chain; attractively furnished, some studios. Restaurant, room service, pools.

**Albert Pick Motel.** *Moderate.* 1119 Government St. 2-level, modern motel. Restaurant, bar, room service, pools, playground.

**Holiday Inn.** *Moderate.* Four locations. Restaurant, pool, pets accepted. Battleship Pkwy., 3339 Government Blvd., 255 Church St., 850 S. Beltline Hwy.

**Howard Johnson's.** *Moderate.* 3132 Government Blvd. Appealing rooms, some with terraces. Pool (heated). Restaurant, room service.

**Mobile TraveLodge.** *Moderate.* 5559 Government St. Restaurant. Pool, seasonal rates.

**Quality Inn.** *Moderate.* Two locations. 3650 Airport Blvd., and 2701 Battleship Pkwy. In both: Airport courtesy car, nice rooms, restaurant, bar, pool, pets allowed.

**BATTLE HOUSE HOTEL.** *Inexpensive.* 26 N. Royal St. Famous hotel tastefully decorated. Restaurant, bar.

**Days Inn.** *Inexpensive.* I–65 & US 90. Member of popular chain. Pool, play area, gift shop, gas station. Pets. Tasty World restaurant.

**Olson Motel.** *Inexpensive.* 4137 Government Blvd. Small attractive motel with TV, telephones, air conditioning. Family units. Restaurant nr.

**Taylor Motel.** *Inexpensive.* 2598 Government Blvd. Comfortable rooms. Pool, restaurant nr. Coffee makers in rooms.

**Town House Motor Hotel.** *Inexpensive.* 1061 Government St. Nice rooms & grounds. Restaurant, bar, room service, pool.

## MONTGOMERY

**Governor's House Motel.** *Moderate.* 2705 E. Southern Blvd. Attractive rooms, many overlooking pool-patio area; some studios. Sauna, golf. Restaurant, bar, dancing, airport courtesy car.

**Holiday Inn.** *Moderate.* Three locations. All have restaurant, pool, and accept pets. Recommended: East: I–85 & US 231. Entertainment. Airport courtesy car.

**Howard Johnson's.** *Moderate.* Two locations. Both have some rooms with balconies. Restaurant, bar, coffeemakers in rooms. Pool. Accept pets. 1110 Eastern Bypass and 995 W. South Blvd.

**Ramada Inn.** *Moderate.* Two locations: 1000 West South Blvd.; and 1355 Eastern Bypass at I–85. Pleasant rooms. Airport courtesy car. Restaurant, dancing, entertainment. Heated pool. Pets permitted.

**Sheraton Motor Inn.** *Moderate.* 1100 W. South Blvd. Airport courtesy car. Multi-story. Restaurant, dancing, entertainment, pool, pets allowed.

**Continental.** *Inexpensive.* 3061 Mobile Hwy. Attractive, comfortable units. Restaurant, entertainment, dancing. Playground and pool. Courtesy airport car. Pets accepted.

**Days Inn.** *Inexpensive.* Two locations: I–65 & 1150 W. South Blvd., and Hope Hall Exit, I–65 & US 31. A good buy. Pool, play area, gift shop, gas station. Pets. Tasty World restaurant.

**Montgomery Coliseum TraveLodge.** *Inexpensive.* 1550 Federal Dr. Attractive rooms. Restaurant nr. Coffee makers in rooms. Pool. Pets allowed.

**Quality Inn–Diplomat.** *Inexpensive.* 3951 Norman Bridge Road. Swimming pool, restaurant.

**Rodeway Inn.** *Inexpensive.* 977 W. South Blvd. Appealing rooms. Restaurant, entertainment some nights. Heated pool. Airport courtesy car. Pets accepted.

**Whitley Hotel.** *Inexpensive.* 231 Montgomery St. Montgomery's largest hotel, with a wide choice of accommodations. Restaurant, coffee shop, bar. Free parking.

## OPELIKA

**Holiday Inn.** *Moderate.* Jct. of I–85 and Rte. 280. Comfortable, attractive rooms. Air conditioning, TV, restaurant, coffee makers in rooms, pool, large grounds.

**Days Inn.** *Inexpensive.* 1107 Columbus Pkwy. One of fine chain.

**Family Inn.** *Inexpensive.* 1105 Columbus Pkwy.

### OZARK

**Candlelight Motel.** *Moderate.* Modern, with pool, restaurant.

**Holiday Inn.** *Moderate.* Some studios. Restaurant, bar, coffee makers in rooms. Entertainment. Airport courtesy car, pool, pets allowed.

### POINT CLEAR

**GRAND HOTEL.** *Expensive.* Large resort hotel with wide choice of accommodations—cottages, cabanas, suites, studio rooms. On Mobile Bay. TV in most rooms. Dining rooms, bar, social program, tennis, golf privileges, pool, beach, dock, rental boats & motors, fishing, water skiing. With advance notice, trains and planes met. Seasonal rates, MAP and EP.

### SELMA

**Holiday Inn.** *Moderate.* Hwy. 80 W. Airport courtesy car, restaurant, bar, heated pool, pets allowed.

**PLANTATION INN.** *Inexpensive.* Hwy. 80 E. Small motel. Restaurant, pets allowed.

**Selma Motel.** *Inexpensive.* Nice rooms, restaurant, coffee makers in rooms, pool, pets allowed.

### TUSCALOOSA

**Holiday Inn.** *Moderate.* Two locations: 2 miles N on 82 bypass, and 3½ miles S at the junction of 82 bypass, I–20 and I–59. Both have restaurant, pool, and accept pets.

**Ramada Inn.** *Moderate.* 631 Skyland Blvd. Nice rooms, restaurant, pool, lounge.

**Sheraton University Inn.** *Moderate.* 4810 Skyland Blvd. E. Restaurant, lounge. pool.

**DINING OUT** in Alabama leads one toward trying traditional Southern dishes, including Southern fried chicken, ham steak with red gravy, and chicken pan pie. You'll soon discover that virtually everything is accompanied by at least a side-dish of the ubiquitous grits. Along the Gulf Coast, you can try creole specialties, so be sure to ask for Gulf flounder, shrimp, and other special seafoods and gumbos. In river towns or nearby, you might try catfish caught fresh from the Tennessee River. For other worthwhile restaurants, re-check our hotel listings. Restaurants are in order of price category. Price categories and ranges for a complete meal are as follows: *Expensive:* $6.50 and up; *Moderate:* $5-$8.50; *Inexpensive:* $2.50-$5.50. For a more complete explanation of restaurant categories see *Facts at Your Fingertips* at the front of this volume.

## ALBERTVILLE

**The King's Restaurant.** *Moderate*. Specialty, steaks and seafood. Closed Christmas.

**Food Basket.** *Inexpensive*. 301 Martlin. Steaks and seafood. Closed Thanksgiving and Christmas.

## ALEXANDER CITY

**Horseshoe Bend Restaurant.** *Moderate*. A daily buffet with large selection of items.

## ANNISTON

**Caro's Annistonian.** *Moderate*. Specialty: steaks, seafood.

**BATTLE HOUSE RESTAURANT.** *Inexpensive*. Roast beef a specialty. Closed Sun. nights and Christmas.

## AUBURN

**Gridiron.** *Moderate*. Specialties are prime ribs and steak.

**The Golden Dragon.** *Inexpensive*. Specialty is Chinese food. Closed Mon.

## BIRMINGHAM

### EDITOR'S CHOICES

Rating restaurants is, at best, a subjective business, and obviously a matter of personal taste. It is, therefore, difficult to call a restaurant "the best" and hope to get unanimous agreement. The restaurants listed below are our choices of the best eating places in Birmingham, and the places we would choose if we were visiting the city.

**CHRISTIAN'S CLASSIC CUISINE**                    French Cuisine
A simple but sophisticated atmosphere complemented by smooth service and waiters who are not afraid to make suggestions. *Expensive*. 2031-E Cahaba Road.

**HUGO'S ROTISSERIE**                             French Cuisine
The dining room, set atop the 14-story Hyatt House, is candlelit and elegant. The menu is ambitious, and the service is first-rate. Dancing. *Expensive*. 901 21st St. N.

**LEO'S**                                          American
Specializing in fresh seafood, this restaurant has a relaxed atmosphere in which patrons are comfortable in casual dress. *Moderate*. 401 18th St. S.

**SHERMAN KAO'S**                                  Chinese
Specializing in authentic Chinese Mandarin food, this is a relatively new but popular establishment. *Moderate*. 112-B Green Springs Hwy.

| **SUMO** | Japanese |

**SUMO** — Japanese
Japanese hibachi-style cooking at table, with an all-Japanese staff. Food preparation at table is a show in itself. *Expensive.* 7767 Eastwood Mall.

**Cork 'N Cleaver.** *Expensive.* 342 Valley Ave. Dinner only. Specialties include aged steaks, seafood, large salad bar selection.

**Gulas.** *Expensive.* 7401 Atlanta Hwy. A varied menu specializing in steaks and chops. Live music and dancing.

**Trader Ku's.** *Expensive.* 1575 Montgomery Hwy. S. Buffet lunch and dinner, featuring Polynesian atmosphere and cuisine.

**King's Inn.** *Moderate.* 2800 20th St. S. A charming dining-out spot, locally popular for a wide variety of menu items. Children's portions.

**Paul's Lamplighter.** *Moderate.* At Ramada Inn South Motel. Serves all meals in nice atmosphere. Children's portions.

**Rossi's.** *Moderate.* 427 S. 20th. Emphasis is on Italian cooking.

**Sarris.** *Moderate.* 600 N. 31st St. Seafood with a Greek flavor. Lunch, cafeteria style, and dinner. Ten blocks from Civic Center.

**Britling.** *Inexpensive.* Seven locations. City's best-known cafeteria. Varied selections. 4620 Ave. V; 2711 Culver Rd.; 2173 Highland Ave. S.; US 11 & Weibel Dr.; Aquarius Dr.; Parkway East; Hwy 31 S in Hoover Mall.

**Ireland's.** *Inexpensive.* Hwy 31 S at junction of State 149. Specialty: steak and biscuits. Entertainment.

**STEVE LEONTI'S SMOKEHOUSE.** *Inexpensive.* 2731 8th Ave. N. Barbecue deluxe with the spotlight on ribs.

## CULLMAN

**All Steak Restaurant.** *Inexpensive.* As you'd expect, steak is emphasized here, aged and in large portions, but they also offer seafood and chicken, plus rolls and pastries baked on premises. Sun. buffet lunch. Children's portions.

**Holiday Inn.** *Inexpensive.* Three attractive dining rooms, overlooking an enclosed pool, provide relaxed dining. Buffet is featured.

## DAUPHIN ISLAND

**Dauphin Sea House.** *Moderate.* Seafood a specialty.

## DECATUR

**Lyon's Dining Room.** *Moderate.* Specialty is steak.

**Gibson's.** *Inexpensive.* Specialty is barbecue, but the Brunswick stew is popular also.

## DOTHAN

**The Cellar.** *Moderate.* 119-B S. Oates St. Specialty: steaks.

**Garland House.** *Moderate.* 200 N. Bell St. Specialty is crepes.

**King's Inn.** *Moderate.* Popular locally for steaks. Dinner only. Entertainment, children's portions. Closed Sun.

## EUFAULA

**The Chewella Restaurant.** *Inexpensive.* Steaks a specialty.

**Town Terrace.** *Inexpensive.* Specialty: steaks.

## FLORENCE

**Dale's.** *Moderate.* Steak served in pleasant atmosphere. Dinners only. Children's portions.

**LAKEVIEW INN RESTAURANT.** *Moderate.* Regional specialties, sandwiches. Children's portions.

**STARKEY'S CAFETERIA.** *Inexpensive.* An inviting atmosphere in which to enjoy Southern fried chicken. Dinners. Children's portions.

## FORT PAYNE

**Black's.** *Moderate.* Located in Best Western Motel. Specialty is steaks and seafood. Open for all meals.

## GADSDEN

**Panorama.** *Inexpensive.* Specialty: steaks.

## GREENVILLE

**Moody's Steak House.** *Moderate.* Like it says, steak.

**Wyatt's Restaurant.** *Moderate.* General menu, casual atmosphere.

**Alabama Grill.** *Inexpensive.* Steaks a specialty. Closed Sun.

## GULF SHORES

**MEME'S.** *Expensive.* On the Bon Secour River. Seafood is the specialty. Evening reservations requested. Closed Mon.

**Gulf Shores State Park Lodge.** *Moderate.* Steaks and seafood.

**Shrimp Boat.** *Moderate.* Specializes in fresh seafood. Closed Wed.

## GUNTERSVILLE

**CATFISH CABIN.** *Inexpensive.* Serves the popular Southern delicacy, catfish, with all the trimmings.

Val Monte. *Inexpensive*. Seafood and steaks.

## HUNTSVILLE

Rib Cellar. *Expensive*. Well-prepared beef and lobster specialties. You can dance here, too. Dinners only.

Britling's Cafeteria. *Inexpensive*. Delicious meals; pleasant. Lunch and dinner.

King's Inn. *Inexpensive*. Specializes in broiled steaks. Private club. All meals.

## JASPER

White Way Restaurant. *Moderate.* Steaks and seafood.

## MOBILE

Gaslite Square. *Expensive*. 271 Azalea Road. Steaks and seafood, with live entertainment in an adjoining lounge. Lunch and dinner.

Eight Kings. *Moderate*. 3209 Airport Blvd. Fine European cuisine. Gracious atmosphere. Bar. Also informal pub and inexpensive sandwich shop.

Rousso's. *Moderate*. Battleship Pkwy. Seafood in a casual atmosphere.

Constantine's. *Inexpensive*. 1500 Government St. An outstanding restaurant for gourmet dishes, both Continental and American. Emphasis is on seafood preparations with shrimp, oysters, or crab. All meals served.

Morrison's. *Inexpensive*. 3282 Springdale Plaza. A regional chain of outstanding cafeterias, with good food attractively displayed and served. A favorite for family dining. Children's portions.

Sea Ranch Restaurant. *Inexpensive*. Battleship Pkwy. An attractive spot for dining and dancing. Seafood well prepared is the specialty. Unusual salads. Children's portions.

Wintzell's Oyster House. *Inexpensive*. 605 Dauphin St. Informal atmosphere and friendly service. Sometimes the atmosphere is better than the food, but it's always a good bet.

## MONTGOMERY

Mr. G's. *Expensive*. 3080 McGehee Rd. A gourmet restaurant featuring seafood and prime rib. Lunch and dinner.

ELITE CAFE. *Moderate*. 129 Montgomery St. A Montgomery tradition. Open for breakfast, lunch, and dinner.

La Chateau. *Moderate*. I–85 at Perry Hill Road. One of a fine chain, specializes in steaks.

Riviera. *Moderate*. 3085 Mobile Hwy. Good varied selection. Entertainment, dancing. Closed Sun.

**Morrison's.** *Inexpensive.* 150 Lee St. Another location in this reputable chain of cafeterias. Good food, attractively displayed. Children's portions. Open for lunch and dinner.

**Sahara Restaurant.** *Inexpensive.* 511 Edgemont. Music and pleasant decor provide a relaxing atmosphere in which to enjoy beef and seafood specialties. Children's portions. Closed Sun.

## ONEONTA

**LITTLE JOE'S.** *Inexpensive.* Family-style meals.

**Round The Clock.** *Inexpensive.* Delicious, buffet-style lunch and dinner.

## OPELIKA

**The Greenhouse.** *Moderate.* 114 N. 9th St. Specializes in Continental cuisine. Closed Sun. It's a good idea to call for reservations.

**Andy's.** *Inexpensive.* 2nd Ave. Steak and seafood.

**WHITE COLUMNS.** *Inexpensive.* 915 Ave. B. Housed in an old home, this restaurant specializes in steaks and seafood. Buffet served daily.

## POINT CLEAR

**GRAND HOTEL RESTAURANT.** *Moderate.* Specialty: steaks and seafood.

**Yardarm.** *Moderate.* Seafood.

**Baron's.** *Inexpensive.* Steaks and seafood. Closed Mon.

## SELMA

**Costa's.** *Expensive.* 1629 W. Highland Ave. Gourmet dining with American-Greek cuisine. Fresh seafood three times a week.

**Mangolds.** *Moderate.* 405 Highland Ave. Seafood, steaks, and country-cured ham.

## TUSCALOOSA

**Joe Namath's.** *Expensive.* 607 15th St. Prime rib au jus, selected steaks, entertainment.

**Nick's.** *Moderate.* Two locations: 4018 Eutaw Hwy., 919 Greensboro Ave. A hideaway for steaks. Bar with restaurant.

**THE PLANTATION.** *Moderate.* 3431 Hargrove Rd. E. Emphasis on down-home Southern-style cooking.

**The Ultimate Place.** *Moderate.* 2301 6th St. Combination restaurant, discoteque. Steaks and seafood featured.

**THE LAMPLIGHTER.** *Inexpensive.* 3408 Univ. Blvd. E. An inviting dining-out spot, charmingly decorated in a theme of the past. Choice steaks, fresh seafood, homemade salad dressing.

**Morrison's.** *Inexpensive.* 111 University Blvd. The good food and pleasant environment usual in this regional chain cafeteria. Open for lunch and dinner.

# ARKANSAS

## Pea Ridge and Prairie Grove

### by
### JUSTIN L. FAHERTY

*Justin Faherty is a former executive of the St. Louis* Globe Democrat.
*the New York* Herald Trubune, *and the Bergen (N.J.)* Record. *He
has written for newspapers on all fifty of the United States.*

Civil War memories and mementoes are not strewn as thickly
across Arkansas as they are across some of the other Southern states,
but those that exist are rich in historic importance and filled with
dramatic substance. Anyone interested in the war, especially its
western phase, must visit the state.

The Battle of Pea Ridge, March 7–8, 1862, was the most
important Civil War engagement west of the Mississippi. It ended
serious Confederate efforts to gain a foothold in nearby Missouri
and was unique in several ways. It was one of the few major battles
in which the South had the larger force. A brigade of Indians was
part of that lineup. They attacked with savage war whoops and
captured a three-gun battery, but then came under artillery fire, a
new experience for them, and broke for the woods where they could
fight from behind trees in a more familiar style. The Union forces
held on in the bloody battle. When the Confederates finally had to
pull back, three of their generals had been killed. (See *Practical
Information* section for details of site.)

A Southern defeat nine months later at neighboring Prairie Grove destroyed the Confederacy's plans for the West. This bitter confrontation just outside Fayetteville is now known as the "forgotten battle." Here ill-clad Arkansas frontiersmen armed only with squirrel rifles clashed with well-equipped Union soldiers and cavalry, managing to hold on until it grew dark, when they slipped away to Van Buren.

Union Gen. J. A. McClernand, on an expedition up the Arkansas River during a lull in the siege of Vicksburg, routed the Confederates on January 11, 1863 in a one-sided battle at Arkansas Post. This ancient and honorable place is the site of the oldest settlement west of the Mississippi, except for the Santa Fe, New Mexico, area.

July 4, 1863 was a momentous day. Gen. Robert E. Lee left Gettysburg in defeat. A Confederate effort to relieve the siege of Vicksburg by attacking Helena, Arkansas, on the Mississippi, was repulsed. On this day, proud Vicksburg surrendered.

More traces and memories of the Civil War can be found in Camden, Fayetteville, Hope, Pine Bluff, Little Rock—indeed throughout the state. Fort Smith is a particular treasure, blending as it does the Deep South with the Far West. There is the shady courthouse square with its towering Confederate monument, and there are the replicas of frontier days where saloons echo with the whoop of big Sam Houston. This former governor of Tennessee abandoned his post, separated from his wife, and came riproaring up the river through Little Rock and Fort Smith on one of the worst brawling drunks in history. He went on to renown as the leader of the Republic of Texas.

The beautiful Bonneville House has been restored, and the Free Ferry Road, which once bore the carriage and freight traffic from the plantations into Fort Smith's business district, is lined with fascinating old homes.

Jefferson Davis, president of the Confederacy, was a familiar figure in Fort Smith, and Gen. Zachary Taylor lived there for a time. There is now a religious shrine at the site of what remains of the home of this man who was the twelfth president of the United States.

## PRACTICAL INFORMATION FOR ARKANSAS

**HOW TO GET THERE.** *By air:* Direct flights to Little Rock, Fayetteville, Harrison, El Dorado, Jonesboro, Pine Bluff, Hot Springs, and Fort Smith by several airlines. Connecting flights and commuter service available.

*By car:* I–40 crosses the state from West Memphis to Fort Smith; I–30 connects Texarkana (Texas and Arkansas), with Little Rock; I–53 continues from the Missouri Bootheel to I–40 at West Memphis. A number of U.S. highways connect Arkansas with Missouri, Oklahoma, Texas, Louisiana, and Tennessee.

*By bus:* Major bus lines serving Arkansas from out of state are: Trailways, Greyhound, Arkansas Motor Coaches, Great Southern Coaches, and Oklahoma Coach Transportation Lines.

*By train:* Like many other states, Arkansas has no passenger railroad service now.

**HOW TO GET AROUND.** *By air:* Within the state service is provided by Frontier, Texas International, Braniff, and commuter lines. There are also air taxis: Central Flying Service and Hiegel Aviation, Inc. at Little Rock; Executive Air Service, Ozark Helicopters, and Spa Flying Service at Hot Springs.

*Car rentals:* Avis and Hertz have offices in El Dorado, Fayetteville, Fort Smith, Hot Springs, Jonesboro, Little Rock, Pine Bluff, and Texarkana. National is at Blytheville, Fayetteville, Fort Smith, Hot Springs, Little Rock, and Texarkana; Thrifty at Harrison, Little Rock, and Fort Smith; Budget at Little Rock.

**TOURIST INFORMATION.** Arkansas Dept. of Parks and Tourism, 149 State Capitol, Little Rock, 72201. Tourist Information Centers are located just inside the border on major highways leading into the state—Ashdown (US 71–59) near Texarkana; Texarkana (I–30); Bentonville (US 71); near Corning (US 67); Van Buren (I–40); near El Dorado (US 167); West Memphis (I–40.)

**STATE PARKS.** Arkansas has 24 state parks, and some are near points of Civil War interest: *Devil's Den,* at Winslow, near Prairie Grove Battlefield; *Winslow Springs,* at Huntsville, not too far from Fayetteville, Prairie Grove, Pea Ridge; *White Oaks Lake,* near Camden, the Confederate Cemetery, and Poison Springs Battlefield, and Hope, the Confederate state capital; *Lake Fort Smith,* near historic Fort Smith.

**CAMPING OUT.** Most state parks offer camping facilities. Write to Arkansas Dept. of Parks and Tourism, 149 State Capitol, Little Rock, 72201, for *Arkansas Camper's Guide.*

**MUSEUMS.** Museums with Civil War interest include: *Arkansas Post National Memorial,* 15 miles north of Dumas on Arkansas River. *Arkansas County Museum,* 2 miles north of Arkansas Post; Civil War memorabilia. *Fort Smith,* Fort Smith National Historic site, free; Old Fort Museum, small fee. *Helena,* Phillips County Museum, Civil War relics; free. *Newport,* Jacksonport Courthouse Museum; delta life; War Memorial Room; small fee.

**SPECIAL INTEREST SITES.** Old Homes. *Conway,* Greathouse Home; weekdays, March–October; free. *Fort Smith,* Bonneville House and the ante-bellum homes along Free Ferry Road (Chamber of Commerce, 613 Garrison Ave., 72901, has a walking-tour pamphlet and a list of old homes, called "Our Town"); *Helena,* many fine old homes. *Mountain Home,* Wolf House, restored two-story log house; artifacts; open May–October for short periods daily; small fee.

**HISTORIC SITES.** *Arkansas Post National Memorial* (see Museums); *Camden,* Confederate Cemetery, includes some 300 markers for unknown soldiers; Poison Springs Battleground State Historical Monument, 11

miles west, under development, diorama of battle. *Fayette,* Headquarters House, used by both sides during war; Civil War displays; daily except Monday, June–October; small fee. Prairie Grove Battlefield, 8 miles southwest. *Fort Smith,* Fort Smith National Historic Site (see Museums). *Hope,* Old Washington State Park; restoration; Confederate State Capitol, 1863–65; Royston House, home of Confederate Gen. Grandison Royston. *Rogers,* Pea Ridge National Military Park, 10 miles north; auto tour; restored Elkhorn Tavern.

**DRINKING LAWS.** Bottles may be purchased Mon. to Sat. from package liquor stores except in those counties voted dry by local option. In the areas of Little Rock, Hot Springs and the city of Eureka Springs, restaurants sell mixed drinks. Elsewhere they are available in private clubs only. Minimum age 21. Beer is served everywhere except in dry counties. No alcoholic beverage may be brought in from another state.

**HOTELS AND MOTELS.** Fine accommodations are available in all the larger cities and at the resorts, particularly at Hot Springs. Hotel and motel rates are based on double occupancy: *Expensive:* $25 and up; *Moderate:* $17 to $25; *Inexpensive:* Under $17.

**CAMDEN:** *Inexpensive:* Airport, Town House.

**CONWAY:** *Moderate:* Holiday Inn, Kings (Best Western), Ramada Inn. *Inexpensive:* Motel 6, Town House Motel.

**DUMAS:** *Inexpensive:* Delta Lodge.

**FAYETTEVILLE:** *Moderate:* Downtown Lodge, Holiday Inn, Ramada Inn, Scottish Inn. *Inexpensive:* Chief Motel.

**FORT SMITH:** *Moderate:* Holiday Inn Downtown, Peddler's Motor Inn (Best Western), King's Row Inn, Ramada Inn, Sheraton Inn, Trade Winds Inn (Best Western). *Inexpensive:* Motel 6, Sands Motel.

**HELENA:** *Moderate:* Holiday Inn.

**HOPE:** *Moderate:* Holiday Inn, Rodeway Inn, Sheraton Inn, Trade Winds (Best Western).

**LITTLE ROCK:** *Expensive:* Americana Inn, Camelot Hotel, Sheraton Inn, Holiday Inn (4 locations). *Moderate:* Coachman's Inn, Howard Johnson's, Magnolia Inn, Ramada Inn, Sam Peck Motel-Hotel, Town House (Best Western). *Inexpensive:* Alamo Plaza, Day's Inn (2 locations), Motel 6, Regal 8.

**MOUNTAIN HOME:** *Moderate:* Carriage Inn (Best Western), Holiday Inn, Mountain Inn, Mountain Home, Town and Country. *Inexpensive:* Carlton, White Sands.

**NEWPORT:** *Moderate:* Downtown Motel, Newport TraveLodge.

**ROGERS:** *Expensive:* Holiday Inn. *Moderate:* Hiway Host Inn. *Inexpensive:* Jan-Lin Motel, Town & Country Motel.

**DINING OUT.** Arkansas restaurants usually are less expensive than those in more heavily populated states. In addition, you will frequently find such popular Arkansas favorites as fresh-fried fish, Hickory-smoked and/or barbecued meats, and hot apple or huckleberry pie. Restaurants are listed according to price category based on a complete meal: *Expensive,* \$8.50–\$12; *Moderate,* \$5.50–\$8; *Inexpensive,* \$3–\$5.50. Drinks are not included and, in Arkansas, are available in restaurants only in Hot Springs, Little Rock, and the Eureka Springs area. Beer is available in restaurants any day except Sunday in areas where it is not banned by local option.

Restaurants listed are other than those at motels and hotels listed above. Most of those inns have their own dining rooms.

**FAYETTEVILLE:** *Expensive:* Farmer's Daughter.

**FORT SMITH:** *Moderate:* Emmy's, Red Barn. *Inexpensive:* Jan's, Furr's (cafeteria), Wyatt's (cafeteria).

**LITTLE ROCK:** *Expensive:* The Leather Bottle. *Moderate:* Bruno's Little Italy. *Inexpensive:* Franke's (cafeteria), Golden Host (cafeteria).

**MOUNTAIN HOME:** *Moderate:* Cedar Grill.

**NEWPORT:** *Inexpensive:* Kelley's Grill.

**ROGERS:** *Moderate:* Lakeside.

**RUSSELLVILLE:** *Moderate:* DEE DEE'S PLACE. Reconverted pioneer boarding house.

# FLORIDA

## *The Confederacy's Southern Flank*

### by
### FLORENCE LEMKOWITZ

*A resident and ardent lover of Flordia, Florence Lemkowitz is a freelance writer whose articles appear in a number of top magazines and newspapers, including a monthly column in* ASTA Travel News *magazine. A former travel editor of the* Hartford Times, *she is the recipient of international and domestic travel writing awards.*

Florida is world famous for its sunny beaches and Number One tourist attraction, Disney World, but the influential role the Sunshine State played in history is often overlooked, the serious being upstaged by the sun-sand-and-sea resorts and magnificent theme parks.

Throughout the centuries, Florida was claimed for kings and by buccaneers, creating a lawless territory. Eventually permanent settlers were attracted to this land of plenty where they could fish, farm, and enjoy the good life, especially when Florida became a territory of the United States in 1821.

Fifteen years later the first railroads began operating in the state, and each year brought more progress. By 1838 a state constitution was drawn up at St. Joseph, and in 1845 Florida became the 27th state.

As a slaveholding state, Florida seceded from the Union on January 10, 1861. It suffered enormous losses during the Civil War. The damage to its economy was surpassed only by Mississippi and South Carolina. More than 16,000 Floridians fought, and one of every eight white male Floridians died. Casualties were said to be more than 5,000. One of the heroines, Mary Martha Reid, was the first female nurse in the Confederate Army. Sun-worshipping tourists now stroll the beaches, but off the Atlantic and Gulf coasts of Florida Confederate blockade runners played dangerous games with the Federal gunboats of the South Atlantic Blockading Squadron and the East Gulf Blockading Squadron. The CSS *Florida,* considered the most successful Confederate blockade runner, captured 75 Union ships.

Fernandina, Jacksonville, St. Augustine, and Key West on the east coast, and Pensacola, Cedar Key, and Fort Myers on the west coast were captured by Federal troops early in the war, but the capital, Tallahassee, was never taken, thanks to the Confederate forces who stopped the Federal troops at Natural Bridge.

The major Civil War battle fought on Florida soil was at Olustee, near Lake City, on February 20, 1864. Each year there is a reenactment at the Olustee Battlefield State Historic Site. More than 300 volunteers set up camp, but there are never enough volunteers to be the Yankees.

Tourism probably began as soon as the Civil War was over, because so many Union soldiers and officers liked the warm, sunny climate, the beaches, and the plantation lands. Quite a few settled along the east coast, from what is now Palm Beach to Titusville. These pioneers were interested in growing coconut palms, pineapple, and citrus.

Harriet Beecher Stowe, who wrote *Uncle Tom's Cabin,* was one of the most enthusiastic Northern visitors. When the War Between the States was over, she stayed near the St. Johns River in a little town named Mandarin where her husband was a preacher. Mrs. Stowe spent her time writing travel stories about Florida for newspapers and magazines up North. She was the first to promote Florida for vacations and as a winter home.

By the 1870s Green Cove Springs was the fashionable resort to see and in which to be seen, and the social set arrived by steamer from Jacksonville.

The Civil War also influenced early settlement of Sanibel Island. Following the death of Capt. Lee Roy Moncure Nutt in Tennessee, his widow, three daughters, mother, and brother-in-law decided to start a new life and homestead on Sanibel, when the war was over. They were such a close family that even during the war the Captain's wife and three daughters accompanied him to every camp and every battle.

Laetitia Nutt never forgave President Lincoln or the North and remained a Confederate until her death. In fact she and her daughters organized the Fort Myers Chapter of the United Daughters of the Confederacy, still in existence today. The home built on

Sanibel Island, Gray Gables, on West Gulf Drive, and the family cemetery on the property, is cared for by The Sanibel Preservation of Historic Sites Committee.

The Civil War certainly left its mark on Florida. One of the best ways to begin your historic sightseeing trip is at the welcome station at Yulee and then drive on to Fernandina Beach and Jacksonville, some of the first Union conquests. Yulee is named for Florida's first senator, David Levy Yulee, a prominent Civil War figure.

On Amelia Island, north of Jacksonville, work began in 1847 on Fort Clinch, named after a Seminole War hero, Gen. Duncan Lamont Clinch. U.S. Secretary of War Jefferson Davis authorized its construction. However, the fort was neither finished nor equipped by the time the Civil War broke out, and the Confederates quickly moved in and tried to finish the job. In the interim, Gen. Robert E. Lee had inspected the site. He was in the area to visit his father's grave on nearby Cumberland Island. The Third Florida Volunteers occupied the fort until 1862 when a strong Union Army force approached. One dark night the Confederates decided to take their guns and evacuate. They confused the Union soldiers by leaving palm logs painted black as decoys on Cumberland Island across from the fort. Much to the Federalists surprise, they took the fort without firing a shot. The Northern forces kept Fort Clinch throughout the rest of the war.

Used briefly during the Spanish-American War, the fort was almost abandoned, but in 1935 the city of Fernandina and the state bought it for a park. During World War II it was used for radar and Coast Guard details.

Now inside 1,086-acre Fort Clinch State Park, the fort makes a pleasant sightseeing and picnicking spot. There are trails and camping areas, a lodge, and a boat ramp. At the fort itself you can see the bricks installed before the Civil War, different from those above the rifle ports, which came from the North and were installed from 1862 to 1867. Inside the guardhouse you can see the original 1859 gun carriage. The fort museum was formerly the soldiers' barracks and houses an historical collection which includes Gen. Clinch's field bed that was carried from battlefield to battlefield.

The ramparts, built up by sand brought in by train from surrounding dunes, include cannons placed here by Confederate troops in 1861. Original plans had called for at least 60 guns on the ramparts to protect Cumberland Sound. Cisterns collected rainwater for drinking. As you can see, Fort Clinch has a strategic location on the north end of the island overlooking Cumberland Sound and the entrance to the St. Mary's and the Amelia rivers. South of the fort, at Fernandina Beach, is fourteen miles of some of the finest bathing beaches you will find anywhere. Depending on the tides, cars at times may be driven over the packed sands. While photographing the old Amelia Island lighthouse you might like to know that it has been doing its job since 1839.

A volunteer Confederate militia regiment, The Third Florida was led by Col. William Scott Dilsworth, a planter's son from Monticello. Not a shot was fired when they captured all defenses on Amelia Island in April 1861. Cases of ammunition were shipped in from Southern sympathizers in the North. One was said to be Fernando Wood, the Mayor of New York, because his first name was similar to Fernandina.

Since Col. Dilsworth had only six companies in his entire regiment, it was impossible for him to hold the fort against the Federal fleet. Also, the Yankees played a trick on the unsuspecting Southerners. A ship flying the French flag entered the harbor and signaled for a pilot. On March 2, 1862, Col. D. F. Holland of the Fourth Florida Regulars and six soldiers went to assist the ship. Needless to say, they were captured.

When reports that U.S. gunboats were headed toward the fort reached Col. Dilsworth, the command was given to evacuate and to destroy the railroad bridge over the inland waterway. Just as the last trainload of residents and soldiers was crossing the bridge, a shell from one of the warships hit. Two men were killed aboard the train, one of them seated next to Sen. David Yulee.

Yulee had started Florida's first cross-state railroad, from Fernandina to Cedar Key. He was imprisoned by the Federalists but later pardoned by President Grant. What was left of his railroad was sold to Northern businessmen in 1866.

But back to Fort Clinch. After the U.S. Land and Naval Forces, under Com. Dupont and Gen. Wright, captured the fort on March 4, 1862, they stayed here victoriously until the end of the war.

## Old Fernandina

When the National Register of Historic Places designated Old Fernandina as an Historic District, city officials had been restoring and refurbishing the old buildings for several years. In addition, the town received a $1.3-million grant to complete the project and "to use history as a resource." Six blocks of Centre Street (Atlantic Avenue) are included in the program, and power lines will go underground to enhance the area's centuries-old atmosphere. The coquina rock sidewalks will be replaced and carved granite curbstones will be installed, and the mercury vapor lights will be replaced by incandescent lighting of the period.

Visitors will be encouraged to take walking tours, and parking on Atlantic Avenue will be limited. The 12 miles of U.S. Highway A1A from the city limits to I–95 will be four-laned, and the Amelia River will be spanned by a new, high-level bridge.

Try a do-it-yourself walking and driving tour, because there are many interesting Civil War sights. The old red brick railroad depot, part of David Yulee's dream of a cross-state railroad between Fernandina and Cedar Key, now houses the Fernandina Chamber of Commerce. Althouggh the Civil War ended the dream of Fernandina becoming a railroad center, the historic depot is a warm, friendly place where visitors are always welcome. This is a good place to stop for information. Nearby Florida House, built by the

Florida Railroad Company before the Civil War, hosted such famous guests as the Rockefellers in the late 1880s.

The Lassenne House (Davis House) built by Dr. Lassenne in the late 1850s, is also pre–Civil War. Constructed of hand-hewn timber and fastened with wooden pegs, the house (as well as the Post Office) is one of the island's oldest inhabited dwellings.

The Williams Home, at 103 S. 9th St., was built in 1859 by a Bostonian. Being against secession, he sold the house to Marcellus Williams, who had come to Florida in 1846 to survey Spanish land grants and, ten years later, to survey the Everglades. He married the great-granddaughter of a Spaniard who had an extensive family grant from King Philip in the Mayport–Jacksonville area. Williams brought his bride to Fernandina because of the Spanish community, and they resided in this fine home. During the Civil War, Jefferson Davis stored his prized possessions with the couple. When Fernandina was occupied by Federal troops, the Williams family was asked to take a loyalty oath to the United States Government.

On the corner of Atlantic and 8th, St. Peter's Parish Episcopal Church was formerly the Church of the Good Shepherd, built in 1859. The bell also dates back to pre–Civil War days and is from one of the old Florida railroad engines. When Federal troops occupied the church, a Black school was formed by the Freedman's Bureau, and classes were held in the building. To the right of the church entrance are two memorial windows, dedicated to the memory of Mary Martha Reid and her son Raymond. The widow of Florida Governor R. R. Reid, Mary Martha was the first woman nurse in the Confederate Army. Eventually, with Dr. Thomas Palmer, she founded a hospital for Florida soldiers. It was located near Richmond, Virginia, where she worked until President Jefferson Davis had to seek refuge away from the Confederate capital. She joined him in his flight. Her son Raymond was mortally wounded in the Battle of the Wilderness. Mary Martha Reid is buried in St. Peter's Cemetery at Alachua and 8th, in Fernandina.

The Presbyterian Church is between Alachua and Atlantic. One of the oldest churches in the state, it is the oldest in Fernandina. David L. Yulee donated the land upon which it was built in 1859. Inside you can see its original Bible, as well as other artifacts. During the Civil War Federal troops were garrisoned in the church. They wanted to melt down the bell for Army hardware but were stopped by their Major W. Duryee. In fact, this Federal officer returned to become one of Fernandina's leading residents.

In 1859, Archibald Baker, the first pastor of the First Presbyterian Church, purchased a home from the bachelor who built it in the mid–1850s. Known as the Baker House, the distinctive landmark is located at 112 North 6th. During the Civil War Federal officers lived there. Some of the sentimental ones returned to visit the home many years later and were welcomed by Archibald Baker's granddaughter.

On 120 North 6th is the Prescott House, built soon after the Civil War by Lt. Josiah Prescott of the Union Army. During the occupation he got to like Fernandina so much that he returned after the war, went into the saw-mill business, and constructed his new home with lumber from his own mill.

Although David Yulee's home was razed because it fell into ruins after his death, you can see the marker on the site at 3rd and Alachua. The plaque reads: "Senator, developer, statesman, and builder of Florida's first railroad."

The Fairbanks Home, on South 7th between Beech and Cedar, was built by the Confederate Major George Fairbanks, who was originally from Watertown, New York. The ornate dwelling is also known as "Fairbanks' Folly," as it was built to surprise his wife. Evidently the yellow and green Italianite residence with a bright red trim was not to her taste, although R. Schuyler was the same architect who had designed St. Peter's Episcopal Church. However, the Fairbanks's kissed and made up, and the former Confederate major founded the Florida Historical Society, edited *The Florida Mirror,* authored *The History of Florida,* and established the citrus industry.

## St. Augustine

Here you should visit old St. Francis Inn, once known as the Dummitt House, headquarters for Civil War spies, before that a jail just after Florida became a U.S. territory, before that a barracks for English soldiers . . . and before that the first church of the Franciscans, in 1577.

Fort George Island's most colorful resident perhaps was Zephaniah Kingsley, a squat little Scotch slave trader who picked the island as headquarters for his business because it was still Spanish territory and he expected the United States to forbid slave imports. The U.S.A. did just that in 1807, but Kingsley was already in action. He had expanded his operation into a combination plantation and training school for slaves by the time the U.S.A. acquired Florida from Spain in 1821. His activities then became illegal, of course, but more profitable as well.

Kingsley married the daughter of an African East Coast king, and she—as Ma'm Anna—oversaw the training of the slaves. Her full name was Anna Madegigine Jai, and she remained Kingsley's favorite despite his propensity for spotting other comely companions among the slave cargo.

The Kingsley plantation buildings are preserved in a state historical memorial and may be seen by taking a paved but unnumbered road from Fort George. The trip takes only a few minutes.

Another pre–Civil War town, Lake View, in 1858 consisted of eight acres and four lakes. Purchased by Northern speculators in 1881, the area was renamed Winter Park.

## Key West

Some historic Old South landmarks are in Key West: Fort Jefferson National Monument, once a Civil War prison, and the lighthouse, dating back to 1856. Dr. Samuel Mudd, who treated John Wilkes Booth's broken leg without realizing Booth had assassinated President Abraham Lincoln, served a term in Fort Jefferson. On South Roosevelt Avenue the Martello Gallery and Museum is housed in what was a fort constructed by Union forces who controlled the island. Key West was the only Southern city continually in Union hands. Originally named Fort Taylor, the East Martello and West Martello towers were never completed. Among the interesting items in the museum are beds and railings from a Civil War hospital.

Should you be traveling north on the Keys to Miami Beach, a visit to Key Biscayne is well worth the trip—about a 20-minute drive from Miami. At the southern tip of Key Biscayne, off US 1, you will find the historic Cape Florida Lighthouse in the 400-acre Bill Baggs Cape Florida State Recreation Area. One of south Florida's oldest structures, it began marking the Cape Florida channel in 1825, when pirates sailed around Biscayne Bay. After being burned by Indians in 1836, the original 65-foot brick lighthouse was replaced by a 95-foot stone structure, completed in 1855.

At the start of the Civil War the lighting system was destroyed, and Cape Florida remained dark for six years. When the Fowey Rocks light was established three miles southeast in 1878, the lighthouse went dark again.

One hundred years later, rangers at the Bill Baggs Cape Florida State Recreation Area agreed that the light should be restored for history buffs and as an extra assistance for boaters. The Coast Guard agreed. They discovered a Fresnel lens, made in Paris in the late 1880s, which had been dismantled from the old Rebecca Shoals Light in Dry Tortugas. The ingenious Coast Guardsmen hooked up a light which will cost only $2 a year to operate but can be seen up to seven miles after being magnified through the Fresnel lens. The Cape Florida Lighthouse blinks again as it did over 160 years ago.

Just across the river from DeSoto National Park on US 41 or 301, turn east for a couple of miles to reach the Gamble Mansion, a plantation-style antebellum museum. Judah P. Benjamin, Confederate Secretary of State, hid out here briefly after the South lost the war and eventually made it to England where he became a successful barrister. The Gamble Mansion is the oldest on Florida's west coast, furnished with treasures to recall the days when this was a flourishing sugar plantation.

South of Bradenton is the important cultural center of Sarasota and its outstanding beaches on Lido Key, Siesta Key, Longboat Key, and Anna Maria Island. There are treasure hunters who believe that during the Civil War a Confederate blockade runner was run aground by a Federal gunboat in Sarasota Bay, just off Anna Maria Island. Some claim the blockade runner had a valuable cargo, but that the captain and crewmen escaped without saving it because they knew the Union troops would hang them if they were captured. Eventually tons of sand covered the small steam vessel and its valuable cargo, but persistent treasure hunters haven't given up.

In East Bradenton you can visit the oldest existing courthouse in Florida, a small frame building canopied by immense oaks in the Manatee Village Historical Park. Beautifully restored with gleaming rubbed yellow pine ceilings and walls and handmade benches, the courthouse was built in 1860 by Ezekiel Glazier, one of the first residents of the county. Old courthouse documents are displayed on the walls. One document describes the case of a runaway slave and the nearby Terra Ceia Islander charged with harboring him. After payment of $750 for the slave, the case was settled.

Along Florida's east coast, most of the Civil War action was blockade running, a dangerous hide-and-seek game against Federal gunboats. In spring of 1861 President Lincoln ordered all Southern ports blockaded from Cape Henry to the Mexican border, a distance of 4,000 miles.

Under cover of darkness, small fast steam vessels with short masts would sneak out of port for a quick cruise to Bermuda, Nassau, or Havana to pick up cargoes from England. Camouflaged with grey paint and helped by their cut-down design, the blockade runners easily slipped by Federal ships at night. If a sailor aboard a blockade runner showed a light as they neared shore, he was shot.

Any shot against the Union ships was considered an act of piracy, and death was the penalty. Crewmen captured from blockade runners were treated as prisoners of war. When blockade runners could not escape Union ships, the crew would scuttle their vessel and use the small boats. When the captain of the blockade runner *Elizabeth* had to abandon ship at Jupiter Inlet north of what is now Palm Beach, he escaped up the river in a small boat, taking along a case of gin to ease the pain of losing his ship.

The South Atlantic Blockading Squadron prowled the area from Cape Canaveral north and the East Gulf Blockading Squadron kept a steady lookout for blockade runners in the waters from Cape Canaveral south as well as to the west coast as far as St. Andrews Bay.

Although it was impossible for the blockading fleet to be everywhere, an especially strict watch was kept on Ponce de Leon Inlet (near what is now Daytona Beach), as this was a favorite port for blockade runners. Arms and ammunition were brought to the inlet and transported by wagon to the St. Johns River, then taken up the Ocklawaha River to Fort Brooks. The cargo went from there to Waldo via wagon and onward to Georgia and other Southern states.

When the *Carolina,* a well-known blockade runner, was being unloaded at Ponce de Leon Inlet, Union sailors arrived, but too late. The Confederates had been warned and had abandoned the ship. The blockade runner was taken over by the Federalists, but a skirmish ensued. In retaliation for the losses, the South Atlantic Blockading Squadron ships shelled some houses at New Smyrna on July 26, 1863.

Captured blockade runners were sent on to Key West, but so many accumulated that some vessels had to be sent up North. Of the 1,000 blockade runners captured during the Civil War, one-seventh were taken along the Florida coast. Profits made on successful runs were so high that a blockade runner's owner could afford the loss if his vessel made two runs and was captured on the third. Some very lucky ships actually made 18 runs.

A blockade runner carrying 800 bales of cotton could earn $420,000 on a successful trip to Nassau or Bermuda. On its return, the ship would be loaded with arms, ammunition, food, and luxury items for Southerners. Most of the blockade runners from Florida sailed to Nassau, bringing great prosperity to that port. Havana was the port for blockade runners from the Gulf of Mexico.

Each man aboard a Federal ship instrumental in the capture of a blockade runner would share in the prize money. The blockade runner *Memphis* earned $510,914 for its Union captors, and the *Banshee* paid off with $104,948.

The *America,* one of the most famous yachts in the world, was involved in Confederate blockade running. After winning the famous *America's Cup* race in 1851, the yacht was eventually sold to an Englishman who re-sold it to the Confederates. She was renamed *Memphis* and did her blockade running on the St. Johns River.

Federal gunboats pursued the *Memphis* so closely on one trip that her crew scuttled her south of Jacksonville in Dunn's Creek. Unfortunately the tall masts protruded above the water and were spotted by the Federals. She was raised, refitted, and re-named— *America.* For the remainder of the Civil War she was part of the South Atlantic Blockading Squadron under the command of Commodore Samuel F. DuPont.

The forerunners of modern destroyers, blockade runners must have been a successful operation. Only half of them were ever caught by the Federals.

A small group of settlers in 1850 named their new hometown "Jernigan," after one of the hardy pioneers. The name was changed to Orlando in 1857, and it was incorporated as a city in 1875.

The first residents raised hogs and cattle and became known as "Crackers" because of the cracking sound they made with their whips to drive the cattle and also to signal each other. When the Crackers came to town in the 1800s, the shootouts in front of the old saloons were like scenes from the Wild West.

Northwest of Orlando, Starkes Ferry is a little rural area between Umatilla and Weirsdale. The fishing is excellent, and you can see a manually-operated swing bridge across the Oklawaha River where it meets SR 42 in south Marion County. This was the site of the old ferry crossing for Confederate Maj. Thomas Starke's plantation when he traveled in the 1860s. Plans call for a modern high-level bridge to be built in the near future, and the hand-cranked bridge that swings open to clear the channel will be a memory. This is bass country, and on either side of the river are rustic fishing camps, and camp and trailer sites.

## The Gulf Coast

Even before the Civil War, Florida's beaches attracted sun-worshippers, and around 1857 a John Gomez of Tampa organized tours to Pass-a-Grille by boat.

Although the important Civil War battles were in the northern part of the state, Confederate sympathizers and guerillas harrassed Union garrisons along Florida's Gulf Coast from the Tampa Bay area all the way to Cedar Key. People in Salt Springs, west of where Port Richey is today, volunteered to make salt and ship it to the Confederate troops.

Some west coast settlers became guerillas by chance. Abel Miranda, a Cuban of Spanish parentage, arrived at Maximo Point (now part of what is the St. Petersburg area) about 1859 to build a home, raise cattle, plant fruits and vegetables, and fish for fun and profit. He was a successful pioneer when the Civil War began and did not take sides. But everything changed after the Federalists captured Tampa and the U.S. Navy anchored across the bay from Miranda's homestead. A group of Union sailors unofficially borrowed a fishing boat, cruised to Egmont Key to steal a cannon, and proceeded to Maximo Point. Miranda's farm was their target. The family was able to escape, but everything was burned to the ground. Needless to say, Abel Miranda was extremely bitter against the Northerners and organized a group of Rebel fighters to harass Union outposts on the Gulf coast. His comrades were other farmers whose property had been ruined by the raiders. After ambushing Union troops near the Weeki Wachee River, he gained notoriety as "Miranda the Cat." All along the Gulf Coast he prevented raids on homesteads and river settlements. When the Civil War ended, Abel Miranda returned to Maximo Point, again cleared the land for his farm and ranch, and lived happily ever after.

Union soldiers fortified 300-acre Egmont Key, an island in the mouth of Tampa Bay, and Union gunboats patrolled nearby waters.

Southwest of Mullet Key (and what is now Fort DeSoto Park), Egmont Key is not connected to the mainland and is accessible to picnickers only by private or rental boat. The towering Egmont Lighthouse, built in 1848, still stands guard over the beautiful blue-green waters of the gulf, bay, and powdery white sands dotted with golden sea oats. Just as it was during the Civil War, the beacon is the guiding light for ships entering Tampa Bay.

Through three wars, Egmont Key was occupied by the military. The tiny island was visited twice by Ponce de Leon in the 16th century, by Spanish explorer Hernando DeSoto, and by the Earl of Egmont, an English land speculator who staked his claim when Spain owned Florida.

Now bird-watchers, treasure-hunters, and beach-lovers consider Egmont Key their own special island.

An interesting trip north from Tampa includes the Greek sponge-fishing village of Tarpon Springs, Weeki Wachee theme park with mermaid shows, Yulee Sugar Mill Ruins, and Homosassa Springs.

You will also be driving through Pasco County, named for Sam Pasco, a popular Florida politician and a Civil War Hero.

Yulee Sugar Mill Ruins, a State Historic Site, was once the more than 5,000-acre plantation of David Levy Yulee, the state's first U.S. Senator. Before the Civil War began, Yulee and his family lived in Fernandina, where he had established the railroad to Cedar Key. He also maintained the sugar mill and plantation in Homosassa, just outside of Homosassa Springs.

Concerned for his family's safety at the outbreak of the war, he sent them to the Homosassa mansion while he stayed in Fernandina. After his railroad was destroyed by the Federalists and Fernandina was captured, Sen. Yulee joined his family in Homosassa. One day when they were away, the Union soldiers set fire to the plantation and everything was ruined except for the sugar mill machinery. The senator and his family moved to a cotton plantation near Archer. The Homosassa manor was never rebuilt, and the beautiful six-acre park is a favorite picnic area. In 1845 the area from the Withlacoochee River north to the Suwannee River was supposed to be named Levy County in honor of Sen. David Levy Yulee, but the surveyors found this to be too complicated because the region included parts of other counties.

## Cedar Key

Cedar Key, actually a town of 40 islands, made its mark in Civil War history books. The Union warship *Hatteras* sailed boldly into Cedar Key harbor and sank a ferry boat, three sloops, and four big schooners. According to local historians, each vessel had a strongbox filled with thousands of dollars worth of gold and silver coins. For over a hundred years anxious treasure hunters have been hoping to retrieve some of this fortune, but so far no one has come up with the loot.

After Atlanta was burned during the war, plantation owners shipped their slaves to Cedar Key. The old Island Hotel, once the Parsons and Hale General Store with upstairs rooms for rent, has been a landmark for almost 140 years. The decor may be contemporary-ramshackle, but the food is excellent, especially the freshly caught fish and seafood.

Just west of Cedar Key is Seahorse Key, once the stomping grounds of pirate Jean Lafitte. At some point during the Civil War Confederate troops brought over a battery of three brass cannon to protect the channel against the expected Federalists' invasion. Now there is added treasure hidden in the sands of Seahorse Key— Lafitte's gold and the brass cannon.

Although it still is photogenic, the lighthouse on Seahorse Key, built in 1855, no longer functions.

Just north of Lake City on US 41, at White Springs, is the Stephen Foster Memorial on the Suwannee River. Carillon recitals from the two-hundred-foot tower feature the composer's work four times daily. Foster never even saw the Suwannee, of course, picking the name for its beauty. As it happened, he picked a good one—the rambling Suwannee, from the Georgia line to the Gulf, is a beautiful stream, and the 243–acre park at the Memorial sets it off well. The Florida Folk Festival, with two thousand or more folk dancers, singers, craftsmen and tale tellers, is held during the first week in May each year. A "Jeannie With the Light Brown Hair" contest is held in February, with Florida lasses of both beauty and musical talent competing for a scholarship.

Less than twenty miles east of Lake City, on US 90, is the Olustee Battlefield Memorial (a State Historic Site), where the only significant Florida battle of the Civil War occurred on February 20, 1864. A museum there has displays of the action, plus newspaper accounts of the battle, in which the Confederates entrenched east of Lake City. There is an annual reenactment, and the public is invited to watch the preliminary skirmish, the battle, and to visit the authentic camps. At night there is a parade, and Civil War songs and entertainment around the campfire.

The Olustee battle had its beginnings when Union troops fanned out from.Jacksonville, captured for the fourth time on February 7, 1864. Union Gen. Truman Seymour wanted to break communication and supply lines between east and west Florida by capturing the territory. Confederate Gen. Joseph Finegan established his camp on Ocean Pond east of Lake City. Union forces got to within 3 miles of Lake City but then had to withdraw to Sanderson after the small skirmish that preceded the main battle.

After much tactical guessing by both sides, the forces met in an open field near noon, and by late afternoon the five-hour battle was over. The Federals, with 5,500 officers and men and sixteen guns, had 1,861 killed, 1,142 wounded and 506 missing. Confederate forces, with a smaller total of 5,200, lost 946 killed, 847 wounded, and 6 missing. The Federals withdrew to Jacksonville, with Rebel Cavalry pursuing, but rather slowly.

The Northern forces remained in command of Jacksonville, St. Augustine and Fernandina for the rest of the war but did not venture into the interior in strength again.

### Tallahassee

You won't want to miss the Museum of Florida History, which opened in early summer 1977, about two blocks from the state Capitol. Admission is free and includes exhibits of a prehistoric mastodon recovered in Wakulla Springs, sunken treasure from Spanish galleons, and uniforms worn by Florida soldiers during the Civil War.

Should you be driving by the Capital City Country Club along Old Fort Drive, you might like to know that this is the Old Fort Site, where Tallahassee residents fortified the capital of Florida.

Along Park Avenue, lined with beautiful trees and shrubs, visitors always admire the antebellum homes. At the Knott House, built in 1840, local residents claim the first camellia bush in Florida was planted. The Murphy House, dating back to 1836, was occupied by Federal troops during the post-war occupation. Their horses were stabled in the basement. The Shine-Chittenden House and the Lewis House were built in the 1830s and 1840s. Unfortunately these old mansions are not open to the public.

While on Park Avenue you may also want to see the May Oak in Lewis Park, site of the May Party, the oldest festival in the South, dating back to 1838. The park is listed on the National Register of Historic Landmarks.

Also well worth a visit is Calhoun Street Historical District. Although the antebellum mansions are not open to the public, visitors are welcome to stroll along what was once the city's most prominent street. The Towle House, built in 1847, belonged to Simon Towle, State Comptroller. The circa-1840 mansion next door was built for Henry Rutgers, City Councilman and Territorial Treasurer. It is now the Tallahassee Garden Club headquarters.

The Randall-Lewis House, built in 1835 for a Federal Judge, was said to have been constructed by George Proctor, a free Negro prominent in local building. Built in the 1840s, the Bloxham House belonged to a well-known Tallahassee merchant and was the governor's residence from 1881 to 1901. In 1894 President McKinley was an honored guest in this lovely home. One of the first "prefab" homes is in this historical district—the Bowen House, circa 1830. The structure of New England white pine was cut in New York state and shipped to Tallahassee coded to be joined by a peg connection system.

While in the Park Avenue—Calhoun Street area you may visit the First Presbyterian Church, constructed in 1838 and the oldest in the city. The original slave gallery has been rebuilt.

At Florida A & M University, a small but notable museum of Black history has interesting Civil War exhibits and the infamous shackles worn by slaves.

Another interesting site is Old City Cemetery, dating back to 1829. Here you can read the tombstones of many early settlers, slaves, and Confederate and Union troops who fell in the battles at Olustee and Natural Bridge.

Black history also was made in the Frenchtown area of Tallahassee. The French settled here in the 1800s, and large pecan groves flourished. When the French left, their slaves stayed on after the Civil War, and Frenchtown is predominantly Black. Even now, hawkers carrying burlap bags of freshly picked pecans wheel and deal with buyers. Daily they cry out the price they want, and the backyard business goes on at a daily rate of 40,000 to 50,000 pounds of pecans. Unfortunately this business is dying because of competition from owners of large groves selling to packers.

Near the airport is the Tallahassee Junior Museum's Pioneer Village, which presents typical farm buildings and implements of Northwest Florida's farm life, circa 1880. The kids will like this, and older folks will enjoy the country store's stock of 19th-century goods.

South on Rte. 61, you can enjoy St. Marks, with its state museum. St. Marks was prominent in Civil War times. Union Naval Commander William Gibson planned to take the fort, but ran hard aground in his gunboat and blocked the river channel for two days. He never got to the fort, which was held by the Confederates.

A turnoff a few miles south of Tallahassee takes you the short distance to the site of the Battle of Natural Bridge, where Confederate soldiers, bolstered by boys from the West Florida Seminary in Tallahassee, repulsed a Union march in 1865 to maintain Tallahassee's record as the only Confederate capital east of the Mississippi never captured by Union troops.

Until March 6, 1865, Tallahassee was far removed from the actual fighting of the Civil War, a fact duly noticed by Brig. Gen. John Newton, commander of Union forces in the district of Key West and Dry Tortugas. He decided that the capture of Tallahassee would surely win a promotion for him and planned to capture the important railroad connecting Tallahassee with St. Marks, a little port about 40 miles south of the capitol. He assumed the railroad and bridges would be lightly defended and a surprise attack would do the trick.

On March 1, Newton and 500 troops sailed out of Key West and met with 10 Union ships at sea. Newton counted on capturing the East River bridge after a sneaky midnight landing of half the troops. At daybreak the remaining troops would land and march on to Newport and St. Marks. Further plans called for destroying the St. Marks railroad and bridges over the Aucilla and Ochlockonee rivers, climaxed by a triumphant march to Tallahassee.

Unfortunately Newton tried to land during a terrible storm. Everything went wrong and was eight hours behind schedule, so the Confederates were alerted and mustered every man or boy capable of carrying a gun to defend the territory. Although there was fierce skirmishing, Newton and his troops advanced to within almost 15 miles of Tallahassee. But he decided to rest his troops and attack in the early morning, and again his timing was bad. The delay gave old and young north Floridians carrying all sorts of firearms the rallying time they needed. In fact, Confederate Commander Gen. William Miller had problems keeping the volunteers organized. Needing professional assistance, he jumped on his horse, got 20 Confederate marines from the gunboat *Spray,* and returned to the Natural Bridge area by daybreak. The first Union shot was fired an hour later.

The Confederates miraculously were able to withstand three attacks by Union troops over the next nine hours. Then Confederate Col. Caraway Smith came to the rescue with the experienced Second Florida Cavalry. Newton realized his predicament and was able to get most of his troops on ships back to Key West. An embarrassed Newton reported that 2,000 Confederate soldiers had been reinforced by 1,000 Confederate troops from Georgia, when actually there were no more than 450 Southerners, including the 200 experienced troops who arrived when the fighting was almost ended. During the two-day battle 23 Confederates were wounded and only three killed, 89 Union troops were wounded, 21 were killed, and 38 were listed as missing.

A proud Governor John Milton praised the Southern soldiers, but the cause was lost when Lee surrendered about a month later on April 9. On May 10, the War Between the States over, Union troops marched into the capital of Florida for the first time.

Somewhere deep in Apalachicola Bay lies a Confederate blockade runner which sank with nearly a million dollars' worth of silver bars and coins. For more than a century now the occasional lucky person has discovered a coin on the beach from this wreck lying in over twelve hundred feet of water.

## Pensacola

At the beginning of the Civil War, Pensacola was the largest city in the state, but, after a brief Confederate takeover, the Federals moved in without violence and kept the town the rest of the war.

Reconstruction days weren't happy ones for Pensacola, and an editor complained that the only sign of growth was among the weeds that grew in the streets. A fire burned much of the business district in 1880, and the city didn't share in the rest of Florida's late nineteenth-century progress.

You can take an interesting driving-and-walking tour of Historic Pensacola with a free map complete with historical descriptions. It is available at the Tourist Information Center at Palafox and Cervantes streets. These offices of the Pensacola–Escambia Development Commission are open weekdays from 8 a.m. until 5 p.m., Saturday from 9 a.m. to 5 p.m.

Some of the highlights are Lee Square, Pensacola's tribute to the Confederacy; the William Franklin Lee House, which belonged to a Confederate officer who lost an arm in the Battle of Chancellorsville; Seville Square, where Union soldiers rode their horses during the Civil War; Old Christ Church (the oldest church in west Florida), seized by the Union troops during the Civil War and used as a hospital and chapel; the reconstructed High House, where Union soldiers were billeted. They called it the "Spanish Barracks" because it was owned by Don Francisco Moreno. In St. Michael's Cemetery, special flags fly over the grave of Stephen R. Mallory, Secretary of the Confederate Navy.

Although Trader Jon's at 511 Palafox Street is not really an historical site, collector's items make it somewhat of a museum. Among the artifacts is a skeleton which belonged to a cousin of Jefferson Davis, the Confederate president.

Driving from Fort Walton Beach on US 98, you can cross over to Santa Rosa Island on State 399 at Navarre and continue to Fort Pickens. This is another one of those brick salesmen's dreams which never really saw much action. The Confederates, who held Pensacola, ordered the Federals to surrender Fort Pickens in 1862 or face the consequences. The Federals said no, so the Rebels said they didn't want the danged thing anyway. Like Fort Jefferson in the Dry Tortugas, it wound up as a sort of prison. Geronimo was among those jailed here.

At the Naval Air Station visitors may take a self-guided tour and see the Pensacola Lighthouse, dating back to 1858 and in operation during the Civil War. It was bombarded by Union forces.

## PRACTICAL INFORMATION FOR FLORIDA

 **FACTS AND FIGURES.** Florida takes its name from the Spanish *Pascua florida*, referring to the Easter Feast of Flowers. Its nicknames are Everglades State, Land of Flowers, and Sunshine State. The state flower is the orange blossom; the state tree, the sabal palm; the state bird, the mockingbird. The horse conch is the state shell. "In God We Trust" is the state motto. Stephen Foster's "Swanee River" is the state song.

Tallahassee is the state capital. State population is over 8,300,000.

Miles of excellent white beaches border Florida's long Atlantic and Gulf of Mexico coastlines, and the seaside plus a mild climate have combined to make the state one of the nation's leading resort areas, with tourism the state's major industry. Most of Florida is flat coastal lowlands, with only a few low hills in the center of the state. Next to its beaches, Florida's most notable natural scenery is in the wild swamps of the vast Everglades National Park at the state's southern tip. The mild climate that attracts tourists also makes it possible for Florida to be the nation's leading producer of citrus fruits and some vegetables, and food processing is the state's leading manufacturing industry.

The famous Florida climate is also noted for being considerably wet, especially in late summer and early fall.

 **HOW TO GET THERE.** *By air:* Air Canada, Allegheny, American, Braniff, Continental, Delta, Eastern, National, North Central, Northwest Orient, Ozark, Southern, Trans World, and United serve the various airports throughout the state, depending on your point of origin. With so many new airline routes you can get to Florida from just about anywhere. For example, National has direct service to Frankfurt, Amsterdam, Paris, and London from both Tampa/St. Petersburg and Miami. Eastern has direct service to Mexico from both Tampa/St. Petersburg and Miami. Because of all the new additions and special money-saving fares, it is best to consult a travel agent for the most up-to-date information.

*By train:* Amtrak has service to Orlando, Winter Haven, Tampa, St. Petersburg, W. Palm Beach, Ft. Lauderdale and Hollywood. You might want to look into the popular "Week of Wheels" package, which includes use of a bar.

A new service is the Auto Train. Passengers can put their car on board at Lorton, near Washington, D.C., and ride with it to Sanford, Fla. The trip takes about 15½ hrs. Dinner, continental breakfast and snacks included in the fare.

*By car:* The speedy way to penetrate to the main East Coast resort area and Central Florida from the northeast is I–95. Not yet completed, in some parts you will have to use US 301, 15 and 17, which will slow you down somewhat. The beautiful, leisurely way is A1A. The frustrating, stoplight way is US 1. If going to the west coast from the northeast, take I–95 to St. Petersburg, then I–85 to Atlanta and I–75 as far as Tampa.

Car rentals are possible in all major cities.

*By bus:* Trailways and Greyhound provide good service and often feature special discounts, such as senior-citizen rates, etc.

**HOW TO GET AROUND.** *By air:* In addition to the airports listed under "How To Get There," within the state, Continental, Delta, Eastern, National, Southern or Commuter Airlines serve Daytona Beach, Eglin A.F. Base, Ft. Lauderdale, Ft. Myers, Gainesville, Jacksonville, Lakeland, Melbourne, Ocala, Orlando, Panama City, Pensacola, Punta Gorda, Tampa/ St. Petersburg, Titusville, Vero Beach, and West Palm Beach. Air Florida, for example, serves Daytona Beach, Ft. Lauderdale, Gainesville, Jacksonville, Key West, Marathon, Miami, Orlando, Panama City, Pensacola, Tallahassee, Tampa, West Palm Beach, also St. Croix in the Virgin Islands, North Eleuthera in the Bahamas, Treasure Cay, Washington, D.C., and Philadelphia.

*By car:* Major routes, some still being perfected are: I–4 from Daytona Beach, on the eastern seaboard, to St. Petersburg, on the Gulf Coast; I–10 from Jacksonville to Alabama line projection, US 301 diverges from US 1 at Callahan, strikes off through Starke, Ocala, Wildwood, Dade City, passes Tampa, to Sarasota. State 60 goes cross-state from Clearwater, on the Gulf Coast, to Vero Beach, on the Atlantic Coast, taking Clearwater–Tampa Bay traffic. State 84 (Alligator Alley) is a toll shortcut from the lower west coast to the Ft. Lauderdale area—access 6 mi. east of Naples, running across the Everglades to US 27 at Andytown.

*By boat:* The intracoastal Waterway parallels the coastline and runs 349 mi. from Jacksonville to Miami. It is 8 ft. deep in the shallower southern portions. Canals abound, connecting to the ocean. Write: Florida Dept. of Natural Resources for *Florida Boating*.

*By bus:* In addition to Greyhound and Trailways, Gulf Coast Motor Lines offers service within the state.

**TOURIST INFORMATION.** Florida makes it easy for the tourist to get information with a proliferation of welcome stations for the motorist, a superbly equipped boaters' station at Fernandina Beach and tourist conscious airlines, which are geared up to answer all sorts of questions. If you are interested in a particular city, town, or area, write to its Chamber of Commerce. They will be happy to provide the information and brochures you request.

Welcome stations, dispensing information and free orange juice, are located on US 17, a few miles north of Yulee; at the junction of US 1, 301 and 23 at Hilliard; at Pensacola on US 90; Campbellton–Jennings on I–75; St. Petersburg, Ulmerton Rd. at US 275 and 688.

Florida Development Commission, 107 W. Gaines St., Tallahassee, 32304; Florida Department of Natural Resources, Rm. 664, Larson Bldg., Tallahassee, 32304.

Visitor Information Center, 10 Castillo Dr., St. Augustine, 32084.

Marine Welcome Station, Fernandina Beach, is at the entrance to the Intracoastal Waterway.

**SEASONAL EVENTS.** *January: Stephen Foster Memorial Week,* White Springs, special musical programs. *Old Island Days,* Key West; city pays tribute to its colorful past with elaborate celebration.
*February:* On the Sunday nearest to the 20th there is an annual reenactment

at the Olustee Battlefield State Historic Site. Hundreds of volunteers set up camp and battle facilities to commemorate the February 20, 1864 encounter between Confederate Gen. Joseph Finegan and his Union opponent, Gen. Truman Seymour. There are Civil War songs and entertainment around the campfire in the evening.

*May: Florida Folk Festival*, Stephen Foster Memorial.

*December: Christmas Concert and Open House of Antiques*, White Springs, at the Stephen Foster Memorial. *Poinsettia Week*, both in Weeki Wachee.

 **MUSEUMS AND GALLERIES.** *Historical: Pensacola Historical Museum.* 405 S. Adams St. Formerly the Old Christ Church, the oldest in west Florida. Occupied by Union troops during the Civil War and utilized as a hospital, prison, and stable. Closed Mon. *Bradenton: South Florida Museum and Bishop Planetarium*, 201 10th St., W. The Civil War, two world wars, and the Seminole days are recaptured in exhibits. Closed Mon. Guided tours. *St. Augustine: Museum of Yesterday's Toys*, in the Rodriquez Avero House, 52 St. George St. Collection of toys dating from the 17th century. *Oldest Store Museum*, 4 Artillery Lane. Over 100,000 mementoes of yesteryear. *St. Petersburg: St. Petersburg Historical Museum*, 335 2nd Ave. NE. Pioneer life, Timuca Indian artifacts, large collection of the area's Civil War relics. *Pinellas County Museum and Heritage Park*, 125th St. N. and Walsingham Reservoir, between St. Petersburg and Clearwater. *Pioneer Village* with old homes furnished with antiques, "cracker" cabins, etc. *Silver Springs: Early American Museum*, Rte. 40. Antique dolls, automobiles and other vehicles. *Tallahassee: Tallahassee Junior Museum*, 3945 Museum Dr. Housed in 1880 farm. Pre-Columbian Indian artifacts, costumes, agriculture. Outdoor museum. Closed Mon., state holidays and 1 wk. at Christmas.

**CIVIL WAR MEMORABILIA.** In the *Stars Hall of Fame* in Orlando near Sea World are realistic statues of Scarlett O'Hara, Rhett Butler, and friends in settings from *Gone with the Wind*, one of the greatest novels and movies about the Civil War. The costumes and props are as authentic as reproductions can be.

One of the new attractions being added to Florida Cypress Gardens in a $5.5-million expansion program is "Legends of the South," a multi-media presentation with animated life-size figures. A hostess will escort visitors through five rooms: "Ghosts of Dixie," "Living Legends," etc. One of the animated figures will depict Gen. Robert E. Lee and the part he played in the Civil War. Scheduled to open late in 1979.

 **HISTORIC SITES.** *Homosassa Springs: Yulee Sugar Mill State Historic Site*, 5 mi. W of US 19 on State 490. Part of sugar-making machinery built by David Levy Yulee, Florida's first U.S. Senator and Confederate leader. Free.

*Olustee: Olustee Battlefield State Historic Site Museum*, off US 90, 2 mi. E. *Port St. Joe: Constitution Historic Memorial.* On US 98. 12 acres of historical and scenic sights, museums exhibits.

*St. Augustine:* All of St. Augustine is, in fact, one enormous historic site, with the early days of American development written indelibly in crumbling or reconstructed stone. The Visitor Information Center has a free Visitor's Guide to help you decide which of dozens of historical buildings you want to personally inspect. The *Historic St. Augustine Preservation Board* has strip tickets to all the historic buildings. *Castillo de San Marcos*, located on site of an original Spanish fort. *Tallahassee: Natural Bridge State Historic Site* marks spot where Confederate forces repulsed a Federal force to prevent capture of the state capitol. Free. There is an historical district at Park Avenue and Calhoun Street where you can see homes which belonged to Civil War notables. Union troops were quartered in the Murphy House. The Old City Cemetery contains the graves of slaves, and Confederate and Federal troops. The Old Fort Site on Old Fort Drive marks what was the second line of defense for Tallahassee citizens during the Civil War.

*Saint Marks Wildlife Refuge: The Saint Marks Lighthouse* is one of the oldest in the southeast. It still uses the same lens used during the Civil War. *Bristol:* In *Torreya State Park* are Civil War gun pits used by the Confederates, and Gregory House, an antebellum mansion, can be visited.

*Fernandina Beach:* Fort Clinch in *Fort Clinch State Park* is one of the best preserved forts of the Civil War. Visitors may stroll around the Ramparts, Parade Ground, Guardhouse, etc. This was the first Florida fort held by the Confederates, and the first Confederate-held fort recaptured by the Union soldiers. Amelia Island Lighthouse functioned during the Civil War. Also in the *Fernandina Beach Historical Centre Street* area, you can take a walking tour past homes which belonged to Civil War figures. A marker denotes the site of the home of David Yulee, Florida's first Senator, first railroad builder, and a prominent figure in Civil War history. The Railroad Depot, constructed in 1853, was a target for Union troops and now houses the Chamber of Commerce. The Presbyterian Church was built in 1859 on land donated by David Yulee. It headquartered Union troops who occupied the city. St. Peter's Parish Episcopal Church, built in 1859, is noteworthy for a window dedicated to Mary Martha Reid, the first female nurse in the Confederate Army. She is buried in the parish cemetery.

*St. Petersburg: Egmont Key,* just off Fort DeSoto Park, was an important blockade headquarters for Union forces. Robert E. Lee visited the area prior to the Civil War and recommended the coastal fortifications. On a clear day you can see Tampa across the Bay. Known as Fort Brooke during the Civil War, it was a strategic post held by Federalists.

*Key West:* The *Martello Gallery and Museum* on South Roosevelt Ave. was a Union fort and blockade headquarters. The museum houses beds from the Civil War hospital here. By boat or seaplane you can visit Fort Jefferson National Monument on Garden Key, about 78 miles west. The fort was a Federal prison where those accused of the assassination of President Lincoln were held. Dr. Mudd, who set John Wilkes Booth's leg, was imprisoned here for awhile.

*Live Oak:* Confederate earthworks may be seen in *Suwanee River State Park. Fort George Island: Kingsley Plantation State Historic Site,* the oldest plantation house in Florida; here slaves were schooled before being sold. *Apopka:* The "Lodge," a meeting place for Masons, was built by slaves in 1859 and is still in use for Masonic meetings. *Ellenton: Gamble Mansion State Historic Site,* once a sugar plantation. The house, the oldest building on the west coast, was the hideout for Confederate Secretary of State Judah P. Benjamin. *Pensacola:* In the *Seville Square Historic District* are many homes connected to the Civil War. One is the Lee House at 420 S. Alcaniz St., owned by Confederate hero William Franklin Lee. The Old Christ Church, Zaragoza and Adams streets, was occupied by Federal troops during the Civil War and used as a hospital and chapel. The grave of Stephen R. Mallory, Secretary of the Confederate Navy, is in St. Michael's Cemetery at Alcaniz and Garden streets. The Edward A. Perry House, corner of Palafox and Wright streets, was owned by Edward A. Perry, a Confederate general and Florida governor. In Lee Square, Palafox between Jackson and Gadsden streets, you can see the memorial to Pensacola's Civil War heroes erected at his suggestion. Inside the Naval Air Station you can visit the Pensacola

Lighthouse, bombarded by Union forces. On nearby Santa Rosa Island, Ft. Pickens was held by Union troops. Neighboring Fort McRae was home base for Col. Theodore O'Hara, author of *The Bivouac of the Dead.*

 **DRINKING LAWS.** City and county establish their own closing times for bars and nightclubs where liquor is sold. It's not unusual in the resort area to find establishments with licenses good until 4 or 5 A.M. In Fort Lauderdale city bars are open until 2; some in the county are open till 4. In the Miami area, the swingers can get service later yet. Package liquor stores, common throughout the area, are under control of State Beverage Commission. Supermarkets can't sell wine 'til past 1 o'clock on Sundays. Under recent legislation, Florida now grants adult privileges to 18-year-olds.

 **HOTELS AND MOTELS.** A Florida vacation means "which hotel" more than a sojourn in any other state, for your entire schedule of activities in the Sunshine State will probably revolve around where you stay. If you want active sports, you will want one kind of hotel; if you prefer to lounge on the beach, you will prefer another. Rule of thumb on prices: the farther from the ocean, the cheaper the room. Good buys can be found up and down US 1 on the east coast. Prices, of course, are always subject to change, but categories generally remain constant. In many locations, offseason prices are as much as 50 per cent cheaper, making an expensive hotel a summer bargain.

We have listed hotels and motels alphabetically in categories determined by double, in-season rates: *Deluxe,* from $35 up; *Expensive,* $20 to $32; *Moderate,* $18 to $28; *Inexpensive,* $12 to $22. For a more complete explanation of hotel and motel categories see *Facts at Your Fingertips* at the front of this volume.

### CEDAR KEY

**THE ISLAND HOTEL.** *Moderate.* You almost expect to see Ernest Hemingway in this 140-year-old picturesque landmark, where artists, locals and characters rendezvous at the antiquated bar. Only 11 rooms. Excellent seafood restaurant.

### CLEARWATER

**BELLEVIEW BILTMORE.** *Deluxe.* A luxury resort since 1897. Built by Henry Plant. 625 acres on Clearwater Bay. Heated pool. Private beach. Fishing pier. Tennis. Golf. Playground. Restaurant. Cocktail lounge. Dancing. Open Jan. through Apr.

### CLEARWATER BEACH

**HEILMAN'S BEACHCOMBER.** *Moderate.* 447 Mandalay Ave. Skillet-fried chicken in butter, an Old South specialty. Steak, seafood. Home-baking. Lunch, dinner.

### KEY WEST

**Marriott's Casa Marina Inn.** *Deluxe.* Resplendent Spanish Renaissance–style inn originally constructed in 1912 by Henry M. Flagler as the Casa Marina. Large pool, private 1,100-foot white sand beach. Old-fashioned charm in

Henry's, the dining room. Calabash Lounge and Sea Hut for cocktails. Registered as an historic landmark.

## PENSACOLA

**Perdido Bay Inn and Country Club.** *Expensive.* 1 Doug Ford Dr. Pool, tennis, golf. Restaurant, lounge. Kitchenettes avail.

**Ramada Inn–North.** *Expensive.* 6550 Pensacola Blvd. Pool. Children's playground, wading pool. Restaurant, lounge with entertainment.

**Sheraton Inn Downtown.** *Expensive.* 224 E. Garden St. Pool. Alhambra Room restaurant; Don Juan Lounge with entertainment, dancing.

**Best Western–Seville Inn** (formerly Ramada Inn). *Moderate.* Convenient to Seville Historic District. 223 E. Garden St. 2 pools (1 enclosed and heated). Restaurant, 3 lounges, nightly entertainment.

**Holiday Inn–North.** *Moderate.* Restaurant, lounge, and all the amenities of this well-known chain.

**Howard Johnson's.** *Moderate.* 7051 Pensacola Blvd. Pool. Restaurant open 24 hours.

**Rodeway Inn.** *Moderate.* Two locations: **Downtown:** 710 N. Palafox. **West:** On SR 297, off Exit 2 on I–10. Both with pool, restaurant, cocktail lounge. Palafox location has Captain's Table seafood and steak restaurant.

**Day's Inn.** *Inexpensive.* 6911 Pensacola Blvd. Pool, restaurant, color TV.

**Scottish Inn.** *Inexpensive.* 6891 N. Pensacola Blvd. Pool, color TV. Restaurant, Lad and Lassie Lounge.

## PENSACOLA BEACH AREA

**Howard Johnson's.** *Deluxe.* 14 Via DeLuna Dr. Directly on beautiful white sand Gulf beach. Large pool. Complete recreation center with 3 lighted tennis courts. Restaurant, cocktail lounge. Suites, kitchenettes avail. Convention facilities.

**Ft. Pickens Cottages.** *Expensive.* At Gulf Breeze. Kitchenettes avail. Daily and weekly rates.

**Galatea Inn.** *Expensive.* Directly on 1500 feet of white sand Gulf beach. Rooms and suites with private balconies. Pool, wading pool. Game room. Waterfront restaurant, two cocktail lounges. Nr. golf, tennis, billfishing, greyhound racing. Convention facilities.

**Mai-Kai.** *Expensive.* 731 Pensacola Beach Blvd. Over 70 units, with kitchenettes, color TV. Also one- and two-bedroom apartments for extended vacations. Sand Shaker cocktail lounge. Pool. Directly on white sand Gulf beach.

**Tiki House Motel.** *Moderate–Expensive.* 2 pools. Restaurant, lounge. Kitchenettes avail. Nr. golf, tennis.

**Del Rey Motor Lodge.** *Moderate.* 23 Via DeLuna. Kitchenettes avail. Pool.

**Dunes Motel.** *Moderate.* 333 Ft. Pickens Rd. Pool. Restaurant, lounge. Nr. tennis, golf.

**Holiday Inn South.** *Moderate.* At Gulf Breeze. Pool. Restaurant.

### PONTE VEDRA BEACH (NEAR JACKSONVILLE)

**Ponte Vedra Club.** *Deluxe.* One of oldest resorts in Florida, but with modern comforts, two 18-hole championship golf courses, tennis, delicious Southern-style food.

### SANIBEL ISLAND

**Casa Ybel Beach & Sport Resort.** *Deluxe.* Named after Sanibel Island's first resort, constructed on this site in 1889. Villas on the Gulf, six all-weather tennis courts, stocked fishing ponds, rental sailboats, children's slide pool. Over 1,500 feet of beach. Same developers as South Seas Plantation Resort on neighboring Captiva Island.

 **DINING OUT.** Eating your way across Florida may not be good for the waistline—or the budget—but what fun you can have hopping a boat to *Cap's Place* in Lighthouse Point for turtle steak and hearts of palm salad, as well as a little history about rum-running days or the time Winston Churchill sampled Cap's cooking during a secret wartime conference! Or maybe the treat will be an old-fashioned farm feed at *Branch Ranch,* just off I–4 between Lakeland and Tampa. Or how about watching the shrimp boats come home as you dine in Florida's southernmost fish house, the A and B Lobster House in Key West? It's all mighty fine fare, and it's hard to find a city without at least one superior eating place. Restaurant categories reflect the cost of a medium-priced dinner at each establishment. Included are hors d'oeuvres or soup, entree and dessert. Not included are drinks, tax and tip. Price ranges for Florida are *Expensive:* $7.50 and higher, *Moderate:* $4.50 to $7.50 and *Inexpensive:* below $4.50. For a more complete explanation of restaurant categories see *Facts at Your Fingertips* at the front of this volume.

### CEDAR KEY

**THE ISLAND HOTEL.** *Moderate to Inexpensive.* For almost 140 years, the restaurant has been noted for seafood—well worth the visit. Antiquated bar is a friendly rendezvous.

### CROSS CREEK

**THE YEARLING.** *Moderate.* Serves Florida recipes that were favorites of Marjorie Kinnan Rawlings, Pulitzer Prize winning author of *The Yearling.* Try the catfish or quail. The tiny village settled by Florida "Crackers" hasn't changed in centuries. Typically rustic. Seats 200.

### HILLSBORO BEACH

**THE MARY CELESTE DINING ROOM.** *Expensive.* In Barefoot Mailman Hotel. Hull of brigantine Mary Celeste forms dining room. Over a hundred years ago, ship was sighted in Devil's Triangle, circling helplessly. Not one human being was aboard, although food was simmering in the galley, the table was set, the sails were trimmed and whole. The Mary Celeste was towed to Florida and sold but the mystery was never solved. Escargots Ocean Ridge, Barefoot Mailman seafood chowder, Hillsboro Salad, are some of the favorites.

## KISSIMMEE

**MRS. MAC'S RESTAURANT.** *Moderate.* Chicken, steaks, home-made pie— family fare in family style.

## LAKE BUENA VISTA

**EMPRESS LILLY RIVERBOAT.** *Moderate–Deluxe.* In Walt Disney World Village, but outside Magic Kingdom gates. (No admission to the village) Authentic 1880s Mississippi sternwheeler. Two family dining rooms (Fisherman's Deck, and Steerman's Quarters). Deluxe gourmet dining in the elegant Empress Room, where reservations are a must.

## OCALA

**1890 BEEF HOUSE.** *Moderate.* Prime ribs, Southern fried chicken, steaks. Hearty sandwiches, too. Closed Sun.

## ORLANDO

**ROSIE O'GRADY'S.** *Moderate.* Church St. Station. Banjo pluckin', Last of the Red Hot Mama singers and oldtime entertainment. Good food and grog. Church St. Station complex also inclues **Lili Marlene's, Apple Annie's Courtyard,** and **Phineas Phogg's** disco.

**TALK OF THE TOWN.** *Moderate.* Turn-of-the-century decor with antiques. Waiters and waitresses in old-fashioned costumes. Horns and cowbells ring out for birthdays. Terrific salad bar. Seafoods, beef. Strawberry shortcake with gobs of whipped cream. Other locations: Clearwater, Lakeland and Winter Haven.

## PENSACOLA

**BARTELS RESTAURANT & WINERY.** *Moderate.* Fried chicken and home-made wines. Bar, with dancing Wed. to Sat. Closed Sun.

**DRIFTWOOD RESTAURANT.** *Moderate.* Good food, cocktails in colonial atmosphere. Closed Sun.

**SEVILLE QUARTER.** *Inexpensive–Moderate.* In historic area. Dining-entertainment complex includes **Rosie O'Grady's, Coppersmith's, Lili Marlene's, Palace Oyster Bar, Palace Courtyard, End O' The Alley Bar, Phineas Phogg's** disco. Gaslight courtyard atmosphere.

## PLANT CITY

**BRANCH RANCH.** *Moderate.* This restaurant, which grew out of Mrs. Branch's inviting a few friends to dinner, is worth the drive from Tampa—or anywhere. Serves chicken, ham, chicken-ham combination. Vegetable dinner has chicken pot pie as side dish. Everything is home grown. Antique shop upstairs.

## ST. PETERSBURG AREA

**AUNT HATTIE'S.** *Inexpensive.* 625 First St. S. Chicken & dumplings, seafood. Victorian decor. No cocktails, but you can get beer, as well as food, next door at **Uncle Ed's.**

**DOE-AL COUNTRY KITCHEN.** *Inexpensive.* 1126 62nd Ave. N. Old South home-style barbecue specialties and sandwiches. Cozy. Family place. New Country Kitchen with white ruffled curtains at South Pasadena Ave.

## TAMPA

**FANNY'S WAREHOUSE.** *Expensive.* Next to Holiday Inn on Cypress St. Floppy-hatted, long-gowned waitresses recall good old days. Nostalgia is the theme. Pianist. Live combo weekends. Lunch, dinner.

**TAMPA BAY STEAMSHIP CO.** *Moderate–Expensive.* Across from Tampa Stadium. Dedicated to Josiah Barleycorn who captained the steamer *Nellie Peck* to Tampa in 1887. Free beverage and cocktails with dinners; help-yourself salad bar. Turn-of-the-century decor. Open for dinner only. Giant shrimp and Trencherman's cut of roast prime rib specialties.

**THE FISHERY.** *Moderate.* 709 Gulf Way. Extensive menu for fish and seafood lovers as well as landlubbers. Across from Pass-A-Grille Beach, visited by Spanish explorers, pirates and tourists as far back as 1857. Lunch, dinner, cocktails. Late supper.

**ROUGH RIDERS.** *Moderate.* Ybor City. In historic, restored Latin Quarter. Teddy Roosevelt and his Rough Riders' memorabilia supply nostalgic decor. Everything from hearty sandwiches and soup to complete lunches and dinners. Cocktails, too.

# GEORGIA

## *Atlanta and Chicamauga*

### by
### CAROLYN CARTER

*Carolyn Carter, a native Georgian, was a staff writer and photographer for* The Atlanta Journal *and* Constitution Sunday Magazine. *She is now a freelancer specializing in travel.*

No scars of the Civil War remain in the bustling metropolitan area that is today's Atlanta. With the world's tallest hotel, with a population rapidly approaching two million people, with skyscrapers of many colors and designs—some with windows like mirrors, some with skytop revolving lounges—with the new Metropolitan Rapid Transit being constructed downtown, Atlanta is a city of the present and the future. Some of the past has disappeared. Loew's Grand Theater, a pseudo–Civil War landmark because it was here that the movie "Gone with the Wind" premiered, has been demolished. Indeed, Scarlett O'Hara would find Atlanta a new and vibrant city, and she would like it. Rising from the ashes after General Sherman's march across Georgia, Atlanta is now considered a "national city" by businessmen, and countless others congratulate this cultural metropolis on its schools, shops, and restaurants.

But while the cosmetics of reconstruction and renovation have removed the blemishes of the War Between the States, it is still simple and thrilling to follow Sherman's path. You will not have to hunt for clues. Civil War homes, buildings, markers, and churches are easily identified. In many places the old streets remain unchanged. Some landmarks have been put to a new use, and others have been restored. The Confederate Iron Works at Columbus is now a convention and trade center with 77,000 square feet of usable floor space and comfortable accommodations for 1,500 people.

Andersonville, the south Georgia village where the infamous Civil War prison was located, has been revitalized, and you can still visit authentic war-time stores and houses. The road to the Civil War cemetery is being resurfaced. Twenty-one miles away is Plains, hometown of Jimmy Carter. The president's maternal great-grandfather was a captain in the Confederate army.

Sherman's March continues to fascinate us today, well over a century after it took place. The march began in May 1864 when Gen. William T. Sherman and his force of 99,000 Federal troops crossed into Georgia from Chattanooga. Confederate Gen. Joseph E. Johnston opposed him with less than half as many men. Both armies followed the route of the Western and Atlantic Railroad, fighting at Chickamauga, Kennesaw Mountain, and along the Chattahoochee River, before entering Atlanta. Here Gen. John B. Hood assumed command of the Confederates. After two months of fighting, Sherman ordered the destruction of buildings, factories, railroad shops, and warehouses. When Atlanta was evacuated, only 400 buildings remained.

Sherman and his troops headed for Savannah and the sea, encountering little organized Confederate opposition. By the time they arrived in December they had demolished $100 million worth of property in 40 central Georgia counties. Sherman telegraphed President Lincoln that he was presenting Savannah to him and the nation for a Christmas gift.

One must realize, however, that the significance of the Civil War in Georgia was much greater than this march. Georgians became involved as soon as the war began. Sons and husbands went to fight. Confederate arsenals were established. Gun powder was made at Augusta. Gunboats and engines were manufactured in Columbus. The sacrifices and demands of war were felt everywhere.

### The Chickamauga Campaign

One week before the surrender of Vicksburg and the Union victory at Gettysburg (both in 1863), General Rosecrans moved out of Murfreesboro, Tennessee, and headed for Chattanooga, one of the most important cities in the south because of its location. It was a main junction on the rail line linking Richmond with Knoxville and Memphis. President Lincoln had long recognized the importance of railroads in this area. In 1862 he said, "To take and hold the railroad at or east of Cleveland [near Chattanooga], in East Tennessee, I think fully as important as the taking and holding of Richmond." Furthermore, at Chattanooga the Tennessee River cuts through the parallel ridges of the Appalachian Mountains and forms a natural gateway to either north or south. By holding the city, the Confederates could threaten Kentucky and prevent a Union penetration of the southeastern part of the Confederacy. If the Union armies pushed through Chattanooga, they would be in position to attack Atlanta, Savannah, or even the Carolinas and Richmond from the rear. As Lincoln told Rosecrans in 1863, "If we can hold Chattanooga and East Tennessee I think the rebellion must dwindle and die."

After the spring and summer campaigns in the east, the Davis government in Richmond approved a movement by Longstreet's corps of Lee's army to the west to reinforce the hard-pressed Bragg. Longstreet's move—a 900-mile trip by rail—involving some 10,000–15,000 men and six batteries of artillery, began on September 9. But a force under Burnside, now commanding the Department of the Ohio, which was not part of Rosecrans' command, had penetrated the Cumberland Gap and driven the Confederates from Knoxville; Longstreet had to go around by way of Savannah and Augusta to Atlanta, Georgia, and did not reach Bragg until September 18. The rail network was rickety, and Longstreet's soldiers quipped that such poor rolling stock had never been intended to carry such good soldiers. Movement of Longstreet's troops from Virginia was nevertheless an outstanding logistical achievement for the Confederates.

Rosecrans had meanwhile reached the north bank of the Tennessee River near Stevenson, Alabama, on August 20. By September 4 his forces were across and on their way toward Chattanooga. After months of delay Rosecrans had accomplished the feat of completely outmaneuvering Bragg without a major battle. He planned to get in behind Bragg from the southwest and bottle him up in Chattanooga, but the Confederate general saw through the scheme and slipped away southward, carefully planting rumors that his army was demoralized and in flight. Rosecrans then resolved to pursue, a decision that would have been wise if Bragg had been retreating in disorder.

There were few passes through the mountains and no good lateral roads. Rosecrans' army was dispersed in three columns over a 40-mile front in order to make use of the various passes. Bragg concentrated his army about September 10 at Lafayette, Georgia, some twenty miles south of Chattanooga. As his force was three times as large as any one of the Union columns, Bragg hopefully anticipated that he could defeat Rosecrans in detail. But his intelligence service failed him; he thought there were two, rather than three Union columns, and prepared plans accordingly. He first planned to strike what he thought was Rosecrans' right—actually the center—then the left, but his subordinates did not support him promptly, and the attacks were made in desultory fashion. Thus, twice in three days Bragg missed a fine opportunity to inflict a serious reverse upon the Federals because of his subordinates' failure to carry out orders.

By September 12 Rosecrans was at last aware that Bragg was not retreating in disorder but was preparing to fight. The Union commander ordered an immediate concentration, but this would take several days and in the meantime his corps were vulnerable. Although Bragg was usually speedy in executing attacks, this time he delayed, awaiting the arrival of Longstreet's corps. He intended to push Rosecrans southward away from Chattanooga into a mountain cul-de-sac where the Federals could be destroyed.

By September 17 Bragg was poised just east of Chickamauga Creek. (Chickamauga, translated from Cherokee into English, means "River of Death.") When Longstreet's three leading brigades arrived on September 18, Bragg decided to cross the Chickamauga and attack. But the Federals, with two corps almost concentrated, defended the fords so stoutly that only a few units got over that day. During the night more Confederates slipped across, and by morning of the 19th about three-fourth of Bragg's men were over.

Rosecrans' third corps went into the line on the 19th, and now Bragg faced a much stronger force than he had expected. The heavily wooded battlefield had few landmarks, and some units had difficulty maintaining direction. Fighting continued throughout much of the day, but by nightfall the Federals still controlled the roads to Chickamauga. That night Lee's "War-horse," Longstreet, arrived in person with two more brigades. He went looking for Bragg to report to him and lost his way in the woods. Encountering some soldiers, he asked them to identify their unit. When they replied with numbers—Confederate divisions were named for their commanders—he realized he was within Union lines, hastily rode off in the darkness, and eventually found Bragg. During the night Rosecrans regrouped and dug in.

Bragg decided to renew the attack the next day and to attack progressively from his right to left (sometimes known in military parlance as "oblique order"). He reorganized the Army of Tennessee into two wings under Polk and Longstreet with little regard for its existing corps organization. The attack began about 9 A.M. and hit Thomas' corps first. The Union line held until Rosecrans received an erroneous report that one of his units was not supported, and ordered another unit to move in and help. In the ensuing confusion, orders designated a unit which was already in line of battle. When this force obediently abandoned its position, Longstreet, just beginning his attack, saw the hole and drove into it at once. Thomas' right flank was bent back and most of the Union right wing simply melted from the field and streamed in rout back toward Chattanooga. Rosecrans, considering himself defeated, retired to Chattanooga to organize it for defense. Thomas, with about two-thirds of the disorganized army, stood fast and checked vicious attacks by Longstreet and Polk until nightfall. This resolute stand and the valorous performance of the U.S. 19th Infantry won for Thomas and that unit the title "Rock of Chickamauga." A Confederate remembered that afternoon how "the dead were piled upon each other in ricks, like cord wood, to make passage for advancing columns. The sluggish Chickamauga ran red with human blood."

Bragg concluded that no decisive results could be attained that day. Polk, Longstreet, and Forrest pleaded with him to push the routed Federals and recapture Chattanooga. But 18,000 casualties (the Federals had lost only 1,500 less) so unnerved Bragg that he permitted Thomas to withdraw unmolested from the field to a blocking position extending from Missionary Ridge west to Lookout Mountain. Next day Thomas retired into Chattanooga. Polk wrote to President Davis of Bragg's "criminal negligence," and Forrest a week later insubordinately told the army commander, "You have played the part of a damned scoundrel, and are a coward and if you were any part of a man I would slap your jaws." Yet nothing could erase completely the fact that the Confederates had won a great victory and had Rosecrans' army bottled up in a trap.

### Sherman's Great Wheel to the East

On March 17, 1864, Grant had met with Sherman at Nashville and told him his role in the grand strategy. Sherman, like Grant, held two commands. As Division of the Mississippi commander, he was responsible for the operation and defense of a vast logistical system that reached from a communications zone at St. Louis, Louisville, and Cincinnati to center on a large base depot at Nashville. Strategically, Nashville on the Cumberland River rivaled Washington, D.C., in importance. A 90-mile military railroad, built and operated by Union troops, gave Nashville access to steamboats plying the Tennessee River. Connected with Louisville by rail, Nashville became one vast storehouse and corral. If the city was destroyed, the Federal forces would have to fall back to the Ohio River line. Wearing his other hat, Sherman was a field commander with three armies under his direction.

With the promise of the return of his two crack divisions from the Red River expedition by May 1864 and with a splendid administrative system working behind him, Sherman was ready to leave Chattanooga in the direction of Atlanta. His mission was to destroy Johnston's armies and capture Atlanta, which after Richmond was the most important industrial center in the Confederacy. With 254 guns, Sherman matched his three small armies, and a separate cavalry command—a total force of more than 100,000 men—against Joseph E. Johnston's Army of Tennessee and the Army of Mississippi including Wheeler's cavalry, consisting of 65,000 men.

Sherman moved out on May 4, 1864, the same day the Army of the Potomac crossed the Rapidan. Johnston, realizing how seriously he was outnumbered, decided to go on the defensive, preserve his forces intact, hold Atlanta, and delay Sherman as long as possible. There was always the hope that the North would grow weary of the costly struggle and that some advocate of peaceful settlement might defeat Abraham Lincoln in the election of 1864. From May 4 through mid-July, the two forces maneuvered against each other. There were daily fights but few large-scale actions. As Sherman pushed south, Johnston would take up a strong position and force

Sherman to halt, deploy, and reconnoiter. Sherman would then outflank Johnston, who in turn would retire to a new line and start the process all over again. On June 27 Sherman, unable to maneuver because the roads were muddy and seriously concerned by the unrest in his armies brought about by constant and apparently fruitless marching, decided to assault Johnston at Kennesaw Mountain. This attack against prepared positions, like the costly failure at Cold Harbor, was beaten back. Sherman returned to maneuver and forced Johnston back to positions in front of Atlanta.

Johnston had done his part well. He had accomplished his missions and had so slowed Sherman that Sherman covered only 100 miles in 74 days. Johnston, his forces intact, was holding strong positions in front of Atlanta, his main base; but by this time Jefferson Davis had grown impatient with Johnston and his tactics of cautious delay. In July he replaced him with Lt. Gen. John B. Hood, a much more impetuous commander.

On July 20, while Sherman was executing a wide turning movement around the northeast side of Atlanta, Hood left his fortifications and attacked at Peach Tree Creek. When Sherman beat him off, Hood pulled back into the city. While Sherman made ready to invest, Hood attacked again and failed again. Sherman then tried cavalry raids to cut the railroads, just as Johnston had during the advance from Chattanooga, but Sherman's raids had as little success as Johnston's. Sherman then began extending fortifications on August 31. Hood, who had dissipated his striking power in his assaults, gave up and retired to northwest Alabama, and Sherman marched into Atlanta on the first two days of September. Sherman hoped that Mobile had fallen, and a shorter line for his supplies by way of Montgomery, Alabama, or still better by the lower Chattahoochee to Columbus, Georgia, was open. Admiral Farragut had entered Mobile Bay on August 5, 1864, but had no troops to take Mobile itself.

The fall of Atlanta gave President Lincoln's campaign for reelection in 1864 a tremendous boost. In addition, the psychological lift given the Union by Admiral Farragut's personal heroism in the battle of Mobile Bay greatly added to Lincoln's prestige.

Atlanta was only a halfway point in Sherman's vast wheel from the western theater toward the rear of Lee's Army of Northern Virginia. Abandoning the idea of catching up with Hood, Sherman by telegraph outlined his next strategic move to Lincoln and Grant in early September 1864. Sherman's two proposals proved him an able strategist as well as a consummately bold and aggressive commander. To defend Nashville, he suggested that he send two corps, 30,000 men, back to Thomas, where that commander would raise and train more men and be in position to hold Tennessee if Hood came north. To carry the offensive against the economic heart of the Confederacy, Sherman recommended that he himself take four corps—62,000 men—cut his own communications, live off the country, and march to the seacoast through Georgia, devastating and laying waste all farms, railways, and storehouses in his path.

Whether he arrived at Pensacola, Charleston, or Savannah, Sherman reasoned he could hold a port, make contact with the U.S. Navy, and be refitted by Stanton and Meigs. Meigs promised to do the logistical job, and Lincoln and Grant, though their reaction to the plan was less than enthusiastic, accepted it in a show of confidence in Sherman.

Before marching out of Atlanta, Sherman's engineers put selected buildings to the torch and destroyed all railroads in the vicinity. On November 12, moving away from the Nashville depots toward Savannah, the Division of the Mississippi troops broke telegraphic contact with Grant. They had twenty days' emergency rations in their wagons, but planned to replenish them by living off the country. Operating on a 60-mile-wide front, unimpeded by any Confederate force, Sherman's army systematically burned and destroyed what it did not need. The march became something of a rowdy excursion. Sherman's campaign, like Sheridan's in the Shenandoah, anticipated the economic warfare and strategic aerial bombardments of the twentieth century. Yet the victims of his methods could hardly be blamed if they regarded Sherman's strategy as an excuse for simple thievery.

On December 10 Sherman, having broken the classic pattern by moving away from his logistical base, arrived in front of Savannah. Confederate forces evacuated the seaport on December 21 and Sherman offered it to the nation as a Christmas present. Awaiting him offshore was Meigs' floating seatrain, which enabled him to execute the last phase of Grant's strategy, a thrust north toward the line of the James River.

### Chicamauga

To retrace Sherman's March, begin at Chickamauga. A State of Georgia Welcome Center located on I–75 at Ringgold can provide directions and guidance for a Civil War tour of the state. The Dixie Highway from Chattanooga to Atlanta (US 41) winds through the green Appalachian Valley, heart of the Cherokee nation until 1838. The Dixie Highway closely follows the route taken in 1864 by General William T. Sherman in his Dalton-to-Atlanta campaign, but few marks of the devastation of war remain.

Chickamauga and Chattanooga National Military Park on US 27 was the scene of a Confederate victory. A Union victory at the Battle of Chattanooga, however, shattered the South's hopes of winning the war. The oldest and largest of the national military parks, this one commemorates the heroic soldiers of both North and South. The park features an eight-mile driving tour, restored Brotherton House, specific battlelines, museum and numerous monuments erected in memory of the state troops that fought in the battle. The park is operated by National Park Service and it's free.

Gordon-Lee Home, located in the battlefield area, served the Union Army first as headquarters and then as a hospital. The Huff House in Dalton (private) served during the winter of 1864 as

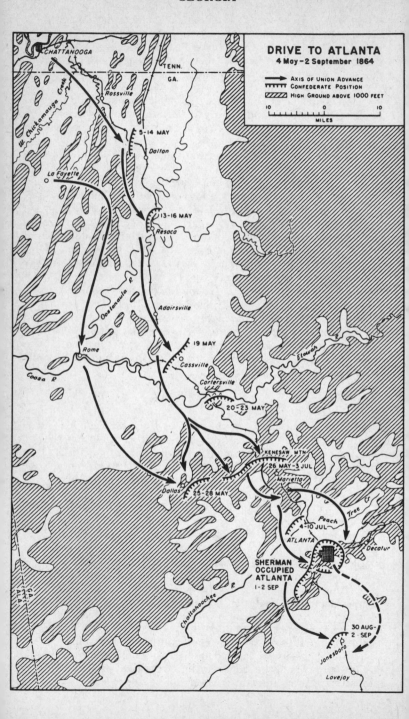

DRIVE TO ATLANTA
4 May – 2 September 1864

→ AXIS OF UNION ADVANCE
ⵜⵜⵜⵜ CONFEDERATE POSITION
▧ HIGH GROUND ABOVE 1000 FEET

10   0   10
MILES

CHATTANOOGA

Rossville

TENN.
GA.

W. Chickamauga Creek

5-14 MAY
Dalton

La Fayette

13-16 MAY
Resaca

Oostanaula R.

Adairsville

Rome

19 MAY
Cassville

Coosa R.

Cartersville

Etowah R.

20-23 MAY

KENESAW MTN.
26 MAY-3 JUL

Dallas

25-28 MAY

Marietta

Peach Tree Cr.

4-10 JUL

ATLANTA

Decatur

SHERMAN
OCCUPIED
ATLANTA
1-2 SEP

Chattahoochee R.

GA.
ALA.

30 AUG-
2 SEP

Jonesboro

Lovejoy

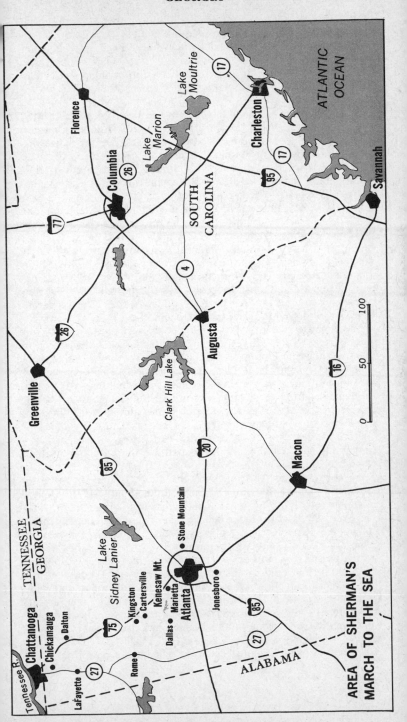

AREA OF SHERMAN'S
MARCH TO THE SEA

headquarters for Gen. Joseph E. Johnston, between the Chattanooga and Atlanta campaigns. Resaca (off US 41 south of Dalton) was the scene of the first major engagement resulting from Sherman's turning movement through Snake Creek Gap, which forced Gen. Johnston to abandon his advanced position along Rocky Face Ridge. Confederate Cemetery here contains the graves of 500 soldiers.

In Rome, the most notable event of the war took place in May, 1863, when Col. Abel D. Straight came up from northeastern Alabama with 1,466 troops prepared to attack the city. This force was captured by 410 men under Gen. Nathan Bedford Forrest who, by a clever trick, convinced Straight that he was outnumbered. A memorial to General Forrest and the event stands at the intersection of Broad Street and Second Avenue.

The Battle of Kennesaw Mountain is commemorated in a national Battlefield Park located on US 41. The museum has slide presentations and exhibits, eighteen miles of hiking trails, picnic facilities. Kennesaw, known for many years as Big Shanty (for the still of the same name), was scene of the first major engagement in the Dalton-Atlanta campaign. The mountain has an altitude of 1,809 feet; the park covers three thousand acres. Big Shanty Museum, at Kennesaw, houses the famous Civil War locomotive "The General," which was involved in "The Great Locomotive Chase."

The highway passes Marietta National Cemetery, twenty-four acres of lavishly landscaped grounds containing the graves of more than ten thousand Union soldiers and many veterans of other wars. Large oaks, magnolias, hollies, evergreen shrubs and a profusion of rose bushes surround the mansion-like main building overlooking the cemetery from atop a hill. A Confederate Cemetery lies a half-mile from the Marietta city square. It has almost three thousand slabs, most of them nameless.

From Marietta turn east eleven miles to Roswell on Ga. 120, a community gradually being enveloped by the suburban Atlanta complex. This town was laid out in 1835 by Roswell King, a Connecticut banker who managed the Pierce Butler plantation on St. Simons Island, almost 350 miles to the south. Envisioning a mountain retreat for himself and his friends from the summer heat of the Sea Islands, Mr. King set up about a dozen homes in the community. One of his neighbors, Martha Bulloch, married the senior Theodore Roosevelt there in 1835. One of their sons was the future president; another was the father of Eleanor Roosevelt. Barrington Hall, built by the town's founder in 1842, housed Union troops during the Civil War. Fourteen Doric columns and wide-planked floors are outstanding features, along with original antique furniture. It is shown by special arrangement. Roswell has a number of privately owned antebellum homes that visitors may see while driving through the town. Mimosa Hall (1846) is Greek Temple style. A tour of homes and gardens is scheduled each spring.

## Atlanta

After Kennesaw, Atlanta was the target. To defend the city, Gov. Joseph E. Brown and the mayor of Atlanta called out all able-bodied men. But Sherman crossed the Chattahoochee River and moved forward. His goal was to cut the city's rail communications. Atlanta was the depot center of the Confederate Army and the location of many factories working on army contracts. Armor plate and rails for the railroads were being manufactured. The city symbolized Confederate strength. General Sherman felt its destruction would bring despair.

He did a thorough job. There are 89 Civil War markers within the city limits. That much of Atlanta was destroyed, and still you can see where it happened and, with a bit of research, why and how.

Three major areas to see are a section around Peachtree Creek; one where the Battle of July 22 took place; and the site of Ezra Church.

Along Palisades Road at Peachtree Creek are two markers which note the battlefield of Peachtree Creek. Here Lt. Gen. John B. Hood, on taking command of the Army of Tennessee, began aggressive action against the Federal approach to Atlanta from upper Chattahoochee crossings. Battle was joined in this area on July 20, 1864, beginning in Clear Creek Valley on the east and progressing west to Howell Mill Road.

Several historic markers in the Peachtree Battle–Howell Mill Road area describe the action here. A few miles away is the spot where Confederates fell back before Federal advances—the famed crossing of the Chattahoochee River at Bolton, on the old Marietta Road. Several markers at Soap Creek and Turner's Ferry Road note the importance of these sites.

The Battle of Atlanta, depicted so graphically in the world-famous Cyclorama, can provide another interesting Atlanta Civil War tour. The area embraced is northeast and southeast Atlanta. From the second story of a house near Oakland Cemetery, Gen. John B. Hood and his staff watched as Brown's and Clayton's divisions moved eastward to attack the Federals. Leggett's Hill is where a major engagement of the Atlanta campaign took place. In eight hours of battle, two generals were killed in this area on July 22, 1864—Walker of the Confederacy and McPherson of the Federals. A monument designates the spot where McPherson died. Fort Walker, at the crown of the hill near the Atlanta Avenue and Boulevard entrance to Grant Park, is a commanding position held by a Confederate battery during the Siege and Battle of Atlanta. The park is honeycombed with breastworks.

Ezra Church was a little Methodist Church where a major Civil War battle was fought, July 28, 1864. An inscription on one of the markers notes that the carcasses of horses remained on the grounds months after the war. The rectangular ground on which the church sat is easily discernible. Markers in southeastern Atlanta chronicle other events of this portion of the Civil War.

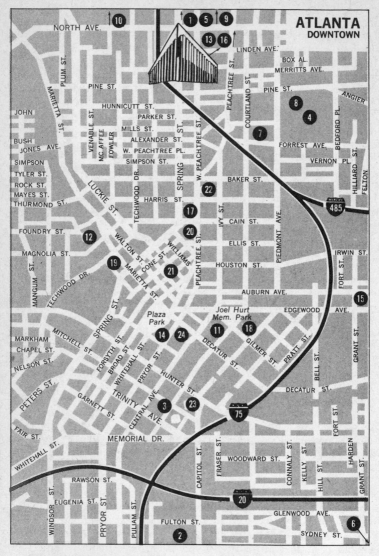

## Points of Interest (Atlanta)

1) Atlanta Historical Society
2) Atlanta Stadium
3) City Hall
4) Civic Center
5) Coach House Restaurant
6) Cyclorama
7) Emory University School of Dentistry
8) Exhibition Hall
9) Fox Theater
10) Georgia Institute of Technology
11) Georgia State College
12) Georgia World Congress Center
13) High Museum of Art
14) Historic Lamp Post
15) Martin Luther King grave
16) Memorial Arts Center
17) Merchandise Mart
18) Municipal Auditorium
19) Omni Hotel and Megastructure
20) Peachtree Plaza Hotel
21) Realto Theater
22) Regency-Hiatt Hotel
23) State Capitol
24) Underground Atlanta

The cyclorama, famous three-dimensional panoramic painting of the Battle of Atlanta, is located at Grant Park. The Swan House (Atlanta Historical Society, 3099 Andrews Dr. NW) has an interesting collection of mementos from Georgia's past housed in the former Edward H. Inman residence. Adjacent is the Tullie Smith Farmhouse which looks essentially as it did in 1840's. Georgia's governor resides in a mansion located at 391 West Paces Ferry Road, a show place opened for tourists several times each week.

East of Atlanta is Stone Mountain Park, where the Confederacy really comes alive. There's an exhibit and map which details Sherman's March. A massive Confederate carving features Gen. Robert E. Lee with Gen. Stonewall Jackson and Confederacy Pres. Jefferson Davis. Lee's likeness is 138 feet from the top of his head to his horse's hoof. His face measures twenty-one feet, his nose, five fcct. Thc stars on his collar are bigger than dishpans and the sword, mcasuring fifty-cight fcct in length and four feet in width, weighs one hundred tons. Stone Mountain is a giant granite dome which rises 650 feet above the surrounding plain. Twenty miles east of downtown Atlanta and visible from the top of many of the city's larger buildings, it is surrounded by a 3,200-acre park that attracts nearly 4 million persons each year. A cable-car lift rises from the base of the mountain to the summit 2,600 feet distant. Two glass-enclosed cars, each carrying fifty passengers, afford a superb view. A replica of the famous Civil War locomotive, "The General," pulls vintage coaches along a railroad that circles the base of the mountain. The seven-mile ride gives an idea of how massive the granite giant really is. A Memorial Building contains a museum featuring Sherman's famous "March to the Sea," depicted in a sixty-foot relief map. There is Magnolia Hall, an authentic antebellum plantation that was moved from its original site at Dickey, Ga., carefully furnished and restored, plus a game ranch, an antique automobile museum, a steamboat operating on an adjoining lake, a marina, a carillon with concerts daily, excellent fishing, horseback riding, golf and camping.

### Outside Atlanta

A short distance west of Atlanta is Dallas. A monument at New Hope Church marks the spot where General Hood's Confederate Corps fought Gen. Joseph Hooker's 209th Army Corps of the Union Army.

At Columbus the Fort Benning Infantry Museum traces the evolution of the Infantry from the French and Indian War to the present. Fort Benning is the Free World's largest infantry training center, covering 282 square miles of varied terrain. An open reservation, it welcomes visitors.

Confederate navy ships are displayed at a museum on US 27. Included are the hull of the iron-clad *Muscogee*. The Ladies' Defender Cannon is shown here, too. It was made from brass articles donated by the women of Columbus during the Civil War. Ladies gave up brass beds, cooking utensils, jewelry and door knobs to be made into this unusual field artillery piece.

A heritage tour of historic points is scheduled regularly and may originate at the Columbus Welcome Center.

Andersonville National Historic Site is on State 49, north from Americus. A Confederate military prison was established here in 1864 and used for fourteen months. Many states have placed monuments.

There's a flagpole on Blakely's Court House Square, the last of the Confederate ones, erected in 1861; and there's a monument to the peanut, which serves as a constant reminder of the product's importance to this area's economy.

Three red brick buildings on Newman's College Street served as a hospital for Confederate and Union soldiers. Buena Vista, an elegant old home of double porches and massive white columns, served as local headquarters for Confederate Gen. Joe Wheeler. Antebellum homes are found throughout the city. Although privately owned, they may be seen on a driving tour of residential areas.

Bellevue in LaGrange was acquired by U.S. Sen. Benjamin H. Hill in 1853 and served as his home for a number of years. Hill later was arrested here by Federal soldiers. On a more festive occasion, Jefferson Davis entertained at Bellevue. It is open daily.

Madison is the town Sherman refused to burn. When Federal forces marching from Atlanta approached Madison, U.S. Sen. Joshua Hill, who did not vote for secession, rode out to meet General Sherman whom he had known in Washington. Sherman favored Hill's plea that the city be bypassed. Some damage was done to the town, however, when General Slocum's troops came through. During this raid a silver service was taken from the Presbyterian church. After the war, General Slocum returned it, and today the service is still treasured and used.

Historic homes abound in Madison, a city chartered in 1809 and located on an old stagecoach road. Owner-maintained antebellum homes may be seen by visitors with the use of a map-keyed brochure. Casulon Plantation was the manor house of an old 10,000-acre plantation with boxwood gardens. The house and sixteen acres are being restored (private). There are tours of homes and gardens in December and in the spring.

Respect for the Confederate past has inspired impressive monuments. The Confederate Powder Works, 1717 Goodrich Street, Augusta, stands in front of the Sibley Mill as a monument to Confederate ideals. The obelisk chimney, 176 feet high, is all that remains of the works which once manufactured more than two million pounds of gunpowder.

Augusta also has a Confederate Monument on Broad Street between 7th and 8th streets. It is a 76-foot marble shaft containing lifesize figures of Confederate heroes.

On the city hall lawn in Athens is a double-barreled cannon, the only one of its kind in the world. Invented in 1863 for use in the Civil

War, it was to have fired simultaneously two balls connected by a chain. It failed to fire accurately, however, and was relegated to its present location as an object of curiosity.

A short distance off I–20 at Crawfordville is the home of Confederate Vice President Alexander H. Stephens. There is also a state park named for him. His home, Liberty Hall, is a focal point of the shrine, and a museum displays mementos relating to Stephens and the Confederacy.

North on State 47 at US 78 is Washington, a gracious city that dates from the late 18th century and was untouched by Civil War destruction. A list of 40 antebellum homes dating back to 1790 is obtainable from its Chamber of Commerce. It is possible to visit a few homes from time to time, but many are open during the spring home tour. The Washington-Wilkes Historical Museum is a rambling 18-room building dating back to 1835. Thirteen doors open to the outside. Civil War relics are displayed.

South on Georgia 22 (at Ga. 15 and Ga. 16) is Sparta, with its Hotel Lafayette first known as the Edwards House and later as the Drummers Home. Currently under renovation, the hotel was a haven for refugees during the Civil War.

There are more than 20 antebellum homes in Milledgeville, on US 441 northeast of Macon. The Mansion, 120 South Clark Street, served as the home of 10 Georgia governors. Built in 1838, it is a superb example of Greek Revival architecture. Restored in 1967, it is open Tuesday–Saturday. The Old Capitol, now rebuilt and a part of Georgia Military College, was used from 1807 to 1867. Milledgeville was planned in 1803 as the state capitol and retains its pattern of parallel streets. The capitol is open daily.

Macon's most notable Civil War landmark is the Cannonball House at 856 Mulberry Street, built in 1853. It was struck by a cannonball during the Federal attack of 1864.

Eatonton, north of Macon on US 129, is the home of Joel Chandler Harris, who was born there in 1848. The Old South plantation atmosphere is accented by an Uncle Remus Museum made up of two log cabins which were formerly slave quarters. There are shadow boxes illustrating tales from *Br'er Rabbit, Br'er Fox* and the others, plus a diorama of a typical Old South plantation.

Fitzgerald, named for a "damyankee" philanthropist from Indiana, originated in the 90s as a summery refuge for aging Union veterans. Located in the south central part of the state, it is proud of its Blue and Gray Museum, housing memorabilia from regiments on both sides in the Civil War.

When General Sherman was in southeast Georgia, General Slocum and his troops made Louisville their headquarters. The business section and many old landmarks were burned, but the Slave Market and the residence used by the general were saved.

The Old Slave Market on Broad Street was built around 1800, though tradition claims it predated the town (1758). Made of heavy timbers, the structure has a roof about 20 feet square supported by square posts. Hanging in the market house is a bell, sent in 1772 by the King of France as a gift to a convent in New Orleans. Captured by pirates and sold at Savannah, the bell was sent to the new capital, Louisville, where slaves were offered for public auction.

Though Sherman followed one route, he sent troops in different directions as they moved toward Savannah and the sea. They left devastation. Clinton, near Macon, had the first iron foundry in Georgia; it manufactured 900 cotton gins a year. It was demolished. Calhoun, north of Atlanta, in the direct path of Sherman's march, was almost completely destroyed in 1864. It was rebuilt after the war. Only two houses in Cartersville survived the Federal occupation of 1864. Most of the houses between Atlanta and Griffin were destroyed. Jonesboro, where combat lasted for two days, August 31 and September 1, often is identified as a source of scenes for Margaret Mitchell's *Gone with the Wind,* but Mrs. Mitchell always insisted that Tara was entirely an imaginative plantation. "GWTW" tours now include this area, plus Madison, Covington, and some Atlanta sectors.

At the beginning of the war, defense of the coast was foremost in Georgians' minds. They knew the U.S. Navy could attack at the Savannah River, which was defended by an inadequate fleet of tugs and river boats. They could not prevent the occupation of Tybee Island, although their major concern was to protect the city and keep the river open.

## Savannah

A tour of Savannah is highlighted by many Civil War sites. St. John's Church and Parish House, 14 W. Macon Street, was built in 1852. The church is famous for its chimes and stained glass windows showing Gothic influence. The Parish House is the former Green-Meldrim House, headquarters of General Sherman after his March to the Sea.

Fort Pulaski, east of Savannah, is now operated by the National Park Service. Built from 1829 to 1849, Pulaski was Robert E. Lee's first engineering assignment after graduation from West Point.

Savannah was an important center for export to Europe and served as a supply center for the Confederacy during the Civil War until the fall of Fort Pulaski in 1862. Fort Pulaski, a monumental engineering feat, guarded the city from the sea from a perch overlooking the Savannah River, while Fort McAllister, a huge earthwork fortress, defended the south. Surviving seven attacks by the Union Navy, Fort McAllister finally fell to Sherman on his march to the sea. In evacuating the city in the face of Sherman's advance, Confederate General Hardee spared the city the battering and burning Sherman had given Atlanta.

Once the coastal area was in Federal hands, effective opposition to Union forces ended in Georgia. Fighting stopped in May, 1865, and the state government was replaced by Federal military authority after the arrest of Governor Brown and other prominent leaders.

## PRACTICAL INFORMATION FOR GEORGIA

**FACTS AND FIGURES.** Georgia was named for King George II of England. It has a long string of mostly less august nicknames; Buzzard State; Cracker State; Goober State; Peach State; Empire State of the South. The state flower is the Cherokee rose; the state tree, the live oak; the state bird, the brown thrasher. "Wisdom, Justice, Moderation" is the state motto, "Georgia" the state song.

Atlanta, the state's biggest city and the leading business center of the Southeast, is the state capital. Population of the state is nearly 5 million.

**HOW TO GET THERE.** *By air:* Atlanta may be reached on direct flights of: Braniff, Delta, Eastern, Northwest, Piedmont, Southern, TWA and United airlines. Delta and Piedmont have direct flights to Augusta; Delta and Eastern to Macon; Delta and National to Savannah; Delta, Eastern and Southern to Columbus; Air South to Brunswick; Southern to Albany, Athens, Moultrie and Valdosta.

From San Juan and Mexico, Eastern has direct flights to Atlanta.

From Montreal and Toronto, Eastern has direct flights to Atlanta.

*By car:* I–95 enters Savannah from South Carolina and continues along the east coast south to Florida. I–85 comes in from Anderson, South Carolina, continues to Atlanta, then goes southwest to Alabama. I–75 enters Georgia from Tennessee, goes through Atlanta and continues south to Florida. I–20 comes into Augusta from Aiken, South Carolina, west to Atlanta and on to Alabama. US 84 enters from Dothan, Alabama, and goes east to Bainbridge, Valdosta and Waycross. US 441 comes in from North Carolina, goes south through Athens and Dublin to Florida.

*By train:* Amtrak from New York and Washington to Atlanta; from New Orleans through Atlanta; another Amtrak train serves Savannah, Thalman, Waycross and Valdosta.

*By bus:* Greyhound and Trailways.

**HOW TO GET AROUND.** *By air:* Delta, Eastern, Piedmont, Southern and Air South serve cities within the state.

*By car:* I–95 goes from Savannah south to the Florida state line; I–16 runs from Savannah northwest to Macon; I–20 goes from Augusta west to Atlanta and on to Alabama; I–85 comes in from South Carolina, proceeds southwest to Atlanta, La Grange and continues to Alabama; I–75 enters from Tennessee, goes south to Atlanta, southeast to Macon and Valdosta and continues south to Florida; US 84 comes in from Alabama and goes east to Bainbridge, Valdosta and Waycross; US 441 enters from North Carolina, goes south to Athens and Dublin and on to Florida.

*Car rental:* You will find Avis, Hertz and National and Budget rental offices throughout Georgia.

*By bus:* Southeastern Motor Lines, Inc., services cities within the state, in addition to Greyhound and Trailways.

*By train:* Amtrak to Atlanta from New Orleans, New York and Washington; also to Savannah, Thalman, Waycross and Valdosta.

**TOURIST INFORMATION.** Welcome Centers, operated by the Tourist Division of the Georgia Dept. of Industry and Trade, offer information on facilities and routing advice. Locations: Savannah—Intersection US

17, 17A; Lavonia—I–85, ½ mi. SW of South Carolina line; Columbus—Intersection of US 280, Us 27; Ringgold—I–75, 2 mi. S. of Tennessee line; Sylvania—US 301, ¼ mi. SW of South Carolina line; Valdosta—I–75, 2 mi. N of Florida line; Augusta—I–20. ½ mi. W of South Carolina line; Kingsland—I–95; Atlanta—Atlanta Airport.

Additional information: Game & Fish, Dept. of Natural Resources, 270 Washington St., Atlanta 30334; State Parks, Dept. of Natural Resources; Ga. Chamber of Commerce, Commerce Bldg., Atlanta 30334; Tourist Division, Georgia Dept. of Industry and Trade P.O. Box 1776, Atlanta 30301.

 **SEASONAL EVENTS.** Many Georgia cities take advantage of the natural beauty of dogwood, peach, camellia and azalea blossoms in the spring to showcase their finer homes. Augusta, Thomasville, St. Simons sponsor camellia shows in January, early February. Home and garden tours are held in Augusta, Columbus, Madison, St. Simons and Savannah in March. Thomasville's Rose Festival is held in April.

There are *Historic Homes Tours* in afternoons and evenings by candlelight during the last three days of April in Athens.

*Summer:* Watermelon Festival in Cordele; frequent watermelon cuttings at Agrirama in Tifton; Buggy Days in Barnesville; Mule Day at Cairo and Dahlonega. In Hiawassee, *Georgia Mountain Fair* draws over a hundred thousand visitors to view the quiltmaking, woodcarvings, soap making, hog rifle shoots. 10 days, early Aug.

*Fall: Powers Crossroads Country Fair & Arts Festival,* in early Sept., is the South's largest arts & crafts festival fair. *Dahlonega's Gold Rush Days* features country music, costumed citizens, pioneer floats, mule races. 3 days, Oct.

 **MUSEUMS AND GALLERIES.** In Columbus is the *Confederate Naval Museum,* 101 4th St., May to Oct., Tues. to Sun. The *U.S. Army Infantry Museum* has exhibits covering the French & Indian War to present. Tues. to Sun. Fitzgerald has two Civil War Museums: *Blue and Gray Museum,* Utility Office, N. Hooker St., is open Mon. to Fri. Free. *Confederate Museum,* Jefferson Davis Memorial State Park, daily except Mon. Savannah's *Factor's Walk Military Museum,* 222 Factor's Walk, houses Civil War mementos. In Washington, *Washington-Wilkes Historical Museum,* 308 E. Robert Toombs Ave., US 78, St. 17, displays Confederate records, antebellum furnishings. Closed major holidays. Free.

*Dahlonega Courthouse Gold Museum* with exhibits from this country's first gold rush. Free. *Uncle Remus Museum,* in Turner Park, Eatonton, has dioramas of 12 Uncle Remus stories, slave cabins, mementos.

*Georgia Dept. of Archives and History,* 330 Capitol Ave. SE. Displays, exhibits. History of Georgia depicted in lovely stained-glass windows. *Cyclorama,* Grant Park, is huge canvas depicting 1864 Battle of Atlanta (temporarily closed). *Swan House,* 3099 Andrews Dr. NW. Period rms. on first floor. *Governor's Mansion,* 391 W. Paces Ferry Rd. Federal furnishings in elegant home. Free. *Emory Museum.* Bishop's Hall, Emory Univ., S. Oxford Rd. NE in Druid Hills. African, American Indian artifacts. Closed school vacations.

 **HISTORIC SITES.** Most famous—or infamous—is undoubtedly *Andersonville National Historical Site,* where in Camp Sumter Confederate prison many Union soldiers died of exposure, hunger and inadequate medical care. On the grounds are Providence Spring, Sundial Monument commemorating Clara Barton's work, and adjoining, Andersonville National Cemetery. Rte. 49, 11 mi. NE of Americus. Free. One of the fiercest battles of the Civil War was fought at *Chickamauga,* nr. the Tennessee border. Part of Chickamauga and Chattanooga National Military Park is in Georgia, the rest in Tennessee. Visitor Center, on US 27, is open daily. Closed Christmas. Free. At *Kennesaw Mountain National Battlefield Park,* US 41, 2 mi. N of Marietta, the Visitor Center has exhibits and a self-guided walking tour. *Fort Pulaski,* 15 mi. E. of Savannah off US 80, was built during colonial days, demolished, rebuilt again 1829–47. It was captured and manned by Union forces, serving effectively in the blockade of the South.

*Fort McAllister,* 17 mi. S of Savannah, is an example of earthen fortification. It withstood the heaviest naval ordnance employed during the War Between the States. Closed Mondays.

Among the houses restored and maintained as State Historic Sites are *Chief Vann House* at Spring Place. *Jarrell Plantation* near Macon, *Lapham-Patterson House* at Thomasville, and *Midway Museum. Meadow Garden,* 1320 Nelson St., Augusta, was restored by the state DAR.

*Traveler's Rest,* 6 mi. NE of Toccoa, off US 123, is a restored plantation house & stagecoach inn. *Callaway Plantation,* W of Washington on US 78, has restored houses, hewn log kitchen with utensils, craft demonstrations, working farm. It illustrates life in this area through the centuries.

**FAMOUS LIBRARIES.** *Margaret Mitchell Library,* adj. to original Fayetteville Academy, between Rte. 85 and Lee St., has over 14,000 author autographed books, and an extensive Civil War reference collection.

**TOURS.** *Columbus:* Two-hour *Heritage Tour* leaves from Georgia Welcome Center, Victory Dr., covers 5 historic houses and Springer Opera House. *Athens, Macon, Madison, Savannah, Fort Gaines,* and *Sparta* offer do-it-yourself maps of historic sites. *Thomasville* Chamber of Commerce sponsors tours of plantations, historic homes and gardens of the immediate area, daily.

**DRINKING LAWS.** Min. age is 18. Liquor stores are generally open from 8 A.M. to 11:30 P.M. daily except Sun. and election days. You can buy a drink during the same hours. State law prohibits the purchase of more than two quarts of liquor at a time.

**WHAT TO DO WITH THE CHILDREN.** Pan for gold with the kids at *Gold Hills of Dahlonega,* Rte. 60. Museum open daily June-Labor Day; wkends. Sept to Nov. *Callaway Plantation,* W of Washington on US 78, open April 15–Oct. 15, offers craft demonstrations, a working farm to visit, two restored houses each with period furnishings. Marietta's *Youth Museum,* Cheatham Hill Rd., also emphasizes American way of life. Valdosta has a *Children's Museum* with 40 exhibits relating to science & history. *Stone Mountain Park,* 16 mi. E of Atlanta on US 78, is a 3,800-acre recreation park with game ranch, antebellum plantation, skylift, lots more. Combination ticket available. *Six Flags over Georgia,* on I–20 outside of Atlanta, is an amusement park with six distinctive areas representing periods of Georgia's history. Rides, live entertainment.

**HOTELS AND MOTELS** in Georgia run the gamut from the deluxe resort on Sea Island to the inexpensive, but attractive, motels found along many of the state's major highways. Accommodations are listed according to price categories, based on double occupancy in the peak season, without meals; *Expensive* $30 to $42; *Moderate:* $18 to $29; *Inexpensive:* $9 to $15. For a more complete explanation of hotel and motel categories see *Facts at Your Fingertips* at the front of this volume.

## ALBANY

**Downtowner.** *Moderate.* 732 Oglethorpe Blvd. (220 rooms.) Pool. Pets. Restaurant, bar, dancing, entertainment. Rms. have refrigerators, snack dispensers.

**Quality Inn.** *Moderate.* 2 locations, each with pool: **Merry Acres:** 1500 Dawson Rd. Restaurant, bar; **Town House:** 701 Oglethorpe Blvd. Cafeteria across street.

**Sheraton Motor Inn.** *Moderate.* 999 E. Oglethorpe Expwy. (150 rooms.) Pool (heated), pets. Restaurant, bar, dancing, entertainment.

**Oglethorpe Motel.** *Inexpensive.* 941 Oglethorpe Ave. There are 34 rooms.

## AMERICUS

**Americus.** *Moderate.* Pool. Restaurant nr.

**Best Western Inn..** *Moderate.* Pool, restaurant.

**King Motel.** *Inexpensive.* US 19N. There are 21 rooms.

## ATLANTA

**Atlanta Hilton.** *Deluxe.* 255 Courtland St. at Harris St. Largest hotel in the southeast (1250 rooms) and new (opened in 1976). Its 29 stories include a spectacular rooftop restaurant with an adjoining nightclub. At lobby level are other restaurants and lounges. Four tennis courts, swimming pool, sauna, health club—and a jogging track!

**Colony Square.** *Deluxe.* Peachtree and 14th St. There are 500 rooms, three restaurants and a cocktail lounge. The *Venetian Room* has big-name entertainment nightly. The *Fairmont Crown,* 27 stories up, has brunch, lunch, dinner and dancing.

**Omni International.** *Deluxe.* There are 471 rooms. Adjoins World Congress Center.

**Peachtree Plaza.** *Deluxe.* Peachtree at Cain Sts. World 's tallest hotel (70 stories), opened in 1975. A truly breathtaking hotel: seven-story atrium lobby with half-acre lake, greenery, tapestries, sculpture. Spectacular three-level revolving restaurant and cocktail lounge, is atop the hotel; *Terrace Room,* multi-level dining room, has waterfall. Swimming pool, sun deck, health club.

**Hyatt Regency Atlanta.** *Expensive to Deluxe.* 265 Peachtree St. NE. (1000 rooms.) Pool. Restaurants, bars, revolving Polaris dining rm. and bar atop roof with panoramic view. Spectacular 23-story atrium is heart of this splendid hotel.

**Sheraton Biltmore.** *Expensive to Deluxe.* 817 W. Peachtree St. NE. (654 rooms.) Pool. Restaurant, bars, dancing, entertainment.

**Admiral Benbow Inn.** *Expensive.* 1470 Spring St. NW. (253 rooms.) Pool, with poolside service. Restaurant, bar, entertainment, dancing. Also at Atlanta Airport and Buford Hwy.

**Atlanta Airport Hilton.** *Expensive.* 1031 Virginia Ave. There are 350 rooms.

**Atlanta American.** *Expensive.* Spring & Carnegie Way. (350 rooms.) Pool with service. Restaurant, bar, dancing, entertainment.

**Guest Quarters.** *Expensive.* 7000 Roswell Rd. NW. (242 rooms.) Kitchen units. Pool. Pets permitted.

**Holiday Inn.** *Expensive.* Four locations, each with pool, kennel, restaurant, bar. **Airport,** 1380 Virginia Ave.; **Downtown,** 175 Piedmont Ave., NE.; **East,** 4300 Snapfinger Wood Dr., Decatur; **I–85,** 1944 Piedmont Circle NE. Total of 10 Holiday Inns in Atlanta area. See moderate-priced ones below.

**Marriott.** *Expensive.* Cain & Courtland Sts. Excellent, lavishly furnished motor inn with in-rm. movies avail. Pool, golf & tennis nr. Restaurant, bar, dancing, entertainment.

**Northlake Hilton Inn.** *Expensive.* 4156 LaVista Rd, Tucker; 4151 Memorial Drive, Decatur. Pool. Restaurant, bar, dancing, entertainment.

**Riveria Hyatt House.** *Expensive.* 1630 Peachtree St. NW. Pool. tennis. In-rm. movies avail. Restaurant, bar, dancing, entertainment.

**Sheraton.** *Expensive.* Three of five; with pool, restaurant, bar. **Northlake Inn:** 2180 Northlake Pkwy.; **Olympic Motor Inn:** at I–285 N. Peachtree exit; **Winchester Inn:** 1200 Winchester Pkwy. Smyrna.

**Holiday Inn.** *Moderate.* Five in this category, with pool, play area, restaurant: **I–75:** 6288 Old Drive Hwy, Jonesboro; **Northeast:** 4422 Northeast Expwy, Doraville; **Northwest:** 1810 Howell Mill Rd. NW; **6 Flags West:** 4225 Fulton Industrial Blvd; **South:** Hapeville.

**Howard Johnson's.** *Moderate.* Five locations, each with pool, restaurant: **Airport:** 1377 Virginia Ave. East Point; **Northeast:** 2090 N. Druid Hills Rd.; **Northwest:** 1701 Northside Dr. NW; **Sandy Springs:** 5973 Roswell Rd. NW; **South:** 759 Washington St. SW.

**Carlton.** *Inexpensive.* 6610 E. Expwy., Jonesboro. Pets welcome. Restaurant near.

**Days Lodges.** *Inexpensive.* Six locations, each with pool, play area, restaurant. I–75 South; I–85 at Clairmont; I–285 and Old Dixie Hwy.; Buford Hwy. & Beverly Hills; Buford & Old Stone Mt. Rd.; Shallow Ford Rd.

## BLAKELY

**Deep South.** *Inexpensive.* Pool. Restaurant nr.

**Quail.** *Inexpensive.* Free in-rm. coffee. Restaurant nr. Pets.

## BRUNSWICK

**Holiday Inn.** *Moderate.* 2307 Gloucester at US 17. (100 rooms.) Pool, restaurant, bar, dancing & entertainment.

**Howard Johnson's.** *Moderate.* US 17N. (128 rooms.) Pool, play area. Restaurant, bar. Pets.

**Sheraton Inn.** *Moderate.* US 341. Pool. Pets. Bar, restaurant, entertainment, dancing.

**Day's Inn.** *Inexpensive.* I–95 and US 341. There are 122 rooms.

**Sands Motel.** *Inexpensive.* 2915 Glynn Ave. There are 35 rooms.

## CALHOUN

**Holiday Inn.** *Moderate.* Pool (heated). Pets. Restaurant.

**Days Inn.** *Inexpensive.* I–75 at Ga. 53. (120 rooms). Pool, play area. Pets. Restaurant.

**Ramada Inn.** *Moderate.* I–75 at Ga. 53. (100 rooms.)

## CARTERSVILLE

**Quality Inn.** *Moderate.* US 41S. There are 86 rooms.

**Crown Inn Best Western.** *Inexpensive.* 1214 N. Tenn. Rd. There are 42 rooms.

**Pioneer Inn.** *Inexpensive.* I–75, Cassville-White exit. There are 60 rooms.

## COLUMBUS

**Best Western Martinique.** *Moderate.* 1011 4th Ave. (180 rooms.) Pool (heated). Restaurant bar, dancing, entertainment. Pets.

**Black Angus.** *Moderate.* Pool. play area. Morning coffee & rolls free. Restaurant.

**Heart of Columbus.** *Moderate.* 1024 4th Ave. (65 rooms.) Pets. Restaurant.

**Holiday Inn.** 2 locations: Airport (173 rooms) and US 27–280, 3170 Victory Dr. (172 rooms.) *Moderate.* Pool, play area. Pets. Restaurant, bar.

**Sheraton-Ralston Inn.** *Moderate.* 1325 4th Ave. (156 rooms.)

**Motel 6.** *Inexpensive.* Pool (heated). Small fee for TV. 24-hr coffee shop.

## DALTON

**Davis Bros.** *Moderate*. Pool, play area. Pets. Free morning coffee & rolls. Restaurant.

**Camelot Inn.** *Moderate*. Pool. Restaurant nr. Pets.

**Holiday Inn.** *Moderate*. (200 rooms.) Pool. Pets. Restaurant, serving beer & wine only. I–75 & Walnut Ave.

**Howard Johnson's.** *Moderate*. Pool. Restaurant. Free airport transportation. Pets.

**Ramada Inn North.** *Moderate*. (103 rooms.) Pool. Restaurant, serving beer & wine. Pets limited. 2201 Chattanooga Road.

**San Quinton Hotel.** *Moderate*. Pool. Restaurant.

**Best Western.** *Moderate*. (97 rooms.) Pool. Pets. Restaurant. 2306 Chattanooga Rd.

## DILLARD

**Dillard House.** *Moderate*. Motel rooms and several rooms in house. Pool, sauna, play area, free in-room coffee in most motel units, golf nr. Restaurant, featuring homegrown vegetables, Southern food. Seasonal rates.

**Dillard Motel.** *Moderate*. Pool nr. Free in-rm. coffee. Rooms have mountain view from private patios. Seasonal rates.

## GAINESVILLE

**Days Inn & Lodge.** *Moderate*. Cafe. Pool. Pets.

**Holiday Inn.** *Moderate*. Pool (heated), play area; tennis & golf nr. Kennel. Restaurant, bar, entertainment. Free airport transportation.

**Georgiana.** *Inexpensive*. Pool. Restaurant. Fam. rates.

## MACON

**Davis Bros..** *Moderate*. Chambers Rd. I–475 at US 80. Pool. Cafe. Pets.

**Holiday Inn.** *Moderate*. 2 locations with all the amenities typical of this chain: **Warner Robins:** 2024 Watson Blvd. 7 mi. E of Warner Robins-Centerville exit; **West:** 4775 Chambers Rd. at Jct. of US 80 and I–75.

**Howard Johnson's.** *Moderate*. 2 locations each with pool, play area: **North:** 2566 Riverside Dr.; **West:** Romeiser Dr.

**Quality Inn-Alpine.** *Moderate*. 1990 Riverside Dr. Pool. Restaurant nr.

**Ramada Inn.** *Moderate*. 2 locations, each with pool, restaurant, bar: 1440 Watson Blvd., dancing, entertainment; **North:** 2400 Riverside Dr.

**Sheraton Motor Inn.** *Moderate*. 2737 Sheraton Dr. There are 120 rooms.

**Brown's.** *Inexpensive.* 1232 Jefferson Rd. Pool, restaurant.

**Courtesy Court.** *Inexpensive.* 2240 Gray Hwy. Play area. Restaurant nr.

## MARIETTA

**Master Hosts Inn.** *Expensive.* 2375 Delk Rd. at I–75. (100 rooms.) Pool. Pets. Restaurant, bar.

**Ramada Inn.** *Expensive.* Pool (heated). Restaurant, bar, dancing, entertainment.

**Squire Inn.** *Expensive.* 2767 Windy Hill Rd. (199 rooms.) Pool. Pets. Restaurant, bar.

**Bon Air.** *Moderate.* Pool, play area. Pets limited. Restaurant nr. Family & seasonal rates.

**Holiday Inn.** *Moderate.* 2360 Delk Rd. (329 rooms.) Pool, play area. Kennel. Restaurant, bar, entertainment, dancing.

**Pacemaker.** *Moderate.* Pool. Pets limited. Restaurant, bar, dancing, entertainment.

**Quality Inn-Marietta.** *Moderate.* Pool, play area. Pets. Restaurant.

**Georgian Oaks.** *Inexpensive.* 1141 South Cobb Pkwy. There are 100 rooms.

**Marietta Motel.** *Inexpensive.* 637 Cobb Pkwy. SE, with 45 rooms.

## MILLEDGEVILLE

**Days Inn.** *Moderate.* Pool. Pets. Cafe.

**Holiday Inn.** *Moderate.* (117 rooms.) Pool, play area. Pets. Restaurant, bar.

**Milledgeville Motel.** *Moderate.* Pool. Playground. Pets.

## PINE MOUNTAIN

**Holiday Inn.** *Expensive.* Pools, heated, play area. Kennel. Restaurant. Free admission to Gardens & facilities. AP, MAP, seasonal, pkg. rates avail.

**Callaway Cottages.** *Moderate.* A family recreation park with kitchen cottages, supervised recreation program, entertainment, free admission to Gardens and its facilities. Fee for TV. Restaurant. Fam. rates only with 1-wk min., 2-wk max. in summer; S & D daily rates Sept. to June. No liquor on grounds. Free terminal transportation.

**Davis Inn.** *Moderate–Expensive.* State Park Rd. There are 22 rooms.

## ROME

**Elstonian Motel.** *Moderate.* TV, pool.

**Holiday Inn.** *Moderate.* 707 Turner-McCall Blvd. (155 rooms.) Pool. Golf nr. Pets. Restaurant, bar. Fam. rates avail.

**Roman Inn.** *Moderate.* US 441. (118 rooms.) Pool. Restaurant, bar. Pets.

**Sheraton-President Inn.** *Moderate.* 840 Turner-McCall Blvd. (107 rooms.) Pool. Cafe.

**Riverview Hotel.** *Moderate.* 105 Osborne. There are 18 rooms.

## SAVANNAH

**Savannah Inn.** *Deluxe.* 612 Wilmington Island Rd. Resort hotel with villas & cottages on Wilmington River. Pool, sauna, play area. Golf, tennis, riding, hunting, fishing, boating, marina. Restaurant, bar, dancing, entertainment. Seasonal, family, golf pkg. rates avail.

**De Soto Hilton.** *Expensive.* (254 rooms.) Liberty & Bull St. Rooftop pool (heated). Golf nr. Free in-rm. coffee. Restaurant, bar.

**Downtowner.** *Moderate.* 201 Oglethorpe Ave. (204 rooms.) Pool. Restaurant, bar. Pets.

**Heart of Savannah.** *Moderate.* (53 rooms.) Pool. Free morning coffee & rolls. 300 W. Bay St.

**Holiday Inn.** *Moderate.* 2 locations, each with pool, restaurant, bar: 121 W. Boundary St. just S of Talmadge Bridge; at Jct US 17 & I-95.

**Medical Arts Motel.** *Moderate.* (50 rooms.) 5000 Waters Ave.

**Howard Johnson's.** *Moderate.* 2 locations, each with pool, restaurant: **Downtown:** 224 W. Boundary St. 232-4371; **West:** Rte. 204 at I-95. Bar. Golf nr.

**Peddler's Town & Country Motel.** *Moderate.* (76 rooms.) 4005 Ogeechee Rd.

**Quality Motel.** *Moderate.* At Travis Field. Pool. Restaurant, bar.

**Sheraton Oasis Village.** *Moderate.* 1 Gateway Blvd., 15 mi. SW on GA 20 at I-95 Abercorn exit. Pool. Pets. Cafe.

**John Wesley Hotel.** *Moderate.* (75 rooms.) 29 Abercorn St.

**Days Inn.** *Inexpensive.* Mall Blvd. Pool, play area. Restaurant. Pets.

## STONE MOUNTAIN

**Stone Mountain Inn.** *Moderate.* There are 89 rooms.

## SYLVANIA

**Quality Inn Paradise.** *Moderate.* Pool, play area. Restaurant nr. Secluded, in 14-acre pecan grove. Pets.

**South Manor Motel.** *Inexpensive.* Pool. Restaurant.

## THOMASVILLE

**Downtown Motor Inn.** *Moderate.* Restaurant, bar.

**Holiday Inn.** *Moderate.* US 19 & 319. (140 rooms.) Pool (heated), play area. Restaurant.

**Days Inn.** *Moderate.* US 19 & 319. (120 rooms.)

**Cotton Patch Motel.** *Inexpensive.* It has 36 rooms.

## TIFTON

**Davis Bros.** *Moderate.* Pool, play area. Morning coffee & rolls free. Fine cafeteria.

**Holiday Inn.** *Moderate.* Pool, play area. Free in-rm coffee. Free airport transportation.

**Tifton TraveLodge.** *Moderate.* Pool (heated). Restaurant nr.

**Ramada Inn.** *Moderate.* (100 rooms.) I–75 & US 82. Pool. Pets.

**Days Inn.** *Inexpensive.* Pool, play area. Restaurant. Pets.

**howard Johnson's.** *Inexpensive.* I–75 at A.B.A.C. exit. (80 rooms.) Pool, play area. Free airport transportation. Restaurant.

**Lankford Manor.** *Inexpensive.* 401 Love Ave., US 41. There are 20 rooms.

**Tifton Motor Inn.** *Inexpensive.* I–75 and 2nd St. It has 120 rooms.

## TOCCOA

**Sheraton Motor Inn.** *Moderate.* Hwy. 175. (80 rooms.) Pool. Restaurant. Fam. rates avail.

## UNADILLA

**Days Inn.** *Inexpensive.* I–75. It has 60 rooms.

## VALDOSTA

**Holiday Inn.** *Moderate.* Pools, play area. Pets. Restaurant, bars, dancing, entertainment.

**Howard Johnson's.** *Moderate.* Pool, play area. Restaurant. Pets.

**Quality Inn.** *Moderate.* Pool, play area, fishing, putting green. Restaurant, bar.

**Sheraton Valdosta Motor Inn.** *Moderate.* I–75 & US 84. (75 rooms.) Pool, play area. Restaurant, bar. Free airport transportation.

**Days Inn.** *Inexpensive.* Pool. Pets. Restaurant.

**Outpost.** *Inexpensive.* Pool, play area. Restaurant. Golf nr. Pets.

**Big 7.** *Inexpensive.* Attractive rms. Pets. Restaurants nr.

## WAYCROSS

**Holiday Inn.** *Moderate.* (103 rooms.) Pool, play area, putting green. Pets. Restaurant, serving beer & wine. 1725 Memorial Dr.

**Quality Motel Arcade.** *Moderate.* Pool, play area. Golf, bowling nr. Pets. Free in-rm. coffee.

**Pine Crest.** *Moderate.* Pool, play area. Free morning coffee. Restaurant.

**Palms Court.** *Inexpensive.* Pool, play area. Golf nr. Restaurant nr. Pets.

 **DINING OUT** in Georgia usually means fine Southern-style foods in a rural atmosphere, or charming plantation house, or sophisticated French cuisine in an elegant urban dining room. Many worthwhile restaurants may be found at the hotels we have listed. Our price categories are for a complete dinner: *Expensive* means a complete dinner may run over $10; *Moderate* will run about $8; *Inexpensive,* below $5. A la carte meals will, of course, bring the bill up. For a more complete explanation of restaurant categories see *Facts at Your Fingertips* at the front of this volume.

## ATLANTA

**LICKSKILLET FARM.** *Expensive.* Southern Cooking.
Reservations are a must at this small, restored farmhouse, where the limited menu offers simple, though elegant, entrees and fresh vegetables. It is wise to call for directions, and the ride takes about half an hour from the city center. Old Boswell Road (Alpharetta)

**AUNT FANNY'S CABIN.** *Moderate.* Southern Cooking.
Dining room is created inside a genuine former slave's cabin, and the fare is first class southern specialties with an emphasis on traditional recipes. The experience is more than just a good meal. Bring your own liquor. 375 Campbell Rd. (Smyrna)

**HERREN'S.** *Moderate.* American Cuisine.
This long-established restaurant includes its own art gallery. The food is first class, and the service exemplary. 84 Luckie St. N.W.

**PITTYPAT'S PORCH.** *Moderate.* 25 Cain St. N.W. in Peachtree Center. Excellent southern specialties. Entertainment.

**Ma Hull's.** 122 Hurt St. NE, in Inman Park. Specialties are biscuits, cobblers, souffles, casseroles. All you can eat for a fixed price. Lunch every day but Saturday; dinner, Mon–Fri.

**Mary Mac's Tea Room.** *Inexpensive.* 224 Ponce de Leon Ave. NE. Cornbread with potlikker; eggplant souffle. Mon.–Fri. only, 11:30–2, 5–8.

## AUGUSTA

**St. Andrews Room.** *Moderate.* Augusta Hilton.

**Town Tavern.** *Moderate.* Popular, attractive.

## BAINBRIDGE

**"OUR " TARA.** *Moderate.* Southern specialties. Homemade bread and ice cream. Children's portions.

## BRUNSWICK

**The Deck.** *Moderate.* St. Simons Causeway. Specializes in seafood.

**The Forks.** *Inexpensive.* 4270 Norwich Street Extention. Home-style cooking, seafood, steaks.

## CARTERSVILLE

**Cartersville Market Square Cafeteria.**

**Howard Johnson's Restaurant.** *Inexpensive.* I–75 at US 411.

## CEDARTOWN

**Old Mill.** Two miles south on US 27. *Moderate.*

## CLARKESVILLE

**CHARM HOUSE DINING INN.** US 441. Buffet lunch and dinner, all you can eat including dessert. Antebellum home, downsouth cuisine, with specialties molasses muffin, barbecued ribs, ham, vegetables.

**Adams Rib.** Highway 441 S.

**La Prade's.** Highway 197 N. Specializes in fresh mountain trout, country ham. Closed during winter months.

## CLAYTON

**Kingwood Inn.** US 76 E.

## COLUMBUS

**Goetschius House Restaurant.** *Expensive.* In an 1839 home, Old South Dining at its best. Gourmet food and drink in historic restoration district.

**Black Angus.** *Moderate.* Steaks and seafood.

**Emmy's Schnitzel Haus.** *Moderate.* First Ave. on Rankin Square. Authentic German.

**Spano's.** *Moderate.* Family-owned, Italian.

## DAHLONEGA

**Smith House.** Just off the square. Family-style home cooking for the hungry traveler. 10 vegetables, 3 meats, biscuits, honey, cobbler, preserves, pickles, iced tea.

## DALTON

**Howard Johnson Restaurant.** *Inexpensive.* 2003 Chattanooga Road.

**Oakwood Cafe.** 201 W. Cuyler.

## DILLARD

**THE DILLARD HOUSE.** *Moderate.* Family-style, ham is the specialty. Ham and sausage made by the Dillard family. Apple sauce, pickles and relishes are homemade, too. Open every day, 3 meals.

## HAZLEHURST

**Village Inn.** Plantation mansion with columns, some antiques, country dishes. US 341.

## HIGH FALLS

**Falls View.** 1½ miles off I–75. Catfish dinners.

## JACKSON

**Fresh Air Barbecue.** US 23. Outstanding Brunswick stew.

## LA GRANGE

**In Clover.** Old Victorian mansion, restored. Fried finger sandwiches named "Prince Albert" and "Queen Anne".

## LUMPKIN

**June's.** On Main Street. Country cooking for visitors to Westville, the village where the clock stopped in 1850.

## MCDONOUGH

**Hampton House.** I–75 at Ga. 20 and Ga. 80. Barbecue.

## MACON

**Beall's 1860.** Located in an antebellum, columned mansion at 315 College St. Fine salad bar; peanut soup.

**Len Berg's.** *Moderate.* In an alley behind the old post office. Country specialties; during the season, homemade fresh peach ice cream. Macaroon pie and stewed corn are outstanding.

**Cag's Open Hearth.** 4330 Forsyth Road.

**La Vista.** 3040 Vineville Avenue. Catfish.

**Peking Garden.** 2772 Riverside Drive.

## MADISON

**Ye Old Colonial.** On the square, country fare served family-style from steam tables. Confederate money for sale at table.

## PERRY

**New Perry Motor Hotel.** *Moderate.* Linen tablecloths, camellia prints on wall. Country specialties with blackberry pan pie a must.

## PINE MOUNTAIN

**Plantation Room.** *Moderate.* At Callaway Gardens. Buffet.

## PLAINS

**Back Porch Cafe.** Main St.

## ROME

**Carriage House.** Holiday Inn, Turner-McCall Blvd.

**Morrison's Cafeteria.** Riverbend Mall.

**Partridge Cafe.** 330 Broad St.

## ST. SIMONS ISLAND

**Bennie's Red Barn.** *Moderate.* N. Frederica Rd. Steaks, homemade apple pie.

**Emmeline and Hessie.** *Moderate.* Golden Isles Marina, overlooks Intercoastal Waterway. Excellent muffins.

**Blanche's Courtyard.** 440 Kings Way. Entertainment weekends in the evening.

**Old Plantation Supper Club.** Steak, seafood, and you may be served collard greens as well.

## SAVANNAH

**De Soto Hilton's Pavillion.** *Expensive.* Waitresses wear elaborate Colonial costumes. Sunday buffet.

**Hester's Martinique.** *Expensive.* 20 Jefferson St. Colonial atmosphere.

**Olde Pink House.** *Expensive.* 23 Abercorn St., 18th-century mansion.

**Shrimp Factory.** *Moderate.* 313 East River St.

**Pirate's House.** *Moderate.* 20 E. Broad at Bay St., in historic Trustee's Gardens.

**JOHNNY HARRIS RESTAURANT.** *Moderate.* 1651 Victory Dr. Savannah landmark.

**Tassey's Pier.** *Moderate.* 3122 Riverroad in Thunderbolt, overlooking Intercoastal Waterway.

**Mrs. Wilkes' Boarding House.** 107 W. James St. Sausage, grits, fresh vegetables, chicken. Mon–Fri., breakfast and lunch.

## SUCHES

**Granny's Farmhouse.** Ga. 60. Barbecue and fried trout served in rustic cabin; sweet potato pie. Open weekends only.

## THOMASVILLE

**Old Strawbridge House.** Restored 1899 Victorian edifice.

## THOMPSON

**Knox Terrace.** 204 Jackson St., Ga. 17 at US 78.

## TOCCOA

**Cherokee Room.** *Moderate.* Sheraton Motor Inn.

**Davis Cafeteria.** *Inexpensive.* US 123.

# KANSAS

## Raiders and Abolitionists

by
### CAROLYN R. LANGDON

*Ms. Langdon, a free-lance author, was formerly on the staff of the Kansas City Star. Her great grandparents settled in "Bleeding Kansas" at the time of the Civil War.*

The territory of Kansas was organized in 1854 when the Kansas-Nebraska Act was passed. The document repealed the Missouri Compromise, which prohibited slavery north of 36° 30′ except in Missouri, and provided for popular sovereignty which permitted resident voters to decide if slavery would be allowed.

The ensuing strife in the territory was ensnared with the activities and opinions in neighboring Missouri. Settlers, many from Missouri, formed communities in Kansas according to their stand on the slavery question. A natural climate of suspicion and hatred developed. In effect, antislavery towns were founded to counteract proslavery ones. Leavenworth, Lecompton, Kickapoo, and Atchison tended toward proslavery, while Osawatomie, Lawrence, Manhattan, and Topeka leaned against it.

Violence was inevitable. Bands of proslavery ruffians attacked free-staters who in turn led raids against their foes. One of the most infamous marauders was John Brown, a staunch abolitionist. In the spring of 1856 he and a band of seven men brutally murdered 5 proslavery settlers along the Pottawatomie Creek. The massacre set off a terrible border war, and the territory became known as Bleeding Kansas. The guerilla warfare, widely reported in the eastern newspapers, gained national attention for the territory.

On January 29, 1861, Kansas was admitted as the 34th state in a troubled union. In response to Lincoln's first call for troops, in April, 1861, Kansas immediately supplied 650 men for the Union Army and continued doing so throughout the conflict. Although there were few major battles on Kansas soil, the state had the highest mortality rate of any in the Union. Her regiments saw action in Arkansas, Mississippi, Alabama, Tennessee, Kansas, and Missouri.

During the war, bands of Kansans frequently crossed the border into Missouri to free slaves and raid farmers who they believed were sympathetic to the Confederacy. However, in many cases they also stole horses and property, even from Missourians who were not Confederates. These bands of Kansans became known as Jayhawkers.

But Kansas paid the price for this Jayhawking as opposing bands raided Kansas towns. One of the most notorious incidents was the work of Willliam C. Quantrill, who raided Lawrence on August 21, 1863. He and a band of nearly 300 Confederates entered the town at dawn, shot down every man they saw, and rode by firing into windows. Banks, stores, saloons, and dozens of houses were looted and most of the town set afire. By mid-morning Quantrill had escaped back into the Missouri hills.

### Exploring the Border

A tour of Civil War sites in Kansas will take in the eastern and southern sections of the state, because what are now wheat fields and cities in western Kansas were not yet cultivated or settled at the time of the War Between the States.

Within an hour's drive west of Leavenworth is Lawrence. The town was established in 1854 as a free-state stronghold and was sacked and burned twice by proslavery forces. The most disastrous was Quantrill's raid in 1863. A stone marker at 935 New Hampshire Street marks the area where his men shot 20 unarmed boys, and many other victims are remembered by a monument in Oak Hill Cemetery.

The University of Kansas was established in 1866 in Lawrence. Later, when athletic teams were established and named, officials apparently remembered history by choosing the name Jayhawks for the athletic squads.

A few miles north and west of Lawrence off US 24 is Lecompton, a hotbed of proslavery activity during the territorial period. A proslavery constitution was drafted by the territorial legislature in

Lecompton, but rejected by the electorate. Constitution Hall on Elmore Street still can be seen.

### Antislavery Stronghold

Return to I–70 and travel west past Topeka. Turn north on State 99, then west on State 18 to Wabaunsee. The little town was founded in April, 1865, by 70 antislavery followers of the Rev. Henry Ward Beecher of Connecticutt. He urged his congregation to support a westward expedition to settle Kansas in the hopes of making it a free-state. The settlers completed construction of a church in 1862 that still is used for services. The Beecher Bible and Rifle Church is on the southeast corner of Chapel and Elm Streets.

These immigrants played an important role in the slavery feud. They brought with them rifles, known as "Beecher's Bibles" because Beecher's congregation in the East had raised money to give each member of the colony a rifle and Bible. But it also was believed that rifles were being shipped into the territory in boxes marked "Bibles." These reports stirred up their opponents and led to open clashes.

### Fort Scott to Osawatomie

Leave Wabaunsee and pick up I–70 east to Topeka. Turn south on US 75 and continue to its junction with US 54. Head east to Ft. Scott.

The fort was built in 1842 to keep peace on the Indian frontier and served as a half-way point between Ft. Leavenworth and Ft. Gibson. The area was the scene of many savage attacks on settlers by proslavery ruffians in the days just prior to the Civil War because it was headquarters for militant free-state forces. During the war it was a key Union outpost in the West, and later it was used to keep order during the settler-railroad disputes.

Reflecting the split of the town over the slavery question, the Free-State Hotel was a stopping point for John Brown's antislavery followers, while directly across the parade ground, in an old barracks next to the hospital, stood the Pro-Slavery Hotel (renamed the Western Hotel in 1862). During the war Ft. Scott was a headquarters, supply and troop depot, prisoner-of-war camp, general hospital, training center for black and Indian troops, recruiting point and refuge for displaced Indians and Union sympathizers from Arkansas. The fort was never under direct attack, but served as an important link between men and supplies in the north and battles in Arkansas, Missouri, and the Indian Territory.

Today the old fort hospital has museum items and an audio-visual presentation of the fort's history. A squared-log blockhouse Civil War fortification called Ft. Blair has been completely reconstructed. Southeast of town is the Fort Scott National Cemetery, which was established in 1862 as one of the first in the country. It contains the graves of servicemen who served in wars from the Civil War to present.

Highway 69 north will take you to Pleasanton. The road follows much the same route that dragoons from Ft. Scott patrolled.

The most significant battle fought on Kansas soil took place at Mine Creek, about 2 miles south of the present town of Pleasanton, which did not exist at that time. On October 25, 1864, 25,000 Confederate and Union troops met a few days after the Battle of Westport in Missouri. The ensuing Union victory ended the threat of a Confederate invasion of Kansas. A marker notes the site of the Battle of Mine Creek.

Eight miles southwest of Pleasanton on State 52 is Mound City, where some victims of the Mine Creek Battle are buried. Also marked is the school where the wounded were tended. In the eastern part of town is the home of Charles (Doc) Jennison, a leader of the Jayhawkers.

Out of Mound City take State 7 North to Osawatomie, which was the headquarters of John Brown. At 10th and Main is the John Brown Memorial Park, with a log cabin (moved from its original site) used by the abolitionist. Osawatomie was sacked and burned in August, 1856, in retaliation for a massacre led by John Brown in May of that year in which he killed settlers on the Pottawatomie Creek.

Among other historical points of interest in the town is the Old Stone Church at 6th and Parker. It is a restored pioneer structure dedicated in 1861.

## PRACTICAL INFORMATION FOR KANSAS

 **FACTS AND FIGURES.** Kansas gets its name from the Kansas Indians. Kansas means "people of the south wind." The state's nicknames are *Sunflower State* and *Jayhawker State*. The sunflower is the state flower; the cottonwood, the state tree; and the western meadow lark, the state bird. *Ad Astra per Aspera* ("To the stars through difficulties") is the state motto. "Home on the Range" is the state song.

Topeka is the state capital. The state population is 2,327,471. In area Kansas ranks fourteenth, with 82,264 square miles, of which 477 square miles are water. A land of wide-open spaces, small towns, and a big sky, Kansas is made up mostly of rolling plains, rising to higher land in the west, with occasional hilly areas. Chiefly a farm and ranching state, Kansas boasts some of the finest grazing land in the country, and its wheat fields are famous. It is one of the biggest wheat-producing states in the country. Food processing also plays an important role in the economy, and in recent years the aircraft industry around Wichita has leaped into prominence. Kansas is also rich in petroleum, natural gas and helium.

Kansas climate is seasonal with cold snowy winters and warm humid summers. Tornadoes and hail-storms occur occasionally in warm weather months. The average annual temperature is 55 degrees.

The state is located in the Central time zone except for a small western portion which is in the Mountain time zone.

**HOW TO GET THERE.** *By car:* I–70, one of the busiest east-west highways, runs through Kansas City in the east through the middle of Kansas and on to Denver in the west. If you are coming from the south, I–35 comes from Oklahoma City, passing through Wichita and intersecting I–70 at Salina. From the north, US 81 joins I–35 near Salina.

*By air:* Wichita and Kansas City have airports for long-haul carriers. Most flights from Wichita stop at Kansas City or Denver. Braniff, United, TWA, and Continental handle the longer flights to Kansas.

*By train:* Amtrak has service to Kansas City (the station is in Missouri), Emporia, Lawrence, Topeka, Newton, Hutchinson, Dodge City, Garden City, Wichita, Arkansas City.

*By bus:* Kansas is served by Trailways, Greyhound, and numerous other smaller lines, including Short Way, North Star, and Missouri Transit.

**HOW TO GET AROUND.** *By car:* Driving in Kansas is easy. The terrain is relatively flat, and most roads run either north-south or east-west. The Kansas Turnpike, however, runs northeast from Wichita to Topeka.

*By air:* There are airports in Parsons, Liberal, Garden City, Goodland, Hays, Manhattan, Salina, and Topeka, besides the larger ones in Kansas City (Mo.) and Wichita. Frontier does most of the short-hop flying.

*By train:* Amtrak trains stop at Kansas City (Mo.), Emporia, Lawrence, Topeka, Newton, Hutchinson, Dodge City, Garden City, Wichita, and Arkansas City. Amtrak's toll-free number is (800) 421-8320.

*By bus:* Midwesterners depend upon good bus service. Trailways, Greyhound, Short Way, Missouri Transit, and numerous other small lines provide it.

**TOURIST INFORMATION SERVICES.** You may write *Kansas Department of Economic Development,* State Office Bldg., Topeka, Kansas 66612, or chambers of commerce in major cities for maps and literature. State universities at Lawrence and Manhattan have information on sports events, museums, drama, lectures. Write the president's office.

**SEASONAL EVENTS.** *Summer:* Old Fort Days Celebration, Ft. Scott in early June; John Brown Jamboree in Osawatomie in late June; Territorial Day Celebration in Lecompton in early July.

**HISTORIC SITES.** *Dodge City* tops the Kansas list perhaps. The *Fort Larned National Historic Site* is important for its role in guarding the Santa Fe Trail from Indian raids between 1859 and 1882. On view there are original gun collections, Indian artifacts and old wagons. *Council Grove,* itself a National Historic Landmark, was the last stop on the Santa Fe Trail between Kansas City and Santa Fe and the *Madonna of the Trail* statue here is especially impressive.

In Wabaunsee, you may visit the *Beecher Bible* and *Rifle Church,* organized by followers of Henry Ward Beecher in 1862. *Marysville* was the first station on the Pony Express Route, but there is no evidence remaining of the site itself. A log cabin used by John Brown before he went East to fame and death is at Osawatomie in a memorial park bearing his name. At Smith Center you can see the restoration of the cabin where Brewster Higley wrote the words for "Home on the Range" in 1872.

**DRINKING LAWS.** Until recently, Kansas was dry, but now there are package sales in stores. Many hotels and motels have "private" clubs and most grant temporary memberships for a small fee.

**HOTELS AND MOTELS** in Kansas are dotted across the landscape. There are scores of comfortable accommodations in old-style hotels, up-to-the-minute motels and modernized hostelries catering to the businessman and tourist. The price categories in this section, for double occupancy, will average as follows: *Expensive* $22 and up, *Moderate* $14 to $22, *Inexpensive* below $14. For a more complete description of these categories see *Facts at Your Fingertips*.

## DODGE CITY

**SILVER SPUR LODGE.** *Moderate.* An excellent medium-sized motel on Front Street restoration. 122 air conditioned rooms. Color TV, heated pool, pets, restaurant, private club, package store.

## FORT SCOTT

**Downtowner.** *Moderate.* 48 rooms; pets, restaurant.

**Red Ram.** *Moderate.* Pool, playground, pets, restaurant.

**Colonial.** *Inexpensive.* A small motel. Pets, restaurant.

**Ramada Inn.** *Expensive.* 6th and Iowa Streets. 110 rooms.

**Holiday Inn.** *Moderate.* Iowa & 23rd St. 119 rooms.

**Lawrence Travelodge.** *Moderate.* 801 Iowa St. 70 rooms.

## LEAVENWORTH

**Cody.** *Moderate.* 71 rooms.

**Hallmark Inn Motel.** *Moderate.* Near Ft. Leavenworth.

**Ramada Inn.** *Moderate.* 100 rooms.

**DINING OUT** in Kansas means plenty of good country food. In addition to such farm specialties as breaded steak, griddle cakes, corn fritters, fried chicken, corn on the cob and apple pan dowdy, try to eat at one of the Swedish-style restaurants. Restaurant price categories are as follows: *Expensive* $7.50 and up, *Moderate* $3.50 to $7, *Inexpensive* under $3.50. These prices are for hors d'oeuvres or soup, entree and dessert. Not included are drinks, tax and tips. For a more complete explanation of restaurant categories refer to *Facts at Your Fingertips*.

## ALMA

**Alma Hotel.** *Expensive.* Gourmet French cooking in a plush Victorian period setting is featured at this historic restaurant, built in 1887. Drinks served under private club operation (small membership fee required). Reservations required. Dinner only, closed Tuesdays.

## BROOKVILLE

**Brookville Hotel Dining Room.** *Moderate.* There is a historic frontier ambience at this hotel, which has been family-owned since 1870. Specialties are family-style chicken dinners, picnics and hot meals to go.

## COUNCIL GROVE

**Hayes House (Old Hays Tavern).** *Expensive.* Oldest continuously operated eatery West of the Mississippi. Built in 1857, authentically restored. Walnut and oak exposed-beam construction recreates the "fine dining" atmosphere of the Old West. Dining room features full-service, menu-type meals.

## FORT SCOTT

**Red Barn.** *Moderate.* Chuck wagon dinners are fun for all in the great atmosphere of this renovated barn, where specialties are chicken, charcoal-broiled steak, and barbecued ribs.

## LAWRENCE

**Eldridge House.** *Expensive.* 701 Massachusetts. Originally built in 1854 and called the Free-State Hotel, this establishment was burned four times, once by Quantrill during his savage raid on Lawrence because he thought it contained the presses that published an anti-slavery newspaper. The present structure was built in 1926. Today continental cuisine and flaming desserts are featured.

## WATERVILLE

**Weaver Hotel.** *Moderate.* Leisurely dining in authentic Victorian atmosphere characterizes this restaurant housed in historic railroad hotel built in 1905. Known locally for family-style chicken dinner. Private room available for drink service on private club basis (small membership fee). Reservations usually required.

## WELLINGTON

**Slate Creek Depot.***Expensive.* 3 miles west of Wellington on Hwy. 160. Specialties change monthly and include quail and pheasant. Building is renovated depots transported from the Kansas towns of Sharon, Mayfield, and Argonia. Rustic atmosphere.

# KENTUCKY

## *A Star in Both Flags*

.

### by
### BETTY ELLISON

*Betty Ellison is a native of Tennessee, now living in Lexington, Kentucky. Before becoming a freelance writer she was chief travel writer for the Commonwealth of Kentucky.*

Kentucky, just below the Mason-Dixon Line, was very much in the middle during the Civil War. Passions ran high for both North and South. The state first tried to adopt a neutral policy, but it was drawn inevitably into the conflict.

Ironically, both Abraham Lincoln, President of the United States, and Jefferson Davis, President of the Confederacy, were born in Kentucky—and only a year apart.

As a 400-mile buffer zone between North and South, Kentucky was a battlefield from the start. Union troops eventually won the state, but about 45,000 Kentuckians went south to join the Confederates. Typical of the house-divided tragedies that rent so many Kentucky families was that of Kentucky-born Mary Todd Lincoln, the President's wife. Her brother, three half-brothers, and the husbands of three half-sisters all served in the Confederate army.

Kentucky was a great breeding ground for Civil War generals—41 on the Union side and 38 with the Confederates. Most famous was the South's Albert Sidney Johnston, who commanded the rebel Army of the Tennessee.

The state was represented by a star in both the Union and Confederate flags. While Kentucky remained officially loyal to the Union, the Confederates hopefully established a "provisional government," which never came to power.

## The War in Kentucky

At first things went well for the Confederates in the west. Gen. Braxton Bragg caught Gen. Don Carlos Buell off guard and without fighting a battle forced Federal evacuation of northern Alabama and central Tennessee. But when Bragg entered Kentucky he became engaged in "government making" in an effort to set up a state regime which would bind Kentucky to the Confederacy. Also, the Confederate invasion was not achieving the expected results since few Kentuckians joined Bragg's forces and an attempt at conscription in east Tennessee failed completely.

Buell finally caught up with Bragg's advance at Perryville, Kentucky, on October 7. Finding the Confederates in some strength, Buell began concentrating his own scattered units. The next morning fighting began around Perryville over possession of drinking water. Brig. Gen. Philip H. Sheridan's division forced the Confederates away from one creek and dug in. The battle as a whole turned out to be a rather confused affair as Buell sought to concentrate units arriving from several different directions upon the battlefield itself. Early in the afternoon, Maj. Gen. Alexander M. McCook's Union corps arrived and began forming a line of battle. At that moment Maj. Gen. Leonidas Polk's Confederate corps attacked and drove McCook back about a mile, but Sheridan's troops held their ground. Finally a Union counterattack pushed the Confederates out of the town of Perryville. Buell himself remained at headquarters, only two and half miles from the field, completely unaware of the extent of the engagement until it was nearly over. The rolling terrain had caused an "acoustic shadow" whereby the sounds of the conflict were completely inaudible to the Federal commander. While the battle ended in a tactical stalemate, Bragg suffered such severe casualties that he was forced to retreat. Coupled with Van Dorn's failure to bypass Federal defenses at Corinth, Mississippi, and carry out his part of the strategic plan, this setback forced the Confederates to abandon any idea of bringing Kentucky into the Confederacy.

Perryville Battlefield State Shrine, west of Danville on US 150, has a museum containing battle relics, displays and a diorama of the battle. There are monuments to both the Confederate and the Union fighting men. A reenactment of the Battle of Perryville is staged annually in October. Near the park are two shrines: the Crawford

House, used by General Bragg as his headquarters, and the Squire H. P. Bottom House.

## City of Culture

Some of Lexington's distinguished old homes are open to travelers. Ashland, Henry Clay's estate, has a beautifully furnished twenty-room mansion, smoke-, carriage- and icehouses and a well-kept garden. Ashland is closed only on Christmas Day.

Hopemont was the home of both the famed Confederate raider John Hunt Morgan and the first millionaire in Kentucky, John Wesley Hunt, who built the house in 1814.

From the Lawrenceburg interchange, thirteen miles from Lexington on the Bluegrass Parkway, US 127 offers a delightful side trip. To the north lies Kentucky's capital, Frankfort, on the Kentucky River. In South Frankfort, a section that seceded from North Frankfort during a turbulent period in the city's history, stands the new State Capitol, erected in 1909. A bronze statue of Abraham Lincoln, Kentucky's greatest native son, dominates the rotunda of the Capitol, which allegedly causes some unreconstructed Rebels to refuse to enter the building by the front door. A statue of Jefferson Davis, the President of the Confederacy and another native Kentuckian, stands on a lesser pedestal in a corner. One modern-day Kentuckian explains: "The Commonwealth is proud of him, too, but after all, he lost."

Back on the Bluegrass Parkway, head west to the Springfield exit. Six miles north of Springfield is the Lincoln Homestead State Park where Abraham Lincoln's paternal grandparents settled after coming to Kentucky from Virginia in the early 1780's. Lincoln's father, Thomas, grew up here, and Lincoln's grandfather, Captain Abraham Lincoln, who had served in the Revolutionary War, was killed here by hostile Indians. Log cabins with pioneer furnishings, among them several pieces made by Abe Lincoln's father, have been erected on the homestead site.

## The Bourbon Capital

Bardstown, another twenty miles or so west of Springfield, is generally agreed to be one of the highlights of any visit to Kentucky. Second oldest community in the state (settled in 1778), it is cosmopolitan and filled with historic buildings, wide streets and fine trees. Among other distinctions, it proudly proclaims itself "The Bourbon Capital of the World." Fourteen distilleries are located in the small town of 4,800 and there are several more in the environs. An off-beat but fascinating place to visit is the Barton Museum of Whiskey History, operated by a distillery open seven days a week and free. In it is a rare collection of whiskey-making and drinking paraphernalia. Even more fascinating is the Star Hill Distilling Co. just outside nearby Loretto, where Maker's Mark sour mash whiskey is made according to traditional methods, and you can watch the mash fermenting in great wooden barrels.

A free Tourmobile makes scheduled tours of Bardstown, leaving from the Information Center on the Courthouse Square. On the itinerary is a visit to My Old Kentucky Home State Park, with its mansion, Federal Hill, which inspired Stephen Foster to compose the ballad, "My Old Kentucky Home." Built in 1795 by one of Kentucky's famous judges and United States Senators, John Rowan (a friend of Jefferson, Madison, Monroe and other Presidents), the mansion was occupied by the family until it was purchased with its grounds as a state park in 1922. Costumed hostesses give entertaining and educational lecture-tours of the handsome house which has been restored to its mid-nineteenth century elegance. Note the children's room upstairs, with its unusually wide crib and tin bathtub.

In the park's amphitheater, *The Stephen Foster Story,* an outdoor drama built around famous songs of the composer, is presented nightly (with Sunday matinees) from June to September. You can buy tickets for the unreserved seats on the day of the performance.

## Lincoln Country

From Bardstown it is about twenty-five miles south over US 31E to Hodgenville, where, three miles south of town, the Abraham Lincoln Birthplace National Historic Site is located. Here, at Sinking Spring Farm, Abraham Lincoln was born on Feb. 12, 1809. Fifty-six steps, one for each year of the martyred President's life, lead up to a granite memorial building overlooking the old spring. Inside is the log cabin that was the actual birthplace. A magnificent oak, an old boundary landmark when Lincoln was born, still grows nearby. The National Park Service also maintains a small museum building here, in which an excellent short film on Lincoln's early life in Kentucky is shown throughout the day.

In the Hodgenville area there is also another log cabin which is preserved as a reconstructed version of the home Lincoln lived in as a small boy. It stands by the roadside at Knob Creek, just a few miles from Sinking Spring, and it is the spot to which the family moved when Lincoln was four years old. "My earliest recollections is of the Knob Creek place," the President wrote in 1860. It was here that Lincoln and his sister first went to a "subscription" school. Each February a festive Lincoln Day Celebration is held.

In Elizabethtown, nine miles northwest of Hodgenville via Route 61, are several Lincoln family home sites: (1) the historic Helm Mansion—birthplace of Abraham Lincoln's brother-in-law, Confederate General Benjamin Hardin Helm; (2) the site of the mill and millrace which Thomas Lincoln supposedly built prior to his marriage, on Valley Creek just off 31W on Race Street; (3) the farm where Tom lived with his mother, sister and brother-in-law (follow Miles Street to the Battle Training Road and turn left); (4) on Main

Street one block north of the courthouse, the site of the Patton home, where Thomas Lincoln was married to his second wife, Sarah Bush Johnston.

Southwest of Elizabethtown via I—65 and US 31 is Bowling Green, seat of Western Kentucky University. The Kentucky Building at the college contains a 16,000-volume library of Kentucky history and a museum of Indian and Moundbuilder artifacts as well as pioneer relics and antique furniture.

Across from the Kentucky Building, on top of College Hill, are about seventy-five feet of trenches that were once a part of a key position maintained by Confederate General Albert Sidney Johnston from September 1861 to February 1862, while Bowling Green was the Confederate capital of Kentucky.

Lost River Cave, two miles south of town, is said to have been a hideout of the James brothers, Frank and Jesse. Lost River itself disappears into the ground about three miles south of Bowling Green.

## Davis Country

In the town of Fairview, on US 68, is a 351-foot tower, said to be the world's largest concrete obelisk, honoring the birthplace of Jefferson Davis, President of the Confederacy. An elevator carries tourists to the top of the monument. It was built at a cost of $200,000, the sum raised by public subscription. Dedication ceremonies took place in 1924. Its appearance is very much like the Washington Monument. A twenty-two-acre park surrounds the obelisk.

## Western Kentucky

Any trip to western Kentucky should include a visit to Paducah, on a beautiful bend of the Ohio River, and one of the ports of call for the sternwheel paddleboat *Delta Queen,* and its newer sister, the *Mississippi Queen.* Paducah, Kentucky's fifth largest city (pop. 35,000), is called the gateway to the Mississippi, which is just fifteen miles farther west. Though hunters and trappers established temporary camps at this spot as early as 1817, not until 1821 were the first log dwellings erected here. The early riverbank settlement catered to the occasional flatboats of settlers bound for the upper Mississippi and to trappers and hunters.

In the Civil War, General Ulysses S. Grant took possession of Paducah on Sept. 6, 1861. After the war Paducah became a railroad center, and by 1925 had developed the largest railroad repair shops in the world.

Market House, S. 2 St. and Broadway, consists of the William Clark Museum with a collection of early Americana items and an art gallery.

### "Gibraltar of the West"

In September 1861 Confederate General Leonidas Polk moved his forces up from Tennessee to occupy the heights at Columbus, Kentucky, overlooking the Mississippi River, and establish a camp at Belmont on the Missouri side. Throughout that autumn and winter 19,000 Confederate troops labored to make the position impregnable. A floating battery was positioned and several river steamboats were converted into gunboats. 140 heavy guns were placed on the bluffs, and a huge chain, anchored on the shore and resting on rafts, was stretched across the river. The Confederate stronghold was known as "the Gibraltar of the West"; it was the most heavily fortified area in North America.

General U. S. Grant, who then occupied Cairo, Illinois, to the north, attacked the Belmont camp in November 1861. After a skirmish the Confederates were forced to retreat, and Grant turned his guns on the main stronghold at Columbus. He was overpowered by the Confederates and withdrew up the river, but not before burning the camp at Belmont.

This battle marked the major opening of the war's Western Campaign and was the scene of Grant's first active engagement in the Civil War. It also ended all Union ideas of taking Columbus by direct force.

In February 1862 the Confederates, being severely outflanked, evacuated Columbus. One month later Union troops occupied the area.

To reach Columbus-Belmont Battlefield State Park, take US 62 from Paducah to State 80, from the Purchase Parkway, exit on US 51 or State 80. A Confederate cannon, a network of earthen trenches, and the massive chain and anchor still stand in the park. There is a museum in a building that served as an infirmary during the war; on display are Civil War relics and also some Indian artifacts. There is an audiovisual slide program on the Battle of Belmont.

### Home of Cassius Clay

Just a mile west off I-75, five miles north of Richmond, is White Hall State Shrine, the former home of the anti-slavery advocate, Cassius Marcellus Clay (1810-1903). The forty-room Italianate mansion has been restored with many of the original furnishings and other items of the period. Clay, a cousin to Henry Clay, was the son of Green Clay, one of Kentucky's largest slave owners. This youngest son, who received the excellent education of a Southern planters' scion, fell under the master spell of William Lloyd Garrison while he was a student at Yale. Clay returned to Kentucky, established an antislavery newspaper, lectured far and wide on the evils of slavery and helped establish a college for all races at Berea. He is credited with making a stirring speech that swung the 1860 Republican Convention to Abraham Lincoln as the Party's presidential nominee. He served as Lincoln's minister to Russia, and he is credited with playing a major part in America's purchase of Alaska from Russia.

The mansion is a composite of two architectural styles and two structures that were separated by half a century, resulting in a three-story building with five levels. Green Clay built the first portion of the house and called it Clermont, in 1799. This was integrated into a much larger residence, Italianate in design, when Cassius Clay was U. S. Minister to Russia, in the 1860's.

### Fort Knox

From Elizabethtown, follow US 31 W northward and pause en route for a visit to Fort Knox, where all the gold is buried. More than $11 billion in pure gold bars is stored in the Fort Knox Bullion Depository; but you can't see it, and there are absolutely no free samples! Actually, Fort Knox is one of the biggest military installations in the United States, and was the site of two battles during the Civil War. It houses about 60,000 military personnel and is about thirty miles south of Louisville. Kentucky state officials are working on the Federal Government to put some gold bars on display.

### Louisville

Farmington, on Louisville's Bardstown Road, was designed by Thomas Jefferson for the John Speed family and was built in 1810. It was here that Abraham Lincoln came to mend a broken heart during his courtship of Mary Todd, a Kentucky belle from Lexington. Lincoln was a friend of the Speed brothers; John Speed served in his cabinet as Attorney General. The house has been restored and is furnished with many fine antiques originally in the home.

## PRACTICAL INFORMATION FOR KENTUCKY

**FACTS AND FIGURES.** Kentucky translated from the Wyandot Indian word *Kah-ten-tah-teh* means "Land where we will live tomorrow" or "Land of Tomorrow." Kentucky is called the "Bluegrass State" because of the abundant growth of bluegrass on its rich limestone soil. Fields of bluegrass have a bluish-green hue during the spring. The state bird is the Kentucky cardinal; state tree, the Kentucky coffee tree; state flower, the goldenrod; state song, "My Old Kentucky Home," by Stephen C. Foster; state fish, Kentucky bass; state wild animal, the gray squirrel, and the state motto, "United We Stand, Divided We Fall."

Frankfort has been the capital of Kentucky since it became a state in 1792. Kentucky has an area of 40,395 square miles, and its population is around 3,380,000.

Kentucky is generally divided into four sections. The Western Waterlands is covered with those two giants of Kentucky waters, Kentucky Lake and Lake Barkley, which jointly hold more than 220,000 surface acres of water. The Ohio and Mississippi rivers form the border for this section of Kentucky.

South central Kentucky includes the Cave Region, with the most famous of all caverns, Mammoth Cave. Five major lakes and some whitewater rivers are in this area.

Kentucky's most famous region is the Bluegrass, which reaches from the mountains to the Ohio River. When thoroughbreds are mentioned, the first thought is of sleek horses grazing in white-fenced pastures with a background of cross fences and colorful barns—a Kentucky landscape. There are more than 350 horse farms that surround Lexington.

The Eastern Highlands, once famous for mountain moonshine and feuding families, now includes the Daniel Boone National Forest resort parks and streams for both fishing and canoeing, shops selling original mountain crafts.

**HOW TO GET THERE.** *By air:* Louisville can be reached from out of the state on flights of Allegheny, American, Delta, Eastern, Ozark, Piedmont and TWA; Lexington via: Allegheny, Delta, Eastern and Piedmont; Owensboro via Ozark; Paducah via Delta or Ozark.

*By car:* Two major north/south interstates, I-75 and I-65, carry heavy traffic from the Ohio state line to the Georgia and Tennessee state lines. I-64 runs west/east from the West Virginia state line to the Illinois state line. US 41 enters the state in the north from Indiana and runs south to Tennessee.

*By bus:* Greyhound and Trailways operate into the state.

**HOW TO GET AROUND.** *By air:* Delta, Ozark and Piedmont serve cities within the state.

*By car:* A network of interstate highways and state turnpikes and parkways make traveling in Kentucky a pleasure. Over 80% of Kentucky's planned 1,387 mi. of interstate highways and parkways is completed. From Princeton, in western Kentucky, it is possible to travel on four-lane highways all the way to the state's eastern border at Ashland. I-75 and I-65 run north/south and are connected by I-71 from Louisville to Cincinnati. I-24 is under construction. The interstate highways are integrated with nine equally modern state parkways.

*Car rental:* Avis and Hertz have rental offices in Frankfort, Lexington, Louisville and Paducah. In addition, Hertz has offices in Ashland, Bowling Green, Calvert City, Owensboro and Somerset. National and Budget have offices in Louisville and Lexington.

*By bus:* Greyhound, Trailways, Bowling Green-Hopkinsville Bus Co., and Tennessee Trail Blazers.

**TOURIST INFORMATION SERVICES.** Travel Dept of Public Information, Capitol Annex, Frankfort, Ky. 40601. Lexington Area Chanber of Commerce, 239 N. Broadway, Lexington, Ky. 40508. Visitor's Bureau, Founders Square, Louisville, Ky. 40202. Northern Kentucky Convention and Visitors Bureau, 129 East Second St., Covington, Ky. 41011.

**SEASONAL EVENTS.** *February: Lincoln Day Celebration,* Hodgenville, weekend nearest Lincoln's Birthday.

*May: Big Singing Day,* Benton, *Kentucky Guild of Artists' and Craftsmen's Fair,* Berea.

*June: American Folksong Festival,* at Grayson, near Ashland.

*July: Blue Grass Fair,* Lexington, *Old Time Fiddlers' Convention,* Renfro Valley.

*September: Kaintuck Territory Septemberfest,* Gilbertsville. *Kentucky Highlands Folk Festival,* Prestonburg. *All-day Singing Marathon,* Renfro Valley. *Tobacco Festival* (late Sept.) Russellville.

*October: Daniel Boone Festival,* Barbourville. *Court Day,* Mt. Sterline. Re-enactment of Battle of Perryville, Perryville Battlefield State Shrine.

**NATIONAL PARKS.** The *Abraham Lincoln Birthplace National Historic Site,* Hodgenville, on US 31E is about 10 miles from the juncture of the Western Kentucky Turnpike, I-65 and the Bluegrass Parkway via Rte. 61. A marble and granite monument covers the tiny log cabin where the 16th president was born in 1809. Leading up to the cabin are 56 steps, representing each year of Lincoln's life. Facilities here include a picnic area, hiking trails and the museum—all open year around.

**STATE PARKS.** *General Burnside State Park,* named in honor of the Union officer who was a close friend of Abraham Lincoln, is on Lake Cumberland, on the western edge of Daniel Boone National Forest. He fortified a settlement here; but unfortunately the original site is covered by the waters of the manmade lake.

**MUSEUMS AND GALLERIES.** Historical. *Kentucky Museum,* Western Kentucky University, Bowling Green. Closed University holidays. *Columbus-Belmont Battlefield State Park Museum,* June to Aug. *Kentucky Historical Society Museum,* St. Clair St. & Broadway, Frankfort. The *Kentucky Military History Museum,* located in the Old State Arsenal (1850), East Main St., Frankfort, *Harrodsburg Historical Society Museum,* located in one of the Morgan Row bldgs., S. Chiles St. June to Labor Day. Closed Mon.

**HISTORIC SITES.** *Abraham Lincoln Birthplace National Historic Site,* Rte. 1 Hodgenville. Birthplace cabin of Abraham Lincoln. Closed Christmas. Free. *Lincoln Heritage House,* Freeman Lake Park, Elizabethtown. *Mary Todd Lincoln House,* Frankfort, where Mary lived with her parents before her marriage.

*Old Fort Harrod Mansion Museum,* in Old Fort Harrod State Park, Harrodsburg, Historical museum housed in 1830 mansion. *Morgan Row,* 220 S. Chiles St. Oldest standing row houses used for a commercial purpose.

**Historic Shrines and Monuments:** *Jefferson Davis Monument State Park,* Fairview. *Perryville Battlefield State Shrine,* Perryville. On US 150W. Site of Kentucky's bloodiest Civil War battle. Each October a reenactment of the battle is staged in the park. *White Hall State Shrine,* Richmond, Winchester-Boonesboro Interchange of I-75. Home of Cassius Marcellus Clay, Kentucky's great abolitionist who served as Abraham Lincoln's minister to Russia and helped accomplish America's purchase of Alaska. *Lincoln Homestead State Shrine,* Springfield. Park museum featuring the Francis Berry House; Lincoln Home, blacksmith shop.

**DRINKING LAWS.** Liquor is available in Kentucky at package stores and by the drink at bars until midnight. No liquor is sold on Sundays and no liquor is served in any of the state parks. Age limit is 21 years.

**HOTELS AND MOTELS.** Finding a place to stay in Kentucky is not difficult, as the state has an abundance of fine hotels and motels. It also has state-operated accommodations at several state parks, and these are noted for their attractiveness and comfort.

Accommodations are listed according to price categories, based on double occupancy in the peak season, without meals, i.e.: Deluxe, $40 and up; Expensive $30 to $40; Moderate, $25 to $30; Inexpensive, under $25. For a more complete explanation of hotel and motel categories see *Facts at Your Fingertips* at the front of this volume.

## BARDSTOWN

**OLD TALBOTT TAVERN.** *Inexpensive.* Built in the late 1700s as a stagecoach stop and reputedly the oldest hotel in continuous operation west of the Alleghenies. Rooms furnished in Colonial style. Private baths but no room phones or TVs.

## BEREA

**Boone Tavern Hotel.** *Moderate.* Operated by Berea College (founded by Cassius Clay) and staffed mainly by students. Charming. Restaurant serves regional food. No tipping. Pets accepted.

## DANVILLE

**Holiday Inn.** *Moderate.* Restaurant. Pool (heated), play area. Kennel.

## ELIZABETHTOWN

**Holiday Inn.** *Moderate.* Jct. US 62 & I-65. Restaurant, entertainment. Pool (heated). Kennel.

**Quality Inn Cardinal.** *Inexpensive.* Attractive rooms. Restaurant, coffee shop. Pool (heated), play area. Pets allowed.

**Ramada Inn.** *Inexpensive.* Nicely decorated, spacious rooms. Restaurant. Pool (heated). Pets permitted. Seasonal rates.

## FRANKFORT

**Holiday Inn.** *Moderate.* Some studio rooms. Restaurant, entertainment. Pool. Seasonal rates.

**Ramada Inn.** *Moderate.* Restaurant, entertainment. Pool (heated), play area. Pets accepted. Seasonal rates.

**Quality Inn.** *Inexpensive.* Restaurant, coffee shop, bar. Pool. Pets accepted.

## HARRODSBURG

**BEAUMONT INN.** *Expensive.* Historic inn, period furniture. Closed Dec. through Feb. Dining room. MAP available.

**ASPEN HALL.** *Moderate.* 558 Aspen Hall Drive. Southern mansion, antique furnishings. 6 rooms. Restaurant near.

**SHAKERTOWN AT PLEASANT HILL.** *Moderate.* At Shakertown, Rte. 4. Authentic furnishings. Some family units. Restaurant serves all meals.

## HODGENVILLE

**Lincoln Memorial Motel.** *Inexpensive.* Choice of motel or cottage rooms. Pool (heated), play area. Restaurant nr. Some pets accepted. Seasonal rates.

## LEXINGTON

**Hilton Inn.** *Deluxe.* 1938 Stanton Way. Cafe, dining room, bar, entertainment, dancing. Pool.

**Hyatt Regency Lexington.** *Deluxe.* In New Lexington Center, downtown, Opened 1977. 380 rooms; restaurants, lounges.

**Campbell House.** *Expensive.* 1375 Harrodsburg Rd. Nice surroundings and decor. Suites available. Restaurant. Pool (heated). Some pets permitted.

**Holiday Inn-North.** *Expensive.* Jct. I-75 & Newton Pike. Restaurant, bar, entertainment. Pool. Pets allowed.

**Hospitality Motor Inn.** *Expensive.* 2143 N. Broadway. One of chain. Courtesy airport transportation. Nice decor, spacious rooms. Round-the-clock restaurant, bar, entertainment. Pool (heated), sauna, putting green, games. Pets allowed.

**Ramada Inn.** *Moderate.* Two locations. Restaurant, bar, entertainment, pets allowed at both: 1) 232 New Circle Rd., N.W. Courtesy airport transportation. 2) 525 Waller Ave.

**Days Inn.** *Inexpensive* 1675 N. Broadway. Pool. 4 wheelchair units. Pets allowed. A good buy.

## LOUISVILLE

(Most rates are higher and 3-day min. stay required during Kentucky Derby week.)

**Breckenridge Inn.** *Expensive.* 2800 Breckenridge Lane. Fairly new. Courtesy airport transportation. Pools, health center, tennis, putting green. Restaurant, bar, entertainment.

**Holiday Inn-Midtown.** *Expensive.* 200 E. Liberty St. Heated pool. Pets allowed.

**Stouffers Louisville Inn.** *Expensive.* 120 Broadway. Twelve-story complex. Handsomely appointed rooms & suites. Pool (heated). Free parking. Restaurant, bar. Some pets permitted.

**Admiral Benbow.** *Moderate.* 3315 Bardstown Rd. Courtesy airport transportation. Some studios and suites. Coffee maker in rooms. Restaurant, entertainment.

**Middletown Manor Motor Court.** *Inexpensive.* 12010 Shelbyville Rd., Middletown. A Best Western member. Nice rooms & grounds. Pools, tennis, putting green. Restaurant nr.

## MAYFIELD

**Holiday Inn.** *Moderate.* Jackson Purchase Pkwy. Nice rooms; some studios. Restaurant. Pool (heated), play area. Kennel.

**Mid-Towner Motel.** *Inexpensive.* 512 E. Broadway. Choice of rooms, studios or efficiencies. Restaurant nr. Coffee maker in rooms.

## OWENSBORO

**Holiday Inn.** *Moderate.* Appealing rooms. Free airport transportation. Restaurant, bar, entertainment. Pool (heated), play area. Kennels.

**Quality Inn Imperial.** *Inexpensive.* Some studios. Play area, pool (heated). Coffee shop; restaurant nr.

## PADUCAH

**Ramada Inn.** *Moderate.* Usual good quality. Restaurant, entertainment. Pool (heated). Pets accepted.

## RICHMOND

**Holiday Inn.** *Moderate.* Pleasant rooms & studios. Restaurant. Pool. Kennel.

**University Inn.** *Inexpensive.* Very nice accommodations. Pool (heated). Restaurant nr. Pets accepted.

## SOMERSET

**Holiday Inn.** *Moderate.* Courtesy airport transportation. Pool (heated), play area. Restaurant. Some suites. Kennel.

**Somerset Lodge.** *Inexpensive.* Courtesy airport transportation. Good selection of rooms. Pool (heated), games. Restaurant. Pets accepted. Seasonal rates.

## WILLIAMSBURG

**Holiday Inn.** *Moderate.* Dependable standards. Some suites. Restaurant. Pool (heated). Kennel.

**Williamsburg TraveLodge.** *Inexpensive.* Nicely furnished. Restaurant. Pets allowed. Pool (heated), play area.

## WINCHESTER

**Holiday Inn.** *Moderate.* Customary quality. Pool (heated). Restaurant. Kennel.

**Skylit Motel.** *Inexpensive.* Restaurant nr. Pets allowed.

**DINING OUT.** Kentucky is proud of its "country cooking," with items like Kentucky Country Ham (cured for days per pound), fried corn, Sally Lunn muffins, chess pie, corn dodgers, and jam cake. You may also enjoy hush puppies, Mississippi and Ohio River catfish and barbecued pork chops. Kentucky eating is hearty and healthy. Many worthwhile restaurants may also be found at the preceding hotels we have listed.

Restaurants are listed by price category as follows: A complete dinner may cost over $15 in our *Deluxe* category; up to $15 in *Expensive;* up to $10 in *Moderate;* up to $7.50 in *Inexpensive.* A la carte meals will bring the tab up. For a more complete explanation of restaurant categories see *Facts at Your Fingertips* at the front of this volume.

## BARDSTOWN

**OLD TALBOTT TAVERN.** *Moderate.* Regional specialties, home baking. Pleasant environment in historic bldg. Children's portions. Lunch and dinner.

**THE OLD STABLE.** *Moderate.* Regional specialties in converted stable. Friendly informal atmosphere. Entertainment in evening with much audience participation.

## BEREA

**BOONE TAVERN.** *Moderate.* Delightful colonial atmosphere. Try the spoon bread and chicken flakes "in birds' nests." Children's portions. No tipping. Jackets required at dinner.

## DANVILLE

**ELMWOOD INN.** *Moderate.* Old fashioned meals served in 1880s building.

## HARRODSBURG

**BEAUMONT INN.** *Moderate.* Delicious cuisine in elegant colonial dining room; gracious service in the southern tradition.

**TRUSTEES HOUSE.** *Moderate.* At Shakertown. A part of reconstructed Pleasant Hill Family Houses. Excellent traditional Shaker and Kentucky food served by waitresses in Shaker dress. Open for all meals at set hours. Children's portions. No tipping.

## WINCHESTER

**OLD SOUTH INN.** *Moderate.* Country ham, home-baked goods served in Southern mansion. Open from lunch through dinner. Closed Wed.

# LOUISIANA

## *Red River and the Mississippi*

### by
### CHARLES C. PHILLIPS

Louisiana seceded from the Union on Jan. 26, 1861. On that date, Alfred Mouton, president of the Secession Convention, meeting in New Orleans, declared: "In virtue of the vote just announced (it was 117 to 13), I now declare the connection between the State of Louisiana and the Federal Union dissolved; and that this is a free, sovereign and independent Power."

Events, of course, were moving rapidly toward the outbreak of the Civil War. On Jan. 23, three days before Louisiana seceded, Gen. Pierre Gustave Toutant Beauregard, a dashing Louisianian with a name to match his fervor, a man who was to become one of the South's famous soldiers, was named superintendent of the U.S. Military Academy at West Point.

Because of his pro-Southern views, he was removed the following day and became a full general in the Southern army. At 4:30 A.M. on April 12, 1861, he ordered the Southern Forces to fire upon Fort Sumter.

On Jan. 18, eight days before secession, Gen. William Tecumseh Sherman resigned as superintendent of the Louisiana State Seminary of Learning and Military Science (now Louisiana State University) and went North, saying to his Southern friends "This will pass,"

The war did not come soon to Louisiana, which was situated a thousand miles from the fronts in Northern Virginia. On April 13, 1862, more than a year after secession, federal gunboats advanced up the Mississippi River bent on carrying out the grand strategy of the Union Forces, which was the capture of the Mississippi, thus cutting the Confederacy in two. The naval engagement is illustrative of one of the two factors which made it nearly impossible for the South to win in a long war.

One was the lack of industry, and the other was the lack of a navy. While many Southerners in the U.S. Army, including some of its most able men, joined the Confederacy, that was not true of their naval counterparts. In fact, it was a Southerner, Admiral David G. Farragut of Knoxville, Tenn., who forced the surrender of New Orleans, which took place on April 29, 1862.

The failure of the Confederacy to fortify New Orleans was one of the vital mistakes of the South. Forts Jackson and St. Philip, which the Southerners used in an attempt to stop Farragut, may still be seen and are of immense interest architecturally, having been built not long after the British were turned back at the Battle of New Orleans in 1815.

Farragut turned the command of the city of New Orleans over to Union Gen. Benjamin Butler, who instituted a repressive occupation. He had a man hanged for tearing down a U.S. flag, and his famous—or infamous—Woman's Order decreed that the ladies of New Orleans who poked fun at the Union troops were to be treated no better than common prostitutes. So harsh was his rule that he was criticized in the North, and in London, Lord Palmerston told the House of Commons that he "blushed to think that such an act had been committed by a member of the Anglo-saxon race." It must be noted, however, that the Union soldiers were treated more courteously following Butler's orders.

Since many of those coming to Louisiana stop first at New Orleans, and since chronologically the events of the Civil War start there, this article will take the same route.

Generally, those interested in Civil War sites and events may divide the war in Louisiana into three sections. First is the capture of New Orleans. Second is the advance up the Mississippi, resulting in a bloody battle at Fort Hudson near Baton Rouge, the fall of the state capital there, and Gen. U. S. Grant's advance through Louisiana, ending in the capture of Vicksburg, located across the Mississippi from Louisiana.

## A Drive for Cotton

The third event and one which many history books treat lightly is Gen. Nathaniel P. Bank's Red River Campaign, beginning in the spring of 1863 and ending at the Battle of Mansfield (or Battle of Sabine Crossroads) on April 8, 1864.

The Red River Campaign has been widely studied by Civil War historians. Many believe that President Lincoln ordered it under pressure from New England industrialists, whose mills were rusting for lack of cotton. The mill owners wanted the Red River opened to commerce and the Union flag planted in Texas so that cotton could be shipped down the Red and up the coast to New England.

Banks was a "political" general. He had been governor of Massachusetts and Speaker of the U.S. House of Representatives. It is believed that he envisioned the Red River Campaign and the capture of Shreveport (then the Confederate capital of Louisiana), as a stepping stone to the presidency.

Banks, whose initials N. P. were said by the Union soldiers to mean "nothing positive" was welcomed in only one place in Louisiana—New Orleans, where he supplanted Butler.

His long march northwestward toward Shreveport and the Texas border was subject to continued harrassment by troops of Gen. Dick Taylor, son of Zachary Taylor and one of the South's most capable commanders. He was a brother-in-law of Jefferson Davis. Taylor, with far smaller forces, kept retreating while recruiting, especially in Texas. He did not choose to make a stand until Banks was within 40 miles of Shreveport.

With Texas cavalry and Louisiana infantry, Taylor waited for Banks. The battle was joined in the afternoon of April 8, 1864. Some tactical errors by Banks and the fact that Taylor was a fine military craftsman led to a miserable defeat for the Union Army. Banks allowed his supply trains to come too far forward and any stand that his army might have made was thereby hindered. Banks fell back to Pleasant Hill, a few miles south of Mansfield. The next day the tactical errors were on the other side, and Taylor's forces fought to a draw. However, Banks called a council of war and decided that morale was too low for another fight, and he headed back toward New Orleans.

### New Orleans and Vicinity

Fort Pike State Commemorative Area, located on U.S. 90, is 26 miles east of New Orleans, features interesting architecture. The fort was started in 1819; the museum contains dioramas, battle scenes and uniforms from the War of 1812 to the present. (Open 9 A.M. to 5 P.M., Monday-Saturday and from 1-5 P.M. Sunday. Admission charge.)

Fort Livingston is situated on Grand Terre Island, a five minute ride by boat from Grand Isle, the Southernmost point on La. Hwy. 1 and one of Louisiana's few stretches of open Gulf beach. This huge masonry fort was built in 1861. It was garrisoned by the Confederates until its capture by Union Forces on April 27, 1862. (Visits are permitted during daylight hours only.)

Fort Jackson, located on the west bank of River Road (La. Hwy. 23) six miles below Buras, was built in 1822-23 to guard the Mississippi River approaches to New Orleans. Confederate Forces inside the massive fort underwent a shelling April 18-28, 1862 from Federal gunboats commanded by Admiral Farragut. There is a museum on the inside. (Open 10 A.M. to sundown daily. No admission.) Fort St. Philip, on the opposite side of the river, is in ruins and a visit is inadvisable.

The City of New Orleans Confederate Museum, at 929 Camp St., has much memorabilia of the Confederacy. Located in a handsome structure erected in 1890, it contains the personal effects of Jefferson Davis. The body of the Confederate president lay in state here on May 27, 1893, before being moved to Richmond for burial. There are currency and silver coins of the Confederacy, as well as paintings. Located one block from Lee Circle, where Lee's statue was erected in 1885, it is open from 10 A.M. to 4 P.M., Monday through Saturday. (Admission charge.)

The Beauregard House, 1113 Chartres St., was built in 1827. By all odds, its occupants have been among the most varied of any residence in the nation. Gen. Beauregard lived here, as did Paul Morphy, one-time world chess champion, who was born here. Frances Parkinson Keyes, the novelist who wrote "Dinner at Antoines," "Crescent Carnival," "Steamboat Gothic," and other novels set in this region, lived here until her recent death. (Open 10 A.M. to 4 P.M., Monday through Saturday. Last tour starts at 3:40 P.M. Admission.)

The U.S. Customs House, located at 423 Canal St., was built in 1848 under the direction of the young army engineer, P. G. T. Beauregard. The house was used as headquarters for Gen. Benjamin Butler, Union commander of New Orleans, beginning in 1862. The exterior is modified Egyptian motif. (Open 9 A.M. to 5 P.M., Monday through Friday.)

The Cabildo occupies the 700 block on Chartres St. facing Jackson Square. Built in 1795-99, this is one of New Orleans' most famous museums and was the seat of government of the Confederacy in New Orleans. (Open 9 A.M. to 5 P.M., Tuesday through Sunday. Admission.)

### North of New Orleans

Camp Moore Confederate Museum, located on U.S. 51 between Kentwood and Tangipahoa, is a plantation-style home. The adjoining log cabin contains relics of the Civil War. This was the site of a Confederate training ground from 1861-64. The cemetery contains the graves of more than 500 Confederate soldiers. (Open 8 a.m. to 4 p.m., Monday through Friday, and 1 p.m. to 5 p.m. on weekends.)

### Baton Rouge Area

The Port Hudson Battlefield Museum is located on U.S. Hwy. 61, half a mile south of the intersection with La. 68. The museum contains a large collection of relics from the battle fought here, described by President Lincoln as one of the bloodiest of the war. The museum is open by appointment only.

Port Hudson National Cemetery lies west of U.S. 61 on La. 3113. The cemetery contains the graves of nearly 4,000 Union soldiers and many Confederates and is situated on a part of the Port Hudson Battlefield. The fort was under siege longer than Vicksburg and was the last Confederate bastion on the Mississippi to surrender. Its capture by the Union forces completed the plan to cut the Confederacy in half by controlling the Mississippi. Open 1 to 5 P.M., Tuesday through Sunday.

### Baton Rouge

The Old State Capitol on River Road at North Boulevard was built in 1847. It has been described by one architect as "49 percent Gothic and 51 percent bad." Mark Twain observed that, except for the capitol building, Baton Rouge was an "otherwise" honorable place." The building houses the Baton Rouge Tourist Information Center. (Open 9:30 A.M. to 5 P.M. Monday through Friday, 10 A.M. to 5 P.M. Saturday, and from 1 to 5 p.m. Sunday.)

The Old Pentagon Barracks are sited on the corner of River Road and State Capitol Avenue, across from the new State Capitol. Originally there were five buildings, hence the "Pentagon." Now there are four. Built in 1822, they are quite handsome, with double galleries and Doric colonnades. They were army barracks for many years, and visitors included Lafayette, President Taylor, Lee, Grant, Sheridan, Custer and Jefferson Davis. It was surrendered by the Federal forces at the beginning of the war and was retaken by the Union during the fall of Baton Rouge. It now serves as state offices. (Open 8 A.M. to 4:30 P.M., Monday-Friday.) A (free) stroll around the buildings any time is pleasant. The magnificent State Capitol grounds are across the street.

The Maryland Oak, a magnificent tree, stands beside La. Hwy. 1, which at this point parallels False River near Parlange Plantation, south of New Roads. Early in the war, a young Marylander who was teaching school nearby stopped beneath the tree and wrote the verses to "Maryland, My Maryland," one of the most stirring of Confederate war songs. The music, of course, is "Tannenbaum." Plaque. Locust Grove Cemetery, is east of St. Francisville on La. Hwy. 10, 4.2 miles east of the US 61 intersection. An unnumbered road leads to the cemetery, the burial place of Sarah Taylor Davis, daughter of President Taylor and wife of Jefferson Davis.

### Newellton Area

Winter Quarters Plantation, on La. Hwy. 608, three miles southeast of Newellton, was Gen. U.S. Grant's headquarters for a time during the siege of Vicksburg. It contains 19 rooms, fine antiques, and is one of the few plantations spared the torch. (Open 9 A.M. to 5 P.M., daily. Admission.) Nearby Tallulah was an important supply point for the Confederate Army. (US 65,80.)

At Lake Providence, you can see Grant's Canal, which Gen.

Grant started in 1862 to get gunboats safely past Vicksburg. The project still may be seen and the Parish (county) of Madison has sued the U.S. government in recent years to fill it up.

## Red River Campaign

In Washington is Magnolia Ridge, situated on La. Hwy. 103, five and one half blocks west of La. Hwy. 10. This Greek Revival mansion was completed in 1830. Six handsome Doric columns line the lower and upper galleries. It was used by both Union and Confederate forces for headquarters. (By appointment only.)

Grand Ecore, on La. Hwy. 6, on the west bank of the Red River west of Natchitoches, is the site of the presentation of "Louisiana Cavalier," performed during summer months, nightly except Mondays. Confederate breastworks here are still visible, as are the gift shop and concessions. (Admission charge to "Cavalier" performance; admission to area free.)

Bailey's Dam lies just west of the Red River bridge at Pineville, across from Alexandria. This was the scene of an important engineering feat carried out by Union forces. As they retreated toward New Orleans, the water in the Red River dropped to a point where the Union gunboats could not proceed. A Union engineer constructed a dam which narrowed the river and made it navigable. Some of the rocks of the dam are still visible.

The Carriage House Museum is located at Eden Street and St. Martin St. (on La. Hwy. 1) on the town of Plaquemine. Indian relics and Civil War items are on display. (Open 9 A.M. to 5 P.M., Monday-Friday, and 9 A.M. to 4 P.M., Saturday.)

Natchitoches is the oldest town in the Louisiana Purchase, having been founded in 1714, and predating New Orleans. There are many antebellum homes in this area, and some are kept open the year around. Some have historical connections with the Civil War, since it was in the route of retreat for Union forces heading back to New Orleans after the Battle of Mansfield.

Trinity Episcopal Church is located at Second Street and Church Street, in Natchitoches. Built in 1857, it was consecrated by the "Fighting Bishop," Gen. Leonidas K. Polk, a West Pointer-turned-clergyman, then soldier.

The Fort Jessup State Commemorative Area is located six miles east of May on La. Hwy. 6. This restoration has no direct connection with the Civil War except that Lee, Grant and many others who participated in the war—on both sides—were stationed here. Its main historical connection is with the Mexican War, and it was from this point that troops departed to engage in that conflict. (Open 9 A.M. to 5 P.M., Monday through Saturday; and 1 to 5 P.M., Sunday. Admission.)

Rebel State Commemorative Area is located three miles north of Marthaville on La. Hwy. 1221. This site has no military significance, but it was created out of pure sentiment and is perhaps the only monument of its kind. Its background is this: At 2 P.M. on April 2, 1864, a Confederate soldier who had been separated from his unit during skirmishes, was wandering in the forest near some houses. Union forces shot and killed him within view of some of the housewives in the area. The soldier was promptly buried. He had no identification on him, and his name was never learned. The incident illustrates something that Americans for the most part have been spared—war arriving at their front door. A festival is staged here during the summer months. The dates vary. (The area is open 9 A.M. to 5 P.M., Monday-Saturday, and 1-5 P.M., Sunday. Admission.)

Mansfield Battlepark and Museum is the site of the most important military engagement of the Civil War in Louisiana. As described earlier in this article, it was the turning point of the Red River Campaign, in which Union forces aimed at capturing Shreveport, the Confederate capitol of the state, and marching westward to Texas. (Open 9 A.M. to 5 P.M., Monday-Saturday, and 1 to 5 P.M., Sunday. Admission.)

Keatchie Presbyterian Church, on La. Hwy. 5 in the town of Keatchie, is known as the place where Confederate wounded from the Battle of Mansfield were treated. Just west of the town of Keatchie is the Confederate Memorial Cemetery, with the graves of 76 soldiers. In a separate plot are buried "three carpetbaggers."

### Shreveport

Shreveport was the last Confederate capital of Louisiana, and some say the last Confederate flag was furled here. It was headquarters for the Trans-Mississippi Department of the Confederacy, commanded by Gen. Edmund Kirby-Smith. A new Parish (county) courthouse stands on the site of the courthouse which housed the Louisiana capital and the Louisiana Confederate legislature. Fort Humbug is located on Youree Drive (La. Hwy. 1) south of the main business district. The beautiful grounds also house a Veterans Administration Hospital. As the Union forces advanced toward Shreveport, the Confederates erected gun emplacements overlooking the Red River to challenge Union gunboats. However, the Southerners had only a few cannon. Hoping to frighten off the Yankees, they painted logs black and placed them alongside the cannon. Hence, the name "Fort Humbug." The northerners were turned back at the Battle of Mansfield and neither the real cannons nor the "humbugs" were used.

Land's End Plantation lies south of Shreveport on Red Bluff Road. Built in 1847, this home was the scene of a brilliant ball the night before the Battle of Mansfield. Confederate wounded from that battle were treated here. (Open by appointment.)

"The Birthplace of the Secession is located on La. Hwy. 16 at the intersection of La. 157 in Rocky Mount. Before the State of Louisiana seceded, the Town Council of Rocky Mount, on Nov. 26, 1860, passed a resolution to secede. Many believe that this was the first documented act of secession. The Hughes home on the site has been restored. (Open 1:30 to 5 P.M., Saturday and Sunday during the summer months. Admission.)

## PRACTICAL INFORMATION FOR LOUISIANA

 **FACTS & FIGURES.** Louisiana was named for Louis XIV of France. Its nicknames are *Bayou State, Sportsman's Paradise, Pelican State*. The magnolia is the state flower; bald cypress, the state tree. The pelican is the state bird. "Union, Justice, and Confidence" is the state motto; *Give Me Louisiana,* the state song.

Baton Rouge is the state capital. The state population is about 3,800,000.

With the exception of some low hill country in the northern part of the state, Louisiana is flat, low Mississippi Delta country. The extreme southern area is a watery region of swamps, marshes, and bayous, the home of trappers, fishermen, and oil (Louisiana is second only to Texas in petroleum output). Cotton, rice and sugar-cane fields line the fertile banks of the broad Mississippi, which courses down the state to the great port of New Orleans and the Gulf of Mexico. The climate is one of mild winters, hot summers and high humidity. Louisiana is a frequent victim of tornadoes, and the coastal areas lie in the tropical hurricane belt.

 **HOW TO GET THERE.** *By air:* New Orleans may be reached from cities within the U.S.A. on direct flights of: Braniff, Continental, Delta, Eastern, National, Southern, Texas International and United Airlines. Baton Rouge and Monroe on direct flights of: Delta, Southern and Texas International airlines; Shreveport on direct flights of: Braniff, Delta and Texas International; Alexandria on Delta and Texas International airlines; Lake Charles on Texas International and Commuter airlines; Fort Polk and Lafayette on Commuter airlines, which also serve other cities.

To New Orleans, Delta has direct flights out of San Juan, Puerto Rico; Eastern out of Mexico City and Montego Bay; Aviateca and Pan Am out of Merida.

*By car:* From Picayune, Miss., you can get to New Orleans via I–59. I–55 will take you from McComb, Miss., south to Kentwood and Hammond. I–20 comes in from Vicksburg, Miss., and cuts through the state west to the Texas state line. I–10 enters the state at Vidor, Texas, and goes through the state to Slidell. In the northern part of the state I–20 comes into Shreveport from Texas and continues east to Monroe, then US 80 to the Miss. state line. US 71 comes in from Kiblah, Ark., goes south to Shreveport and then east to Alexandria. US 61 enters the state at Woodville, Miss., goes south to Baton Rouge and then east to New Oreans.

*By train:* Amtrak and Southern Railways trains enter the Union Passenger Terminal in New Orleans.

*By bus:* Greyhound and Trailways provide frequent service. In addition, Baton Rouge and New Orleans can be reached on: "Arrow Coach, Central Texas Bus Lines, Inc., Great and Southern Coaches, Inc., Jefferson Lines, Inc., Kerryville Bus Co., Inc., Oklahoma Transport Co., Orange Belt Stages and Salter Bus Lines. Several other bus lines operate into New Orleans.

 **HOW TO GET AROUND.** *By air:* Delta, Southern, Texas International and Commuter airlines service cities within the state. Aircraft charter and rental services, including helicopter, are available.

*By car:* I–55 will take you from Kentwood to Hammond. I–20, in the north, runs west from Monroe, Ruston, Minden to Shreveport. On I–10 you can go from Slidell east through New Orleans, Baton Rouge, Lafayette, Jennings to Lake Charles. I–12 leads from Baton Rouge east to Hammond and Covington. US 61 goes from New Orleans west to Baton Rouge, then US 190 west to Opelousas.

*Car Rental:* You can rent an *Avis, Hertz* or *National* car in Baton Rouge, Lafayette, Lake Charles, Monroe, New Orleans and Shreveport. Hertz and National also have rental offices in Alexandria, Morgan City, New Iberia and Opelousas.

*By bus:* Greyhound and Trailways, as well as Arrow Coach, Central Texas Bus Lines, Inc., Great Southern Coaches, Inc., Orange Belt Stages and Salter Bus Lines serve some cities within the state.

*By ferry:* The Mississippi River may be crossed by ferry at St. Francisville or at Lutcher.

**TOURIST INFORMATION SERVICES.** The Greater New Orleans Tourist and Convention Commission at 334 Royal St. will help you plan. The Chamber of Commerce at 334 Camp St., 524-1131, is also helpful. For the rest of the state, inquiries to specific chambers of commerce of cities and towns and to the Louisiana Tourist Development Commission, Box 44291, Baton Rouge 70804, will bring desired information.

**SEASONAL EVENTS.** In April, *Lake Charles* has a *House & Garden Tour; Shreveport* a 10-day, *Holiday in Dixie* festival celebrating the Louisiana Purchase. Balls, parades, water shows, art exhibits are part of festivities. *Lake Charles* celebrates *Contraband Day* late May to early June with a water sports carnival.

*Summer: Many* has its *Arts & Crafts Festival* the first weekend in June.

*Fall: Natchitoches* offers its *Historic Plantation Tour* the 2nd weekend in Oct.

**STATE PARKS.** *Audubon Memorial State Park,* nr. *St. Francisville* on State 965, is the site of Oakley Plantation House, a museum of Audubon memorabilia, with period furnishings. Formal garden, picnicking, hiking trails. *Fort Jesup State Monument,* 6 mi. E of *Many* on State 6, is the site of the antebellum garrison. Replicas of 2-story brick and frame building and of army field kitchen. Museum, picknicking. *Fort Pike State Monument,* US 90, 30 mi. E of New Orleans. Picnicking. *Longfellow-Evangeline State Park,* 3 mi. NE of *St. Martinville* on Rte. 31, on banks of Bayou Teche, has restored Acadian house, kitchen garden, craft shop, replica of Acadian cottage. Museum, picnicking, swimming, boating, fishing, camping. *Fontainebleau State Park* in *Mandeville* on US 190, has nature trails, ruins of a plantation brickyard and sugar mill, camping, picnicking, water sports. *Niblett's Bluff Confederate Memorial State Park,* site of Civil War ammunition supply point, on Sabine River. Picnicking, boating, fishing, undeveloped camping facilities.

**MUSEUMS AND GALLERIES.** *Herbert S. Ford Memorial Museum,* 502 N. 2nd. St., *Homer,* maintains history, medicine, military, Indian artifact collections. Tour. Closed national holidays.

*Lafayette Museum,* 1122 Lafayette St., *Lafayette,* was home of Gov.

Alexandre Mouton. Furniture, historical documents, portraits, Indian artifacts. Tours. Closed Mon. & holidays.

In *Reserve, San Francisco Plantation* house is 2 mi. upriver on State 44. 18th-century furnishings, landscaped grounds.

*New Orleans: Confederate Museum,* 929 Camp St. Relics pertaining to military history; Civil War memorabilia. Closed Sat., Sun. and holidays. *Musee Conti Museum of Wax,* 917 Conti St. Period settings of local history. Closed Mardi Gras and Christmas.

**HISTORIC SITES.** In New Orleans the *Vieux Carré* (Old Quarter) represents a concentration of historic sites, with the apex at Jackson Square, where the old *St. Louis Basilica* has housed the Catholic See of New Orleans continuously since 1794. It was around this square that Bienville had engineers lay out the city in 1718. For over two and a half centuries the city's history has centered here. Uptown, the *Garden District's* great homes are still maintained as showplaces of the antebellum period. *U.S. Custom House,* 423 Canal St. 4-story 1849 building of granite. The site was once occupied by Fort St. Louis. Used as an office by General Benjamin F. Butler during the Union Army's occupation of New Orleans. Closed wknds. and holidays. Free.

**DRINKING LAWS.** Liquor sold by package and drink at stores or establishments with a license. Sunday sales optional in some locations. None may be imported from another state. The minimum age is 18.

**WHAT TO DO WITH THE CHILDREN.** *Louisiana Purchase Gardens and Zoo,* off I–20, *Monroe,* exhibits rare animals in modern buildings, some glass-fronted, some moated. Nocturnal animals are shown under red lights. The entertainment section has a Lewis & Clark Railroad, boat rides, and other amusement rides.

**TOURS.** New Orleans:*Bus. Gray Line* offers five tours covering various sections of city. Three night-life tours cover the Bourbon St. area, various clubs and cafes. Hotel pickup and return. *Orleans Tours* offers two 2½-hr. tours of French quarter and Garden District, plus a *Lagniappe Tour,* combining both. Hotel pickup and return.

*Boat. MV Voyageur* leaves from foot of Canal St. for cruise into Intercoastal waterway, Bayou Barataria, and return through Harvey Canal. 5 hrs. Harbor cruise to Chalmette Battlefield, 2 hrs. *Mark Twain,* diesel-powered replica of sternwheeler steamboat, leaves Canal St. Dock for bayou trip, 4 hrs. *S.S. President,* large sidewheel steamboat, offers two 30-mi. harbor cruises, leaving Canal St. dock. Sat night cruise with jazz band, drinks, dancing. The 1600-passenger sternwheeler *Natchez* leaves from Toulouse St. Wharf at Jackson Square 3 times daily for 2 and 2½ hr. cruises on the Mississippi from Chalmette Battlefield to Huey P. Long Bridge. Moonlight dance cruise Sat. only. Dining rooms, cocktail lounges, snack bar. The smaller *Cotton Blossom* makes 1 daily 5½ hr. trip into bayou country.

*On foot.* Louise S. McGehee School, 2343 Prytania St., conducts tours of interiors and gardens of Garden District antebellum homes. Costs vary.

*Elsewhere: Delcambre,* 15 mi. W of New Iberia on Rte. 14, offers tours aboard paddlewheeler *Cajun Belle.* In *Monroe, Twin City Queen Excursion Boat* cruises the Ouachita June to Sept., Sun. *Passe Partout Touring Co.,* 329 Beverly Dr., Lafayette, offers special interest & offbeat tours in Acadian country.

**HOTELS AND MOTELS.** *New Orleans:* Rates are higher at Carnival (and during the Sugar Bowl football and sports events at the New Year) than at any other time of the year. Almost all the better hotels and motels in New Orleans have French- and Spanish-speaking staff members. Most people in South Louisiana are bilingual, speaking English and French.

Listings are in order of price category. Based on double occupancy without meals price categories and their ranges are as follows: *Superdeluxe,* $50 and up; *Deluxe,* $40-49; *Expensive,* $30-39; *Moderate,* $20-29; *Inexpensive,* under $20. For a more complete explanation of hotel and motel categories see *Facts at Your Fingertips* at the front of this volume.

Outside New Orleans: Most of the state's establishments are less expensive outside New Orleans. There are many "chain" motels along I–10 and I–12. One practical note: virtually all the motels in Baton Rouge are along US 61 from New Orleans north and US 190, which runs east-west. Both of these routes pass along the edge of the city on US Bypass 190. A few hotels and motels are within the downtown or capitol area. An Airline Highway address in Baton Rouge is located along the US 61 and 190 bypass.

Based on double occupancy without meals, price categories and ranges are as follows: *Deluxe:* $26 and up; *Expensive:* $20-$26; *Moderate:* $15-$20; *Inexpensive:* under $15. Listings are in order of price category.

## NEW ORLEANS

**ROYAL ORLEANS HOTEL.** *Superdeluxe.* Royal & St. Louis Sts. Located on the site and using some of the masonry of the historic old St. Louis hotel (once the state capitol), this plush hotel has a fine restaurant, cocktail lounge with jazz, and coffee shop. Second lounge and pool on rooftop.

**MAISON DE VILLE.** *Deluxe.* 727 Rue Toulouse. 18th century building, furnished with antiques. Complimentary breakfast, coffee, tea, soft drinks. Suites with kitchens available. Pool.

**MAISON DU PUY.** *Deluxe.* 1001 Rue Toulouse. In French Quarter, near Superdome. Furnished in French Provincial style. Restaurant, cabaret. Food and drinks served in garden courtyard. Pool.

**BIENVILLE HOUSE.** *Expensive.* 320 Decatur St. In French Quarter. European atmosphere with iron balconies and courtyard. Restaurant, pool.

**PROVINCIAL MOTEL.** *Expensive.* 1024 Chartres St., in French Quarter. Very pleasant rooms with antiques as part of the decor. Restaurant, pool, list of sitters.

**HEDGEWOOD HOTEL.** *Moderate.* 2427 St. Charles. Babysitters, family plan, free parking. Stately mansion furnished with antiques in Garden District.

**LAMOTHE HOUSE.** *Moderate.* 621 Esplanade Ave. Small but special. Restored old New Orleans mansion with English and French antique furnishings, canopy beds, balconies overlooking courtyard. Continental breakfast. Closed June to Aug.

## ALEXANDRIA

**Howard Johnson's Motor Lodge.** *Expensive.* Free library. Olympic pool, nightly entertainment, free local calls.

**Rodeway Inn of America.** *Expensive*. Pool. Restaurant and cocktail lounge adj. Free parking.

**Sheraton Inn.** *Expensive*. 2716 MacArthur Dr. Cafe, bar, entertainment, pool.

**Alexandria TraveLodge.** *Moderate*. Lounge and restaurant. Pitt Grill and shopping area nr.

**Holiday Inn.** *Moderate*. Member of chain. Restaurant and bar.

## BATON ROUGE

**Baton Rouge Hilton.** *Deluxe*. I–10 at College Drive. In Corporate Square, 31-store enclosed mall. 3 restaurants, 2 cocktail lounges, nightclub with live entertainment. Tennis courts, pool, health spa. Fully stocked bars in rooms.

**Sheraton Baton Rouge Hotel.** *Deluxe*. I–10 at College Dr. Large motor inn. Suites. Restaurant, lounge with entertainment, coffee shop. Pool (heated). Golf nr.

**Chateau Capital.** *Expensive*. Convention & Lafayette Sts. (downtown). Roof deck pool over Mississippi River. Elegant cocktail lounge and restaurant. Free lobby-entrance garage. 24-hr. cafe.

**Howard Johnson's Motor Lodge.** *Expensive*. 2365 College Dr. Babysitter list, restaurant, pool, shuffleboard.

**Prince Murat.** *Expensive*. 1480 Nicholson Dr. Nicely decorated rooms. Pool, dining room, coffee shop, bar.

**Rodeway Inn.** *Expensive*. I–10 and S. Arcadian Thruway. Pool, restaurant, cocktail lounge, live entertainment.

**Baton Rouge TraveLodge.** *Moderate*. 427 Lafayette St. (downtown). Some rooms have river view. Pool, café, coin laundry.

**Holiday Inn.** *Moderate*. At three locations: Siegen Lane, I–10 at Siegen. **South:** 9940 Airline Hwy. **West:** I–10 & State 415. Coffee shop, pool, bar, free airport transportation. Kennel.

**Oak Manor Motor Hotel.** *Moderate*. 8181 Airline Hwy. Luxurious rooms and suites on 14 acres of landscaped grounds. Old English Manor restaurant. Bar, pool, free parking.

**Alamo Plaza Hotel Courts.** *Inexpensive*. 4243 Florida Blvd. Pool. Free continental breakfast.

## NATCHITOCHES

**Holiday Inn.** *Moderate*. Very pleasant rooms with color TV. Suites. Restaurant, lounge with live entertainment. Kennels. Free airport transportation.

**Revere Inn Motel.** *Inexpensive*. Restaurant. Kitchenettes available.

## NEW IBERIA

**Holiday Inn.** *Expensive.* Decor follows railroad theme in Park Station Restaurant and Railhead Lounge.

**Acadiana Motor Lodge.** *Moderate.* Restaurant, bar, pool. Entertainment.

## OPELOUSAS

**Downtowner Motor Inn.** *Inexpensive.* Pool, restaurant, and bar.

## SHREVEPORT

**Chateau.** *Deluxe.* 201 Lake St. Cafe, bar, entertainment, pool. Free in-room movies. Free airport transportation.

**Sheraton Inn-Shreveporter.** *Deluxe.* 3880 Greenwood Rd. Children free; play area and pool. Luxurious rooms.

**Captain Shreve Hotel.** *Expensive.* Jct. of US 80, 71, & State 1. Free garage. Barber and beauty shop. Bar.

**Holiday Inn.** *Expensive.* Three locations. **West:** 4900 Greenwood Rd. N off I–20. **North:** 1906 N. Market St. US 71 & State 1. List of babysitters, kennel. **Bossier City:** 150 Hamilton Rd. (off I–20). All with restaurant, bar, pool, color TV and free airport transportation.

**Howard Johnson's Motor Lodge.** *Expensive.* 5101 Monkhouse Dr. Pool, kids playground; restaurant and lounge. Local calls are free and there is a free library and morning paper. Rates increase during State Fair.

**Palace Inn.** *Expensive.* 1968 Airline Dr., Bossier City. Pleasant rooms. Complimentary coffee. Babysitter list. Restaurant. Pool.

**Sheraton-Bossier Inn.** *Expensive.* 2015 Old Minden Rd., Bossier City. Attractive rooms, some with king-size beds. Suites. Restaurant, lounge with dancing and entertainment. Pool with service at poolside. Free airport transportation.

**Days Inn.** *Moderate.* Also in Bossier. Pools, restaurant.

**Western Hills Inn.** *Moderate.* 3515 E. Texas St., Bossier City. Restaurant, lounge, and pool.

 **DINING OUT.** *New Orleans:* Fine creole cooking is a treat in New Orleans, but other cuisines can also be found here. Classic French fare is also a specialty, and French restaurants are included here because the heritage of *this* part of the Old South is, of course, so predominantly Gallic. See the previous hotel listings for some other good restaurants. Price categories and ranges (for a complete dinner) are as follows: *Deluxe,* $15-19; *Expensive,* $10-14; *Moderate,* $5-9; *Inexpensive,* under $5. Listings are in order of price category.

*Elsewhere:* Louisiana often means the same fine creole cooking you can experience in New Orleans, as well as more conventional southern cuisine.

Restaurants are listed in order of price category. Price categories and ranges, for a complete dinner, are as follows: *Expensive:* $7-$12.75; *Moderate:* $4-$7; *Inexpensive:* $1.70-$4. For a more complete explanation of restaurant categories see *Facts at Your Fingertips* at the front of this volume.

## BATON ROUGE

**BELLEMONT RESTAURANT.** *Expensive.* Louisiana seafood. Photos of antebellum mansions and historic Louisiana sites decorate the walls.

## LAFAYETTE

**JACOB'S FINE FOODS.** *Moderate.* 1600 Cameron St. Very popular in the area. Relaxed and friendly atmosphere. Acadian and French cuisine. Seafood is their specialty. Children's portions. Closed Christmas and New Year's Day.

## LAKE CHARLES

**CHATEAU CHARLES RESTAURANT.** *Expensive.* On US 90 at the Sheraton Chateau Charles Motor Inn. Locally popular. Serves a variety of well-prepared American and Louisiana French dishes. Children's portions.

## NEW IBERIA

**THE FRENCH HOUSE.** *Moderate.* Cajun dishes are featured at this pleasant dining spot. Try the crawfish, gumbo or other seafood as well as their steaks. Closed first 2 weeks in July; Christmas, New Year's Day; Labor Day.

## NEW ORLEANS

**LeRUTH'S.** *Expensive.* The chef-owner operates this establishment with a menu which perfectly compliments the intimate environment. The restaurant is three miles south of the center of the city, across the Mississippi River. Specialties include stuffed soft-shell crab, frog's legs meuniere, and a noisette of lamb for two. Excellent appetizers include Crabmeat St. Francis, and the bread is baked on the premises daily. Franklin St. (Gretna).

**GALATOIRE'S.** *Expensive.* French/Creole. This old-fashioned, traditional dining room accepts no reservations, but patrons don't seem to mind standing in line watching the passing scene on Bourbon St. Excellent seafood includes Trout Marguery and broiled pompano. Excellent appetizers are topped by Shrimp Remoulade, and the Creole gumbo is in a class by itself. 209 Bourbon St.

**ANTOINE'S.** *Deluxe.* French/Creole. This is dining in the opulent old tradition, and regular customers even have their own personal waiters. The large wine cellar is open to the public and worth a visit. This restaurant can accurately be described as a local landmark, and specialties include Oysters Rockefeller, Pompano en Papillote, and the Tournedos. Crepes Suzette are a favorite sweet, and the menu is full of dishes that are specifically associated with this exceptional establishment. 713 St. Louis St.

**BRENNAN'S.** *Expensive.* French/Creole. Actually a gracious old home in the Vieux Carré (the old French Quarter), with a quaint patio where drinks are served while diners wait for their tables. Actually best known for its bountiful breakfasts, which have occasionally been described as "the eighth wonder of the world," the morning's repast includes Eggs Hussard, Eggs Sardou, and an appetizing omelet of eggs and crabmeat. Flaming desserts are also a specialty, and the most famous of these are the Crepes Fitzgerald and the Bananas Foster. Don't miss the Buster Crabs Bearnaise, poached redfish, or the poached pompano at dinner.

**MASSON'S.** *Expensive.* French Cuisine. Owned and operated by the talented chef, and a fine place for a leisurely and elegant suburban dinner. The quiche is exceptional, and every seafood item is delicious—especially the "marvels of the seas" and sauteed crab "fingers." 7200 Pontchartrain Blvd. (West End).

**ELMWOOD PLANTATION.** *Expensive.* Continental/Creole. Located on the grounds of the oldest plantation (1762) in the Mississippi Valley, complete with oak-shaded elegance. Game dishes are the specialties, including locally raised quail, Cornish hen, and squab. Oyster Mosca and Veal Elmwood are also staples of an interesting menu. Desserts offer an excellent bread pudding and custards. 5400 River Road (9 miles west off US 90).

**ANDREW JACKSON.** *Expensive.* 221 Royal St. Elegant service and atmosphere. Tour the kitchen to see the chef prepare trout Meuniere, lump crabmeat or Creole gumbo.

**ARNAUD'S RESTAURANT.** *Expensive.* 811 Bienville St., at Bourbon St. World renowned French restaurant in the French Quarter. Wide selection of delectable dishes on their menu. Specialties: oysters Bienville, shrimp Arnaud and filet mignon Clemenceau. *The Richelieu Room* requires black tie. Children's portions.

**COMMANDER'S PALACE.** *Expensive.* 1403 Washington Ave., at Coliseum St. Located in the historic Garden District. Popular restaurant decked out in the elegance and grandeur of the 1880s. Creole menu. Dine inside or outside on a lovely patio. The Crayfish Etoufée or Crabmeat Imperial are tempting taste treats. Children's portions. Closed Christmas and during Mardi Gras.

**CORINNE DUNBAR'S.** *Expensive.* 1617 St. Charles Ave. Creole dishes served in a lovely Victorian dining room. Reservations required. Closed Sun.

**COURT OF TWO SISTERS.** *Expensive.* 613 Royal St. French and Creole menu. In the French Quarter.

**ETIENNE'S.** *Expensive.* 3100 19th St., Metairie. French and Creole menu.

**T. PITTARI'S.** *Moderate.* 4200 S. Claiborne. Creole cuisine, lobster, beef.

**SCLAFANI'S.** *Moderate.* 1315 N. Causeway Blvd. Variety of Italian, American and Creole dishes, served in a Louisiana plantation-style dining room.

**TUJAGUES.** *Moderate.* 823 Decatur St. Est. 1856. Well-prepared Creole and French dishes served family style. There is no menu choice. Children's portions. Sun., holidays dinner served from 11 A.M. Closed during Mardi Gras.

**COFFEE HOUSES.** Across the square from St. Louis Basilica and down the street are the outdoor coffee houses of the *Café du Monde,* St. Peter and Decatur, and the *Morning Call,* where South Louisiana coffee (and chicory) and *beignets* (square, puffy doughnuts) are served through the night, the latter sprinkled with powdered sugar. Native *Orléanais* get their coffee and gumbo at the *Gumbo Shop* at 630 St. Peter and at the pancake shops in the Quarter.

## OPELOUSAS

**PALACE CAFE.** *Moderate.* 167 W. Landry St. Gumbo, crawfish, seafood and steaks are specialties at this restaurant. Creole and Cajun menu.

# MARYLAND

## Antietam and Gateway to Gettysburg

### by
### VICTOR BLOCK

*Victor Block, a lifelong resident of the Maryland area, has contributed articles about the state to leading newspapers and magazines for a decade. He has written and edited several books, and currently writes the* Joyer Travel Report, *a monthly newsletter that stresses tips on stretching the budget and travel to out-of-the-way destinations.*

The Civil War hurt and divided Maryland. Most people in the state did not wish to secede, nor to fight the South. Despite this majority opinion, a number of Marylanders—especially in Baltimore, the Eastern Shore and southern counties— *were* in favor of secession once it became clear that compromise no longer was possible. In fact, so strong was sentiment for the Southern states that in September 1861, several members of the General Assembly were placed under arrest in order to undermine any effort to pass an act of secession. After a quixotic try at remaining neutral, Maryland finally officially sided with the Union. Even then, many of its citizens went into the Confederate army, so that there were Maryland regiments on both sides, but Union troops outnumbered Confederate about three to one. On September 17, 1862, Lee's first attempt to capture Washington was stopped in western Maryland at Antietam. The land is today a National Monument and Historic Battlefield Site. The emancipation of slaves did not much affect Maryland's economy, for, prior to the war, the state's slaveholders had been freeing slaves on their own, while the state itself was appropriating $10,000 annually to transport to Liberia all freed men who wished to go.

### The Mason-Dixon Line

This 233-mile line was surveyed and marked during 1763–67 by English surveyors Charles Mason and Jeremiah Dixon, to settle a boundary dispute between the Calverts and the Penns, proprietors respectively of Maryland and Pennsylvania. Later it popularly came to be regarded as the dividing line between North and South, although it does not extend west of the Ohio River. The original stones still are in place, one a mile. Every fifth marker is a "crownstone" bearing the arms of the Calverts on one side, of Penn on the other. On the eastern shore of the Chesapeake Bay, turn off US 50 onto State 313 and then onto State 54 and you will come upon the very first of the stones. A shelter has been erected over it, and a plaque gives the history. Look well. Along this line the United States almost split in two.

Fort McHenry in Baltimore, whose resistance to the British in 1814 inspired Francis Scott Key to write "The Star Spangled Banner," served as headquarters during much of the Civil War for the commanding general of the Maryland Military District. It also was used as a prison for Confederate prisoners of war and sympathizers—including, ironically, a son-in-law and grandson of Key. The prisoner count at the fort usually hovered around 300, but after the Battle of Gettysburg in July 1863, it soared to nearly 7,000.

### The Western Shore

Go to Point Lookout, at the southern tip (end of State 5) of the western shore of Chesapeake Bay. Here the 10-mile-wide Potomac River rolls into the 20-mile-wide Bay, and the nearby state park offers excellent camping facilities. This was the site during the Civil War of a hospital and prison camp for Confederate soldiers. Small traces of the once sprawling facilities still are visible, and in Point Lookout Confederate Cemetery are monuments to commemorate the suffering of prisoners who died. Built to hold 10,000 men, the overcrowded camp by the end of the war housed twice that many. Food and living conditions were horrible, and nearly 3,400 prisoners died during the camp's existence.

### North of Baltimore

Leave Baltimore by US40 East and go to the Aberdeen Proving Grounds, where, in the Army Ordnance Museum, you will see the greatest collection of weapons of war in the world. All American history is there, in the arms not only of our own forces but in those of our enemies as well. Examples of the latter include "Anzio Annie," still mounted on a flatcar, and the Congreve rocket that made the "red glare" above Baltimore Harbor in the War of 1812. Also at the museum is a limited collection of muskets and ammunition from the Civil War.

### Antietam

On the field of Antietam on September 17, 1862, the Union Army repulsed the first Confederate attempt to invade the North. The field may be reached by State 65 out of Hagerstown, or State 34 out of Boonsboro. The Battle of Antietam (sometimes called the Battle of Sharpsburg) was the most fiercely fought, and bloodiest, single-day battle of the war. Losses on both sides were staggering: 12,410 Federals (15% of those engaged) were killed or wounded, as were 10,700 Confederates (26% of those who fought). Gen. Robert E. Lee's failure to carry the war effectively into the North had two major results. It caused Great Britain to postpone recognition of the Confederate government. Almost equally important, it gave President Lincoln the long-awaited opportunity to issue the Emancipation Proclamation, warning the South that on January 1, 1863, he would declare free all slaves in territory still in rebellion against the United States.

The Visitor Center is the best place to begin your tour. It features exhibits and a slide program pertaining to the battle. Antietam National Cemetery, established in 1865, contains the graves of 4,776 Union soldiers, and a monument to Civil War dead. The 810-acre Antietam National Battlefield Site is marked with 200 tablets and 80 monuments, as well as vertical cannon barrels indicating where three Federal and three Confederate generals lost their lives. A self-drive tour includes stops at main points of interest, several of which have tape players with information about the battle.

### Frederick

While Frederick is not directly identified with any major Civil War battle or incident, it served in 1863 as headquarters for the Union Army, and has a number of buildings and sites closely related to the War Between the States. Kemp Hall (S. Market and Church streets) was where the Maryland legislature convened in 1861 to vote on whether the state should secede. Their decision made Maryland the only Southern state to remain in the Union.

In Frederick City Hall (S. Market and 2nd streets), city fathers met in 1864 to hear the demands of Confederate Gen. Jubal Early. On his way to invade Washington, he asked for ransom in exchange for Frederick's safety from fire. He left town with $200,000, only to find his path blocked by Union troops. While Early's forces won the ensuing Battle of Monocacy, the fight lasted long enough for Union reinforcements to reach Washington and prevent its capture.

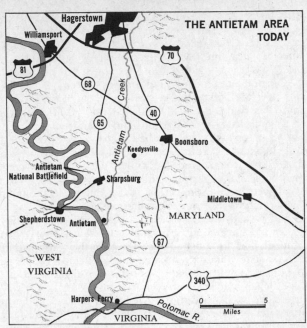

THE ANTIETAM AREA TODAY

The restored Hessian Barracks (S. Market Street) served as a hospital and sometimes prison for captured Confederate soldiers. The Barbara Fritchie House and Museum (154 W. Patrick St.) is a restoration of the home and glove shop of Barbara and her husband, John Fritchie. Barbara, a devoted Unionist, is immortalized by John Greenleaf Whittier in the poem named for her, with the lines, "Shoot if you must this old grey head, but spare your country's flag." The house is furnished with Civil War–period antiques.

## Lee Invades Maryland

Until the Battle of Antietam, the Confederates in the east had been following defensive strategy, though tactically they frequently assumed the offensive. But Davis and Lee, for a complicated set of political and military reasons, determined to take the offensive and invade the North in co-ordination with Bragg's drive into Kentucky. Militarily, in the east, an invasion of Maryland would give Lee a chance to defeat or destroy the Army of the Potomac, uncovering such cities as Washington, Baltimore, and Philadelphia, and to cut Federal communications with the states to the west.

The Army of Northern Virginia, organized into two infantry commands (Longstreet's consisting of five divisions, and Jackson's of four divisions) plus Stuart's three brigades of cavalry, and the reserve artillery, numbered 55,000 effectives. Lee did not rest after Manassas but crossed the Potomac and encamped near Frederick, from where he sent Jackson to capture an isolated Federal garrison at Harpers Ferry. The remainder of Lee's army then crossed South Mountain and headed for Hagerstown, about twenty-five miles northwest of Frederick, with Stuart's cavalry screening the right flank. In the meantime McClellan's rejuvenated Army of the Potomac, 90,000 men organized into six corps, marched northwest from Washington and reached Frederick on September 12.

At this time McClellan had a stroke of luck. Lee, in assigning missions to his command, had detached Maj. Gen. D. H. Hill's division from Jackson and attached it to Longstreet and had sent copies of his orders, which prescribed routes, objectives, and times of arrival, to Jackson, Longstreet, and Hill. But Jackson was not sure that Hill had received the order. He therefore made an additional copy of Lee's order and sent it to Hill. One of Hill's orders, wrapped around some cigars, was somehow left behind in an abandoned camp where it was picked up on September 13 by Union soldiers and rushed to McClellan. This windfall gave the Federal commander an unmatched opportunity to defeat Lee's scattered forces in detail if he pushed fast through the gaps. McClellan vacillated for sixteen hours. Lee, informed of the lost order, sent all available forces to hold the gaps, so that it was nightfall on the 14th before McClellan fought his way across South Mountain.

Lee retreated to Sharpsburg on Antietam Creek where he turned to fight. Pinned between Antietam Creek and the Potomac with no room for maneuver, and still outnumbered since Jackson's force had yet to return to the main body after capturing Harpers Ferry, Lee relied on the advantage of interior lines and the boldness and the fighting ability of his men.

McClellan delayed his attack until September 17, when he launched an unco-ordinated series of assaults which drove back the Confederates in places but failed to break their line. Heavy fighting swelled across ripe fields and up through rocky glens that became known to history as the West Wood, the Cornfield, the East Wood, Bloody Lane, and Burnside's Bridge. One southerner remembered the attacking Union columns: "With flags flying and the long unfaltering lines rising and falling as they crossed the rolling fields, it looked as though nothing could stop them." But when the massed fire of field guns and small arms struck such human waves, a Union survivor recalled, it "was like a scythe running through our line."

McClellan, like too many leaders during the Civil War, could not bring himself to commit his reserve (the V Corps under Porter) at the strategy moment. Although adored by his men, as one of the veterans wrote after the war, he "never realized the metal that was in his grand Army of the Potomac." Jackson's last division arrived in time to head off the final assaults by Maj. Gen. Ambrose Burnside's corps, and at the end of the day Lee still held most of his line. Casualties were heavy. Of 70,000 Federal troops nearly 13,000 were killed, wounded, or missing, and the 40,000 or more Confederates engaged lost almost as many. Although Lee audaciously awaited new attacks on September 18, McClellan left him unmolested, and that night the Army of Northern Virginia withdrew across the Potomac.

## PRACTICAL INFORMATION FOR MARYLAND

**MARYLAND FACTS AND FIGURES.** Maryland was named for Queen Henrietta Maria of England. Its nicknames are *America in Miniature; Free State; Old Line State*. The state flower is the black-eyed susan; the state tree, the Wye Oak, a 400-plus-year-old white oak at Wye Mills; the state sport, jousting; the state bird, the Baltimore oriole. *Fatti maschii parole femine* ("Manly deeds, womanly words") is the state motto. "Maryland, My Maryland" is the state song.

Annapolis, home of the U.S. Naval Academy on Chesapeake Bay, is the state capital, The state population is about 4,100,000, 18th in the U.S.; its area of 10,577 square miles is 42nd in size among the 50 states.

Chesapeake Bay, the long arm of the Atlantic that runs through the state from north to south, dominates the topography, economic and social character of Maryland. In 1608 Captain John Smith described it thus: "Here are mountains, hills, plaines, valleyes, rivers and brookes all running most pleasantly into a Faire Bay compassed but for the mouth with fruitful and delightsome land." The flat land of the Eastern Shore is primarily agricultural and fishing country (Maryland is famous for its oysters, crabs, and now clams), and the region is a paradise for sportsmen—sailing, fishing, hunting—including fox hunting. The Eastern Shore is the "southern" part of the state, a land of old antebellum mansions, rich in reminders of the South's colonial past. To the west of Chesapeake Bay, the land rises to rolling hills in the center of the state, a pleasant landscape dotted with historic old towns like Frederick. Western Maryland is a skinny mountainous panhandle squeezed between Pennsylvania and the Potomac River, which come to within less than two miles of each other near Hancock. The state's highest point, Backbone Mountain (3,360 feet) is here; and on Marsh Mountain there is skiing well into March. Despite its rural aspects, industry plays a dominant role in the state's economy, with most industrial activity centered around the port of Baltimore.

The climate is moderate, with cold winters and warm summers.

**HOW TO GET THERE.** *By Car.* I-95 enters the state near Wilmington, Delaware, passing through Aberdeen and Baltimore and leaving the state at Washington, D.C. I-70 connects central Pennsylvania and Baltimore, entering Maryland at Hancock. US 301 is the primary north-south route on the Eastern Shore, entering the state from Middletown, Delaware. The Chesapeake Bay Bridge-Tunnel connects Cape Charles, Virginia (near Salisbury, Maryland), and Cape Henry, Virginia (Bayside).

*By air:* There is scheduled air service to Baltimore, Hagerstown and Washington, D.C. Numerous airlines fly to Baltimore and Washington, D.C. *Allegheny* flies to Hagerstown and Salisbury.

*By bus: Greyhound* and *Continental Trailways* are the major carriers to Maryland and Baltimore is the major terminal.

*By train: Amtrak* has service to Wilmington, Delaware, Baltimore and Washington, D.C.

**HOW TO GET AROUND.** *By car:* A network of good roads, which makes it possible to speed through Maryland en route to Florida or New England, also makes it convenient to get to all parts of the state. Maryland boasts the first Federally-financed road in the original 13 United States, the National Road (US 40), which still provides a scenic route to western

Pennsylvania, Ohio and the West. The new I-70 west from Baltimore also traverses the same route. I-95 does the same north and south.

*By boat:* The Inland Waterway traverses the Chesapeake Bay from the Chesapeake and Delaware Canal to the Virginia Capes. There are approximately 60 yachting centers and 350 marinas and marine facilities along the way. Boats can be rented in Annapolis, Chestertown, Edgewater, and Ocean City.

 **TOURIST INFORMATION.** Maps, brochures and information of all kinds are available from The Division of Tourist Development, Maryland Department of Economic & Community Development, 1748 Forest Dr., Annapolis 21401. Tel (301) 269-2686.

 **SEASONAL EVENTS.** *January.* Open house at the Governor's mansion in Annapolis is a tradition on New Year's Day.

*March. Maryland Day,* Anniversary of the landing of the first settlers in 1634, is celebrated at St. Mary's City and before the State Court House at Baltimore on the 25th.

*April. The Maryland House and Garden Pilgrimage* gets under way the last few days of April and continues into May, while as soon as the weather gets balmy the brigade of 4,000 midshipmen turns out many Wednesday afternoons at 3:45 P.M. to parade at the U.S. Naval Academy.

*May.* Meanwhile, the *House and Garden Tours* to more than 100 old homes and gardens continue.

*June.* In southern Maryland, at La Plata, Hughesville, Upper Marlboro, and Wayson's Corner, tobacco auctioneers sing-song their distinctive chant over Maryland leaf from mid-April to mid-June, Monday to Friday. Fair Hill also is site of sheepdog trials and the *Delaware Highland Gathering* with traditional Scottish games, dances and bagpipes. Maryland farms are open for visiting. The Frederick Fairgrounds is the site of the *National Craft Fair. Flag Day* is occasion for festivities in Baltimore.

*July.* County fairs and jousting by this time are going strong. The state sport requires skilled horsemen or horsewomen, who ride nearly every Saturday for the benefit of country churches, to spear a small ring at full gallop.

*August.* The original jousting or tilting tournament on the Eastern Shore is still held at St. Josephs's Catholic Church, Cordova, the first Wednesday. Another is at Port Republic in southern Maryland.

*September.* Down at St. Clement Island, where Maryland's first settlers landed in 1634, they hold a blessing of the fleet. But the oldest annual commemoration is *Old Defenders' Day* on Sept. 12, which marks the successful defense of Baltimore against the British, and on the Sunday nearest that date a *mock bombardment at Fort McHenry* recalls the historic day. The last weekend of September is *Heritage Weekend* in Annapolis, when homes not usually open on other tours welcome visitors inside to see where history often was made more than two centuries ago.

*October. Autumn Glory Time,* always in the first two weeks, celebrates the fall scene in the Appalachian Mountains. Grantsville takes the opportunity to display its handicraft at the *Folk Arts Festival.*

*December.* Try the *Holly Tour* of downtown Baltimore homes, the candlelit *Hammond-Harwood House,* and "A Child's Christmas" at the Paca House in Annapolis, the 18th-century *Mount Clare* and *Charles Carroll mansions* in Baltimore and the old farm home at *Carroll County Farm Museum.* The custom of Christmas gardens in firehouses has been consolidated in recent years so that Engine Co. No. 45 provides one for the entire city. Another is at Towson Fire Headquarters.

**NATIONAL PARKS AND HISTORICAL ATTRACTIONS.** The bloodiest single day's fighting of the Civil War occurred along *Antietam Creek* near the town of Sharpsburg. While *Antietam National Battlefield Site* has its share of modern encroachments, much of it is still farm land as it was on September 17, 1862, when Gen. Robert E. Lee made his first unsuccessful invasion of the North. Tours are self-conducted, but start at the Visitors' Center, which can be reached by State 34 from Alt. US 40 at Boonsboro, by State 65 from Alt. US 40 at Hagerstown.

*Catoctin Furnace,* US 15, 7 mi. south of Thurmont. There are several iron furnaces in the state but this one, in the town of Catoctin, where several old log houses are sole remnants of a once thriving community, is the best preserved. Cannon balls for the Yorktown campaign and plates for the ironclad *Monitor* were made here. *Gathland Correspondents' Memorial Arch,* near Burkittsville. Reached via Rte. 17 from Middletown on Alt. US 40. On a hilltop, novelist George Alfred Townsend raised this curious monument to correspondents who, like himself, covered the Civil War. Names of World War I and II war reporters have been added by State of Maryland. Now in a state park.

*Fort Frederick,* on State 56 off I-70. Now a state park on the Potomac River, the stone fort was built in 1756 as a defense against the French and Indians, later used as prison during Revolutionary and Civil Wars. Revolutionary period military drills are presented several weekends in summer.

*Roger Brooke Taney House,* 123 S. Bentz St. Frederick. Memorabilia of Francis Scott Key and his brother-in-law, Chief Justice Taney, who administered the oath of office to seven Presidents, including Abraham Lincoln. Slave quarters in the rear are furnished as they were about 1812. Open June through October. "Schifferstadt" at 1110 Rosemont St. in Frederick, a German-style farmhouse built in 1756, serves as the county visitors' information center.

*Williamsport.* Here the Civil War nearly ended 10 months before Appomattox. Following the Battle of Gettysburg, Lee's Army of Northern Virginia was unable to recross a rain-swollen Potomac River. But Union Gen. George Gordon Meade delayed his attack, and Lee escaped under cover of night.

**STATE PARKS AND FORESTS.** Maryland has 35 parks and recreation areas, some of them small historic sites that are free. Others levy a small charge for day shelters, fireplaces, picnic tables and charcoal. Many parks have separate areas for campers. Improved campsites are $4.50 per day, unimproved $2.50 a day. Assateague campsites are $5.50 per day, as are those at Point Lookout with water and sewer hookups. Trailers, when permitted, are limited to 28 feet in length. Dogs, except seeing-eyes, are not allowed in developed areas of parks. Hunting is allowed in some state parks.

The parks provide a variety of topography, scenery and recreational experiences. There are parks on the tidewater flatlands; parks in the mountains and parks on beautiful lakes. Others are on the Chesapeake Bay and its tributaries, the Atlantic Ocean and one on an island. They include within their boundaries old forts, lighthouses, mansions, Civil War battlefields, a monument to George Washington and several famous trout streams. In *Cunningham Falls State Park,* Big Hunting Creek, with a 40-foot waterfall, has lured five presidents of the United States. Across the road is the late President Franklin Roosevelt's *Shangri-La,* later renamed *Camp David* for his grandson by President Dwight D. Eisenhower.

Maryland also has nine state forests that provide primitive camping and permit licensed hunting and fishing in season. For a complete list of parks, forests and details, write Maryland Park Service, Tawes State Office Building, Annapolis, Md. 21401.

*Catoctin Mountain Park,* just 3 miles west of Thurmont, includes the site of Camp David, the Presidential retreat. But for the public there is still a 7-mile scenic drive, 12 miles of well-marked hiking trails, a 6-mile long snowmobile trail, two picnic areas and a modern camp for 5-day family camping from mid-April through October, Girl and Boy Scouts and other groups have primitive areas. The National Park Service conducts several interesting programs during the summer season. Of course, Camp David is strictly off limits. The park is about equidistant, 65 miles, between Washington and Baltimore, and about midway between Frederick and Gettysburg, Pa., on US 15.

 **MUSEUMS AND GALLERIES.** *Army Ordnance Museum,* Aberdeen Proving Ground, off US 40 at Aberdeen. Free. Some 15,000 weapons of our allies and enemies from the Revolutionary War to the present, including tanks from World War II to "Anzio Annie," a German V-2 rocket and the car Gen. John. J. Pershing used in Mexico in 1916.

*Carroll County Farm Museum,* off US 140 on Center St. Extended in Westminster. A century-old farm where blacksmithing, weaving, quilting and candlemaking can be seen.

*Calvert Marine Museum,* Solomons. A museum dedicated to preservation of local marine history, featuring a lighthouse, boat models, Chesapeake Bay boats, paintings and other exhibits.

*Naval Academy Museum,* just inside Gate 3, U.S. Naval Academy, Annapolis. Free. An outstanding collection of incredibly detailed model ships, plus many mementos of naval battles and heroes, such as Admiral "Bull" Halsey's saddle.

*Chesapeake Bay Maritime Museum,* on State 33 off US 50, in St. Michael's. Established in 1965 to keep alive the memories, adventures, romance and artifacts of America's great inland sea, the museum already has an impressive collection of boat models, name boards, bells and figureheads, but it also now has a retired lightship, lighthouse and several sailing craft which can be boarded.

*Julia A. Purnell Museum,* on US 113 in Snow Hill. An interesting collection of local rural ca. 1800 memorabilia and artifacts, such as dentist's pliers, flatirons, hair curlers, gingerbread molds, high-wheel bicycyles and Tom Thumb's bathtub.

 **HISTORIC SITES.** Central Maryland, all within less than an hour's drive from Baltimore, *Clara Barton House,* MacArthur Blvd. in Glen Echo, 3 mi. north of District of Columbia line. Home of the Civil War nurse who founded the American Red Cross, erected for her by the grateful survivors of the 1889 Johnstown flood using lumber from emergency barracks erected while she was director. Used as Red Cross headquarters from 1897 to 1904.

The 21-room *Shriver Homestead and Mill,* on US 140 in Union Mills, once a post office, stage stop, school, magistrate's office, and home of the Shriver family (Sargent Shriver was first director of the Peace Corps) since 1797.

*White's Ferry.* The only crossing of the Potomac River between Washington and Point of Rocks, this ferry has been in operation since at least 1830.

Used by Gen. Jubal Early to escape after an unsuccessful raid on Washington in the last days of the Civil War. Can be reached from US 15 north of Leesburg, Va., or via State 107 from Poolesville, Md. Toll $1.25 for car and passengers, 25¢ for foot passengers.

*U.S. Naval Academy and Chapel,* with crypt of John Paul Jones. Entrance through Maryland Ave. gate. Bancroft Hall is the largest dormitory in the world. The *Big E* ship's bell from the aircraft carrier *Enterprise* is rung after a Navy victory over Army. *Tecumseh,* a bronze replica of the figurehead from the USS *Delaware,* is the god of "C," the passing grade for midshipmen. Dress parades, Wednesday afternoons in spring. Noon meal formation in front of Bancroft Hall.

*Farmer's Market,* on State 5 at Charlotte Hall. St. Mary's County Amish farmers and their wives bring produce, home-baked bread and rolls, and homemade preserves, jellies, and cheese to sell. It operates on Wed. and Sat., but the weekend attracts its share of hucksters and junk dealers.

*Point Lookout,* the southern tip of southern Maryland, on State 5. Monument marks site of Civil War prison, whose prisoners Gen. Jubal Early hoped to free during raid on Washington. A state park is now located here.

*Fredericktown and Georgetown* (US 213) are picturesque waterside villages on opposite sides of the Sassafras River, said to be the prettiest river in Maryland. Both were raided by the British fleet during the War of 1812. Today they are yachting centers.

*Centreville,* on US 213. An 18th-century town with an old courthouse and lawyers' row still in daily use. On Main St. is *Wright's Chance,* an excellent example of a colonial Eastern Shore plantation home, now a museum. In 1977, a larger-than-life statue of Queen Anne—for whom the county was named—was placed in front of the courthouse.

*Wye Mills,* on State 404 off US 50. Here is the location of the *Wye Oak,* Maryland's official tree, said to be well over 400 years old. Nearby is a restored 18th-century grist mill which ground flour for George Washington's army, a one-room schoolhouse and restored *Wye Church* (1721).

*Old Trinity Church,* Church Creek, State 16, 7 miles south of Cambridge. The oldest active church in use, built about 1675, it was restored in 1960 by daughter of Walter P. Chrysler, the auto magnate. Its 15 picturesque slip and roundabout pews seat only 100. Burial place of Anna Ella Carroll, close friend of Abraham Lincoln's who conceived the successful Tennessee campaign during the Civil War.

**TOURS.** The *Annapolitan* leaves from Pier One, Annapolis City Dock, for a cruise to *St. Michaels Maritime Museum.* The *Harbor Queen* makes 40-minute tours of *Annapolis harbor.* Sights include Naval Academy and Bay Bridge. The *Mustang,* a Chesapeake Bay log canoe, is available for daytime charter at a rate of $15 an hour for groups up to six people. Passengers must supply own food. Cruises to *Smith Island* aboard the *Captain Tyler* can be made from Crisfield.

**DRINKING LAWS.** It is best to inquire locally about legal drinking restrictions, for they vary from county to county and even differ in towns in the same county. But generally, most bars, restaurants, hotels and other places serving alcoholic beverages are open from 6 A.M. to 2 A.M., except on Sundays and election days, when they are closed. Nothing can be consumed on the premises between 2 A.M. AND 6 A.M. except on New Year's Day, when there are few restrictions. Persons under 21 are prohibited from purchasing distilled spirits for themselves or others. The minimum age for buying light wine and beer is 18.

**HOTELS AND MOTELS** in Maryland range from first class to inexpensive, and include resorts over a century old and the latest in up-to-the-minute motels. As elsewhere in this book, hotels and motels are arranged alphabetically by community. Price categories for double-occupancy rooms in Maryland are divided into the following ranges: *Deluxe* $28 and higher, *Expensive* $19-27, *Moderate* $10-18 and *Inexpensive* $9 and lower. For a more complete explanation of price categories, refer to *Facts at Your Fingertips* at the beginning of this volume.

## ANNAPOLIS

**MARYLAND INN.** *Moderate.* Church Circle. Originally built in 1778, this lodging still retains the old flavor with its hand-hewn beams and large fireplaces. There is a bar with entertainment and you can play golf nearby.

## HAGERSTOWN

**Holiday Inn.** *Expensive.* 1 mi. E on US 40. Swimming pool, cocktail lounge, room service, restaurant, and all the other Holiday services, as well as convenience to Hagerstown, Antietam National Battlefield, Harpers Ferry National Park, and other historic points of interest.

**Sheraton Motor Inn.** *Expensive.* 1910 Dual Hwy. All the comforts and conveniences of this well-known chain service.

**Ramada Inn.** *Moderate.* 1 mile east on US 40. The adjacent Tortuga Restaurant attracts area residents as well as motel guests.

**Venice.** *Moderate.* ½ mi. E on US 40. Good restaurant, cocktail lounge, and beautiful swimming pool with golf course just across the road from this 2-story, air-conditioned motel. Several other good eating places in the area. Rates lower from November to March.

## ROYAL OAK

**PASADENA INN.** *Deluxe.* Eight mi. W. of Easton on State 33. This big, rambling, old resort inn is open spring, summer and fall, making available a plain but comfortable place to stay in the Chesapeake Bay country, close by such seafood centers as Tilghman's Island or the yacht races at St. Michaels. This is the kind of place to take it easy, go crabbing, fishing, visiting old estates, or playing shuffleboard. Dancing Saturday nights. Board includes three huge meals a day.

**DINING OUT** in Maryland can involve not only fine local dishes, but also the pleasure of a country drive culminating in the discovery of a charming restaurant or inn. There are plenty of fine spots along the highways as well, but if you have the time you should definitely try to sample some of the more out-of-the-way places.

Restaurant price categories are as follows: *Deluxe* $9 to $12.50, *Expensive* $6.50 to $9, *Moderate* $5 to $6.50, *Inexpensive* below $5.00. These prices are for hors d'ouevres or soup, entree and dessert. Not included are drinks, tax and tips. For a more complete explanation of restaurant categories refer to *Facts at Your Fingertips*.

## ANNAPOLIS

**THE GALLEON.** *Deluxe.* Md. 2 at S. River Bridge. From an interior that looks like a Spanish galleon, the view is superb of the beautiful South River, S of Annapolis. Features prime rib, one full rib, and imperial crab. Come by boat or car—docking or parking free.

**MARYLAND INN.** *Deluxe.* On Church Circle, Annapolis. An inn serving the public for 200 years on historic Church Circle in the Maryland capital, the menu features 18th-century St. Mary's crab imperial, lobster, corn sticks, fish from the Chesapeake Bay and pecan pie. Entertainment Fri., Sat. and Sun. nights in the King of France Tavern.

**MIDDLETON TAVERN.** *Deluxe.* 2 Market Place, Annapolis. A registered historic landmark, this fine eating place has a cozy atmosphere with large fireplaces.

## BALTIMORE

**HAUSSNER'S.** *Expensive.* Continental Cuisine. The dining room is a veritable art gallery, with the walls covered with paintings that range from modest to great value. Less intellectual art (nudes, to be precise) adorn the walls of the bar. Food is well prepared, and the variety of the menu is impressive, from a wide selection of seafood to pig's knuckle, quail and rabbit. 3244 Eastern Avenue.

**DANNY'S.** *Deluxe.* Continental Cuisine. Each dish is carefully prepared, many at tableside, and the portions are more than ample. The selection of wines is as expensive as it is extensive. Eating here is an experience that will be remembered—but so will the bill, which can escalate rapidly. Charles and Biddle Streets.

**SCHELLHASE'S.** *Moderate.* German-American Cuisine. The original family is still operating this restaurant, which was once the favorite of H.L. Mencken. Sauerbraten is still the overwhelming favorite, and the dining room is comfortable and beautifully lit. Beer is the favorite beverage, and the Chincoteague oysters (caught nearby) are also popular. 412 North Howard Street.

**HAMPTON HOUSE TEA ROOM.** *Inexpensive.* Hampton Lane, off Dulaney Valley Rd. The very good food here is just a part of the experience. Meals are served in the former kitchen of a Georgian mansion that is now a National Historic Landmark. You'll see a beautiful fireplace and real colonial furnishings. Lunch only.

**PEABODY BOOK SHOP, BEER STUBE AND BAR.** *Inexpensive.* 913 N. Charles St. Unique and unusual. The eatery is hidden behind the book shop. An old-time institution in downtown Baltimore, its specialties are T-bone and haddock platters for under $3.00. Nightly entertainment.

**THOMPSON'S SEA GIRT HOUSE.** *Inexpensive.* 5919 York Rd., at Belvedere Ave. Only a few restaurants serve homemade crab cakes made with backfin meat. This is one of them, and it has become nationally known since it was established in 1885. Imperial crab is another delicacy.

## BOONSBORO

**OLD SOUTH MOUNTAIN INN.** *Deluxe.* Alternate US 40 on top of South Mountain. A picturesque setting for an inn that dates back to the French and Indian Wars. American and Continental fare, with al fresco dining in summer.

## FREDERICK

**PETER PAN INN.** *Moderate.* 7 mi. S on Rte. 80, Urbana exit off I-270. Using century-old family recipes, noted for country-cured ham and fried chicken, served family style with corn fritters, this unusual restaurant has become a Maryland tradition and institution. Popular with church and other groups, which drive more than a hundred miles to eat here; there is often a wait of an hour or more to get in by the number. There are only five choices and the menu hasn't changed in 47 years. Children's portions half price.

## GEORGETOWN

**KITTY KNIGHT HOUSE.** *Moderate.* Rte. 213. Good menu and pleasant atmosphere in large dining room that presents a good view of yachts moored in the Sassafras River. It is said Kitty Knight saved this house from burning by the British.

## GRANTSVILLE

**PENN ALPS.** *Moderate.* US 40, one-half mi. east. In a dining room of early-American appointments in the Swiss-German tradition, this is one of the few places in the state where the desserts include that Pennsylvania Dutch delicacy for the sweet tooth, shoofly pie. Also, other home-style cooking of the Amish, who populate this area.

## HAGERSTOWN

**TORTUGA.** *Expensive.* US 40. An old establishment that serves prime ribs of beef and live Maine lobsters.

## OXFORD

**ROBERT MORRIS INN.** *Expensive.* On St. 333. Seafood is the specialty in this restored tavern, where bread is baked on the premises. Try the soft shell crabs, oysters (in season) prepared several ways, and homemade strawberry pie, famous in these parts.

**PIER STREET MARINA AND RESTAURANT.** *Moderate.* Pier St. Steamed crabs and beer in historic old town on the Tred Avon River, where old homes and old boatyards draw almost as many visitors as the small ferry that still operates across the river.

## RED HOUSE

**CHIMNEY CORNER, RED HOUSE.** *Moderate.* Junction of US 50 and 219. After sampling dry sugar-cured and hickory-smoked hams, bacon and sausage, you can buy buckwheat flour, home-made preserves, corn relish, and old-fashioned candy in this rustic country-store-like dining room.

## SHARPSBURG

**FERRY HILL INN.** *Expensive.* Rte. 34. On a high bluff overlooking horseshoe bend of the Potomac River and the college in Shepherdstown, W. Va., on the opposite bank, this pre-Civil War home was a hospital following the Battle of Antietam, where Gen. Robert E. Lee's son recuperated.

## SILVER SPRING

**MRS. K'S TOLL HOUSE.** *Deluxe.* 9201 Colesville Rd. (US 29). Beautifully decorated and highlighted with early American pressed glass and other antiques. Highway tolls actually once were collected at this location. The best entrees are the excellent fried chicken, ham, turkey, and other typical American fare. Hot buttered rolls, garden-fresh mix-it-yourself salad with the popular house dressing, and a wide selection of desserts top off the meal. Reservations necessary.

# MISSISSIPPI

## Vicksburg, Natchez and More

by

**BERN KEATING**

*Mr. Keating, the author of many books on historical subjects, is also Mississippi editor for several Fodor guides.*

Contrary to widespread belief, sentiment for secession in Mississippi was by no means unanimous. Large segments of the population, ranging from wealthy slave-owning planters of the Yazoo–Mississippi Delta to hardscrabble farmers of the piney woods, voted against leaving the Union. Once the majority decided to join the Confederacy, however, Mississippians *almost* to the man banded together in a ferocious defense of their new nation—almost, but not quite. The first invasion of Mississippi soil by Union forces was led by Adm. David Farragut who had spent much of his youth on the Gulf Coast.

Jefferson Davis, during his tenure as U.S. Secretary of War, had built on Ship Island near Gulfport a fortress to defend the Gulf Coast. Confederate militia had occupied the fort on the outbreak of war and named it Twiggs after a Confederate general who was to become known as outstandingly incompetent in a war marked by a wealth of boneheaded generals on both sides.

Farragut's flotilla bombarded the fort and put ashore an assault force that rushed the gates, only to discover the place deserted. Farragut renamed it Fort Massachusetts after his flagship and from there mounted his attack on the lower Mississippi River.

The Union garrison at Fort Massachusetts, converted to a Federal prison, effectively blockaded the Mississippi coast throughout the war. A visitor to the ruins of the fort, now part of the Gulf Islands National Seashore, can understand how its guns dominated the passages from the gulf to the ports that might have served the inland South.

On the Mississippi River, Farragut's fleet blazed its way past forts St. Philip and Jackson, guarding the lower river, and captured New Orleans and Baton Rouge.

Farther upstream in Mississippi, Natchez fell almost without firing a shot, which partly explains why that small city has probably the largest and finest concetration of antebellum southern architecture left standing.

Connelly's Tavern was built in 1795 and flew the first American flag in the lower Mississippi Valley in 1797. The Natchez Garden Club has restored and refurnished the tavern in authentic frontier style and keeps it open to the public. The even older Kings Tavern, dating from 1789, is now a restaurant. The Pilgrimage Garden Club operates Stanton Hall, one of the oldest and grandest of the city's mansions. Its carriage house is now a restaurant. The Union Army used Rosalie as headquarters during its occupation, which does not prevent the United Daughters of the Confederacy from running it as a museum.

On the outskirts of town stands Longwood, a vaguely Moorish octagonal grotesquerie that was to be the home of the eccentric Dr. Haller Nutt. On the outbreak of war, the workmen putting up the structure dropped their tools and joined the colors. Many of the southerners who recount the story as an example of how the region flocked to the flag do not know that the workmen were from Philadelphia and marched off to join the Union.

Dr. Nutt was an open Union sympathizer, so his neighbors burned his crops. He fared little better under the Federal occupation, for Union soldiers burned his gin, sawmill, and three of his plantation houses. Longwood is the sad memorial of a very hard-luck man.

Seventeen of the great mansions of Natchez, most of them still lived in, rotate being open daily for visitors. Jefferson Davis was married at the Briars. The Elliot family silver was buried on the grounds of D'Evereaux and lay there intact through the war. At Green Leaves are letters from Jefferson Davis, Audubon paintings, and a saber from Waterloo. During the spring Pilgrimage, young men dress in Confederate uniforms—most of them as officers, of course, and usually as cavalry officers with sash and saber.

But it was upriver at Vicksburg that the war was fought. A mighty fortress perched atop impregnable bluffs and manned by determined defenders, Vicksburg and its cannon corked the river, blocking passage of the trans-Appalachian North's commerce to world markets. Just as important, the guns protected a crossing where the western half of the Confederacy could send men and supplies to the embattled east. Lincoln himself said that Vicksburg was the key to the whole conflict, and the Union could not win until it had that key in its pocket.

Flushed with victories upriver, Gen. U.S. Grant in 1862 moved toward Vicksburg, but in April collided with a Confederate Army at Shiloh, just across the state line in Tennessee. In a titanic struggle, the combined casualties were 23,700 men. Despite the frightful casualties, neither side could claim a victory. Each nation then realized that it faced a dangerous enemy and the war was not likely to end in the few months everyone had hoped.

The Confederates fell back to Corinth in Mississippi, 23 miles from Shiloh. Early in May 1862, Union forces besieged them there, but the Union general's excessive caution allowed the supposedly trapped Southern force to escape.

It would plague the North for three more years of war. In fact, five months later a strong Confederate force attacked an equal Union force at Corinth. The Union soldiers manned the entrenchments that had been dug by Confederate soldiers during the earlier siege. During a two-day seesaw battle, both sides suffered combined casualties of 6,750, a substantial percentage of them "missing" Confederates who were probably deserters. The Confederates fled the field.

More than 6,000 men from both sides lie in Corinth in the National Cemetery established there in 1866 (one mile east, on Cemetery Street).

General Grant based himself at newly captured Memphis and Corinth and mounted a massive campaign aimed at cutting the Confederacy in two by reducing the fortress at Vicksburg. He sent two forces southward, one going by river transport to assault the fortress at Chickasaw Bluffs on the northern side of the city, the other to march cross-country and take the city from the rear. Grant moved to Oxford, Mississippi, to be closer to the action.

Confederate Gen. Earl Van Dorn, who had suffered the bloody defeat at Corinth, redeemed himself with a brilliant raid on Holly Springs when he destroyed a mountain of Union supplies meant to supply the overland assault on Vicksburg. From Oxford, Grant could see smoke from the fires and knew that the campaign was suspended till he could rebuild his forces. He retreated to Corinth.

The dashing cavalry genius Gen. Nathan Bedford Forrest had cut all telegraph lines in the area, and Grant was unable to warn General Sherman that his amphibious assault on Chickasaw Bluffs on the northern rim of the Vicksburg fortress would not have the support of an overland column hitting the defenses from the other side. Sherman was repulsed with hideous losses.

Today a motorist on US 61 approaching Vicksburg from the north is appalled to imagine troops trying to scale the precipitous wooded sides of the bluffs. A bit farther along, where the woods were cleared to provide a field of fire, the guns of Fort Nogales are perched so high atop the bluffs that no fire from below could touch them.

Desperate to reach the land side of the Vicksburg fortress, Grant studied a map of the network of rivers, streams, ditches and bayous that crisscross the swampy and virtually impenetrable Yazoo Delta country between Memphis and Vicksburg. The river was flowing almost at the top of the levees. He cut the levee near present-day Clarksdale and sent a flotilla of gunboats and loaded troop-transports through the crevasse and down Moon Lake into the swamp. The idea was to zigzag down the inland streams to the Yazoo River, debarking an assault force behind the water fortress. A plaque on US 61 marks where Grant cut his artificial "Yazoo Pass" through the levee. But irregular Confederate troops and local sympathizers felled trees across the narrow twisting bayous; snipers picked off soldiers and sailors. The pilots struggled to keep their awkward craft from running aground.

A few miles west of Greenwood on US 82 stands Fort Pemberton Park, a hastily improvised strong point armed with a battery of Army field pieces. The cannon still standing in the tiny park points down one of the few straight stretches of the Union advance and shows how even that light battery worked devastating damage on the intruders. The gunboats and transports turned back, and Grant gave up the idea, accepting the fact that the only road to conquest was across the high dry ground south of Vicksburg. To get his troops there, he could march them down the west bank, but to get them back to the east bank below the fortress he would have to sail his river transports past its guns, because the craft were all upriver.

To spread confusion about his intentions, Grant launched three cavalry regiments under Col. Benjamin Grierson on a 600-mile dash through the heart of Mississippi, destroying supplies, burning gins, and generally spreading havoc. Their main objective was the railroad that supplied Vicksburg. They cut the link in several places. At Hazlehurst and again at Brookhaven his troops had to turn firemen when sparks from burning freight cars set the town on fire. Enemy soldier and Southern civilian fought the flames side by side.

Grierson met little opposition. Though Jefferson Davis was himself a citizen of Vicksburg, the Confederate president did not seem to have as good a grasp of its importance as the Illinois Yankees Lincoln and Grant. Davis virtually had stripped Mississippi of cavalry to reinforce an inconsequential campaign in east Tennessee.

Grierson succeeded admirably in confusing Pemberton, who sent troops, badly needed on the Mississippi's banks, to run down the elusive raiders. Meanwhile Grant marched his troops past Vicksburg to the river bank below another fortress, at Grand Gulf, Mississippi. His transports made a night dash past Vicksburg's guns and ferried the army across the river to land on the Mississippi shore at the mouth of Bayou Pierre.

A few miles upriver lay the fortress at Grand Gulf that had

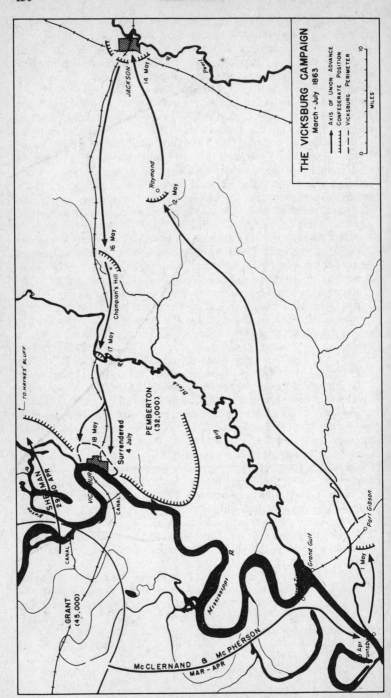

THE VICKSBURG CAMPAIGN
March - July 1863

→ Axis of Union Advance
Confederate Position
Vicksburg Perimeter

0    10
MILES

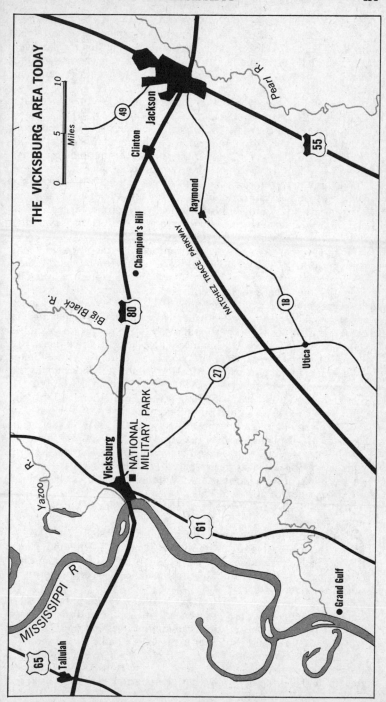

harrassed Grant's river support operations. His river fleet had fired 2,500 shots in a five-hour battle, but had disabled only one of the fort's 13 guns. A landing party had caused some further damage. Once his whole force landed on the east bank, Grant bypassed the fort in the night and left it to be mopped up by Union forces from Baton Rouge.

Fortifications, a sawmill and a museum in Grant Gulf State Military Park preserve mementos of the battles.

On his march upcountry, Grant passed a stately six-story mansion called Windsor. According to local legend he got it into his head that somebody had fired at his troops from the house, and so he prepared to burn it. The mistress of the house used what must have been a prodigiously powerful personality to dissuade him. But in 1890 at a house party, a guest tossed a lit cigarette butt into a pile of shavings left by a carpenter, and Windsor burned to the ground except for its 23 columns. A romantic ruin, they still point starkly to the sky on the Old Rodney road west of Port Gibson.

Grant also spared Port Gibson, supposedly because he said it was "too beautiful to burn." Though it is doubtful the hard-boiled soldier ever harbored so tender a sentiment, visitors universally agree that the town is indeed too beautiful to burn.

Confederate forces in Mississippi were divided between Vicksburg and Jackson. Grant dealt with them piecemeal, first defeating the defenders of Jackson and putting the city to the torch. For years the state capital was known as Chimneyville because the brick flues were almost the only structures left standing. Curiously, the Union soldiers spared the Governor's Mansion, which still does duty as the chief executive's residence, and the Old State Capitol, now a museum. The Ordinance of Secession was passed there in 1861, the "Bonny Blue Flag" was first sung there, the first post-war constitutional convention in the South was held there in 1865, and Jefferson Davis made his final speech to the legislature in 1884. The museum exhibits many Jefferson Davis memorabilia. A Greek Revival cottage, the Oaks, was also spared, probably because General Sherman used it for headquarters. Confederate trenches and cannon are still visible in Battlefield Park.

With the rear now secured, Grant turned toward Vicksburg, 40 miles west.

Plaques on the road between Jackson and Vicksburg mark where forces clashed in bloody battles at Champion's Hill and Black Bayou. Badly mauled in both encounters, the Confederates retreated behind their formidable entrenchments guarding the land side of the river fort.

In one of the finest battlefield parks in the world, today's visitor can circle completely the battle lines that loop around the city in a crescent. The road goes up the Confederate lines and returns by the Union lines. The visitor's center explains the battle with a diorama and a movie. Monuments on the road show where individual units fought. On the battlefield itself stand Shirley House, which survived the fighting, and the oak tree where Pemberton and Grant dickered over the surrender.

Standing in the shadow of the Confederate fortifications, the visitor can understand why massed attacks on May 19 and 22, 1863, were repulsed with losses too heavy even for the hardened Grant to endure. The armies settled down to a siege.

Under the bluffs at the northern end of the park is a beautifully groomed National Cemetery, the resting place for 17,000 soldiers, 13,000 of them unknown.

Within the town stands the Old Courthouse that was the target for Union Army and Navy guns throughout the siege. Now it houses a collection of Civil War relics.

McRaven developed from a frontier cottage built before 1797, with additions in 1836 and 1849. It is in Neo-Greek style. The house still shows scars of the battle. During the occupation, owner John Bobb ran some soldiers off his property and heaved a brick after them. They returned with their muskets and shot him down, the first incident of gross violence after the surrender. The military hanged the murderers.

Cedar Grove was built between 1840 and 1858. It also shows scars of battle. The building now belongs to the Little Theater group.

Planters Hall was built as a bank in 1832. The Vicksburg Council of Garden Clubs maintains it as a museum.

On July 4, 1863, Vicksburg could no longer stand the hunger pangs and surrendered. (For 82 years Vicksburg refused to celebrate Independence Day because it fell on the anniversary of their capitulation.) A few days later Port Hudson in Louisiana fell, and the last Confederate block to river passage was gone. Lincoln said, "The Father of the Waters rolls unvexed to the sea."

With the fall of Vicksburg, the Confederacy's chance for survival vanished, but it took two more years of fighting to convince Southerners that they had lost. Much of that fighting was in Mississippi.

Guerrillas harrassed occupying troops in the western and southern reaches of the state. (Near Laurel, soldiers from Jones County—which openly had opposed secession—deserted and fought a guerrilla war against the Confederacy for the duration.)

Along the Mississippi-Tennessee border, the Southern cause was defended by Regular units, many of them led by the brilliant Confederate tactician, Gen. Nathan Bedford Forrest, who baffled Union forces in a series of slashing raids on Federal communication lines.

To reduce the threat from guerrillas, in February 1864 General Sherman marched 150 miles east from Vicksburg to their stronghold of Meridian. He sacked this railroad and industrial center. (Somehow the Merrehope Mansion survived. It is open to the public.) A column of cavalry sent from Memphis to support him had the misfortune to run into Forrest. The Union cavalry was sent reeling back to base, so Sherman had to withdraw to the defenses of Vicksburg. His train included three hundred wagons lifted from farmers and loaded down with loot. In their wake came a ten-mile-long column of slaves fleeing to freedom; the countryside was losing its labor force.

To pull from their side the very prickly thorn of Forrest's cavalry, the Union sent 8,000 soldiers east from Memphis with the mission of trouncing Forrest's 3,500 men once and for all. Forrest ambushed the column at Brice's Cross Roads south of Tupelo. From dense underbrush on each side of the road, the dismounted cavalry carved the Union column to ribbons with deadly fire from newfangled Colt's six-shooters. The retreat turned into a rout when a supply wagon overturned and blocked the only bridge across Tishomingo Creek. Forrest snatched up all the cannon, the wagon train, and 1,500 prisoners. Among them were the unhappy survivors of a black company that had fought a courageous rear-guard action that allowed some Union soldiers to make it back to Memphis.

The location of the ambush is now a National Battlefield Site; markers and maps explain the course of the battle. In a cemetery nearby are gravestones of unknown soldiers who fell there.

The vexatious Forrest so worried Sherman, who was marching against Atlanta, that he dispatched a 14,000-man force, a column 15 miles long, to deal with the threat to his flank. The Union force had orders from Sherman to "Follow him to the death, if it costs 10,000 lives and breaks the Treasury."

On the night of July 13, 1864, the Union force made camp in what is now Tupelo. Next morning, 9,400 Confederate troopers stormed the camp. They were Forrest's men, but they were led by General Stephen Lee, no match for his brilliant superior. Federal soldiers beat off three attacks, inflicting heavy losses. For some reason, the Union general moved his troops four miles north and camped again. The Southerners attacked the new camp the next day and were again repulsed.

They had beaten off all attacks and had suffered far fewer casualties than their enemy; nevertheless, the Union troops withdrew toward Tennessee, harrassed every foot of the way by the Southerners. Though he fled the field, the Union general is credited with absorbing the energy of Forrest's force, thus making possible the capture of distant Atlanta by Sherman. In the Tupelo National Battlefield, plaques and markers explain the battle.

Despite the bitterness left by the war, some Mississippians made gestures of reconciliation. To mourn the assassination of Lincoln, the lighthouse that still stands at Biloxi was painted black. In Columbus, a year almost to the day after Appomattox, women decorated the graves of fallen soldiers in Friendship Cemetery. Because they decorated the headstones of blue and gray alike, their act of compassion prompted the nationwide observance of what we now call Memorial Day.

On his release from prison in Virginia, Jefferson Davis retired to Beauvoir, in Biloxi, to write his monumental *Rise and Fall of the Confederate Government*. Today Beauvoir is a museum and memorial garden.

## PRACTICAL INFORMATION FOR MISSISSIPPI

**FACTS AND FIGURES.** Mississippi gets its name from the Algonquin Indian *misi sipi,* meaning "father of the waters" or "big river." Its nickname is Magnolia State. The magnolia is also the state flower and the state tree. The mockingbird is the state bird. *Virtute et Armis* ("By valor and arms") is the state motto. "Go, Mississippi" is the state song.

Jackson is the state capital. The state population is 2.2 million. Mississippi is mostly a flat, featureless state, with some low hills in the east and bayous in the west. It is dominated by the Mississippi River that flows along its western boundary, and whose waters created the rich delta cottonland that extends north and east from Vicksburg. Soybeans has surpassed cotton as a money crop in Mississippi, although diversification of agriculture and industrialization has begun. For many reasons, including its long dependence on a single crop, Mississippi is the poorest state in the nation. The southern region of the state, bordering the Gulf of Mexico, is a popular local resort area. Mississippi summers are long, hot and humid; winters are mild.

**HOW TO GET THERE.** *By air:* Jackson-Vicksburg may be reached on direct flights of Delta, Southern and Texas International. Southern has direct service into Columbus, Greenville, Greenwood, Gulfport, Hattiesburg, Laurel, Meridian, Natchez, Tupelo and University-Oxford. Delta also flies into Meridian. Air Illinois rapidly is expanding a feeder line already linking Greenville with Memphis and New Orleans, and Natchez with New Orleans.

*By car:* I–55 will take you from the Tennessee state line to the Louisiana state line. US 45 runs from the Tennessee state line through Meridian and southeast to the Alabama state line. US 61 enters the state at the Tennessee line and goes south to Louisiana. US 82 goes from the Arkansas state line east to the Alabama state line. I–10, I–20, and US 84 and US 90 go from the Louisiana state line east to Alabama.

*Car rental:* Avis and Hertz have offices in major cities.

*By train:* Southern Railway System and Illinois Central Gulf.

*By bus:* In addition to Greyhound and Trailways, Arrow Coach Lines, Great Southern Coaches, inc., Gulf Transport Co., Illini-Swallow Lines, Inc., Ingram Bus Lines, Inc., Jefferson Lines and Salter Bus Lines provide transportation into the state.

*By ferry:* From St. Joseph, La., a ferry crosses the Mississippi River into the state.

**HOW TO GET AROUND.** *By air:* Southern has flights within the state.

*By car:* I–55, US 45 and US 61 go from north to south in the state; US 81, I–10, US 84 and US 90 cross the state from east to west. The Natchez Trace Parkway is lined with historic markers, roadside parks and nature trails.

*By train:* Southern Railway System and Illinois Central Gulf.

*By bus:* Greyhound, Trailways, Arrow Coach Lines, Great Southern Coaches, Inc., Gulf Transport Co., Illini-Swallow Lines, Inc., Ingram Bus Lines, Inc., Jefferson Lines and Salter Bus Lines operate within the state.

**TOURIST INFORMATION.** Mississippi Park Commission, 717 Robert E. Lee Bldg., Jackson 39201, and the Dept. of Tourism Development, P.O. Box 22825, Jackson 39205, can furnish you with any general information you might desire about the state and its facilities for the visitor, especially about the well-known areas. You would do well to contact the individual chambers of commerce in each city if you want specific information about the local points of interest.

Natchez-Adams County Chamber of Commerce, 300 N. Commerce St., Natchez, will supply information re antebellum homes which are open all year.

In Vicksburg, the Hospitality House, Monroe and Clay Sts., has free information on all points of interest. Open 8–5. Closed New Year's, Thanksgiving and Christmas.

 **SEASONAL EVENTS.** In every section of Mississippi *Annual Spring Pilgrimages* are held in early spring (Mar.–Apr.). Hoopskirted attendants greet visitors to the pre-Civil War mansions—filled with rare antiques and treasures of the antebellum past. These Pilgrimages can be enjoyed in the following cities: Bay St. Louis, Biloxi, Carrollton, Columbus, Gulfport, Hattiesburg (homes featured here were built during the first years of the 20th century); Holly Springs, Jackson (through June), Natchez, Oxford, Pascagoula, Pass Christian, Port Gibson, Raymond, Sardis, Vicksburg, Woodville. The *Gulf Coast Pilgrimage,* held during mid-March, covers eleven cities. Tours are marked and are free. The Pilgrimage is sponsored by the Mississippi Gulf Coast Council of Garden Clubs.

 **NATIONAL PARKS.** Vicksburg National Military Park, in Vicksburg, is something truly different for the traveler. As you enter the park, the Visitor Center offers you a pictorial display of the Battle of Vicksburg, fought on the site of the present park. As you walk over the surrounding countryside, dotted with memorial markers, you can see evidence of the lines of battle. Half-covered trenches mark the Union and Confederate emplacements; rusted guns and sabers, ruined forts and cannons are mute testament to the battle which won the war.

 **TOURS.** *By boat:* Excursion boats make two round trips daily, leaving Biloxi and Gulfport to historic Fort Massachusetts on Ship Island. *Jefferson Davis Cruises,* leave from Vicksburg, mid-Apr. to Aug. daily; Sat., Sun. only Sept. to Oct.

 **GARDENS.** *Beauvoir,* Jefferson Davis Shrine and Memorial Gardens, Biloxi. 50 acres of landscaped grounds.

**STAGES AND REVUES.** *Southern Exposure* is presented Mon., Wed., Fri. and Sat. 8:30 P.M. during the Natchez Pilgrimage, Mar. through the first week of Apr.

**DRINKING LAWS.** Privately owned package stores and bars in hotels and restaurants are legal on a local option basis in municipalities and resort areas. Store hours 10 to 10, bars 10 A.M. to midnight. Certain resort areas are allowed to remain open longer. No Sunday sales. The drinking age is 21.

 **WHAT TO DO WITH THE CHILDREN.** Here in Mississippi is the opportunity for youngsters to see first hand one of the most famous sites of the War Between the States. *Vicksburg National Military Park* and the

*Park Museum* are teeming with mementos of the battle. You will find models, maps, and displays showing the course of the battle and the influence of the terrain. After seeing the museum, take the children around the park so they may actually see the trenches and barricades restored to their natural condition.

Those curious about Southern life before the war get an accurate picture from the exhibits and pictures on display in the *Old Courthouse Museum* in Vicksburg.

  **MUSEUMS AND GALLERIES.** *Cottonlandia,* in Greenwood, exhibits the history of cotton cultivation from slave days to modern times. *Florewood River Plantation,* off US 82 west of Greenwood, reproduces antebellum plantation life. *State Historical Museum* in Old State Capitol, Jackson. *Oaks,* 823 N. Jefferson St. in Jackson, houses a museum in one of the few buildings that survived Civil War destruction. *The Old Courthouse Museum,* 1008 Cherry St., Vicksburg. Relics of the siege. Closed holidays. The *Park Museum* in Vicksburg Military Park has memorabilia from the Battle of Vicksburg, including models of the deployment of troops and the terrain during the battle. Free.

 **HISTORIC SITES.** *Baldwyn; Brice's Cross Roads National Battlefield Site,* off Rte. 370. Daily. Free. *Biloxi: Beauvoir,* on US 90, last home of Confederate President Jefferson Davis, now a shrine and museum. Closed Christmas. *Biloxi Lighthouse,* West Beach Blvd. Painted black in 1865 to mourn Lincoln's assassination. *Columbus: Friendship Cemetery,* first site of National Memorial Day. *Corinth: National Cemetery,* the dead of both sides lie in this first national cemetery. *Ship Island: Fort Massachusetts* can be reached by excursion boats twice daily from Biloxi and Gulfport. *Tupelo: Tupelo National Battlefield. Jackson: Battlefield Park. Vicksburg:* the *National Military Park and Cemetery,* daily. Free. *Cedar Grove,* 2200 Oak St. 1842 mansion located at the site of the siege of Vicksburg. Closed Dec. to Feb. 15. *McRaven,* 1503 Harrison. Pre-Civil War home. Closed Nov. 15 to Feb. 15. Near *Woodville: Rosemont Plantation,* the boyhood home of Jefferson Davis. Free. Guided tours. *Meridian: Merrehope.* Open Tuesday through Saturday. Closed Thanksgiving and Christmas. Near *Port Gibson: Grand Gulf State Military Park.* Closed New Year's, Thanksgiving, Christmas.

Seventeen of the Old Southern homes in Natchez are open to the public, including *The Briars,* where Jefferson Davis was married; *Dixie,* the home of Davis' older brother; and *The Elms,* called "one of the loveliest specimens of provincial architecture in Mississippi."

On Ellicott's Hill can be seen *Connelly's Tavern,* which is one of the most interesting historic buildings open to the public. Its rules were simple. Fourpence a night for bed, sixpence with supper. No more than five to sleep in one bed. No boots to be worn in bed. Organ grinders to sleep in the washhouse. No dogs allowed upstairs. No beer allowed in the kitchen. No razor grinders or tinkers taken in. And it was inside these walls that former Vice-president Aaron Burr planned his defense against the charge of treason.

Another antebellum mansion, probably the most lavish remaining in Natchez, is *Stanton Hall,* built in 1851, and now owned by the Pilgrimage Garden Club. Located at Pearl and Monroe Streets, it's an imposing white structure set beneath towering oaks. Among its outstanding features are carrara marble mantles, bronze chandeliers, enormous mirrors from France, and a 72-foot ballroom.

Among the antebellum houses in *Vicksburg,* three are of particular interest—Planters Hall, McRaven and Cedar Grove. *McRaven,* located at the eastern end of Harrison Street, developed from a frontier cottage built before 1797, with additions in 1836 and in 1849, the year during which it developed into its present Neo-Greek style with living wing stairway, exquisite plaster wall moldings, ceiling medallions and graceful marble fireplaces. Caught in a crossfire during the siege of Vicksburg, the house still bears shell marks visible both inside and out. John Bobb owned McRaven when General U.S. Grant came marching into Vicksburg. And on a morning in 1864, he glanced out the window and saw Federal troops in his yard. He ordered them to leave. They refused. So Bobb picked up a brick and threw it at them. When the troops returned they were carrying muskets and as Bobb walked alone in his garden, he was shot to death. It marked the first recorded incident of violence against the civilian populace during the Union occupation of Vicksburg. Grant, outraged, had the soldiers court-martialed and hanged.

*Cedar Grove,* another antebellum home being restored as a civic project, is located at 2200 Oak Street. It was constructed between 1840 and 1858 by John A. Klein, prominent plantation owner and banker. After seeing a succession of owners following the Civil War, the mansion was purchased by the Little Theater group in 1960 with funds resulting from the spring and summer shows. Cedar Grove, too, bears Civil War scars. Mute testimony of the siege of Vicksburg can be seen in the walls, where Federal warships attempted to level the house with cannonballs but failed.

*Planters Hall,* at Main and Monroe streets, the third antebellum showplace in Vicksburg, has had a varied career. It was erected in 1832 as a bank, and contained a special second-story apartment for the bank president. The bank prospered until President Andrew Jackson ordered gold or silver payments for government land instead of bank notes. Banking became difficult, and operations ceased in 1848. The building was bought by the McRae family, and converted into a residence. They in turn sold it to the Vicksburg Council of Garden Clubs, who have maintained it as a museum dedicated to the true South.

 **HOTELS AND MOTELS.** The Gulf Coast of Mississippi boasts several fine resort establishments and a wide selection of excellent motels on or near the gulf. Inland, the state has a more narrow range of accommodations, there being no super deluxe hostelries in the grand tradition. But these are more than compensated for by the abundance of comfortable, more modest accommodations. We have listed hotels and motels alphabetically in categories determined by double-occupancy, in-season rates. Family rates are available at almost all listings. Rates will be $3–$4 higher during Pilgrimages. *Expensive:* $35–$42; *Moderate:* $25–$35; *Inexpensive:* $17–$25. For a more complete explanation of hotel and motel categories see *Facts at Your Fingertips* at the front of this volume.

### BILOXI

**Broadwater Beach.** *Expensive.* West Beach Blvd. (US 90). This large resort has all the facilities, including deep-sea fishing, heated pool, golf, tennis, or you can spend a quiet afternoon walking over the thirty-three acres of terraced grounds. Free airport transportation. In-room coffee. Restaurant. Cocktail lounge with entertainment in evenings, dancing. Supervised play area.

**Hilton Resort Motel.** *Expensive.* 300 Deluxe rooms, gourmet dining room, show lounge, lighted tennis courts, 18 hole championship golf course.

**Sheraton Motor Inn.** *Expensive.* 3634 W. Beach Blvd. (US 90) Pools (heated). Restaurant, cocktail lounge, entertainment, dancing. Playground, pets allowed, balconies, some private patios.

**Buena Vista Hotel-Motel.** *Moderate.* 710 Central Beach Blvd. The spreading shade trees offer a welcome relief from the hot summer sun, while a dip in the pool will certainly be enjoyed. Play area. This large hotel-motel complex offers a wide choice of accommodations including suites. Restaurant, bar, dancing. In-room coffee.

**Holiday Inn.** *Moderate.* 92 W. Beach (US 90). Free airport transportation. Restaurant, bar, dancing. In-room coffee. Pool. Play area. Pets welcome.

**Oak Manor Motel.** Member of Best Western. *Moderate.* 626 Central Beach Blvd. Pool, restaurant nr.

**Quality Inn Emerald Beach.** *Moderate.* 3717 W. Beach Blvd. Restaurant, bar. Limousine, tour service.

**Ramada Inn.** *Moderate.* 3719 W. Beach Blvd. (US 90W). Restaurant, coffee shop, bar, dancing, Pool (heated).

**Sun-N-Sand.** *Moderate.* W. Beach Blvd. (US 90). For those who are interested in salt-water swimming, fishing and boating, this is the place. A large resort with pools. Play area. Restaurant, bar, dancing. Free airport transportation. Beautician.

**Sun Tan Motel.** *Moderate.* 200 Central Beach Blvd. A Well-run medium-sized motel which offers many opportunities for both relaxing and sightseeing. Pool. In-room coffee. Restaurant nr.

**Biloxi Downtowner.** *Inexpensive.* 115 W. Beach (US 90). Pools, play area. Restaurant, cocktail lounge, entertainment, dancing. Pets allowed.

**Sea Gull.** *Inexpensive.* W. Beach Blvd. (US 90). Here is an excellent medium-sized place for the whole family. Outdoor barbecue facilities. Some family kitchen units and cottages. Restaurant nr. Heated pool, play area.

## CLARKSDALE

**Clarksdale Uptown Motor Inn.** Member of Best Western. *Inexpensive.* Central location. Restaurant, bar.

**Holiday Inn.** *Inexpensive.* Restaurant, bar. Free airport transportation. Pool.

## COLUMBUS

**Chief Econo Inn.** *Inexpensive.* Café.

**Columbus.** *Inexpensive.* This well-maintained medium-sized motel seems to cater to the family visitors. Restaurant nr. Pool.

**Holiday Inn.** *Inexpensive.* 5th Ave. N. Central location. Restaurant, Bar. Pets welcome.

**Ramada Inn.** *Inexpensive.* US 45N. Pool. Pets allowed. Restaurant, cocktail lounge, entertainment.

## CORINTH

**Holiday Inn.** *Inexpensive.* Free airport transportation. Pools. Pets welcome. Restaurant, bar.

**southern.** *Inexpensive.* This is a favorite meeting place for many of the local service clubs. Restaurant, bar. Play area. Pets allowed.

**Windsor Inn.** *Inexpensive.* Pool. Pets allowed. Restaurant.

## GREENVILLE

**Gilhara.** *Inexpensive.* Large well-furnished rooms will add much to your comfort while you stay at this spacious motel. Pool. Pets allowed.

## GREENWOOD

**Downtowner Inn.** *Inexpensive.* Restaurant, pool.

**Holiday Inn.** *Inexpensive.*

## GRENADA

**Days Inn.** *Inexpensive.* On Miss. 7, 8 at I–55. TV. Pool, play area. Pets. Café.

**Holiday Inn.** *Inexpensive.* Restaurant, bar. Pool (heated). Pets allowed.

**Hilltop Motel.** *Inexpensive.* Member of Best Western. Restaurant, pool.

**Monte Cristo.** *Inexpensive.* The well-maintained grounds lend the touch of quality to this medium-sized, well-run motel. Restaurant, pool. Play area. Pets allowed.

**Ramada Inn.** *Inexpensive.* Heated swimming pool. Restaurant. Entertainment.

## GULFPORT

**Holiday Inn.** *Moderate.* Pools. Pets allowed. Free airport transportation. Bar, entertainment, dancing.

**Moody's Fountainhead.** *Moderate.* Fishing trips arranged. Restaurant, bar. Pool. Play area. Family units offered by this large motel-cottage combination. Seasonal rates.

**Alamo Plaza Hotel Courts.** *Inexpensive.* Large well-maintained operation, with rooms on Gulf. Family units with kitchens, outdoor barbecue facilities. Pool. Restaurant nr.

**Deep South.** *Inexpensive.* Pool. Restaurant nr.

**Downtowner.** *Inexpensive.* Overlooks Gulf. Restaurant, bar, entertainment, dancing. Pool (heated). Pets allowed. Sundeck. Free airport bus.

**Ramada Inn.** *Inexpensive.* Pools. Play area. Restaurant, bar, dancing. Free airport transportation.

## JACKSON

**Downtowner Motor Inn.** *Moderate.* 225 E. Capitol. Central location, rooftop pool (heated). Restaurant, bar, entertainment.

**Sheraton Motor Inn.** *Moderate.* US 51N, I–55. The large dressing rooms will add much to your pleasure while staying here. A good-sized motor hotel with an excellent restaurant, bar, entertainment. Pool. In-room coffee.

**TraveLodge-Airport.** *Moderate.* Jackson Municipal Airport above terminal blvd. Restaurant.

**Admiral Benbow Inn.** *Inexpensive.* 905 N. State St. Restaurant, bar, entertainment. Pets allowed.

**Coliseum Ramada Inn.** *Inexpensive.* 400 Greymont St. Pool (heated), play area. Bar, entertainment. Pets welcome.

**Heidelberg Hotel.** *Inexpensive.* 131 E. Capitol St. All the necessities, many extras for your pleasure. Children in parents' room free. Fine restaurant, bar. Free parking.

**Holiday Inn.** *Inexpensive.* Four locations. All have restaurant, entertainment. Pool. **North:** 155 N. Frontage Rd. **Southwest:** 2649 US 80W. **Downtown:** 200 E. Amite St. **Medical Center:** 2375 N. State St.

**Howard Johnson's Motor Lodge.** *Inexpensive.* I–55 at McDowell Rd. Restaurant, bar. Pool. Pets allowed.

**Jacksonian Master Hosts Inn.** *Inexpensive.* US 51N, 5 mi. Ideal location for the sportsman, with bowling, golf, other sports to test his skill. Restaurant, bar. Wide choice of accommodations and rates. Pools. Play area.

**Jackson Downtown Travelodge.** *Inexpensive.* 550 W. Capitol St. Central location of this medium-sized motel helps account for its popularity. Excellent staff. Restaurant. pool.

**Quality Inn Drake.** *Inexpensive.* On US 80W. 2 mi W of downtown. Restaurant.

**Ramada Inn.** *Inexpensive.* 2275 US 80W. Pool. Restaurant, bar.

**Rodeway Inn.** *Inexpensive.* 3720 I–55N. Restaurant, bar, entertainment. Pool. Pets allowed.

**Sun-N-Sand Motor Hotel.** *Inexpensive.* 401 N. Lamar St. Restaurant, cocktail lounge, entertainment. Pool (heated). Pets allowed.

**Stonewall Jackson Motor Lodge.** *Inexpensive.* 1955 US 80W. Gracious staff. Medium-sized establishment. Restaurant, bar. Pool.

## LAUREL

**Holiday Inn.** *Inexpensive.* 4 mi. N. on US 11. Free airport transportation. Bar, entertainment. Pets welcome.

**Magnolia Motor Lodge.** *Inexpensive.* Convenient location is just the thing for those who want to explore the area. Medium-sized motel, spacious rooms. Restaurant, bar. Pool.

**Town House.** *Inexpensive.* 340 Beacon St. This medium-sized motel is a favorite among the local gentry. The accommodations are better than average, so is the service. In-room coffee. Restaurant nr. Pool.

## MERIDIAN

**Ramada Inn.** *Moderate.* Hamilton Rd. Restaurant, bar. Pool, play area. Pets allowed.

**Days Inn.** *Inexpensive.* 1521 Tom Bailey Dr. Swimming pool. Restaurant.

**Downtowner Motor Inn.** *Inexpensive.* Convenient location. Restaurant, pool.

**Holiday Inn.** *Inexpensive.* Two locations, 1 blk. N. of I–20 and also 1½ mi. S. on US 45. Both have restaurant, bar, free airport transportation and pool.

**Howard Johnson's Motor Lodge.** *Inexpensive.* 1 blk. N. of I–20. Restaurant, bar. Pool (heated). Play area. Free airport transportation. Pets welcome.

## MISSISSIPPI CITY

**Fairchild's.** *Inexpensive.* Located above the Gulf of Mexico, this well-equipped, medium-sized motel offers splendid views of the blue water below. Pools. Some family kitchen units.

**Worth Motor Lodge.** *Inexpensive.* 2252 E. Beach Dr. Whether your interest lies with golf, lawn games, or just a stroll among trees, this is the place for you. Restaurant nr. Some kitchens and efficiencies. Barbecue facilities. Pool (heated). Play area.

## NATCHEZ

**Holiday Inn.** *Inexpensive.* 249 D'Evereaux Dr. Restaurant, bar. Pool, play area.

**Prentiss Motel.** *Inexpensive.* Restaurant, cocktail lounge, entertainment. Pool (heated).

**Ramada Hilltop.** *Inexpensive.* 130 John R. Junkin Dr. Swimming pool. Restaurant.

## OCEAN SPRINGS

**Gulf Hills Inn and Gold Club.** *Expensive.* ½ mi. N. of US 90. This is Mississippi's only first class resort, with tennis, golf, swimming pool, and horseback riding. Children are offered a summer recreation program.

## OXFORD

**Holiday Inn.** *Inexpensive.* 400 N. Lamar. Free airport transportation. Restaurant, bar.

**Ramada Inn.** *Inexpensive.* Swimming pool. Restaurant.

## PASCAGOULA

**La Font Inn.** *Moderate.* 1½ mi. E. on US 90. Large motel with excellent view of pool from spacious rooms. Family rates. Restaurant, bar. Pools. Play area. Pets welcome. Free airport transportation.

**LONGFELLOW HOUSE.** *Moderate.* 3401 Beach Blvd. Par 3 golf. Pool. Dancing, dinner theater, rich atmosphere. Landscaped grounds, dock area. Restaurant, bar.

## STARKVILLE

**Holiday Inn.** *Inexpensive.* Montgomery St. 1 mi. from Miss. State U. Restaurant, pool.

**Plantation Bell Motor Lodge.** *Inexpensive.* Well-run medium-sized motel caters to families. Restaurant. Play area. Pets welcome.

## TUPELO

**Holiday Inn.** *Inexpensive.* 1¼ mi N. of jct. US 45, 78. Restaurant. Pool. Play area. Free airport transportation.

**Natchez Trace Inn.** *Inexpensive.* 3000 W. Main St. Restaurant, bar, entertainment. Pool, play area. Pets welcome.

**Ramada Inn.** *Inexpensive.* 854 N. Gloster St. Free airport transportation. Pools. Restaurant, bar, entertainment.

**Sheraton Rex Plaza.** *Inexpensive.* 1 mi. N. on US 45. This medium-sized motel offers all the facilities normally associated with larger operations. Restaurant, bar, entertainment. Pool.

**Town House.** *Inexpensive.* 2 mi. S. on US 45. One of the better-run motels in the area, this well-equipped medium-sized establishment features a pleasing decor in both the lobby and rooms. Pool. Restaurant. Recommended restaurant (see Shockley's, below).

**Tupelo TraveLodge.** *Inexpensive.* 401 N. Gloster St. Situated among many historical sites, this medium-sized motel offers an excellent jumping-off place for day trips. Pool. Restaurant nr.

## VICKSBURG

**Downtowner Motor Inn.** *Inexpensive.* 1313 Walnut St. Convenient location. Recommended restaurant (see Old Southern Tea Room, below), bar. Pool. Pets allowed.

**Holiday Inn.** *Inexpensive.* 1 mi. E. on US 80. Restaurant, bar. Pool. Play area.

**Magnolia Quality Inn.** *Inexpensive.* 4155 Washington St. Large dressing areas, tastefully decorated. Family units. Restaurant, bar, coffee shop. Play area. Part of the Best Western chain.

**Ramada Inn.** *Inexpensive.* 2 mi. E. on US 80. Swimming pool. Restaurant.

 **DINING OUT.** Mississippi offers many traditional Southern specialties, as well as all the standard American favorites. Along the Gulf coast, be sure to try the shrimp prepared in the Creole manner, and hot gumbos or other seafood specialties. Among the Southern items to be found on many Mississippi menus: hush puppies, grits, country-style ham, and of course, Mississippi River catfish.

For other worthwhile restaurants, be sure to re-check hotel listings. Restaurants are listed in order of price category. Price ranges and categories for a complete meal are as follows: *Expensive:* over $10; *Moderate:* $5–$8.50; *Inexpensive:* $2.50–$5. For a more complete explanation of restaurant categories see *Facts at Your Fingertips* at the front of this volume.

### BILOXI

**WHITE PILLARS.** *Expensive.* 100 Rodenburg. New Orleans-style seafood. Jambalaya and gumbo.

### JACKSON

**LEFLEUR'S.** *Moderate.* A profusion of flowers and Creole cooking. What could be more appropriate to this area? You will enjoy the beef and shrimp dishes.

### GULFPORT

**Angelo's.** *Inexpensive.* European cuisine served in a semi-Old-World atmosphere, made even more pleasant by the large fireplace and view of the Gulf.

**Simmons Restaurant.** *Moderate.* Overlooks the beach and docks, specializing in seafood.

### MISSISSIPPI CITY

**CONFEDERATE INN.** *Inexpensive.* Rebel flags add atmosphere to this charming place. Southern cooking at its best. Children's portions. Bar. Open for all meals.

### NATCHEZ

**CARRIAGE HOUSE.** *Moderate.* Southern cooking in a Southern setting. At Stanton Hall, historic mansion restoration. Open for lunch and dinner.

**THE SIDE TRACK.** *Moderate.* Turn-of-the-century atmosphere in a former railway depot. Crab, shrimp, steak, pie. Locally popular.

## OCEAN SPRINGS

**FRENCHIE's.** *Moderate.* Cajun-styled delicacies such as lemon fish and crawfish.

**LAGNIAPPE.** *Moderate.* Lagniappe is a Cajun word meaning "something extra." It describes this restaurant's Cajun cooking.

## PORT GIBSON

**Jimhams.** *Inexpensive.* Steak.

## VICKSBURG

**OLD SOUTHERN TEA ROOM.** In Downtowner Motel (see above). *Moderate.* Southern specialties, own baking, music. Locally popular. Chef owned.

# MISSOURI

## *The Bloody State Divided*

### by
### CAROLYN R. LANGDON

In the late 1850's when radical Southern leaders were debating about secession from the Union, the public opinion in Missouri was carefully monitored by North and South alike. The population and wealth of Missouri had grown to where it was first among the 15 slaveholding states. Each side wanted her as an ally.

Missouri, one of the states carved out of the Louisiana Purchase, was admitted to the Union in 1821 under the terms of the delicate Missouri Compromise. The state remained in the Union, but sentiment was by no means unanimous. That division of opinion, coupled with activities in neighboring Kansas, made the border region an area of peculiar violence and bitterness during the conflict.

The violence in Missouri and Kansas began well before those shots fired at distant Ft. Sumter officially opened the War Between the States. In 1854 Stephen A. Douglas pushed through Congress a bill that opened the Kansas Territory to slavery, thereby repealing the Missouri Compromise.

Repeal meant popular sovereignty would determine the dividing line between free and slave territory; in effect it meant the outbreak of sectional conflict. When President Franklin Pierce signed the bill to organize the Kansas Territory, hundreds of proslavery settlers from Missouri flocked to the choice Kansas land on the west bank of the Missouri River to ensure good locations for the new river towns. In reality, many were as interested in economics as in slavery. Nonetheless, other towns farther from the river were established by Northern sympathizers.

Violence, often cold-blooded and hidden by the dark of night, resulted as guerrilla bands formed. Secret societies sprang up—the Blue Lodges, Social Bands, Sons of the South, and Friendly Societies. Free-state settlers labeled Missourians "border ruffians" and assumed they were out to control the new territory by any means.

The border raids that began in the 1850s continued during the war. Men who have become notorious kept the war spirit alive by fueling distrust and hatred. William C. Quantrill, "Bloody Bill" Anderson, and "Little Archie" Clement are among them. These civilians led guerrilla bands in skirmishes against neighbors and small bands of soldiers, often murdering by ambush. Sometimes they carried out their deeds as "favors" to military commanders.

Missouri sent about 60 percent of her men of military age into the armed forces, making the percentage of enlistments relative to total population among the highest of the states. The Union armies counted 109,000 and the Confederates more than 30,000 Missourians in their ranks, in addition to the irregular fighters who were not enlisted.

### Major Battlefield

One of the fiercest struggles of the Civil War in Missouri took place at the Battle of Wilson's Creek, 13 miles southwest of Springfield on US 60. There, on August 10, 1861, Confederate troops led by Gen. Sterling Price engaged in combat the troops of the Union Gen. Nathaniel Lyon. Lyon died in the battle, and a granite monument on Bloody Hill is a tribute to him. Maps for self-guided driving tours are available at the information trailer at the entrance to the 1,700-acre Wilson's Creek National Battlefield.

Many of the casualties are buried in the Springfield National Cemetery, which has monuments to Lyon and Price although neither general is buried there. The Museum of the Ozarks, 603 East Calhoun, contains Civil War artifacts among its collection of pioneer memorabilia. The museum is in a 3-story Victorian home on the northern edge of the Drury College campus.

Leaving Springfield on US 160, travel west to US 71 and proceed north to the town of Nevada. The Bushwhacker Museum, in the old county jail, is open from Memorial Day to November and by appointment at other times. It houses Civil War memorabilia such as coins, shells, guns, flags, and pictures that pertain to the area. Nevada suffered the ravages of the border war, and on May 26, 1863, federal troops burned much of the town. The cell room survived the burning, and today its exhibits recall the area's Confederate bushwhacker past.

## Kansas City

Traveling north on US 71 you will arrive in Kansas City. What are now its suburbs were isolated communities and farms during the Civil War, and little trace remains of the guerrilla warfare that took place in this border region.

The major engagement in the area was the Battle of Westport in what is now Loose Park, about a mile south of the Country Club Plaza. The battle, considered the last full-scale action of the Civil War in the West, was part of a last-ditch effort by the Confederacy. On October 22, 1864, Confederate forces along the Big Blue River near Kansas City met Union forces, and the next day advanced west for the Battle of Westport. The Confederate General Price was beaten and forced to retreat south along the Kansas-Missouri line. A few days later the Battle of Mine Creek took place in Kansas.

Today Loose Park, with its gentle hills and pathways, is a haven for joggers. A rose garden in the center has beautiful foliage in the summer. The park is surrounded by a fashionable residential district.

Several blocks south of the park is the Wornall House at 61st Terrace and Wornall Road. The house was built by John Wornall in the 1850s on his 500-acre farm. During the Battle of Westport it was used as a hospital by both armies. The mansion is restored and furnished with antiques of the 1850s.

## River Towns

Forty miles east of Kansas City on US 24 is Lexington, situated on a bluff overlooking the Missouri River. One of the largest battles of the western campaign took place in Lexington when Union and Confederate troops battled for three days in September, 1861. On the third day the Confederate General Price came up with an idea that was a major factor in his victory. Realizing that the manufacture of hemp bales was one of Lexington's major industries, he commanded that a quantity of the bales be sent to the front lines from the warehouses along the riverfront. These he used as moveable breastworks for the men, and they were able to advance, slowly but surely, on the Union positions. He even had the bales soaked in the river so that when the Federals tried to set them afire they did not burn. Finally at 2 o'clock in the afternoon the Union troops surrendered the Battle of the Hemp Bales.

Much evidence of the historic struggle remains in Lexington. A cannonball is still embedded at the top of the easternmost column of the Lafayette County Courthouse in the center of town. Near the riverfront on the 80-acre battlefield is the Anderson House. It was built in 1853 and used as a hospital during the Battle of Lexington. Bloodstains remain on the floors and walls, and bullets and cannon-shot marks are visible on inside and outside walls. It is furnished in period pieces and is open for tours.

About 1 ½ miles southeast of Lexington is Linwood Lawn, built in 1850. There are numerous other historic homes and sites in the Lexington area, such as the Wentworth Military Academy, and the Chamber of Commerce has excellent literature available. One of the pamphlets is a self-guided walking tour of the downtown area and a driving tour of the battlefield.

When you leave Lexington take US 24 east to Missouri 41 and stop in Arrow Rock. The town is situated on the Old Santa Fe Trail and features the home of frontier artist George Caleb Bingham among its nearly 40 historic buildings. Bingham's brushes were busy during the Civil War; one of his most famous paintings depicts the grief caused by "Order No. 11," which was issued from Kansas City on August 25, 1863. It demanded that all residents of Jackson, Cass and Bates counties and the northern part of Vernon County, with certain exceptions, leave their homes. Persons who could give evidence of their loyalty to the United States were permitted to move to any military post within the district or to any part of Kansas other than counties on the eastern boundary. Others were supposed to move beyond the limits of the District of the Border.

The order was in response to Quantrill's raid in Lawrence, in which 150 civilians were killed, and other acts of violence by guerrilla leaders.

Aside from painting, Bingham's family ties in with the war in another way. His wife owned a wretched building in Kansas City that housed Rebel women prisoners. It collapsed in August, 1863, and among those killed and injured were two sisters of "Bloody Bill" Anderson, a guerrilla leader. It is believed that many of his brutal activities were in revenge.

A walking tour of Arrow Rock takes in the restored courthouse, gun shop, chapel, jail, and private homes in the old town. Among the three Missouri governors who came from Arrow Rock was Claiborne Jackson, who served at the outbreak of the Civil War. He is buried in Sappington Cemetery, near Arrow Rock.

### St. Louis

On I–70 travel east to St. Louis, about 2 hours' drive. The city was named for Louis IX of France and was founded by Pierre LaClede as a fur-trading post. The Jefferson National Expansion Memorial on the riverfront was built in 1966 to commemorate the symbolic starting point of westward expansion. An elevator takes visitors to the top for a commanding view of the city. Under the arch is the Museum of Westward Expansion that tells the story of pioneers, the rise and collapse of fur trading, the waves of immigrants, the settlers, the Indians, the cattlemen, the farmers and miners who later took part in the Civil War.

Near the arch is the Old Courthouse where the Dredd Scott case that triggered the Civil War was tried. It contains two restored courtrooms and exhibit rooms on the Louisiana Purchase, Indians and the West.

About 10 miles south of St. Louis on State 231 is the Jefferson Barracks Historical Park founded in 1826. Two arch foes in the Civil War, Robert E. Lee and Ulysses S. Grant, are among the military leaders whose careers included service at Jefferson Barracks. Although no Civil War battles took place at the facility, it was important during the war as an induction and medical center. The laborers house, stable and powder magazine have been restored and are open for tours. A national cemetery is west of the parade grounds.

## PRACTICAL INFORMATION FOR MISSOURI

 **MISSOURI FACTS AND FIGURES.** Missouri is named for the Missouri Indians, the word meaning "people of the big canoes." Its nicknames are *Center State, Gateway to the West, Mother of the West,* and, most often, *Show Me State.* The hawthorn is the state flower; the flowering dogwood, the state tree; the bluebird, the state bird. *Salus populi suprema lex esto* ("Let the welfare of the people be the supreme law") is the state motto. "Missouri Waltz" is the state song.

Jefferson City (pop, 32,400) is the state capital. The state population is 4.7 million.

A little north of St. Louis is the most striking landmark in Missouri, the dramatic meeting place of the Missisisippi and Missouri Rivers. The two mighty rivers bring products of the entire Mississippi Valley pouring into the great port of St. Louis, the state's cosmopolitan leading city. The flat eastern half of the state, bordering the Mississippi, verges into the eroded Ozark highlands in the southern third of the state, and into the prairies and rolling hill country of the north. The highest spot is Taum Sauk. Mt., 1772 ft.; the lowest is the St. Francis River, 230 feet. Missouri is a leading livestock state, and while much of the state is devoted to farmland, industry has become increasingly more important in the state's economy. The most popular resort area is the region surrounding the manmade Lake of the Ozarks in the center of the state. Missouri's climate produces hot, humid summers, generally moderate winters, and occasional tornadoes during spring and early summer.

Missouri entered the Union in 1821; it was the twenty-fourth state. Its area is 69,674 sq. mi., nineteenth among the states. The average dimensions are about 295 mi. E-W by 170 mi. N-S. It has 114 counties, and its present constitution was adopted in 1945.

**HOW TO GET THERE.** *By car.:* I-70, from Vandalia in central Illinois, enters the state at St. Louis and connects it due west with Kansas City via Columbia and Boonville. It continues to Topeka, Kansas, and beyond. From Oklahoma City and Tulsa, take I-44 northeast to Joplin, Springfield, Rolla and St. Louis. I-55 follows the undulations of the Mississippi River from Memphis to St. Louis, looking in on Cape Girardeau and Ste. Genevieve; then it veers northeast to Springfield, Illinois. Motorists bound for Bull Shoals or Lake of the Ozarks from Little Rock may use US 65, which continues to Springfield. Southeastern Missouri is served by US

67, also out of Little Rock. It goes to Poplar Bluff and joins I-55 at Festus. In the northwest quadrant, Kansas City is express-linked to Omaha and Des Moines by I–29 and I–35 respectively.

*By air:* After St. Louis and Kansas City, the busiest airports are at Springfield and Joplin, both of which have direct service from cities in neighboring states, such as Memphis and Little Rock. Most of this service is provided by *Ozark Airlines,* complemented by *Frontier* and *Delta.* The other interstate terminals in Missouri are at Jefferson City, Cape Girardeau and Columbia-Jefferson City, and St. Joseph.

*By train:* Amtrak's *National Limited* serves Kansas City and St. Louis, and stops in Warrensburg, Sedalia, Jefferson City, and Kirkwood. St. Louis is connected with Springfield, Ill., and Chicago. The *Lone Star* stops daily in Kansas City enroute from Chicago to Houston. Out of Chicago, the *Southwest Limited* runs to Albuquerque and Los Angeles daily, with a stop in Kansas City. The *Inter-American* from St. Louis goes through Poplar Bluff to Dallas.

*By bus:* Coast-to-coast Greyhound and Trailways expresses stop in St. Louis, Springfield and Joplin. Kansas City and northern Missouri (Chillicothe, Hannibal) are on E-W routes that stretch through Chicago and Omaha. Trailways has a diagonal route from Memphis serving Thayer, Cabool, Springfield, Osceola, Warrensburg and Kansas City. North-south routes from central Iowa to either Springfield or Rolla are handled by Missouri Transit. The same line operates an east-west run from Moberly to Kansas City. Another useful regional carrier is Jefferson Lines, with a route from Texarkana and Ft. Smith, Ark., to Joplin and Kansas City.

*By boat:* The *Delta Queen Steamboat Co.* brings cruise passengers to St. Louis from New Orleans and other cities along the Mississippi River, stopping at Hannibal and Cape Girardeau. The *Delta Queen* has been joined by the newer *Mississippi Queen* on this run.

**HOW TO GET AROUND.** *By car:* Missouri has a fine mix of Interstate and Federal highways reaching every corner, crossing every tier. St. Louis, Kansas City and Joplin form a triangle of Interstate service. Across the southern portion, US 60 goes from Springfield to Sikeston. In the north US 36 crosses from Hannibal to St. Joseph, and farther up, near the Iowa border, is US 136. the N-S routes—US 71, 65, 63 and 61—are evenly spaced west to east.

*By train:* Amtrak connects Kansas City with St. Louis and, on its other right of way, with Fort Madison, Iowa.

*By air:* Commuter and interstate airlines combine to connect Missouri's airports—St. Louis, Kansas City, Joplin, Springfield, Jefferson City, Cape Girardeau, Fort Leonard Wood, Sedalia, Poplar Bluff, Lake of the Ozarks, Kirksville, Malden and Columbia. *Ozark* is the busiest major carrier and the commuters are: *Air Illinois, Trans Mo, Semo,* and *Skyway.*

*By bus:* Some of Greyhound's routes along Federal highways include St. Louis to Memphis via Cape Girardeau and Sikeston, St. Louis to Joplin via Rolla, Fort Leonard Wood and St. Louis to Kansas City via Warrenton, Columbia, Boonville, Lexington and Odessa. Trailways has, among others, a run from Hannibal to Kansas City via Shelbina, Brookfield, Chillicothe and Cameron. Regional bus lines are especially numerous in the state. You may find yourself riding *Missouri Transit, Trenton-St. Joseph, V-K,* or *Jefferson Lines.*

**TOURIST INFORMATION SERVICES.** Most of the relevant offices are in Jefferson City: *Missouri Division of Tourism,* Box 1055; *Missouri Dept. of Conservation,* Box 180; *Missouri Division of Parks & Recreation,* Box 176; all Jefferson City, Mo. 65101. For *National Forest information* write *National Forests in Missouri,* Box 937, Rolla. Mo. 65401 and *Ozark National Scenic Riverways,* Box 490, Van Buren, Mo. 63965.

 **SEASONAL EVENTS.** *Spring:* Florissant's *Valley of Flowers Festival* in early May is a combination carnival and historic house tour.

*Summer:* Hannibal's *Tom Sawyer Days* in early July feature a fence-painting contest. Venerable Ste. Genevieve celebrates its French heritage with pioneer exuberance in mid-August with its *Jour de Fête.*

The oldest *county fair* west of the Mississippi, Boone County's, brings its horse show and other events to Columbia each August.

*Fall:* Sikeston's *Cotton Carnival,* late in Sept., has a Deep South atmosphere, with parades and contests. From mid-Sept. for three weeks a *National Crafts Festival* is held in Silver Dollar City. An eagerly awaited mid-October event for exhibitors from coast to coast is the annual *Ozarks Art & Crafts Fair* held in War Eagle, Ark., just south of the Missouri border. From late May well into October, the popular *Shepherd of the Hills pageant* is held evenings at the Old Mill Theater on Shepherd of the Hills Farm, seven miles west of Branson on State 76.

 **MUSEUMS AND GALLERIES.** The *Springfield Art Museum* has American sculpture and paintings and relics of the westward movement. 1111 E. Brookside. St. Joseph reflects its former role as the head of the Pony Express route and Missouri's first railroad at its *Pony Express Stables Museum,* 914 Penn St. It's free. The *Doll Museum* is at 1501 Penn St. Year-round museums are the *Albrecht Gallery,* with its pleasant formal gardens, Charles and 11th Sts., with renowned Indian collections and natural, regional and local history on view as well; the *Bushnell Pioneer Museum* W of St. Charles on I–70.

*The Audrain County Historical Society Museum* in Mexico (501 S. Muldrow St.) is restored ante-bellum mansion housing also the *American Saddle Horse Museum.* In the Jefferson City Statehouse, the *Missouri State Museum* has historic exhibits—military flags and guidons, an old stagecoach, valuable zithers, of interest to music-lovers who may have thought it was just a *kitsch* item, and a display of moon rocks brought back on the Apollo 11 lunar mission. *The Cole County Historical Society Museum,* nearby at 109 Madison St. has genealogical records and fancy dress gowns from the state's Inaugural Balls. Anyone fascinated by the unique culture of the Ozarks will enjoy the *Ralph Foster Museum* in Branson. Both Indian and white societies are represented.

**HISTORIC SITES.** Near Sibley, Off US 24 east of Kansas City, visit the *Fort Osage* reconstruction on the site of the first U.S. outpost in the Louisiana Purchase. Built in 1808 by William Clark. *Jefferson Landing,* in Jefferson City between the Capitol and the Governor's Mansion, is a new site with three mid-19th-century mercantile buildings restored. The Lohman

Building (1834) has a Visitors Center showing history of the state's government and a museum reflecting the era of commercial river trade.

Missouri is not widely known as a Civil War area, but several important engagements were fought within its confines, including the *Battle of Lexington*, 1861. The site may be toured with a guide, and there's a minimal fee. *Wilson's Creek National Battlefield*, also an 1861 event, has self-guided auto tours, with free maps available only during the summer from the Information Trailer. The site is on State ZZ off US 60, 13 mi. SW of Springfield. St. Charles was the state's first capital and the capitol has been restored to its 1820s appearance.

**TOURS.** Bus lines and auto rental agencies are the best sources of information about individual packages and major airlines are getting into the act with "Fly-Drive" deals. Tours *within* individual communities in Missouri usually have to do with its lakes and rivers. Lake Taneycomo in the southwestern region has, in Branson, a *Pirate Cruise* from the Main St. Pier. It operates in summer and the 15-mi. jaunt takes an hour. A similar excursion on the *Lake Queen* puts out from the Sammy Lane Dock in little Rockaway Beach on State 76A. The huge Lake of the Ozarks has its cruise boats too and they leave from *Casino Pier* near Bagnell Dam. Daytime trips and evening dance socials are available. Hannibal has *sternwheeler tours* on the Mississippi and a *train ride* around town, summer only.

**DRINKING LAWS.** Liquor may be bought by the drink from 6 A.M. to 1:30 A.M. on licensed premises ex. Sun., when they may serve 1 P.M. to midnight. Package sales are prohibited Sun.; other days they are legal 6A.M. to 1:30A.M. There are some restaurants which have package depts., but, by local options, cannot allow drinking on the premises.

**WHAT TO DO WITH THE CHILDREN.** Nevada has the *Bushwhacker Museum*, a former jail complete with inmates' graffiti and cuts, scrapings, chippings, and holes recording their efforts at escape. *Hannibal* has several houses, exhibits, and events of interest to readers of Mark Twain. Perhaps the most unusual is the *July Fence Painting Contest*, inspired by the riotously funny episode from Tom Sawyer. In St. Louis there is *Six Flags Over America*, a 200-acre amusement park whose themes include Spanish and French fur traders, English settlements, pioneer trading posts. There are a Runaway Mine Train ride and a log flume water ride. The park is open from 10 A.M. to 10P.M. Sun.–Fri. and to 11 P.M. Sat. from late May to Labor Day, and on weekends from mid-April to mid-May and in Sept. and Oct. Also in St. Louis: *Riverfront Trolley*, a narrated tour on a replica of the 1890's cable cars; the *Delta Queen*, a sternwheeler that makes weekend and longer trips on the Mississippi; 1 to 4 hr. *river excursions* on a replica of a 19th-century sternwheeler. *Silver Dollar City*, 7 mil. W of Branson, is a historic 1880 mining village with a steam train ride and float trip, a tree house, and Marvel Cave. Open daily 9:30 A.M.-7 P.M. from Memorial Day to Labor Day; open to 6 P.M. Wed.–Sun. in spring and fall.

**HOTELS AND MOTELS** outside greater Kansas City and St. Louis range from the lavish *Lodge of the Four Seasons* and *Tan-Tar-A Resort* in the Lake Ozark region to the clean and comfortable establishments to be found in the smaller towns. Price categories for double occupancy are divided as follows: *Deluxe* $30 and up, *Expensive* $20 to $30, *Moderate* $15 to $20 and *Inexpensive* below $15.

Hotels and motels in Kansas City and St. Louis cover the gamut from the inexpensive to the luxurious. Price categories in these two cities are divided as follows: *Deluxe* $30 and up, *Expensive* $20 to $30, *Moderate* $15 to $20 and *Inexpensive* below $15. For more complete explanation of these categories see *Facts at Your Fingertips.*

## COLUMBIA

**Hilton Inn.** *Deluxe.* On 18 acres adjacent to 18-hole golf course.

**Columbia Best Western Inn.** *Expensive.* Pool, restaurant.

**Holiday Inn.** *Expensive.* 2 locations. **East:** Providence Rd. & I–70; **West:** I–70 & Stadium Blvd. exit.

**Ramada Inn.** *Expensive.* Pool, restaurant.

**Tiger Motor Hotel.** *Expensive.* 120 rooms. Close to the M.U. campus. In existence since 1929.

**Howard Johnson's.** *Moderate.* Pool, playground.

## KANSAS CITY

**Alameda Plaza.** *Deluxe.* Wornall Road at Ward Parkway. Heated pool, restaurant and many amenities. Lovely grounds and from the rooftop dining rm. there is a superb view of the city. Free parking and baby sitter list.

**Breckenridge Inn.** *Deluxe.* 1601 N. Universal off I–435 N. Near Worlds of Fun. Heated indoor/outdoor pool, tennis, health club, restaurant.

**Crown Center.** *Deluxe.* 1 Pershing Rd. Heated pool, 24-hr. restaurant, baby sitter list, free garage, barber shop, beauty shop, drugstore, sauna, lawn games, tennis. A luxurious establishment.

**Granada Royale Hometel.** *Deluxe.* 220 W. 43 (north of the Country Club Plaza) 268 units, all suites, restaurant, heated indoor pool, sauna, steam room. Full breakfast and cocktails in evening included in price of a suite.

**Hilton Plaza Inn.** *Deluxe.* 45th and Main Sts. Restaurants, heated pool, barber shop, beauty shop. Well-kept, attractive spot.

**Marriott Hotel.** *Deluxe.* 241 Paris St. 13 mi. N of city at KCI airport. Elegant furnishings. Boating, indoor pool. two restaurants, lounge, nearby tennis facilities.

**Radisson Muehlebach.** *Deluxe.* Baltimore and Wyandotte at 12th St. A well-known, established spot with 24-hr. restaurant, rooftop pool, elegant tower rms., color TV, barber shop, beauty shop.

**Ramada Inn Central.** *Deluxe.* 610 Washington St. Heated pool, some patios and balconies add to the plush atmosphere.

**Raphael.** *Deluxe.* 325 Ward Parkway. Billed as Kansas City's "little elegant hotel." Many suites, gracious atmosphere. Walking distance from Country Club Plaza shops and restaurants. Free parking.

**Sheraton Royal.** *Deluxe.* I–70 at Sports Complex. Saunas, tennis.

**Continental.** *Expensive.* 106 W. 11th St. & Baltimore. Large indoor heated pool, restaurant, baby sitter list, barber shop.

**Executive.** *Expensive.* 509 W. 13th St. Pool, restaurant.

**Granada Inn.** *Expensive.* 115th and S. US 71. Air-conditioned rooms and suites. Steam baths, heated pool. Live entertainment.

**Heritage Inn (Best Western).** *Expensive.* 15201 S. 71 Highway, Grandview. 151 rooms. Restaurant, lounge, indoor heated pool.

**President Hotel.** *Expensive.* Baltimore and 14th Sts. A large, downtown hotel close to the Municipal Auditorium. A convention-goers favorite. Sauna, pets OK, restaurant.

**Prom Sheraton Motor Inn.** *Expensive.* 6th and Main Sts. Pool, restaurant, barber shop, beauty shop, baby sitter list. In the downtown area.

## LEXINGTON

**Holiday Inn.** *Expensive.* Set back from road.

## ST. LOUIS

**Breckenridge Pavilion Hotel.** *Deluxe.* 1 S. Broadway. A 24-story tower built atop the former Spanish Pavilion (moved to St. Louis from the N.Y. World's Fair). Across the street from Busch Memorial Stadium. Three dining rooms, night club, and theater with topnotch live entertainment, pool.

**Chase Park Plaza.** *Deluxe.* N. King's Hwy. at Lindell Blvd. One of the focal points of the social and business life of St. Louis, it has 5 restaurants, coffee shop, 24-hour shopping, pool, live entertainment.

**Lennox Hotel.** *Deluxe.* 9th & Washington St. 270 rooms. Lounge, restaurant, and piano bar.

**Marriot.** *Deluxe.* I–70 at Lambert Airport. 2 pools, sauna, tennis, 3 dining rms., barber shop, beauty shop, entertainment, exercise rm.

**Mayfair Hotel.** *Deluxe.* 806 St. Charles. In the heart of downtown. Recently re-opened after total remodeling. Bar, coffee shop, and restaurant.

**Rodeway Inn-Downtown.** *Deluxe.* 2600 Market St. at Jefferson. A good spot where the decor is Spanish. Pool, restaurant, live entertainment, some oversize beds.

**Sheraton St. Louis at Convention Plaza.** *Deluxe.* Sixth St. & Cass Ave.

Downtown's newest, this ultra-modern hostelry is located next to St. Louis' new convention center and anchors one corner of Convention Plaza East, an extensive commercial development on north edge of downtown area.

**Sheraton-West Port Inn.** *Deluxe.* I–270 & Page in West Port Plaza. Swiss Alpine decor, beautifully furnished rms. Plaza has many dining and entertainment places. 15 mi. west of downtown on outer belt bypass. Near Six Flags Over Mid-America.

**Stan Musial & Biggies' Hilton Inn.** *Deluxe.* 10330 Natural Bridge Rd. Pool, tennis, and shuffleboard, 3-hole golf course, 2 restaurants, live entertainment.

**Bel Air West.** *Expensive.* 4630 Lindell Blvd. Sauna, restaurant featuring German food.

**Breckenridge Hotel.** *Expensive.* Hwy 40 & Lindbergh Blvd. in west suburbs, adjacent to elegant Plaza Frontenac shopping mall (branches of famous stores such as Nieman Marcus, Saks, etc.) Excellent dining rm. Under 18 free. No pets.

**Cheshire Inn and Lodge.** *Expensive.* 6300 Clayton Rd. English decor with restaurant, pool, sauna and many amenities. Pets OK. Sitter list.

## SPRINGFIELD

**Holiday Inn.** *Expensive.* 2 pools.

**Howard Johnson's.** *Expensive.* 2 pools.

**Ramada Inn.** *Expensive.* Attractively decorated.

**Springfield Travelodge.** *Inexpensive.* Pool.

 **DINING OUT** in Missouri can provide unique experience to anyone willing to go off the beaten track. Eating in a plush dining room overlooking the Lake of the Ozarks is a real pleasure but so is sitting down to a plain table of simple, good food. Price categories are divided as follows: *Deluxe* $10 and up. *Expensive* $8 to $10. *Moderate* $5 to $7.50 and *Inexpensive* below $5. For a more complete explanation of restaurant categories refer to *Facts at Your Fingertips.*

## ARROW ROCK

**OLD TAVERN.** *Moderate.* Built around 1834, operated by DAR. Early American decor.

## COLUMBIA

**Katy's Station.** *Expensive.* 402 E. Broadway. In remodeled railroad station dated 1909. Steaks, prime rib, crab.

## HIGGINSVILLE

**Apprill's Oak Barn.** *Moderate.* Jct. of I–70 and Mo. 13. Hitching rails and old farm implements decorate the restored oak barn built about 1917. Barbecued chicken, chops, brisket and ribs are specialties. Homemade barbecue sauce and cinnamon rolls are features.

## JANE

**Stephenson's Cider Mill Restaurant.** *Moderate.* US 71 at Mo. 90. At the Arkansas line near Bella Vista. Rustic atmosphere. Hickory-smoked meats and homemade apple dumpling and apple butter are specialties.

## KANSAS CITY

**SAVOY GRILL.** *Deluxe.* Old-line eating place.

**Dolce's Highland View Farm.** *Expensive.* 1333 N.E. Barry Rd. American cooking in 143-year-old restored antebellum mansion.

**GOLDEN OX.** *Expensive.* Stockyard environment.

**HEREFORD HOUSE.** *Expensive.* Western style.

**Sandy's Oak Ridge Manor.** *Moderate.* 5410 N.E. Oak Ridge Road in Clay County. German and American food served family-style in 10-room farmhouse and restored log cabin dated 1829. Dinner only.

**Stephenson's Apple Farm.** *Moderate.* US 40 at Lee's Summit Rd. Hickory-smoked chicken and meats and homemade apple butter and dumplings. Establishment began as roadside apple stand in an orchard. Rustic atmosphere.

**Stephenson's Apple Tree Inn.** *Moderate.* 5755 N.W. Northwood Rd. Run by same family and similar theme as Apple Farm.

## NEVADA

**Deli 1.** *Inexpensive.* In the old Nevada Hotel built in 1925. Original oak counter and fixtures and marble soda fountain. Deli-type sandwiches, salads and desserts. Lunch only.

## ST. GENEVIEVE

**OLD BRICK HOUSE.** *Expensive.* 180-year-old building with ancient brick walls.

## ST. LOUIS

**BALABAN'S.** *Deluxe.* 405 N. Euclid Ave. Victorian decor.

**BAYOU BELLE.** *Deluxe.* 12341 St. Charles Rock Rd. Nautical atmosphere in paddlewheel boat.

**SCHOBER'S WINE RESTAURANT.** *Deluxe.* 6925 S. Lindbergh Blvd. German-American menu. Old German decor.

**LA SALA.** *Moderate.* 513 Olive St. Early Mexican decor.

## SEDALIA

**OLD MISSOURI HOMESTEAD.** *Expensive.* Rock garden, fountain, fireplace.

## WRIGHT CITY

**BIG BOY'S.** *Expensive.* Old Missouri paintings.

# NEW MEXICO

## *The Confederate's Farthest Gamble*

### by

### BERN KEATING

From the day that the Thirteen Colonies formed a new nation called the United States, Southern dreamers flirted with the idea of splitting away from the North and snapping up the northern states of Mexico and a strip across the continent to the Pacific as a mighty slave-owning empire. When Texas left the Union in 1861, the first part of the dream had come true; Texans began to look westward with a speculative eye, the old dream of empire reawakened.

Besides, the gold and silver of California, Arizona and New Mexico were desperately needed by the fledgling country that couldn't persuade anybody to accept its paper shinplasters.

But standing between Texas and the gold and silver mines was New Mexico, the roadblock to empire.

On July 23, 1861, Lt. Col. John R. Baylor entered New Mexico from El Paso leading a ragtag and bobtail force of about 250 cowboys armed with six-shooters, shotguns, squirrel rifles, tomahawks and bowie knives. They were welcomed into the town of Mesilla by Southern sympathizers.

About 700 Union Regular Army troops from nearby Fort Fillmore fought a brisk skirmish with the Texans and fell back to the fort to spend the night. Unaccountably, though the Union Regulars far outnumbered the Texans and were far better trained and equipped, the morning after their skirmish the Union force fled northward. Their commanding officer was having an outdoor lunch on a table covered with fine linen when the cowboys caught up with them. Apparently he had more stomach for dining than for fighting, because he immediately surrendered his whole force and wagon train over the violent protests of his officers.

On August 1, 1861, Col. Baylor proclaimed all the land south of the thirty-fourth parallel to be the Confederate Territory of Arizona. The territory would stretch to the Pacific, and its capital would be Mesilla.

Today Mesilla is a charming village two miles southwest of Las Cruces. It was already a historic spot when Baylor elevated it to a territorial capital, for Mexico and the United States had signed the Gadsden Treaty there in 1853. Today the central plaza and the buildings around it are designated La Mesilla State Monument.

Back in Texas, Henry Hopkins Sibley had defected from the U.S. Army to the Confederacy and had been named brigadier general to head a campaign into New Mexico. Sibley had been a brilliant engineering officer in the U.S. Army, but he had a drinking problem. He had little trouble, however, in raising a brigade of cowboys armed with the same haphazard collection of weapons Baylor's men had used to frighten the Union commander of Fort Fillmore into surrendering. Sibley took command from Baylor of the Confederate force in New Mexico and moved northward from Mesilla.

Opposing Sibley was Col. Edward Canby, who was at Santa Fe hurriedly scratching together a force of mixed Regulars and volunteers. He called on the governor of Colorado to send reinforcements, and two companies of hardrock miners and frontiersmen began training. More serious problems for Sibley were the sullen passive resistance of the New Mexicans, who loathed Texans; the uselessness of their paper money, which nobody would accept; and the hostility of the New Mexican desert.

Colonel Canby marched a strong force into Fort Craig on the Rio Grande about 30 miles south of Socorro, squarely across the path of the invaders. The Confederates challenged the Yankees to come out and fight in the open, a challenge prudently refused. The Confederates crossed to the east bank and camped opposite the fort.

Colonel Canby had rightly judged that the desert was his best ally and told his officers that every Confederate horse or mule killed or captured, every wagon of supplies destroyed was a victory to be celebrated. He had studied Napoleon's catastrophic Russian campaign and set about scorching the earth to strand Sibley without adequate supplies for the harsh New Mexican winter.

To carry out the plan, Capt. Paddy Graydon, a tough Arizona frontiersman, strapped boxes filled with howitzer shells to the backs of two old mules and stealthily approached the Confederate picket lines. Lighting the fuses, he spanked the mules on the rump, assuming they would join their Southern cousins and blow them all to tartar steak. To his horror, the mules felt cosier with him and refused to leave his side. He galloped off in terror, the mules close on his heels until they vanished in a dazzling blast. Graydon miraculously was spared.

His harebrained scheme did work, however. About 200 mules, frightened by the blast, tore up their picket pins and fled to the river where they were captured by Union troops. This severe blow forced Sibley to abandon several wagons and their stores.

On February 21, 1862, the Confederates marched to Valverde, about seven miles upstream from the fort. To prevent their crossing to the more convenient western bank, Canby drew up his army facing Sibley across the stream. After a ferocious battle with frightful casualties on both sides, Canby conceded defeat and retreated to the fort. Officers had to awaken Sibley from a drunken nap in an ambulance to tell him of his victory. The Confederates then bypassed the fort and moved north again.

Fort Craig stands in ruins today, four miles east of US 85, on a gravel road thirty miles south of Socorro. The battlefield of Valverde is on the east bank of the Rio Grande seven miles north of there and near San Marcial Lake. It is now on private property.

The Texans reached Albuquerque on March 2, 1862, but found that its huge depot of military stores had been burned. On March 13, 1862, Sibley raised the Confederate flag in Santa Fe over the Palace of the Governors, then the seat of government. Now it is a splendid archaeological museum and the oldest public building north of Mexico.

Though the Texans were short of supplies, they went on a senseless orgy of burning and destruction of the very materials they would desperately need within a few days.

Northeast of Santa Fe stood Fort Union, near the Colorado line at Raton Pass. Sibley had to have the huge supply of military stores stocked there, and he knew he outnumbered the meager garrison. The alarmed fort's commandant called on the governor of Colorado for reinforcements. He dispatched the First Regiment of Colorado Volunteers.

A courier met the column of volunteers on the road with the startling information that Albuquerque and Santa Fe had already fallen to the Texans and Fort Union was under immediate threat. The men petitioned their officers to force the march. They discarded all gear but weapons and blankets, and hit the road again, though they had just marched a prodigious 92 miles in 36 hours.

A blizzard struck them at the summit of the pass, but they pressed on. When they arrived at the fort on March 10, 1862, they had marched 400 miles in 13 days, most of that on a rough mountain path in a blizzard. In fact, many of their horses and mules had dropped dead from exhaustion.

After issuance of standard army equipment and 13 days of drill, the garrison marched out of the fort headed for a collision with the cowboy troops coming from Santa Fe.

Fort Union had been built to guard the Santa Fe Trail. That famed roadway ran by the fort through Apache Canyon, at the western end of Glorieta Pass toward the train terminal in Santa Fe Plaza, which still graces the center of the city looking just as it did then.

The miners met a cowboy advance party in Apache Canyon. The first day of battle went in favor of the Colorado volunteers, but Union officers knew strong Confederate reinforcements were on the way, so they fell back and camped for the night at Pigeon's Ranch, which still stands. Nearby atop a bluff is a boulder displaying a plaque that recounts the events of the battle.

The Confederate main body assembled at Johnson's Ranch, today called Canyoncito. It hurried forward in a night march to reinforce its badly mauled vanguard.

Though the Union battle lines had also been reinforced, the miners were outnumbered. The next battle was desperately fought and not going well for the Union. A small detachment of Union soldiers slipped through back trails in the mountains and fell on the Confederate wagon train at Canyoncito, killing 1,000 horses and mules and burning all the stores the Texans depended on to stay alive in that hostile country.

The destruction of the wagon train was decisive. The Texas foray into New Mexico had been a steady series of overwhelming victories, but wound up in total defeat. Canby's scorched earth policy had won, and the Texas invasion collapsed.

Motorists today can drive down US 84 about 19 miles from Santa Fe to Glorieta Pass. Just beyond the village of Galisteo, turn left to Pecos National Monument, 1½ miles off the main road. Here stand the ruins of an early Spanish mission and Indian pueblo. About these ruins in 1862, the Colorado miners thrust back the Texas cowboys and ended the threat of the Confederacy to capture the riches of the Far West. The ruins of Fort Union are now a national monument near Valmora on US 85 beyond Las Vegas.

While white men fought each other, the Apaches, Navahoes and Comanches ravaged the frontier. After the retreat of the Texans, the Union Army's main concern in the Far West was putting down Indian depredations. Chief among the Indian fighters was the New Mexican Kit Carson, who pursued Canby's tactics of scorching the earth. He starved the Indians into submission and forced them to move into reservations. Today his home is a museum in Taos. Around his grave a short distance away is a memorial park with picnic area and playground. In the winter there is ice skating in the park.

## PRACTICAL INFORMATION FOR NEW MEXICO

**FACTS AND FIGURES.** The state's name is derived from the Aztec god Mexitli. It's nickname is "The Land of Enchantment." The yucca is the state flower, the roadrunner the state bird, the piñon the state tree, and *Cresit eundo* (it grows as it goes) is the state motto.

By the latest census the population is 1,133,000. Santa Fe is the state capital. Elevations within New Mexico range from 2,850 feet above sea level up to 13,151 feet—a fact that also gives the state a wide range of climate. While second to Arizona in year-round sunshine, it has the nation's sunniest winters.

Racially, its population is 90.1 percent white, 7.2 percent Indian and 2.7 percent other nonwhite. Ethnically, however, it has a Hispano (Spanish and Mexican-American) population of about 40 percent, and the state's culture strongly reflects this Spanish colonial heritage.

**TOURIST INFORMATION.** Brochures and information are available from the Tourist Division, Dept. of Tourism, 113 Washington Ave., Santa Fe, NM 87503, phone 800-545-9876. They will provide free of charge an information packet, maps and a calendar of events.

**STATE PARKS.** New Mexico is well endowed with thirty-four state parks, of which 12 are products of the state's recent campaign to improve its attractiveness to tourists. Seventeen are based on lakes, most of the others include streams, and all but two have facilities for camping. Service fees are similar throughout the system, with the charge for camping $2 or $3 if utility hook-ups are available, even if not used by the campers. If no facilities are used, there's no charge. Several of the parks are unusual. Among them is *Rio Grande Gorge,* which stretches seventy mi. S from the Colorado border to Velarde along the Rio Grande Canyon. The stream was one of the first to receive the federal "wild river" designation, but a preexisting highway (US 64) parallels several miles of it, as does State 96. The upper end is less easily reached, but there is access to the rim on an improved road northwest of Questa. The canyon is spectacular, and the lower reaches of the river offer safe rafting possibilities after the spring runoff season.

There are a number of state parks close to Civil War sites. Those in the northern part of the state include *Morphy,* thirty-one mi. N of Las Vegas; *Kit Carson Memorial,* at the site of the frontiersman's grave in Taos; Santa Fe's winding and shady *River Park,* which spreads through downtown and past the capitol building; *Villanueva,* at the old riverside village of that name, thirty-three mi. S of Las Vegas; the *Coronado Park,* at the site of the ruined pueblo where the explorer made his first base, fifteen mi. N of Albuquerque; *Indian Petroglyph Park,* on the Albuquerque "west mesa"; and San Gabriel park in Albuquerque's north valley. The Truth or Consequences area includes in the southern part of the state *Caballo Lake Park, Elephant Butte,* and *Percha Dam,* on the Rio Grande lakes. Also on the Rio Grande is *Leasburg Dam Park,* thirteen mi. N of Las Cruces.

**CAMPING OUT.** There are camping and trailer parking facilities throughout New Mexico. Hundreds of camp-sites are available in the national forest, for example, and can be reached within a few hours from almost any spot in the state.

In addition, campsites are provided in areas managed by the U.S. National Park Service and by the Bureaus of Land Management, Indian Affairs, Reclamation and Sports-Fisheries and Wildlife.

There are also camping areas under the jurisdiction of the New Mexico Department of Game and Fish and the State Park and Recreation Commission.

Many municipalities have also arranged to have camping areas for visitors, and there are a number of private campgrounds.

**DRINKING LAWS.** Liquor, beer, wine retailers and dispensers are open daily, except Sundays. Maximum hours, 7 A.M. to 2 A.M. Proof of age required. Age limit is 21, or 18 when accompanied by parent, legal guardian, or spouse of legal age. Sundays, by local option, liquor served by drink only, noon to midnight.

 **HOTELS AND MOTELS.** New Mexico and other less populous states of the Southwest had a deserved reputation for inadequate overnight facilities. The rapid rise of the tourist industry in the state and the spread of the motel chains, however, have eliminated this situation. Accommodations now range from American-Standard in towns of little tourist interest, to colorful, charming, and unique in places like Taos and Santa Fe. In all these places, however, it's a good idea to have reservations. It's not at all uncommon to see nothing but NO VACANCY signs in Santa Fe on a summer evening. Cost figures are generally for moderately priced rooms unless a range is indicated. Listings are in order of price category.

The price categories in this section, for double occupancy, will average as follows: *Deluxe $24, Expensive $18, Moderate $14,* and *Inexpensive $10.* For a more complete description of these categories see *Facts at Your Fingertips.*

## ALBUQUERQUE

**Rodeway Inn–Old Town.** 1015 Rio Grande Blvd. N.W. Handy to the old town preserved from pioneer days.

**Sheraton–Old Town Inn.** 800 Rio Grande Blvd. N.W. Within the area occupied by Texas troops more than a century ago.

## LAS CRUCES

**Holiday Inn.** 201 University Plaza. Civil War–style saloon. Patio is duplicate of Mexican town plaza.

## LAS VEGAS

**Best Western Town House.** 1215 N. Grand Ave. Near Fort Union, Pecos Monument and the Glorieta Battlefield.

## RATON

**Holiday Inn.** Clayton Rd. On the Santa Fe Trail near the pass where the Colorado Volunteers set the all-time record for forced marches.

## SANTA FE

**Inn of the Governors.** *Expensive.* 234 Don Gaspar Ave. at the Alameda. On the Santa Fe River Park, adjoining capitol, within three blocks of the Plaza. A lovely example of what can be done with Santa Fe's historic architecture. Rooms have both air conditioning and fireplaces. Pool, patio dining, restaurant, bar, atmosphere.

**La Fonda.** *Expensive.* 100 E. San Francisco. One of the most historic hotels in the West, once used by Santa Fe Trail drivers. At the corner of the Plaza, a huge, cool, interesting old pile built around a central patio and offering the ultimate in Santa Fe atmosphere. Pool, beauty and barber shops, travel services, and gift shops, excellent restaurant and bar.

 **DINING OUT.** In theory, traditional dishes of New Mexico are Mexican—enchiladas, tacos, burritos, and a variety of other applications of green chiles, corn meal, fried breads, pinto beans, and pork. As a matter of fact, as anyone who has traveled extensively on both sides of the border has learned, the years have brought a unique evolution to New Mexican recipes. Something as simple as a "bowl of chile" is as different in Mexico and New Mexico as it is in New Mexico and Texas. A Santa Fe enchilada is hardly third cousin to a Chihuahua enchilada. In New Mexico traditional dishes have come to blend Spanish, Indian, and Anglo-American.

Restaurant price categories are as follows: *Deluxe* $10 and up, *Expensive* $8–$10, *Moderate* $5–$7.50, and *Inexpensive* $3–$4.50. These prices are for hors d'oeuvres or soup, entree and dessert. Not included are drinks, tax and tips. For a more complete explanation of restaurant categories refer to *Facts at Your Fingertips*.

## ALBUQUERQUE

**CASA VIEJA.** *Expensive*. In Corrales (about 20 min. drive northwest of town). Literally the "Old House," the dining room is set in a 200-year-old house with adobe walls two feet thick. A historical atmosphere pervades the entire place, and the general feeling is a return to bygone days. The food is excellent.

**LA HACIENDA.** Old Town Plaza. Reeking with atmosphere. Mexican menu.

**LA PLACITA.** Old Town Plaza. Hacienda dating from Spanish rule days. Superb New Mexican version of Mexican menu.

## LAS CRUCES

**LA POSTA.** Near Mesilla. Converted Butterfield Stage Coach Lines station.

## SANTA FE

**EL FAROL.** *Expensive*. Mexican-American cuisine. Rustic decor.

**THE PALACE.** *Expensive*. The luxurious, Viennese-style velvet interior is housed in a historic building near the Santa Fe Plaza. Seafood is a specialty. A restored Western saloon adjoins the premises.

**THE LEGAL TENDER.** *Expensive*. Lamy, 18 mi. SE of Santa Fe on I-25. An authentic old saloon located in a genuine ghost town. The long, traditional bar is staffed by girls in the dance hall costumes of 100 years ago. Reservations necessary.

**THE STEAK SMITH.** *Expensive*. Old Vargas Hotel. The dining room has been restored to resemble an old forge. The menus are made of wrought iron and feature steaks, naturally.

**The Compound.** *Expensive*. Stunning rancho-style architecture.

**Ernie's.** *Expensive*. Adobe building with patio.

**Pink Adobe.** Fireplaces, music.

**RANCHO DE CHIMAYO.** *Expensive*. 28 miles from Santa Fe in pictur-esque Chimayo. An old hacienda. Cuisine of first order.

**FORGE RESTAURANT.** *Moderate*. In the Inn of the Governors. Tradi-tional Spanish decor unusually well handled, with a lovely dining patio. Mexican and American menus, bar.

**LA TERTULIA.** *Moderate*. Across from the Guadalupe Church. New Mexico menu served in an old adobe building. Great cooking.

**Grand Central Station.** *Moderate*. Converted gas station. Dining outdoors in summer. Guitarists. French crepes and quiches. Standing-room-only at lunch.

**La Cocina.** *Moderate*. Mexican menu. Patio dining.

**Periscope.** *Moderate*. Italian and French cuisine. Adobe with wooden floor. Possibly best in Santa Fe but serves lunch only.

**The Palace Swiss Bakery.** *Moderate*. Also a restaurant. Pizza made from fresh tomatoes. Soup and sandwiches. Pastry tray.

**Guadelupe Cafe.** *Inexpensive*. Green enchiladas and other New Mexican cuisine.

## TAOS

**LA DONA LUZ.** *Expensive*. One of the state's most famous restaurants. Excellent European cooking in a colorful old setting across from the Kit Carson Memorial Museum.

**El Pinto.** *Moderate*. Spanish decor, Mexican food.

**Michaels Kitchen.** *Inexpensive*. Sturdy fare, especially good for breakfast. Own bakery.

## TRUTH OR CONSEQUENCES

**LOS ARCOS STEAK HOUSE.** *Expensive*. Steak, lobster tails. Mexican decor.

# NORTH CAROLINA

## Fort Fisher and the Blockade

by

### JOHN PHILLIPS

*John Phillips is a native North Carolinian living in Raleigh. He is in the staff of* State Magazine, *vice-president of the North Carolina Travel Council, and is on its Board of Directors.*

North Carolina, a slumbering giant, started awakening in the early to mid-1800s with the building of roads, public schools, ports and cotton mills. During these years there were numerous free negroes, many of them skilled craftsmen. North Carolina was coming into its own just before the Civil War.

She shared with other Southern states the problems which brought war even though many of her people were devoted to the Union. She believed in states' rights, but refused to join Virginia in a protest against the Alien and Sedition Acts of 1798 and refused to endorse South Carolina's nullification of federal tariff laws in 1832–33. For the most part, North Carolina did align herself with the South in disputes with the North. When President Lincoln asked for troops to attack Southern States, Gov. John W. Ellis replied, "You can get no troops from North Carolina."

North Carolina was the last Confederate state to secede from the Union—on May 20, 1861—and re-entered it in 1868. Among seceding states she ranked third in population. One-sixth of the soldiers in the Confederate Army were "Tar Heels," and one out of every four casualties was from North Carolina, a higher percentage than from any other state.

Most of these young men lost their lives fighting in other states. There were few major battles fought on North Carolina soil. The state furnished food, supplies and men.

One of the most dramatic chapters in Civil War history was that of the blockade runners, who supplied the Confederacy through the port of Wilmington until the fall of Fort Fisher on the Cape Fear River in 1865.

In March, 1864, the largest battle ever fought on North Carolina soil took place in Bentonville near the small town of Newton Grove. It was a battle of desperation, and the last major engagement of the Civil War.

North Carolina was under federal military authority during the Reconstruction years. The Republican Party controlled the government and drew up a new state constitution that abolished slavery. The Civil War brought not only death and destruction to the state but also caused many of the large plantations to be divided into small farms due to the lack of labor. The North Carolinians quickly rebuilt their state, and by 1880 had equaled its farm production of the pre-Civil War days.

## Fort Fisher and South

South of Carolina Beach are the smaller resorts of Wilmington Beach, Kure Beach and Fort Fisher State Historic Site. At Fort Fisher, a museum displays ammunition, weapons and other artifacts brought up from the submerged wrecks of Confederate blockade runners close to shore. Several embankments and gun emplacements of the Fort have been marked. The largest land-sea battle in history, up to that time, took place at Fort Fisher in January, 1865. Below Fort Fisher, US 421 dead-ends at the Rocks, a breakwater built in 1875–81 to close the New Inlet and save Wilmington's harbor by insuring a sufficient depth over the main bar at the mouth of Cape Fear. There is automobile ferry service between Fort Fisher and Southport.

The Blockade Runner Museum, on US 421 at Carolina Beach, offers exciting surprises for those who think they don't like museums. It was presented a national award in 1967 as an outstanding contribution to national, state and local history. The museum presents the story of how over 2,000 ships attempted the Carolina ports through the Northern blockade, how the massive fort sought to protect them as they approached the coast and what the city was like that received the vital supplies which meant so much to the Confederacy. The presentation is done with dioramas, each with its own tape explaining the action, displaying expertly crafted models of ships that were twenty years ahead of their time. The highlight of a visit to the museum is the forty-foot diorama of Fort Fisher. The history of the fort and the blockade is presented in a fifteen-minute narration accompanied by martial music, projected pictures, the sounds of battle and smoke from the guns of the fleet. It is open all year and well worth a visit.

## Brunswick

On the east side of lower Cape Fear River in Brunswick County, the town of Brunswick was founded in 1725. It was a flourishing river port until the American Revolution, when it was partly burned by the British. After the Revolution, the town never recovered, and it became extinct about 1830. Walls of St. Philip's Church and numerous house foundations remain. Also remaining are the massive works of Fort Anderson, a Civil War fortification erected by the Confederates; they have been improved for exhibit. There are historical markers in the area and trailside exhibits, plus a visitor-center museum off Hwy. 133 south of Wilmington.

Fort Caswell, constructed in 1825 and manned during the Civil, Spanish-American and both World Wars, is a religious assembly grounds operated by the Baptists of North Carolina. Many of its frame buildings are in use.

## Central Coast

North of Wilmington is the port of Morehead City. Near Morehead is Fort Macon State Park at Atlantic Beach. The fort played a significant role in the Revolutionary and Civil wars. The park offers picnic facilities and a bathing beach, as well as the historic fort museum.

## New Bern, a Colonial Capital

New Bern, settled in 1710, is the second-oldest town in North Carolina. Here, the first permanent colonial capital, the first state capitol building has been restored to its original elegance, and it is open (except Mondays) to visitors all year. Now known as the Tryon Palace Restoration, its gardens are on the site where Governor William Tryon supervised construction of a "seat of government and residence of the royal governor." New Bern was captured by the Union forces early in the Civil War, but the town survived the war with little damage. This old town is a historian's delight, where one can go back 200 years into the nation's past. The Fireman's Museum with horse-drawn fire equipment, the John Wright Stanly House of the 1770's and numerous other structures of classic Georgian architecture executed in brick and wood are also in New Bern.

## Kinston

In Kinston, one of several eastern towns captured early in the war, Civil War buffs can see the hull of the only Confederate ship built in North Carolina, the CSS *Neuse*. She is the largest remaining Confederate naval vessel and can be seen at the Gov. Richard Caswell Memorial historic site off US 70A, 2 mi. W of Kinston. The site is open year-round Mon.–Fri. from 9 a.m. to 5 p.m. and weekends from 1 to 5 p.m.

### Smithfield–Newfield Grove–Godwin

On N.C. Hwy. 82 north of the small rural town of Godwin is the Averasboro Battleground. It was here a small Confederate force under Gen. W. J. Hardee resisted a wing of Sherman's troops under General Slocum. The Confederates were defeated, but this battle set the stage for the Battle of Bentonville. Map markers located in the area describe the battle.

On US 701 off I–95, approximately 20 miles south of Smithfield at the town of Newton Grove, is the Bentonville Battleground with a Visitor Center, nearby Confederate cemetery and the Harper House. The home of John and Amy Harper was used as a field hospital by the Union; and after the Battle of Bentonville it became a hospital serving the Confederate wounded. The Harper House has been preserved and furnished circa-1865.

### Battle of Bentonville

Gen. Joseph E. Johnston hoped to stop General Sherman who had captured Fayetteville and skirmished with Confederate troops at Averasboro, about 30 miles north. Sherman's troops were led by General Slocum. The Confederates were defeated at Averasboro, and the Union forces moved north to Bentonville, General Sherman commanding 60,000 troops and Johnston commanding 30,000 Confederates. Bad roads forced two wings of Sherman's troops to become separated by a half day's march. Johnston heard this and took his troops toward Bentonville hoping to capture one wing of Sherman's army. The right wing fell into Johnston's trap, but the Confederates did not overrun the Union line before darkness. The following morning the remainder of Sherman's troops arrived, and the fight continued for two days. On March 21 the Confederate troops started their withdrawal. The "Battle of Desperation" was over.

### Raleigh

In the Archives Building on Jones St. is the North Carolina Museum of History, which houses many artifacts from the Civil War. One block south is the State Capitol. On the grounds is a statue of

Henry L. Wyatt of Tarboro who, at twenty years of age, was the first Confederate soldier killed in battle in the Civil War.

About one mile from Raleigh's Capitol Square is the Andrew Johnson House, a tiny gambrell-roofed building where the 17th President was born. This historic shrine is located in Mordecai Park on Person St. and is open to the public. On N. Blount St., two blocks from the Capitol is the official residence of North Carolina's, governors. This "gingerbread" mansion (1880's) has been restored recently and is adjacent to Historic Oakwood, a section where many homes of the same era have been restored. Raleigh has a marked "Capital City Trail" keyed to a leaflet describing points of interest.

## Durham

Durham, only twenty-three miles from the capital, is a ranking industrial center, leading tobacco market of the Middle Belt and home of Duke University, one of the largest institutions of higher learning in the Southeast. The history of Durham is a fascinating chapter of the "American success story." Durham was only a small village when, in 1865, General W.T. Sherman received the surrender of General Joseph E. Johnston a few miles west at Bennet Place, a historic site off US 70 W and open all year. Among the Durham County residents mustered out of the Confederate Army when the Civil War ended was Washington Duke, who walked 137 miles home to his farm to begin civilian life again. The Dukes, like most of their neighbors, grew tobacco. Washington Duke began grinding tobacco which he packaged and sold. By 1874, Duke and his three sons were established in Durham as manufacturers of smoking tobacco. Within a few years, they were producing cigarettes for domestic sale and export; the growth of the huge American Tobacco empire and other manufacturing enterprises began in their city. It has been said that James B. Duke did with tobacco what Rockefeller did with oil and Carnegie with steel. He endowed the University (formerly Trinity College), which bears his family name and is principal beneficiary of the Duke Endowment.

Duke University has a Gothic West Campus and Georgian East Campus on 7,500 acres of rolling land a few miles west of Durham. Duke Chapel, a Gothic structure, has a spire rising 210 feet above the West Campus. Nearby are the Sarah P. Duke Memorial Gardens with extensive formal and informal landscaping. The gardens offer a succession of blooms from early spring through late autumn.

The Duke family homestead, three miles north of Durham via US 501, is a small white frame dwelling built in 1851 by Washington Duke. Restored and containing its original furnishings, it is open on Sunday afternoons, April through September.

## Weaverville

In the western section of the state, near the resort city of

Asheville, is Weaverville. Here is located the Appalachian mountain home of the "War Governor of the South", Zebulon Baird Vance. Through his leadership and motivation, North Carolina made great contributions in men and spirit to the Southern cause. The home and other log buildings are preserved and nearby is a visitor center and museum portraying Governor Vance's life. This State Historic Site is open from 9 to 5 Tuesday–Saturday and from 1 to 5 on Sundays. There is a picnic area for visitors. The area can be reached by Business US 19 to State Road 1103.

## PRACTICAL INFORMATION FOR NORTH CAROLINA

 **FACTS AND FIGURES.** The state was named for Charles I of England. Its nicknames are the "Old North State" and the "Tar Heel State." The state flower is the dogwood; the cardinal is the state bird. *Esse Quam Videri* ("To be, rather than to seem") is the state motto. Raleigh is the state capital, and the population of North Carolina is 5,082,059.

 **HOW TO GET THERE.** *By air:* Raleigh-Durham, Charlotte and Greensboro may be reached by direct flights of Delta, Eastern, Piedmont and United from various cities in the U.S. In addition, Southern flies into Charlotte. United and Piedmont have direct flights into Asheville; Piedmont into Fayetteville, Goldsboro, Hickory, Jacksonville, Kinston, New Bern, Rocky Mount, Wilmington and Winston Salem from out of the state. Limousine service available at all airports.

Out of Montreal, Eastern has direct service to Charlotte; Eastern and Nordair connecting flights out of Hamilton. Greensboro may be reached from Montreal on Allegheny, Eastern and Piedmont connecting flights. Air Canada and Eastern connecting flights go into Raleigh out of Montreal.

*By train:* Amtrak trains go into Rocky Mount, Raleigh, Fayetteville, Hamlet and Pinehurst. Southern Railway also has passenger service.

*By car:* A tourist is given a taste of "Tar Heel" hospitality at the state's lovely Welcome Centers located on I–95 and I–85 on the Virginia and South Carolina state lines and on I-40 on the Tennessee line. I–26 and I–77 come in from South Carolina.

*By bus:* Good service by Greyhound and Trailways. Ingram Bus Lines also go into Charlotte.

 **HOW TO GET AROUND.** *By air:* Delta, Eastern, Piedmont, United and Commuter airlines have flights within the state. There is local service into Morehead City and Pinehurst. Limousine service available at all airports.

*By car:* North Carolina's state-administered highway system has more than 75,000 mi. of roads and bridges, all toll-free. I–26, I–40, I–77, I–85 and I–95, as well as US 17, US 19, US 64–264, US 70, US 220, US 221, US 258 and US 421 all have delightful rest areas with picnic tables and barbecues.

*By ferry:* The state operates toll-free ferries daily across Currituck Sound from Currituck to Knotts Island, Hatteras Inlet, Pamlico River, at Bayview, and Neuse River, at Minnesott Beach. Toll ferry service is available from Cedar Island to Ocracoke Island and Southport to Ft. Fisher. All state ferries carry automobiles.

*By bus:* In addition to Greyhound and Trailways, Seashore Transportation Co. operates within the state.

 **TOURIST INFORMATION.** For information regarding historical points of interest, write to Historic Sites, N.C. Dept. of Cultural Resources, Div. of Archives and History, Raleigh, N.C. and also to the N.C. Travel Division, Dept. of Commerce, Raleigh, N.C. 27611. A pamphlet listing vacation events in North Carolina can be obtained by writing: "N.C. Calendar of Events" from the Travel Division. The N.C. Dept. of Transportation, Raleigh, N.C. 27611, can supply ferry information and highway-condition bulletins.

Welcome Centers are located on I–95 and I–85 on the Virginia and S.C. state lines and on I–40 on the Tennessee line.

 **STATE PARKS AND FORESTS.** North Carolina's twenty-seven State Parks and two nature preserves range from mountaintop to seacoast. The five listed below are located near the state's Civil War Historic Sites. All are open year-round, daily and Sunday. For more specific information write to Dept. of Natural Resources & Community Development, Division of State Parks, P.O. Box 27687, Raleigh, N.C. 27611, or call 919/733-4181. All State Parks are wildlife sanctuaries. Firearms are prohibited.

*Carolina Beach*—Formerly known as Masonboro State Park—15 mi. S. of Wilmington, at junction of Intracoastal Waterway and the Cape Fear River. A naturalist's delight. The Venus Fly Trap is endemic to this area. Year-round tent-trailer camping, fishing, boating, nature study, hiking & picnicking.

*Cliffs of The Neuse*—In Wayne Co., 14 mi. SE of Goldsboro off N.C. 111. Scenic, recreation, picnicking, swimming, tent, trailer & organized camping, boat rentals, fishing, hiking, nature study & museum.

*Fort Macon*—on Bogue Island, opposite Morehead City and Beaufort, 4 mi. from Atlantic Beach, via US 70 and State road. Historic Fort with museum, bathing, beach, surf fishing, picknicking, snack bar.

*Raven Rock*—In Harnett County, 6 mi. W of Lillington on US 421, then 3 mi. N by Rte. 1250. Outstanding 125-ft. rock formation on south bank, at "fall line" of Cape Fear River. Mountain-type trees and shrubs. Undeveloped. Picnicking, hiking, nature study, fishing in Cape Fear River.

*William B. Umstead (Crabtree Creek Section)*—12 mi. NW of Raleigh on US 70. Tent-trailer camping, organized group camping, picnicking, boating, fishing, hiking, nature study.

*William B. Umstead (Reedy Creek Section)*—10 mi. NW of Raleigh near Cary, off US 70–A & Rte. 54, also I–40. Picnicking, organized group camping, fishing, hiking, nature study.

 **CAMPING OUT.** There are many campgrounds in North Carolina, and visitors to the Tar Heel State can write to the Travel Division, Department of Commerce, Raleigh, N.C. 27611 for brochures listing these campgrounds.

 **MUSEUMS AND GALLERIES. Historical:** *Museum of History* in N.C. Archives Building, 109 E. Jones St., Raleigh. Closed national holidays. A historical museum in the *Burgwin-Wright House and Garden (1771).*

*Admission charge.* **Wilmington-New Hanover Museum,** *814 Market St., Wilmington. Regional History museum. Closed Mon. and national holidays.*

**Special Interest Museums:** *Blockade Runner Museum,* on US 421, Carolina Beach. Year around. Admission charge. *Museum of the Cherokee Indian,* US 441, Cherokee. Open year around. Admission charge.

**HISTORIC SITES.** *Historic Bath State Historic Site,* Bath. Admission charge. *Fort Fisher State Historic Site,* on US 421, 6 mi. S of Carolina Beach. Coastal defense fort that provided protection for Confederate blockade runners. Visitor center museum. Daily, all year. *Somerset Place State Historic Site,* Creswell. *Bennett Place State Historic Site,* Durham, has a visitor center and is open Sept to May wknds., during June to Aug. Tues. to Sat.; The Bennett House is also open to visitors. *Market House,* Market Square, Fayetteville, open on a restricted basis. A square building with cupola, it is a rare example of the English form of town hall with open, arcaded ground floor surmounted by public rooms on the 2nd floor. *Caswell-Neuse State Historic Site,* Kinston. Closed Mon. *Attmore-Oliver House,* 511 Broad St., New Bern. Closed on national holidays. Admission charge. *Stevenson House,* 611 Pollock St., New Bern. Admission charge. *Bentonville Battleground State Historic Site,* Newton Grove. Free. *James K. Polk Birthplace State Historic Site,* Pineville. *Andrew Johnson Memorial,* Raleigh. Closed Sat. Admission charge. *The State Capitol,* Capitol Square, Raleigh, is open to the public and guides are available. Built 1833–40, this building is one of the country's finest Greek Revival structures. *Brunswick Town State Historic Site,* 225 Pine Grove Dr., Southport. Free. *Zebulon B. Vance Birthplace State Historic Site,* Weaverville. Closed Mon.

**SPECIAL INTEREST TOURS.** *Chinqua-Penn Plantation House,* Rte. 3, Reidsville. Closed Mon.

*Tryon Palace Restoration,* 613 Pollock St., New Bern. Admission charge. Tryon Palace. Admission charge. Tryon Gardens. Admission charge. Stanly House. Admission charge. Closed Mon.

*Historic Bath* has visitors center where tour information is available.

*Hope Plantation,* (1803) located 4 miles west of Windsor. Open Tues.-Sun.

*Somerset Place,* off US 64 south of Creswell. Early Greek Revival style house. Open daily. Closed Thanksgiving and Christmas.

**DRINKING LAWS.** Local option under state control governs the sale of alcoholic beverages. Distilled spirits are sold legally in package stores controlled by the N.C. Board of Alcoholic Control, the "ABC." There are ABC stores in approximately half the coastal and Piedmont counties and in some cities and towns of the mountain counties. Some municipalities allow "mixed beverages" to be served in properly licensed restaurants. Under state law, no person under 21 years of age may purchase any alcoholic beverage containing over 14% alcohol.

**HOTELS AND MOTELS.** Travelers in North Carolina will find accommodations in all price ranges. National chains, such as Quality Courts, Ramada Inns, Holiday Inns, Howard Johnsons, Hilton Inns and the "Economy" motels such as Scottish Inns and Econotels are located throughout the state. Television, telephones, heat and air conditioning are standard equipment. Except at a very few inexpensive hotels in downtown locations, free parking is standard.

The accommodations below are listed according to price categories. Based on double occupancy, without meals, categories and price ranges are *Deluxe:* $45 up; *Expensive:* $35 to $45; Moderate: $25 to $35; *Inexpensive:* $20 to $25. For a more complete explanation of hotel and motel categories see *Facts at Your Fingertips* at the front of this volume.

## BELHAVEN

**RIVER FOREST MANOR.** *Moderate.* Gracious old mansion, 600 E. Main St. Antique furnished rooms. 25 rooms. Famous for its three-tiered buffet table laden with the fresh seafood of the area and other delicacies.

## BLOWING ROCK

**GREEN PARK INN.** *Deluxe.* A spacious white-frame resort hostelry built in 1882. Remodeled in 1952 to modernize conveniences, but old charm has been retained. Good family hotel. Season June to Oct. American Plan.

## BURNSVILLE

**NU-WRAY INN.** *Moderate.* On village square. A charming old inn with early American atmosphere. Meals served family-style are famous featuring Southern specialties (no Sun. night meal). Season is mid-April thru Dec.

## CHAPEL HILL

**CAROLINA INN.** *Moderate.* Owned and operated by University of North Carolina. Restaurant. Lovely old inn, typical of a small university town.

## CLEMMONS

**TANGLEWOOD MANOR HOUSE.** *Moderate.* Manor House was part of the William N. Reynolds estate. Guests enjoy colonial decor in bedrooms and dine in the elegance of gracious Southern living.

## DILLSBORO

**JARRETT HOUSE.** *Moderate.* A comfortable inn built in 1890, well known for its dining rm. featuring Southern specialties. Season is mid-April thru Dec.

## DURHAM

**Howard Johnson's Motel.** *Moderate.* On I–85. Double-story motor inn. Rms. have balconies or patios.

**Ramada Inn.** *Moderate.*af18Two locations. I–85 at Guess Rd. and I–40 at Duke St.

## FAYETTEVILLE

**Bordeaux Motor Inn.** *Moderate.* Complete family recreation. Shopping center.

### FLAT ROCK

**WOODFIELDS INN.** *Moderate.* Historic inn near Flat Rock Playhouse. Dining rm. Season June to Nov. 1.

### HILLSBOROUGH

**COLONIAL INN.** *Inexpensive.* A small, pleasant inn built in 1759. Dining rm. Year round.

### KINSTON

**Kinstonian Motel.** *Moderate.* Convenient and comfortable. Restaurant.

### NEW BERN

**Holiday Inn.** *Moderate.* Restaurant, pool, year round.

**Quality Inn Palace.** *Moderate.* Pool, play area, restaurant.

**Ramada Inn.** *Moderate.* Overlooking Neuse River. Convenient.

### RALEIGH

**Plantation Inn.** *Moderate.* US 1N. Restaurant, putting green, lake.

### SAPPHIRE

**FAIRFIELD INN.** *Moderate.* Elegant old mountain inn in beautiful Sapphire Valley. Cottages and very good dining room.

### SMITHFIELD

**Howard Johnson's Motor Lodge.** *Moderate.* Comfortable rooms. Restaurant, play area.

### WASHINGTON

**Holiday Inn.** *Moderate.* US 17N. Near Historic Bath.

### WILMINGTON

**Wilmington Hilton.** *Moderate.* Comfortable rooms. Convenient to historic area.

**DINING OUT.** The choice of good places to eat in North Carolina is extremely varied, including restaurants specializing in international cuisine in several of the larger cities. Local specialties in Eastern North Carolina and a number of Piedmont localities include barbecued pork and chicken, fresh seafood, fried chicken and country ham. Hush puppies, made from corn meal batter and fried in deep fat, almost always accompany both fish and barbecue here. Grits is another Southern specialty widely served in North Carolina, usually with breakfast. There is also a wide selection of places which feature steaks and roast prime ribs of beef. Some of the restaurants listed serve continental cuisine. We have listed them because of the period buildings in which they are housed. Example: Seth Jones 1847 Restaurant in Raleigh serves French and American food. The price range for restaurant meals in North Carolina is somewhat lower than in metropolitan areas of the Northeast. Restaurants are listed according to price category. Categories and ranges for a complete evening meal are as follows: *Moderate:* $4 to $9; *Expensive:* $9 and up. For a more complete explanation of restaurant categories see *Facts at Your Fingertips*.

## ASHEVILLE

**WEAVERVILLE MILLING COMPANY.** *Expensive.* A few mi. N. of Asheville on Hwy. 19–23. A 1900's grist mill presents a rustic atmosphere for its patrons enjoying live entertainment and gourmet buffet dinners. Open nightly except Mon. All ABC permits. Reservations.

## BURNSVILLE

**THE NU-WRAY INN.** *Moderate.* This old inn on Burnsville's Town Square is one of North Carolina's best known landmarks. Food served family style. No menus. Beef, chicken and hickory smoked ham presented in this "Southern-board" style. Breakfast and dinner served except on Sundays and holidays, when breakfast and lunch are served. Open mid-April thru Dec.

## DILLSBORO

**JARRETT HOUSE.** *Moderate.* A comfortable old inn which has been in operation for more than 70 years. Mountain trout, country ham and Southern fried chicken, fresh vegetables, hot biscuits and regional specialties bring visitors from near and far to enjoy a family-style meal in this old inn.

## DURHAM

**THE OLDE HOUSE.** *Moderate.* 2701 Chapel Hill Rd. Continental food served in atmospheric setting. Reservations suggested.

## FLAT ROCK

**WOODFIELDS INN.** *Moderate.* This is the oldest continuously operated inn in the state. Southern food served, though beef stroganoff and home-grown vegetables are a specialty.

## GLENDALE SPRINGS

**GLENDALE SPRINGS INN.** *Moderate.* On N.C. 16, this old house has been recently opened as a family-style restaurant. Enjoy a relaxing swing on the wide veranda after feasting on trout, fried chicken, ham, fresh vegetables, homemade soup and yeast rolls. Open daily.

## GREENSBORO

**DARRYL'S 1808.** *Moderate.* 2102 N. Church St. Lunch & dinner. Good sandwiches and steaks, in period restaurant. These restaurants are always fascinating as they are appointed with furnishings of the period (1808).

## HILLSBOROUGH

**THE COLONIAL INN.** *Moderate.* Historic 1759 Inn serving typical "old south" food such as chicken and dumplings, ham, Southern fried chicken and fresh vegetables.

## NEW BERN

**HENDERSON HOUSE.** *Moderate.* Peanut or peach soup? These are specialties of this 18th-Century inn for lunch. (During the Civil War the inn housed officers of the 45th Massachusetts Militia.) Lunch served Tues. through Sat. Dinner, Fri. and Sat. Reservations requested for dinner.

## RALEIGH

**ANGUS BARN.** *Expensive.* Raleigh-Durham Hwy. (US 70). Unique atmosphere and fine food in a spacious big red barn; collection of antiques and old farm tools. Steaks and rare prime ribs of beef are specialties. Open every night, reservations recommended.

**SETH JONES 1847.** *Expensive.* House is part of a plantation and a visitor can still see the tobacco barns and farm equipment of the past. Food is well prepared and the atmosphere delightful. Reservations advisable.

**DARRYL'S 1849 RESTAURANT,** U.S. 70 W. and **Darryl's 1906 Restaurant.** *Moderate.* 1906 Hillsborough St. Delightful atmospheric restaurants.

**Balentine's.** *Moderate.* 410 Oberlin Rd. Specializing in Southern food. Attractive cafeteria located in Cameron Village Shopping Center.

## SMITHFIELD

**FRENCH COUNTRY INN, LTD.** *Expensive.* Excellent French food. Old colonial home is setting for intimate dining. Reservations only. The inn is located in the small town of Selma, near Smithfield.

## TRYON

**OAK HALL HOTEL.** *Moderate.* Overlooking Tryon and commanding fine views of the mountains surrounding the resort. This is one of North Carolina's oldest hotels and the atmosphere is leisurely and gracious. Menus are not elaborate but food is noted for its fine quality.

## WILMINGTON AND WRIGHTSVILLE BEACH

**THE GRAY GABLES.** *Expensive.* Airlie Rd. Excellent food in an old colonial house. Reservations suggested.

**CORTLEY'S OLD FASHIONED DELI.** *Moderate.* 316 Nutt St. in Cotton Exchange, Wilmington. Located in newly restored area of Old Wilmington waterfront.

## WINSTON-SALEM

**SALEM TAVERN.** *Moderate.* Old Salem. Following Germanic traditions of the Moravians, good German food served in 1784 tavern; a registered National Historic Landmark.

**ZEVELY HOUSE 1815.** *Moderate.* Corner of 4th & Summit Sts. Menu is apropos of the era, and fresh vegetables are cooked as in colonial times. Pumpkin muffins, beef, cheese dishes all delectable. Enjoy the casual atmosphere in this authentically restored oldest house in Winston-Salem.

# OKLAHOMA

## *The Last Surrender*

#### by

#### AL FIEGEL

Oklahoma, the forty-sixth state, was admitted to the Union in 1907. In the Choctaw Indian language, *okla* means people and *homa* means red. Freely translated, Oklahoma means "home of the red people," and was Indian Territory during the Civil War.

Oklahoma first was the home of prairie grass, great buffalo herds, and the Plains Indians. Then, between 1817 and 1837, it also became the home of the "Five Civilized Tribes"—the Cherokees, Chickasaws, Choctaws, Creeks and Seminoles forced by the federal government to move from the Carolinas, Georgia, Alabama, Mississippi, Tennessee and Florida. Upon their arrival in Indian Territory, the tribes formed their own independent nations and governments.

The Plains Indians in what is now western Oklahoma became hostile at having to share their hunting domain with the Five Civilized Tribes in what is now eastern Oklahoma. To protect the latter, the federal government in 1824 established the frontier posts of Fort Gibson and Fort Towson. These forts later were to become military headquarters for Union and Confederate troops during the Civil War.

When the war began, the Indians were divided in their loyalties. Had they remained neutral, as John Ross of the Cherokees proposed, they might have avoided involvement, but wealthy Indian slaveowners—and hence the Five Civilized Tribes for the most part—allied themselves with the Confederacy. The land was ravaged as a consequence. When the Confederacy lost, its Indian allies had been driven into Texas, while Indians aligned with the Union were pushed into Kansas.

To pay for their defection, the Five Civilized Tribes were compelled to sell much of their land—for fifteen to thirty cents an acre—on which savage Indians from elsewhere were then relocated, contributing to more friction.

There are eighty-six historic sites associated with the Civil War in Oklahoma, most of which are identified by Oklahoma Historical Society highway markers. Twenty-nine of these are combat locations, many of which are situated on private property. None of the engagements were regarded as decisive insofar as the outcome of the war.

More than a dozen skirmishes were fought near Fort Gibson (temporarily renamed Fort Blunt in 1863–65 after its commanding officer). It was from here that Gen. James G. Blunt learned of an impending Confederate attack on the fort by five to six thousand poorly equipped soldiers. They proved to be no match for Blunt's three thousand well-fed, well-equipped Union troops, and were defeated at the Battle of Honey Springs in July, 1863. The Oklahoma Historical Society Marker commemorating this engagement is on US Highway 69, south of Oktaha, in Muskogee County.

## Civil War Tour of Oklahoma

Sites of Civil War significance which one can actually still see in the Sooner State are confined largely to the eastern one-fourth of Oklahoma from Tahlequah south. This "tour" starts in Tahlequah and ends at Millerton in the southeastern corner of the state—or, if you're coming from the other direction, can begin at Millerton.

Tahlequah was capital of the Cherokee Nation from 1841 to 1907, when Oklahoma became a state. Its capitol building on the city square, now the Cherokee County Courthouse, was built in 1872. Across from the southeast corner of the square are the Cherokee Supreme Court Building, erected in 1844, and the Cherokee National Prison, built in 1874. The administration building of Northeastern State College, circa 1888, originally served as the Cherokee Female Seminary.

From Tahlequah, drive south on US 62 about four miles, jogging left a short distance on SH 82. Here is the Murrell Home, the aristocratic southern mansion of a daughter of the famed Cherokee Ross family in pre–Civil War times, and center of activity during the war. The home of this influential family has been fully restored inside and out, including its slave quarters and spacious surrounding lawns.

Return to US 62, which becomes SH 10 as you continue southwest toward Fort Gibson, 17 miles away. When established in 1824, Fort Gibson was the westernmost outpost of the United States, and an important Arkansas River port. The fort's stockade is rebuilt and many of the original post buildings remain, including barracks, officer's quarters and a powder house. Headquarters for Union Army activity in Indian Territory during the Civil War, the fort stands on Garrison Hill, which rises above the old town. Many important military men and Indian chieftains of that day are buried in the National Cemetery, a short drive across town. One grave is identified as that of Tiana Rogers, the Cherokee wife of Sam Houston. Much favored by the Cherokees, Houston spent many years with the tribe prior to his heroic career in the Texas war for independence.

Fort Chickamauga, on SH 82 near Cookson, might best be called an anachronism. It is a full-time, functioning, frontier military post, serving as headquarters for the reactivated 4th Cavalry—the only horse cavalry post in the U.S. It is manned by the Sons of Veterans Reserve, a quasi-official military organization the duties of which are primarily ceremonial. The troopers wear authentic period uniforms, use regulation period equipment, and are qualified experts in the use of the lance, the 1861 cavalry saber, and the 1873 Springfield rifle. The women seen in 1870 costumes are either wives and family of garrison troops or members of the WAC contingent. Some of the fort's old buildings, earmarked for destruction elsewhere, were moved in. The post is geared to tourism and offers essentially the same services to civilian guests that would have been offered 100-plus years ago on the frontier.

Dwight Mission is situated in a remote area three miles SW of Marble City. The road to it angles NE from US 64 east of Vian. Already a landmark by the time of the Civil War, it occasionally housed Confederate troops during the conflict. Established by the Presbyterian Church in 1821 to serve the Cherokees, its cemetery contains many graves of early missionaries, some dating back to the 1830s.

About thirteen miles NW of Durant on SH 78 and three miles W on SH 199 is Fort Washita, a Confederate post during the Civil War. The site was selected by Gen. Zachary Taylor in 1842, and the fort was built a year later to protect the Chickasaw Indians from marauding Plains Indians. Here Gen. Albert Pike negotiated the Confederate Treaty with the Five Civilized Tribes. Abandoned by the War Department in 1870, the fort has been dramatically reconstructed by the Oklahoma Historical Society.

Goodland Mission, three miles SW of Hugo, is the oldest school with continuous service in Oklahoma. Founded by the Presbyterian Church in 1848, two companies of Choctaw troops trained here for Confederate service. The old church and log-cabin office of the Choctaw governor still stand on the campus.

About one mile northeast of the town of Fort Towson on US 70 are the ruins of the old fort and relics of the army post for which the town was named. Fort Towson was Indian Territory's second fort, active from 1824 to 1854. Reactivated by the Confederacy during the Civil War, it was here that the Indian General Stand Watie surrendered his troops in 1865, the last Confederate general to lay down arms in the Civil War.

## PRACTICAL INFORMATION FOR OKLAHOMA

 **FACTS AND FIGURES.** In the Choctaw language, Oklahoma means "home of the red man." The state's nickname is the Sooner State. The state flower is the mistletoe; the state tree, the redbud; the state bird, the scissor-tail fly-catcher. The state song is Rodgers and Hammerstein's "Oklahoma!" The state motto is *Labor Omnia Vincit* ("Labor Conquers All").

Oklahoma City, one of the largest cities in area in the U.S., is the state capital. The state population is 2,559,463.

A skyline of oil wells symbolizes Oklahoma, the booming southwestern state that is equally known for rodeo champions, Rhodes scholars and Indian ceremonials. Farming, ranching and oil are the chief sources of wealth, although Oklahoma is striving to diversify its industry, and a major step has been taken with the completion of the Arkansas River Navigation System, which links Oklahoma's Port of Catoosa to the Mississippi River and thus opens Oklahoma to world shipping trade. The state enjoys increased popularity because of the fresh image that many man-made lakes have given it. Oklahoma now boasts more miles of shoreline than either the Atlantic or Pacific coast of the U.S.

 **HOW TO GET THERE.** *By car:* Except for the panhandle and northwest quadrant, Oklahoma has an adequate skeleton of interstate highways. From Dallas, I–35 heads due north past Lake Texoma, Ardmore and Norman. You may still have to use city streets in Oklahoma City, but the interstate resumes thereafter, passing Stillwater and Ponca City on its way to Wichita, Kansas. From the east comes I–40, out of Ft. Smith, Arkansas, through Henryetta, Shawnee, Oklahoma City, El Reno, Clinton and Elk City before reaching the Texas border. I–44 connects Oklahoma City and Tulsa with Joplin, Missouri. East-west Federal highways are: in the north, US 60 from Lake of the Cherokees to its junction with US 64 twenty-five miles N of Enid. US 64 goes on to northeastern New Mexico. In the south, US 70, from Hot Springs, Arkansas, crosses the state to the Wichita Falls, Texas, area. North-south roads include: US 75 from Dallas, which connects with US 69 for McAlester and Muskogee; US 81, also from Dallas goes past Lawton (US Army's Fort Sill), Chickasha, El Reno and Enid. Its first major stop north of the state is Wellington, Kansas. From central Texas, US 83 crosses the Oklahoma panhandle and passes fifty miles SW of Dodge City, Kansas.

*By air:* There are direct flights to Oklahoma City and Tulsa from both coasts: Boston, New York, Washington, D.C., Los Angeles, San Diego, San Francisco, Portland and Seattle. You can jet in from almost every city in Texas and Arkansas, while *Braniff* has service to Oklahoma City from Monterrey and Mexico City. Mid-south and Midwest cities directly served include Chicago, Denver, Colorado Springs, Memphis, Nashville, St. Louis,

Kansas City and Wichita. Smaller Oklahoma airports receiving direct flights are: Muskogee, from Dallas, Memphis, Denver, Little Rock and Ft. Smith (Ark.); Lawton, from Dallas, Kansas City Lincoln (Neb.), Midland-Odessa and Wichita Falls (Texas); Enid, from Lincoln, Kansas City and Dallas.

*By bus:* Greyhound and *Trailways* serve the major cities on their through service and connections to local service or affiliated lines will get you to any area of the state and almost any small town. The best regional line schedules are maintained by *M. K. & O.* and *Oklahoma Transportation*.

*By train:* Amtrak's *Texas Chief,* on its run between Chicago and Houston, stops at Ponca City, Perry, Guthrie, Oklahoma City, Norman, Purcell, Pauls Valley and Ardmore. There is no train station in Tulsa.

**HOW TO GET AROUND.** *By car:* Modern multi-lane turnpikes, state and Interstate highways crisscross Oklahoma. Both Avis and Hertz *Rent-A-Car* facilities, as well as independent dealers, are located in Oklahoma City and Tulsa.

*By bus: Continental Trailways* and *Greyhound* bus service is available, as well as that provided by smaller bus lines.

*By air:* Serving Oklahoma City by air are *American, Braniff, Continental, Frontier, Pan American* and *Trans World Airlines.* Tulsa is served by *American, Braniff, Frontier, Continental, Ozark, Pan American* and *Trans World. Frontier* also serves several smaller cities. Landing strips are also provided at many state-owned resort lodges to make vacationing there convenient.

**TOURIST INFORMATION.** Persons planning a trip to or through Oklahoma can obtain tourist brochures and information by writing Tourism & Recreation Department, 504 Will Rogers Building, Oklahoma City 73105.

The tourist information centers on major interstate and highway routes offer on-the-spot suggestions for travelers. Centers are located on I–35 at the Kansas and Texas borders; on I–40 at the Arkansas and Texas border; on US 69–75 at the Texas border; on US 277 in Lawton; east of Miami on the Will Rogers Turnpike, and at the intersection of Will Rogers Turnpike and U.S. 66. Travel brochures are also available at the Glass House Restaurant on the Will Rogers Turnpike, Howard Johnson's Midway on the Turner Turnpike and in the Capitol Rotunda in Oklahoma City.

**SEASONAL EVENTS.** Old-fashioned 4th of July celebration each year, with pink lemonade, a band concert and fireworks at Fort Chickamauga, on SH 82 near Cookson.

**HISTORIC SITES.** Bacone College Indian Museum, Five Civilized Tribes Museum, Honor Heights Park, *Muskogee.* Creek National Capital Building, *Okmulgee.* Choctaw National Capital Building, *Tuskahoma.* Chicasaw National Capital Building (now the Johnston County Courthouse), *Tishomingo.* Oklahoma Historical Society Museum, State Capital Complex; National Cowboy Hall of Fame, 1700 NE 63rd; Oklahoma Heritage Center, 201 NW 14th St., all in *Oklahoma City.* Philbrook Art Center; Gilcrease Institute of American History and Art, both in *Tulsa.*

**DRINKING LAWS.** Prohibition was repealed in Oklahoma in 1959 and liquor is available in package stores between 10 A.M. and 10 P.M. except Sundays, holidays and election days. Bars, as such, do not exist, but private clubs are in abundance. Memberships are easily obtained through hotels or motels, or by paying a modest membership fee, which is frequently comparable to a cover charge. Where mixed drinks are not served, the "bring your own bottle" rule exists.

 **HOTELS AND MOTELS.** Many hotels and motels have private clubs (the Oklahoma version of a bar) on the premises. Guests automatically become members upon registering. Cost figures generally are for moderately priced rooms, unless a range is indicated.

The price categories in this section, for double occupancy, will average as follows: *Deluxe* $36 and up, *Expensive* $25 to $35, *Moderate* $18 to $24, and *Inexpensive* under $17. For a more complete description of these categories see *Facts at Your Fingertips*.

## ALTUS

**QUARTZ MOUNTAIN LODGE.** *Moderate.* Outdoor and indoor pools, restaurant, and private club. Guests may choose from modern lodge facilities or cottage units. Lodge dining room overlooks Lake Altus and granite peaks of the area.

## ARDMORE

**LAKE MURRAY LODGE.** *Expensive.* Pool, air conditioning, restaurant. Variety of cottages or lodge accommodations. Complete park and lake facilities available. Golf course and paved airstrip.

## DURANT

**LAKE TEXOMA LODGE.** *Expensive.* Pool, air conditioning, restaurant, Ping-Pong, shuffleboard, horseback riding, tennis. Located in Lake Texoma State Park, a complete resort hotel with excellent view of the lake. Lodge accommodations, cottages, and a fisherman's lodge. Complete lake facilities are available, as well as an airstrip.

## EUFAULA

**FOUNTAINHEAD LODGE.** *Expensive* to *Deluxe.* Multi-level facility curved around huge pool. Airstrip, golf, tennis, boating, horseback riding, private club, trailer hookups, cottages.

**ARROWHEAD LODGE.** *Moderate.* Pool, air-conditioning, restaurant, private club, Ping-Pong, pool table, playground, tennis court. A state-operated lodge situated in Arrowhead State Park on Lake Eufaula. Guests may choose from one of the many hexagonal-shaped rooms or from three types of cottages, including tree houses. Golf course, park, and lake facilities are available.

## WAGONER

**WESTERN HILLS LODGE.** *Expensive.* Pool, air-conditioning, private club, riding stables. On top of wooded peninsula extending into Lake Fort Gibson. Guests may take advantage of golf course, airstrip, and complete park and lake facilities of Sequoyah State Park.

## WATONGA

**ROMAN NOSE LODGE.** *Expensive.* Pool, air-conditioning, restaurant, riding stables. On rim of canyon overlooking twin lakes in Roman Nose State Park. Guests may choose from modern lodge accommodations or cabins. Golf course, lake and park facilities available.

 **DINING OUT.** Oklahomans do not eat steak at *every* meal; in fact, a traveler will find some surprising items on many menus, including catfish, lobster, fettuccine and even Indian dishes. Categories denote medium-priced meals. For other worthwhile restaurants, check the hotel listings. Restaurants are listed in order of price category.

Restaurant price categories are as follows: *Deluxe* $10 and up, *Expensive* $6–$7.50, *Moderate* $3 to $6, and *Inexpensive* under $3. These prices are for hors d'oeuvres or soup, entree, and dessert. Not included are drinks, tax and tips. For a more complete explanation of restaurant categories refer to *Facts at Your Fingertips*.

## ALTUS

**QUARTZ MOUNTAIN LODGE RESTAURANT.** *Moderate.* Scenic surroundings overlooking the lake add to the enjoyment of specialties which include southern-fried chicken, seafood, steak.

## ARDMORE

**El Palacio.** *Expensive.* Mexican decor. Steak, chicken, chili rellenos.

**LAKE MURRAY LODGE RESTAURANT.** *Moderate.* Smorgasboard nightly during summer season. Attractive surroundings. Children's menu. Specialties: catfish, steak, roast beef.

## CLAREMORE

**HAMMETT HOUSE.** *Expensive.* Fried chicken, steak, lemon pecan pie. Early American decor.

## MC ALESTER

**GIA COMO'S.** *Expensive.* Specialty is charcoal steaks in a pleasant and picturesque setting.

## OKLAHOMA CITY

**CHRISTOPHER'S.** *Deluxe.* 2920 N.W. Grand Blvd. Though located right in the heart of the city, the swan-filled lake and surrounding park areas convey the ambiance of a country inn. Menu includes representative American dishes, including steaks, chops, chicken and seafood.

**THE WHITE HOUSE.** *Deluxe.* Artichokes, scampi, steak, chicken Kiev. In converted mansion.

**SLEEPY HOLLOW.** *Expensive.* 1101 N.E. 50th St. This is genuine Americana, with a relaxed, "down home" atmosphere and southern-style cooking. Specialties are steaks, southern-fried chicken, fresh greens, and hot biscuits.

**GLEN'S HIK-RY INN.** *Expensive.* Steak (choose your own), chicken, shrimp. Western decor.

## TAHLEQUAH

**RESTAURANT OF THE CHEROKEES.** *Moderate* to *Expensive.* 4 mi. SW on 62. In an authentic Indian setting, this restaurant operated by the Cherokee nation specializes in game and fried chicken. They also do their own baking.

## WAGONER

**WESTERN HILLS LODGE.** *Expensive.* In Sequoyah State Park, State 51. A charming spot with view of the lake. Children's menu.

## WATONGA

**ROMAN NOSE LODGE RESTAURANT.** *Moderate* to *Expensive.* In Roman Nose State Park on State 8A N. Steak, chicken, and rainbow trout in scenic surroundings beside Lake Boecher.

# PENNSYLVANIA

## *Decision at Gettysburg*

### By
### GLORIA HAYES KREMER AND RICHARD HAAZ

*Gloria Hayes Kremer is a syndicated writer, contributing travel articles to* The Philadelphia Inquirer, *and writing in* The Bulletin *as well as national publications. She has written and produced numerous television programs, industrial shows and children's educational records.*

When the Civil War tore the states asunder, Pennsylvania was the pivotal hinge in a decisive conflict. Not only was it a chief source of guns and military supplies for the North, with its three major cities of Philadelphia, Pittsburgh and Harrisburg, but Pennsylvania was also a strategically important target for the South. Harrisburg, the state's capital, was a rail, canal and highway center. Through it passed many of the supplies needed by the Union Army. The Confederacy hoped to break the back of the Union in Pennsylvania by seizing one or more of these centers.

From a military standpoint, Lee gambled for victory by trying to draw the military might of the North away from Washington. It was a big risk and the South went for broke. Lee had to stake his all in the battle for Pennsylvania, the richest prize in the war. From July 1st to 3rd, 1863, Robert E. Lee played the deadly game across the board. Backed by some of his most brilliant generals, "Jeb" Stuart, C. Fitzhugh Lee and G.E. Pickett, he met the Union forces at a little town called Gettysburg. This was the turning point of the Civil War, one of the most important battles in American—and world—history.

On the green sloping hills around Gettysburg, one-third of the Union Army, many of them from Pennsylvania, commanded by General George Meade, himself a Pennsylvanian, clashed with the Army of the South. Pickett made his memorable charge in the face of certain death. When the smoke cleared, 22,000 men of the Union Forces were killed, wounded or missing. The Grays lost 28,000 men "on this hallowed ground," and the war itself. Thus Pennsylvania was not only where our country began, but also where it was preserved.

## Battle of Gettysburg

Gettysburg National Park is undoubtedly the most famous Civil War monument in the state, and perhaps in the nation. It was here, on July 3, 1863, that the greatest artillery battle ever held on this continent was fought.

The Battle of Gettysburg began on July 1, 1863. General Robert E. Lee had marched his army up the Valley of the Shenandoah, across the Potomac, through Maryland and into Pennsylvania. His hope was to take Harrisburg and then Philadelphia, but he and his host were met at Gettysburg by the Union army under General George C. Meade. For three days the relentless fighting went on and when the last shot had been fired, one man out of every four of the 159,000 who took part in the engagement had been killed or wounded or was missing. The Union army had taken the worst the Confederates could inflict on them—and the Blue line held. Lee was forced to retreat; his hopes for victory were now dashed; the tide had turned.

Within a few weeks of the battle, it was decided to make a cemetery on seventeen acres of the battlefield, bought by the State of Pennsylvania for that purpose. Today, the Gettysburg National Military Park covers more than sixteen thousand acres. On November 19, 1863, at dedication ceremonies, President Lincoln spoke a few words that became immortal and known around the world as the *Gettysburg Address*.

Practically all of Gettysburg is a museum. There are regular guided bus tours of the battlefield that leave the terminal near US 15 and US 140. At the Visitors' Center, designed by Philip Neutra, a cyclorama portrays Confederate General George Pickett's charge up Cemetery Ridge. After hours of furious gunfire, the Union guns had become silent and the Confederates assumed that they were out of ammunition. Not so. A barrage of artillery and musket fire ripped apart the advancing line of men in gray; the attackers were forced to retreat, with heavy casualties.

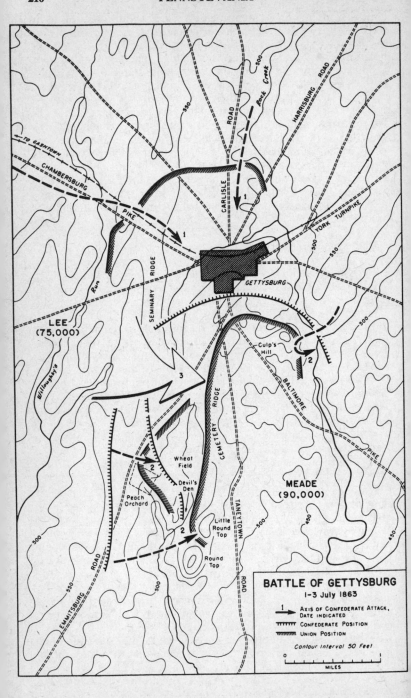

BATTLE OF GETTYSBURG
1-3 July 1863

Axis of Confederate Attack, Date indicated

Confederate Position

Union Position

Contour Interval 50 Feet

0                    1
MILES

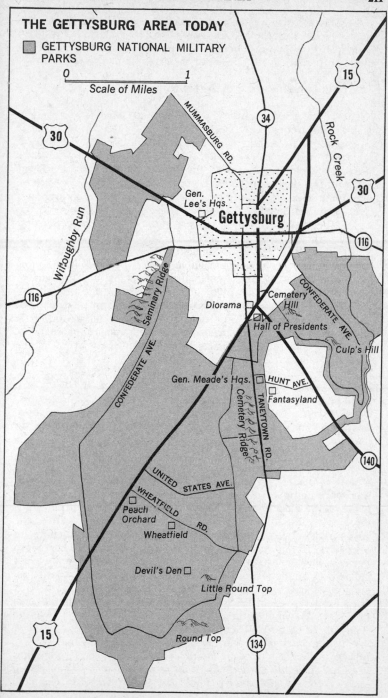

THE GETTYSBURG AREA TODAY

GETTYSBURG NATIONAL MILITARY PARKS

0 _____ 1
Scale of Miles

A more recent tourist attraction at Gettysburg is the farmhouse now occupied by Mamie Eisenhower, wife of the late President Dwight D. Eisenhower. Thousands of people flock here annually for a look at it. Neither the house nor the grounds is open to visitors.

## Lee's Second Invasion of the North

By 1863 the war had entered what Sherman called its professional phase. The troops were well trained and had ample combat experience. Officers had generally mastered their jobs and were deploying their forces fairly skillfully in accordance with the day's tactical principles. Furthermore, the increased range and accuracy of weapons, together with the nature of the terrain, had induced some alterations in tactics, alterations which were embodied in a revised infantry manual published in 1863. Thus, by the third year of the war, battles had begun to take on certain definite characteristics. The battle of Gettysburg was a case in point.

Gettysburg was, first of all, an act of fate—a three-day holocaust, largely unplanned and uncontrollable. Like the war itself, it sprang from decisions that men under pressure made in the light of imperfect knowledge. It would someday symbolize the war with all the blunders and heroism, hopes and delusions, combativeness and blinding devotion of the American man in arms of that period. With its enormous destruction, tactical maneuvers, and use of weapons, Gettysburg was one of the most dramatic and most typical of the 2,000-odd land engagements of the Civil War.

After the great victory at Chancellorsville, the Confederate cause in the eastern theater looked exceptionally bright. If 60,000 men could beat 134,000, then the Confederacy's inferiority in manpower was surely offset by superior generalship and skill at arms. Vicksburg was not yet under siege, although Grant had ferried his army over to the east bank of the Mississippi. If Davis and Lee were overly optimistic, they could hardly be blamed. Both men favored another invasion of the North for much the same political and military reasons that led to invasion in 1862. Longstreet, on the other hand, was concerned over the Federal threats in the west. He proposed going on the defensive in Virginia and advised taking advantage of the Confederacy's railroads and interior lines to send part of the Army of Northern Virginia to Tennessee to relieve pressure on Vicksburg. But he was overruled and Lee made ready to move into Pennsylvania. By this time Union strategy in the east was clearly defined: to continue operations against Confederate seaports—an attempt to seize Fort Sumter on April 7 had failed—and to destroy Lee's army. President Lincoln's orders made clear that the destruction of the Army of Northern Virginia was the major objective of the Army of the Potomac. Richmond was only incidental.

On June 30, 1863, the Army of the Potomac numbered 115,256 officers and enlisted men, with 362 guns. It consisted of 51 infantry brigades organized into 19 divisions, which in turn formed seven infantry corps. The cavalry corps had three divisions. The field artillery, 67 batteries, was assigned by brigades to the corps, except for army reserve artillery. The Army of Northern Virginia, numbering 76,224 men and 272 guns in late May, comprised three infantry corps, each led by a lieutenant general, and Stuart's cavalry division. (The Confederacy was much more generous with rank than was the U.S. Army.) In each corps were three divisions, and most divisions had four brigades. Of the 15 field artillery battalions of four batteries each, five battalions were attached to each corps under command of the corps' artillery chiefs.

In early June Lee began moving his units away from Fredericksburg. In his advance he used the Shenandoah and Cumberland Valleys, for by holding the east-west mountain passes he could readily cover his approach route and line of communications. Hooker got wind of the move; he noted the weakening of the Fredericksburg defenses, and on June 9 his cavalry, commanded by Brig. Gen. Alfred Pleasonton, surprised Stuart at Brandy Station, Virginia. Here on an open plain was fought one of the few mounted, saber-swinging, cut-and-thrust cavalry combats of the Civil War. Up to now the Confederate cavalry had been superior, but at Brandy Station the Union horsemen "came of age," and Stuart was lucky to hold his position.

When the Federals learned that Confederate infantrymen were west of the Blue Ridge heading north, Hooker started to move to protect Washington and Baltimore and to attempt to destroy Lee. Earlier, Lincoln had vetoed Hooker's proposal to seize Richmond while Lee went north. As the Army of Northern Virginia moved through the valleys and deployed into Pennsylvania behind cavalry screens, the Army of the Potomac moved north on a broad front to the east, crossing the Potomac on June 25 and 26. Lee, forced to disperse by the lack of supplies, had extended his infantry columns from McConnellsburg and Chambersburg on the west to Carlisle in the north and York on the east.

After Brandy Station, and some sharp clashes in the mountain passes, Stuart set forth on another dramatic ride around the Union army. With only vague instructions and acting largely on his own initiative, he proved of little use to Lee. It was only on the afternoon of July 2 with his troopers so weary that they were almost falling from their saddles, that Stuart rejoined Lee in the vicinity of Gettysburg, too late to have an important influence on the battle. His absence had deprived Lee of prompt, accurate information about the Army of the Potomac. When Lee learned from Longstreet on June 28 that Hooker's men were north of the Potomac, he ordered his widespread units to concentrate at once between Gettysburg and Cashtown.

After Chancellorsville, Lincoln, though advised to drop Hooker, had kept him in command of the Army of the Potomac on the theory that he would not throw away a gun because it had misfired once. But Hooker soon became embroiled with Halleck and requested his own relief. He was replaced by a corps commander, Maj. Gen. George G. Meade, who before dawn on June 28 received word of his promotion and the accompanying problems inherent in assuming command of a great army while it was moving toward the enemy. Meade, who was to command the Army of the Potomac for the rest of the war, started north on a broad front at once but within two days decided to fight a defensive action in Maryland and issued orders to that effect. Not all his commanders received the order, and events overruled him.

### Gettysburg

Outposts of both armies clashed during the afternoon of June 30 near the quiet little Pennsylvania market town of Gettysburg. The terrain in the area included rolling hills and broad shallow valleys. Gettysburg was the junction of twelve roads that led to Harrisburg, Philadelphia, Baltimore, Washington, and the mountain passes to the west which were controlled by Lee. The rest was inevitable; the local commanders sent reports and recommendations to their superiors, who relayed them upward, so that both armies, still widely dispersed, started moving toward Gettysburg. *(See Map)*

On July 1, Union cavalrymen fought a dismounted delaying action against advance troops of Lt. Gen. Ambrose P. Hill's corps northwest of town. By this stage of the war cavalrymen, armed with saber, pistol, and breech-loading carbine, were often deployed as mounted infantrymen, riding to battle but fighting on foot. The range and accuracy of the infantry's rifled muskets made it next to impossible for mounted men to attack foot soldiers in position. With their superior speed and mobility, cavalrymen, as witnessed in the Gettysburg campaign, were especially useful for screening, reconnaissance, and advance guard actions in which they seized and held important hills, river crossings, and road junctions pending the arrival of infantry. During the morning hours of July 1, this was the role played by Union horsemen on the ridges north and west of Gettysburg.

By noon both the I and the XI Corps of the Army of the Potomac had joined in the battle, and Lt. Gen. Richard S. Ewell's Corps of Confederates had moved to support Hill. The latter, advancing from the north, broke the lines of the XI Corps and drove the Federals back through Gettysburg. The Union infantry rallied behind artillery positioned on Cemetery and Culp's Hills south of the town. Lee, who reached the field about 2 P.M. ordered Ewell to take Cemetery Hill, "if possible." But Ewell failed to press his advantage, and the Confederates settled into positions extending in a great curve from northeast of Culp's Hill, westward through Gettysburg, thence south on Seminary Ridge. During the night the Federals, enjoying interior lines, moved troops onto the key points of Culp's Hill, Cemetery Hill, Cemetery Ridge, and Little Round Top.

Meade had completed his dispositions by the morning of July 2, and his line was strong except in two places. In the confusion, Little Round Top was occupied only by a signal station when the supporting cavalry was dispatched to guard the army trains and not replaced; and the commander of the III Corps, Maj. Gen. Daniel E. Sickles, on his own responsibility moved his line forward from the south end of Cemetery Ridge to higher ground near the Peach Orchard, so that his corps lay in an exposed salient. By early afternoon, seven corps were arrayed along the Union battle line.

On the Confederate side, Lee had not been able to attack early; reconnaissance took time, and Longstreet's leading division did not arrive until afternoon. Generals in the Civil War tried to combine frontal assaults with envelopments of flanking movements, but the difficulty of timing and co-ordinating the movements of such large bodies of men in broken terrain made intricate maneuvers difficult. The action on the second day at Gettysburg graphically illustrates the problem. Lee wanted Longstreet to outflank the Federal left, part of Hill's corps was to strike the center, while Ewell's corps was to envelop the right flank of Meade's army. The attack did not start until 3 P.M. when Longstreet's men, having deployed on unfamiliar ground under a corps commander who preferred to take a defensive stance, advanced toward Little Round Top. The brigade was the basic maneuver element, and it formed for the attack with regiments in a two-rank line. Divisions usually attacked in columns of brigades, the second 150 to 300 yards behind the first, the third a similar distance behind the second. Skirmishers protected the flanks if no units were posted on either side. But such textbook models usually degenerated under actual fighting conditions, and so it was with Longstreet's attack. Divisions and brigades went in piecemeal, but with savage enthusiasm. Attacks started in close order as most men were using single-shot muzzle-loaders and had to stand shoulder to shoulder in order to get enough firepower and shock effect. But intervals between units soon increased under fire, troops often scattered for cover and concealment behind stone walls and trees, and thereafter units advanced by short rushes supported by fire from neighboring units. Thus, by late afternoon the smoke of battle was thick over the field south of Gettysburg and the cries of the wounded mingled with the crash of musketry. The whole sector had become a chaos of tangled battle lines.

At this point Meade's chief engineer, Brig. Gen. Gouverneur Warren, discovering that no infantry held Little Round Top, persuaded the commander of the V Corps, Maj. Gen. George Sykes, to send two brigades and some artillery to the hill. They arrived just in time to hold the summit against a furious Confederate assault. When this attack bogged down, Longstreet threw a second division against Sickles' troops in the Peach Orchard and Wheatfield; this cracked the Federal line and drove as far as Cemetery Ridge before Meade's reserves halted it. Lee then ordered his troops to attack progressively from right to left and one of Hill's divisions assaulted Cemetery Ridge in piecemeal fashion, but was driven off. On the north Ewell attacked about 6 P.M. and captured some abandoned trenches, but Federals posted behind stone walls proved too strong. As the day ended the Federals held all their main positions. The Confederates had fought hard and with great bravery, but the progressive attack, which ignored the principle of mass, never engaged the Union front decisively at any point. The assaults were delivered against stoutly defended, prepared positions; Malvern Hill and Fredericksburg had shown this tactic to be folly, although perhaps Lee's successes against prepared positions at Chancellorsville led him to overoptimism.

Meade, after requesting the opinions of his corps commanders, decided to defend, rather than attack, on July 3. He also estimated that Lee, having attacked his right and left, would try for his center. He was right. Lee had planned to launch a full-scale, co-ordinated attack all along the line but then changed his mind in favor of a massive frontal assault by 10 brigades from four divisions of Longstreet's and Hill's corps against the Union center, which was held by Maj. Gen. Winfield Scott Hancock's II Corps. The assault was to be preceded by a massive artillery barrage.

The infantry's main support during the war was provided by field artillery. Rifled guns of relatively long range were available, but the soldiers preferred the 6-pounder and 12-pounder smoothbores. Rifled cannon were harder to clean; their projectiles were not as effective; their greater range could not always be effectively used because development of a good indirect fire control system would have to await the invention of the field telephone and the radio; and, finally, the rifled guns had flat trajectories, whereas the higher trajectories of the smoothbores enabled gunners to put fire on reverse slopes. Both types of cannon were among the artillery of the two armies at Gettysburg.

At 1 P.M. on July 3 Confederate gunners opened fire from approximately 140 pieces along Seminary Ridge in the greatest artillery bombardment witnessed on the American continent up to that time. For two hours the barrages continued, but did little more than tear up ground, destroy a few caissons, and expend ammunition. The Union artillery in the sector, numbering only 80 guns, had not been knocked out. It did stop firing in order to conserve ammunition, and the silence seemed to be a signal that the Confederates should begin their attack.

Under command of Maj. Gen. George E. Pickett, 15,000 men emerged from the woods on Seminary Ridge, dressed their three lines as if on parade, and began the mile-long, 20-minute march toward Cemetery Ridge. The assault force—47 regiments altogether—moved at a walk until it neared the Union lines, then broke into a run. Union artillery, especially 40 Napoleons on the south end of the ridge and some rifled guns on Little Round Top, opened fire, enfiladed the gray ranks, and forced Pickett's right over to the north. Despite heavy casualties the Confederates kept their formation until they came within rifle and canister range of the II Corps, and by then the lines and units were intermingled. The four brigades composing the left of Pickett's first line were heavily hit but actually reached and crossed the stone wall defended by Brig. Gen. John Gibbon's 2nd Division of the II Corps, only to be quickly cut down or captured. Pickett's survivors withdrew to Seminary Ridge, and the fighting was over except for a suicidal mounted charge by Union cavalry, which Longstreet's right flank units easily halted. Both sides had fought hard and with great valor, for among 90,000 effective Union troops and 75,000 Confederates there were more than 51,000 casualties. The Army of the Potomac lost 3,155 killed, 14,529 wounded, and 5,365 prisoners and missing. Of the Army of Northern Virginia, 3,903 were killed, 18,735 wounded, and 5,425 missing and prisoners. If Chancellorsville was Lee's finest battle, Gettysburg was clearly his worst; yet the reverse did not unnerve him or reduce his effectiveness as a commander. The invasion had patently failed, and he retired at once toward the Potomac. As that river was flooded, it was several days before he was able to cross. President Lincoln, pleased over Meade's defensive victory and elated over Grant's capture of Vicksburg, thought the war would end in 1863 if Meade launched a resolute pursuit and destroyed Lee's army on the north bank of the Potomac. But Meade's own army was too mangled, and the Union commander moved cautiously, permitting Lee to return safely to Virginia on July 13.

Gettysburg was the last important action in the eastern theater in 1863. Lee and Meade maneuvered against each other in Virginia, but there was no more fighting. After Gettysburg and Vicksburg the center of strategic gravity shifted to Tennessee.

### Carlisle

The Court House on the square at High and Hanover streets was built in 1845. It is Georgian in design and replaced the original building which was destroyed by fire. The columns bear the scars of General Fitzhugh Lee's shelling of Carlisle in 1863. The Soldier's Monument bears the names of 17 officers and 325 private soldiers and is typical of Civil War–period markers.

The Elks Home, midway on High Street near Pitt Street, was the home of Isac B. Parker. This lovely home was famous for its hospitality and is prominently mentioned in a story of Civil War days, "In Old Bellaire" by Mary Dillon. Walking on East Street to Hanover, turn right to the War College, which belongs to the U.S. Government and has been in use in various capacities since 1757. See the Cavalry station used in the Civil War and barracks which were abandoned and taken over by Capt. Richard Pratt. The Hamilton Library at 21 N. Pitt Street contains early newspapers, historical documents and souvenirs of early days. Historical lectures are presented on the third Thursday of winter months at 7:30 P.M.

### Pittsburgh

At the Stephen Foster Memorial Hall, Forbes and Bigelow Blvd., you will find a valuable collection of this famous Pittsburgher's memorabilia in the west wings.

Foster was born on July 4, 1826, in the Lawrenceville section of Pittsburgh. In his brief life—he died in 1864—he wrote 235 songs, including such favorites as "Old Black Joe" and "My Old Kentucky Home." Each January, a special program is presented in the auditorium of the memorial, recalling the day of his death. He died in New York from a fall in a lodging house, and was found with only 38 cents in his pocket and the lyric of a song that began, "Dear hearts and gentle people . . ."

## PRACTICAL INFORMATION FOR PENNSYLVANIA

**PENNSYLVANIA FACTS AND FIGURES.** Pennsylvania—"Penn's Wood"—is named for William Penn, the Quaker founder of the state. Its nickname is *Keystone State*. The mountain laurel is the state flower; the hemlock, the state tree; the ruffled grouse, the state bird. "Virtue Liberty, and Independence" is the state motto. Pennsylvania is in the Eastern Time Zone.

Harrisburg is the state capital. The state population is almost 12 million.

Pennsylvania's landscape begins with thousands of square miles of level or gently rolling agricultural land in the east and south-central parts of the state. There are three mountainous areas: the recreation-filled Poconos in the northeast; and the Appalachians and Alleghenies, which slant diagonally across the center. In the west, the Allegheny and Monongahela rivers join at Pittsburgh to form the mighty Ohio, and the northwest corner flattens out into the industrial belt along the shore of Lake Erie. Pennsylvania is third in population in the U.S., and third in industrial production. It is 307 miles from east to west, 169 from north to south. Its area of 45,330 square miles is 33rd in size among the 50 states. The climate is one of cold winters and warm summers, with heavy snow in the mountains and northern part of the state.

**HOW TO GET THERE.** *By car:* There is easy access to Pennsylvania by Interstate Highway. From New York on the east, I–95 runs to Philadelphia, in the northeast I–81 passes through Binghamton, N.Y., to Scranton and down the state to Harrisburg. I–80 bisects the state on an east-west axis. I–79 has its northern terminal in Erie, Pa., passing through Pittsburgh and leaving the state near Morgantown, West Virginia.

*By train: Amtrak* has service to Philadelphia, Harrisburg, and Lancaster on interstate routes.

*By bus: Greyhound* and *Trailways* are the major carriers to Pennsylvania. *Continental* also has service to the major cities.

*By air:* Philadelphia and Pittsburgh have the major airports. *Allegheny, Eastern* and *TWA* are some of the major airlines serving Philadelphia and Pittsburgh.

**HOW TO GET AROUND.** *By car:* A word of caution: the Pennsylvania Turnpike west of Harrisburg can be a hair-raising experience. The road is narrow and large trucks roar down the steep grades and through the tunnels. Leave yourself plenty of time to enjoy the mountain scenery but keep an eye out for the trucks.

*By train: Amtrak* has good service in the southern half of the state between Philadelphia and Pittsburgh. There is also commuter service in the Philadelphia suburbs. Contact your travel agent or Amtrak office for rates and schedules.

*By bus: Trailways, Greyhound* and *Continental* provide fairly complete coverage within the state.

*By air: Allegheny Airlines* is the major interstate carrier. Besides Philadelphia and Pittsburgh, *Allegheny* flies to: Erie, Bradford, Williamsport, Scranton and Wilkes-Barre, Hazelton, Allentown, Reading, Lancaster, Harrisburg, Johnstown, Altoona, Clearfield, Dubois and Franklin.

**TOURIST INFORMATION.** The Travel Department Bureau, Pennsylvania Department of Commerce, 206 South Office Building, Harrisburg, Pa. 17120, is ready to answer any questions you might have. A list of county tourist bureaus is available from the same source, 717-787-5453.

**TOURS.** For a free walking tour of historic downtown Gettysburg or a 36-mile driving tour of scenic Adams County, stop at the Gettysburg Travel Council Information Center for maps and further information.

*Gettysburg Bus Tour Center.* Hollywood actors have recorded "The Battle of Gettysburg" which accompanies the 35-mile, 2-hour tour in an air-conditioned bus. Main terminal on Baltimore St. 717-334-6296.

*Association of Gettysburg Battlefield Guides.* You can take a guide in your own car for an informative, pleasant tour. Licensed guides at Lincoln Square, 1½ miles west on Rt. 30 and at Park Service Visitor Center. 717-334-9920 or 717-334-1124.

*Audio-Tronic Tour.* Original tape-recorded tour of the Battlefield in your car, at your leisure. Human interest stories and battle sound effects. 240 Steinwehr Ave., Bus. Rt. 15, south 7 blocks. 717-334-5800.

*CCInc. Auto Tape Tours.* Hear historic 3-day battle vividly recreated in your own car. Rent player and tape at National Civil War Wax Museum. Bus. Rt. 15 south. 717-334-6245.

*Helicopter Tours.* Unobstructed, spectacular views of the battlefield. 3 miles south on Bus. Rt. 15.

*Steve Wolf's Sightseeing Tours.* Excursions from campgrounds arranged daily in economy or air-conditioned buses. R.D. 2, Gettysburg, 17325. 717-334-5296.

**NATIONAL PARKS.** *Gettysburg National Military Park* surrounds the town of Gettysburg at the junction of US 30 and 15 and 140 about 7 miles north of the Maryland border. It comprises the battlefield on which, on July 1, 2 and 3 of 1863, was fought one of the bloodiest and most decisive battles of the Civil War. Here, too, is the spot on which President Abraham Lincoln delivered his most famous speech, the *Gettysburg Address,* on November 19, 1863. The park covers 25 square miles and has almost 30 miles of roads through the fighting areas, with monuments, markers, and tablets of granite and bronze; and 400 cannon in battle positions are located on the field. Battlefield guides, licensed by the National Park Service, conduct two-hour tours to all the points of interest, describing the troop movements and highlights of the battle. Tours are also available in air-conditioned sightseeing buses that supply the sounds of the battle and a dramatized description in stereophonic sound. A helicopter service is also available which gives the tourist a superior view of the battlefield. Tours are also available at the Gettysburg Wax Museum. A *Park Visitors Center,* located on US 15 and State 134, features many instructive exhibits and dioramas in a large museum, as well as a 356-foot cyclorama painting of *Pickett's Charge.* The center is open 8 to 5 p.m. daily and is free, but adults pay 50¢ admission to the cyclorama. During June, July, and August there is a free *Campfire Program* in the ampitheater in *Pitzer's Woods*. It is held nightly at dusk, weather permitting, and features a brief talk on the Civil War soldier and the 45-minute MGM film *The Battle of Gettysburg*.

**CAMPING OUT.** There are private campgrounds throughout the state; most have facilities for both tents and travel trailers. Campgrounds range from merely an open space to pitch a tent to elaborate facilities including movies, churches, organized social activities, in fact, all the amenities of a resort. The Travel Development Bureau publishes a *Pennsylvania Campground Association Guide* that lists over 100 private campgrounds. Write: The Travel Development Bureau, Department of Commerce, 206 South Office Building, Harrisburg, Pa. 17120.

*Drummer Boy Camping Resort,* 100 acres, 300 shaded sites for family camping. Pool, fishing, lake, mini golf. 1½ miles E of Gettysburg on Rt. 116 at US 15 R.D. 5, Gettysburg, Pa. 17325. 717–642–5713.

*Gettysburg Koa Kampground.* Quiet, wooded setting. Pool, laundry, store. Full hook-ups, tent sites. Nitely historical program. Battlefield Bus and Tape Tours, R.D. 3, Gettysburg, Pa. 17325. 717–642–5713.

*A-O.K. Campground.* 49 acres, centrally located near Visitor Center. Hot showers, elec. & water, pool, laundry. 717–334–1288.

*Colonel's Creek Campground & Cottages.* Cool mountain comfort along shady stream. Hook-ups, cottages, fishing. US 30, 12 miles W of Gettysburg. R.D. 2, Fayetteville, Pa. 717–352–8938.

*Granite Hill Family Campground & R.V. Resort.* Complete family camping. Hook-ups, tennis, hayrides, mini golf, pool. Located 6 miles W on Rt. 116. 717–642–8749.

*Round Top Campground.* R.D. 1 Jct. US Bypass 15 & Pa. 134, 3 miles south of Gettysburg. Wooded sites, dump station. Playground, pool, tennis, rec. building. 717–334–9565.

*Welcome Traveller Camp Site.* Hiking trails adjacent to Battlefield. Ten sites, restrooms, laundry. Pool, playground. 1½ miles S on Rt. 140. 717–334–9226.

**TRAILER TIPS.** The increasing popularity of trailer travel in recent years is evidenced in Pennsylvania by an ever-growing number of accommodations and facilities for this pleasantly informal mode of travel and vacation. All of the state parks that provide camping facilities accommodate the smaller and moderate-size travel trailers at the same rates as for tent camping. However, no electricity or hookups are provided. In addition, there are many private, well-equipped trailer and mobile home parks through the state. *Melody Lakes Mobile Park* is in Quakertown, in beautiful Bucks County. Another working farm that features a campground is *Twin Bridge Meadow Valley Campground,* R.D. 4, Chambersburg, Pa.

**MUSEUMS AND GALLERIES.** In Gettysburg, site of the largest battlefield shrine in America, you may tour the Gettysburg National Military Park, six miles by seven miles, and also visit countless museums unlike any in the world. There are some privately owned museums, for which there is an admission charge. Begin your tour at the *Visitor Center*. See the electric map-orientation program; a *Cyclorama Center* features Sound-and-Light program of Pickett's charge. The *Gettysburg Battlefield Tower* has a dramatic sound program in a sky capsule. The *National Civil War Wax Museum,* Bus.

Rt, 15 S, has an audio-visual presentation of the entire Civil War. The *Hall of Presidents,* at the main gate of the *National Cemetery* on US 140, has life-size figures in wax of all the presidents. *General Lee's Headquarters,* Rt. 30 W, 7 blks., houses a collection of Civil War relics. The *Lincoln Train Museum* offers a 'ride' with Lincoln in sound, sight and motion. The *Lincoln Room,* downtown on Lincoln Square, records the "Spirit of Lincoln" where he wrote his Gettysburg Address. The *Gettysburg Battle Theatre* presents a film and diorama, "America at Gettysburg," and the *Jennie Wade House* pays tribute to the only citizen killed during the battle, with a tape of the poignant story. *Fort Defiance Museum,* Rt. 134 just south of the Visitor Center offers view of 1863 Gettysburg with the battle in progress, in miniature.

**DRINKING LAWS.** The legal drinking age in Pennsylvania is twenty-one. Bottled liquor is sold only in state stores.

**HOTELS AND MOTELS** in Pennsylvania range from deluxe resorts, mostly in the southeast quarter, to the plain highway accommodations that blend with the less glamorous life-style of the northern half of the state west of the Poconos. Price categories are, for double occupancy, *Super Deluxe* over $45, *Deluxe* $28–45, *Expensive* $22–27, *Moderate* $17–21 and *Inexpensive* under $17. A 6% state tax will be added to your bill.

## GETTYSBURG

**Gettysburg Motor Lodge.** *Expensive.* 380 Steinwehr Ave. (US 15 Business). A mile S of midtown, this motel may charge extra during big college events like graduation. It has a heated pool and newsstand; a cafe is next door, coin laundry a block away.

**Holiday Inn.** *Expensive.* 516 Baltimore St. (US 140 at US 15 Business). Swimming pool, newsstand, suites available. College events may occasion a 2-day minimum. There's a ramp for guests with wheelchairs.

**Howard Johnson's.** *Expensive.* 301 Steinwehr Ave. (US 15 Business). Practically across the street from the above, they offer a sun deck and some private patios as well as a heated pool.

**Sheraton Inn-Gettysburg.** *Expensive.* 5 mi. S. on US 15 Business. Facilities include indoor heated pool, sauna, entertainment, beauty shop, par-3 golf, tennis, and lawn games. 28 rooms with balconies, and an Old English motif.

**Stonehenge.** *Expensive.* Baltimore Pike (US 140). Just S of downtown, it has a pool with snack and drink service and a sauna. Entertainment enlivens the bar on weekends; the restaurant is open 11 A.M. to midnight in summer, from 4 P.M. other seasons.

**Gettysburg TraveLodge.** *Moderate.* 10 E. Lincoln Ave. (US 15 Business). As usual, this is the least expensive in town among representatives of the big motel chains. There's a pool (heated) and it's one block to a café.

**Blue Sky Motel.** *Inexpensive.* 4 miles north on Rt. 34. Comfortable, reasonable family-type atmosphere. TV, pool, picnic and play area. RD 6, Gettysburg, Pa.

**Criterion Motor Lodge.** *Inexpensive.* (3 blocks north on US Bus Rt. 15 at 337

Carlisle St.) Comfortable rooms at a convenient downtown location. Tours arranged.

**Heritage Motor Lodge.** *Inexpensive.* (Junction Bus. Rt. 15 and 140). Heart of the historical and museums area.

**Homestead Motor Lodge.** *Inexpensive.* (R.D. 5, 2 miles east on Rt. 30, ¼ mile east of US 15.) Reasonable rates, 10 units.

**Lincolnway East Motel.** *Inexpensive.* (1½ miles east on US 30, ½ mile west of US 15 bypass.) Cable TV, picnic area. Will arrange tours.

**Peace Light Inn.** *Inexpensive.* Reynolds Ave. ½ mi. N. of US 30. At the entrance to Peace Light Memorial, some of its cottages are on the battlefield. There's a stocked pond to fish from. (R.D. 8)

**Penn Eagle Motor.** *Inexpensive.* (1½ miles east of Lincoln Square on US 30). Attractive accommodations, swimming pool. Reasonable rates. Plant and craft shop.

**Perfect Rest Motel.** *Inexpensive.* (4½ miles south Bus. Rt. 15.) Country surroundings near National Park. Close to leading sites. Pool. Large family rooms. RD 2, Box 64, Gettysburg, Pa.

**Quality Inn Larson's.** *Inexpensive.* 401 Buford Ave. (US 30). Next door you'll find the house where Gen. Lee stayed during the Civil War battle here. Larson's offers a pool, putting green, bar and dining room. One mi. W of town. Beautifully landscaped. Dutch Pantry kitchen.

 **DINING OUT** in Pennsylvania encompasses several regional influences: the cosmopolitan flavor of the Boston-Washington urban corridor, the specialties of Pennsylvania Dutch tradition and, along the southern border, hints of the Midwest and Dixie.

For mid-priced dinners on each menu, the following categories apply: *Deluxe* $9.25–13, *Expensive* $7.25–9.25, *Moderate* $5.75–7.25 and *Inexpensive* under $5.75. These costs include hors d'oeuvres or soup, entree and dessert; they do not include drinks, tax and tip.

**Dutch Pantry.** *Expensive.* 8 blks. west of Lincoln Square on US 30 West. Enjoy "Country Cooking" in an original Penna. Dutch style.

**FARNSWORTH HOUSE DINING.** *Expensive.* 40l Baltimore St., Gettysburg. 334-8838. Restored battle-scarred Civil War house where you dine among original Civil War artifacts.

**HISTORIC FAIRFIELD INN.** *Expensive.* Main Street, Fairfield. 8 miles west of Gettysburg on Rt. 116. Old stagecoach stop in continuous operation since 1823!

**Dutch Cupboard.** *Moderate.* 523 Baltimore St., Gettysburg. Penna. Dutch food is featured; candy and gift shop adjoin restaurant.

**Elby's Big Boy.** *Moderate.* Famous for the "Big Boy" double-deck hamburger. (Adjacent to National Civil War Wax Museum.)

**HICKORY BRIDGE FARM.** *Moderate.* Family-style meal served in a century-old barn. "Like the old times." West of town, off Pa. 116.

**Jennie Wade Village Kitchen.** *Moderate.* 591 Baltimore St., Gettysburg Bus Tour Center. Adjacent to Streets of "63" and Museums. Outdoor seating in season.

# SOUTH CAROLINA

## *Cradle of the Confederacy*

Though partisans of each state in the Confederacy may have good arguments for advocating Georgia, Virginia, or Mississippi as representing the quintessence of the Old South, no one can deny South Carolina its claim to a leading role in the tragedy of the Civil War. Sheltered by distance from federal supervision and by choice from Northern manners, South Carolina was actively internationalist, relying as she did on foreign trade for much of her wealth. Since the early part of the 19th century, South Carolina had been unhappy with rising tariffs, and saw its hero, John C. Calhoun, achieve a compromise with the federal government in his doctrine of nullification, by which a state could ignore a national law it felt was disagreeable. At the very time this settlement between Washington and South Carolina was effected (1833), federal ships were steaming toward Charleston with the purpose of enforcing the tariff laws, even if it meant imposing order through strength.

With the election of Abraham Lincoln in 1860, however, those favoring secession were convinced that no further compromises with Washington were possible. Beginning in December of that year, South Carolina patriots instigated the chain of events which was to lead to the firing on Fort Sumter.

## Abbeville

On November 22, 1860, some three thousand persons gathered on Abbeville's Magazine Hill—now Secession Hill—to hear orators of the Southern cause and to choose delegates to a state convention. When the cry for secession went up in the South, the first formal voice came from Abbeville. A monument marks the event at the entrance on Secession Ave. Abbeville did not stop with lighting the fuse of secession. Many of its men fought in the War Between The States, and its women served in hospitals.

Death gasps of the Confederacy rattled clearly when President Jefferson Davis and his cabinet moved out of Richmond, Virginia, southward. On May 2, 1865, Armstead Burt invited President Davis and his cabinet to spend the evening in Abbeville, and it was decided that further resistance was useless. Jefferson Davis, President of the Confederacy, his full cabinet and six Confederate generals held their last formal meeting here. The government was disbanded, and cabinet members split up the next day to go their own way. The Burt House, now known as Stark House, with the room where the fateful decision was made, is kept much as it was that evening. Built more than 100 years ago by Squire Lesley, a lawyer from Ireland, and later purchased by Burt, it stands at the fork of State 28 and 20.

(For a full description of the Jefferson Davis Trail, see the end of this chapter.)

Many old churches and homes 150 years old are located in and around Abbeville. Trinity Episcopal, just off the square, one of the most visited, was organized October 16, 1842. There are historic names on the interior walls and tombstones. Organized in 1768, Upper Long Cane Church on State 20, two miles north of Abbeville, has a graveyard with veterans of ten wars. William Randolph Hearst's great-great-grandfather lived in the area. The Hearsts moved west to Missouri and California. Patric Noble's home—he became governor in the early 1800's—still stands. His son, Edward, was a signer of the Ordinance of Secession. Murals on the wall of the State Bank and Trust Co. depict historic people and incidents in and around Abbeville.

The Opera House was once one of the grandest in the Southeast. This showplace, on the square, retains some of its original majestic grandeur amidst fallen plaster, creaking hinged doors and gilded box seats. Show troupes came from up north in the 1900's and through World War II and performers paraded in the square before the 5 P.M. opening. Every show was standing room only, with as many as 1,500 arriving by special train from other cities.

Tourists interested in heraldic art and family ancestral designs should see Mrs. James Austin, a talented artist and a specialist for over 30 years in coats of arms. Her husband specializes in upstate family names. An unusual antique store, Noah's Ark, lies just off the square. The contents change constantly and range from history books to iron bath rubs, old locks and keys to a church pew.

On State 10 near Greenwood is Promised Land, a Civil War

Federal Government Negro relocation project of several thousand acres.

### Edgefield

Oakley Park, in Edgefield, is the Red Shirt Shrine Museum. Maintained by the Daughters of the Confederacy, it has many portraits, furnishings and interior decorations. On the second floor are maps, histories and clothes of bygone days. The house was built in 1835 by Daniel Byrd, descendent of the Virginia Byrds. Carroll Hill, Bumcomb and Pickens Sts., was built by Chancellor James Parsons Carroll, signer of the Ordinance of Secession and representative in both branches of the legislature.

Many tourists go to Edgefield to check ancestral dates in five church graveyards. Trinity Episcopal, Simpkins at Wigfall Streets, is one of the largest—Edmund B. Bacon deeded the land in 1836 for one dollar. Others are at Willowbrook Cemetery, the First Baptist Church, the Presbyterian Church on Church Street, the Methodist Church at Norris Street, and St. Mary's Catholic Church on Bumcomb Street.

Halcyon Grove on Bumcomb St. was the town house of Governor Andrew Pickens, Jr., the son of General Andrew Pickens. It was later bought by Governor Francis Wilkinson Pickens, Minister to the Russian Imperial Court in St. Petersburg from 1858 to 1860. Pickens' beautiful third wife, the former Lucy Holcomb, was the toast of Russia. Their daughter, born in Russia, was named Olga Liva Lucy Holcomb Douschka Francesca Pickens. This young, beautiful American Joan of Arc, clad in red silk, stood beside Wade Hampton on the balcony of Oakley Plantation House as he rallied the crowd with his spirited talk. The Pickens beauty mounted her horse, held the Red Shirt Banner high, and led 1,500 men in a triumphant parade. She is buried near her father in the Willowbrook cemetery. The tombstone reads simply "Douschka."

In Pendleton, on State 88, is the Old Farmer's Hall, oldest in the United States, with a post office on the first floor; the original banner carried by Wade Hampton's Red Shirts and the cannon used by the Red Shirt Company during the Civil War—it was last fired in celebration of Grover Cleveland's election as President. Near the cannon is a sun dial given the Farmer's Society by Col. Francis Huger, known as the liberator of the Marquis de Lafayette, from the dungeon of Olmütz.

Also visit the Old Stone Church and cemetery with its many historic graves. Of Presbyterian faith, it was founded in 1789. The building of rough field stone erected by John Rusk replaces the original log church two miles away. "Printer" John Miller, publisher of the famous *Junius Letters* in England, donated seventeen acres to the church and cemetery. The Calhoun Chapter of the United Daughters of the Confederacy erected an ampitheatre on the church grounds for Memorial Day meetings.

Among many historic homes in this section is Woodlawn, near the

Old Stone Church—once the residence of a famous clergyman, the Reverend Jasper Adams. San Salvadore, on the Seneca River, was built by Major Samuel Taylor and named for a soldier killed by Indians on his place.

Recently opened by Pendleton Foundation for Historic Preservation is Ashtabula House, three miles north on State 88. It holds antiques and relics, and the dining room and outside kitchen are restored.

In Mayfield, on State 19N, visit the town's museum, which has relics of the Confederacy, and an Andrew Jackson collection.

## Port Royal

During the Civil War, while the Confederates were concentrated in Charles Towne, Federal forces landed sixteen ships with 12,000 men at Port Royal. They kept possession of the Sound for the duration of the war.

## Columbia

The State House, a three-story granite building of Italian Renaissance style, was designed by John R. Niernesee, begun in 1851, but not completed until 1907. Bronze stars on the south and west facades mark scars made by Sherman's shells in 1865. On the first landing, north of the building, is a life-sized bronze statue of George Washington, his staff broken by Sherman's men. In front of the building is the Monument to the Confederate Dead, and on the grounds is a Memorial to the Women of the Confederacy.

The convention to draw up an Ordinance of Secession met in Columbia at the First Baptist Church on December 17, 1860, but, because there was an epidemic of smallpox in the city, the convention moved to Charleston where, on December 20, the fateful document was signed.

When Sherman entered Columbia on February 17, 1865, he promised to respect the city's surrender and keep it intact, but on the following night, fire of "unknown origins" destroyed more than two-thirds of the city, including every house save one on Main Street.

Highlight of Columbia for Civil War buffs is the Confederate Relic Room and Museum in the World War Memorial building on the corner of Sumter and Pendleton streets. Here you can view the cannonballs fired at the State House by Sherman's troops, Confederate money, battle flags, costumes of the period and other items.

The Governor's Mansion, 800 Richland Street, is all that remains of a military school burned when Sherman occupied the city. Open by appointment only.

For genealogists, the South Carolina Department of Archives and History is a storehouse of information. Early South Carolina was a melting pot for people of English, French, Scottish, Welsh, Eastern European, Swiss, and German stock. The American Revolution, the plantation era and the War Between the States caused South

Carolinians to migrate to all parts of the country. It could just be that you and South Carolina are linked by family ties, and you can find out by visiting the State Archives Department.

Three Confederate generals are buried in the graveyard of Trinity Episcopal Church, on Sumter Street, as is Henry Timrod, author of the state song, "Carolina."

The Confederate Bureau of Engraving and Printing, where all that money was made, was located in the Old State Dispensary Building, corner of Gervais and Pulaski Streets.

Four miles east of town are the ruins of Millwood, home of Wade Hampton. Sherman's troops burned the house in 1865, but you can still see its vine-covered columns and some remnants of the gardens.

### Charleston

The first action of the War Between the States came as a symbolic blow, sought by South Carolinians eager to assert their independence from the United States, not because Fort Sumter itself was a threat to secession. The decision to take the fort stemmed, in fact, from an earlier attempt by federal forces to send supplies to Sumter. On January 9, 1861, Washington ordered an unarmed steamship, the *Star of the West*, to carry supplies, especially food, and reinforcements to Fort Sumter. Cadets of the Citadel, "the West Point of the South," fired the college's cannon at the ship, forcing her to withdraw.

Commanded by Maj. Robert Anderson, himself a Southerner, Fort Sumter faced starvation; Anderson refused several offers to surrender. Finally, on April 12, 1861, at 4:30 in the morning, mortar fire from neighboring Fort Johnson, in South Carolinian hands, began to shell Sumter. Thirty-four hours later, his barracks burning and his flag shot down, Major Anderson surrendered. Amazingly, there was not a single fatality during the entire action. The Confederacy kept Sumter throughout the war, but at its conclusion, Anderson returned with his tattered Union flag, raising it once again above the post he had commanded.

Fort Sumter, where the Civil War began, can be reached by sightseeing boats departing from the Charleston Municipal Marina several times a day. Both the Fort Sumter cruise and Gray Line's 25-mile Harbor of History Tour give the visitor a delightful boat trip and spectacular offshore views of Charleston's famous Battery mansions.

A beautiful monument to the Battle of Fort Sumter can be seen at Battery Park, at the meeting place of the Ashley and Cooper rivers.

The Hunley Museum, located in one of the oldest bank buildings in the United States (1798), houses a full-scale replica of the first submarine ever used in warfare, the Confederate's *H. S. Hunley*, and other artifacts of the Civil War.

Other historic points of interest include the Charleston Museum, oldest municipal museum in America; the old City Market; the

Confederate Museum and the Old Slave Mart Museum and Gallery.

Also open to the public are Charleston's three famous house museums—the Joseph Manigault House (1803), the National Russell House (1809), and the Heyward-Washington House (1770).

Those who prefer to simply walk or ride through the historic sections of Charleston may do so at their leisure by following the Walking Tour route or by taking romantic horse-drawn carriage tours. Also available are tape-recorded walking tours and bus tours. For persons interested in more comprehensive touring and individualized attention, the Charleston Guide Service offers well-trained professional guides who provide transportation and guided tours for individuals, families or larger groups.

A statue of the city's defender throughout the war, Gen. P. G. T. Beauregard, stands in Washington Square (also known as City Hall Park). Nearby is a monument to the Washington Light Infantry, a leading Confederate unit.

Charleston's biggest attraction, Charles Towne Landing, was opened in 1970, having been built on the original 1670 landing site to commemorate the city's 300th birthday. One of the most unusual parks in the country, Charles Towne Landing includes a theater with a 25-minute film showing the beauty of the state's Low Country; an Exhibition Pavilion, whose outstanding artifacts illustrate the first century of settlement; a Reception Center with gift shop, restaurant, and rental carts or bicycles; a 1670 Experimental Garden showing various crops grown by the early settlers; the original 1670 Settlement Site; the *Adventure,* a reproduction of a 17th-century trading ketch; the Animal Forest, with animals indigenous to South Carolina in 1670; and nearly 100 acres of beautifully landscaped English park–type gardens with paths circling placid lagoons.

One of the reconstructed buildings, the old Planters Hotel, is said to be the place where Planter's Punch originated. The hotel, built in 1810, was a rendezvous for plantation owners until the end of the War Between the States.

The chimes of nearby St. Philip's Church, on Church Street, were removed in 1863 and cast into Confederate cannon. They were never replaced. Robert E. Lee attended church at St. Michael's, corner of Broad and Meeting streets. So did George Washington and Lafayette.

Pringle House, on King Street, was headquarters for the Union commander when Charleston was occupied in 1865. Before that the house, built in 1765, served as headquarters for Lord Cornwallis in 1782.

Old Magnolia Cemetery, established in 1850, contains the graves of many Confederate soldiers.

Located in Charleston Harbor not far from Fort Sumter is Castle Pinckney National Monument, on Shute's Folly Island. The fort, built on a site selected by George Washington, was captured from federal engineers, the only persons there, while they were attempting to fortify it seven days after South Carolina had seceded from the

Union. It was thus the first military action of the Civil War, but there was no firing, so Fort Sumter remains the scene of the first battle of the conflict.

### City of Ghosts and Plantations

Georgetown, north on US 17, is a city of memories, ghosts and fine plantations. Many prominent figures from pre-Revolutionary days and the Civil War were born, lived or visited here. Lafayette and DeKalb landed where Winyah Bay empties into the Atlantic. The waterway from Brookgreen to Georgetown was traveled by Theodosia Burr as she came to town to board the *Patriot*. Many legends are told of this beautiful daughter of the famous Aaron. It is even said that she was captured by pirates and made to walk the plank, but who can believe that? Francis "Swamp Fox" Marion also lived here.

Georgetown is also home of Belle Isle Gardens, off US 17, 5 miles south of town, a 5,000-acre expanse of landscaped grounds planted in azaleas and other flowers. It occupies the old rice fields of a plantation. Located here was Battery White, a 16-battery Confederate fort, during the Civil War. The gardens are open from November to August every day except Christmas. Small admission charge.

Several graves of Confederate soldiers can be seen in the grave-yard of Prince George Winyah's Church, Broad Street and High Market Street.

### Florence and Beaufort

The museum of this fine old town specializes in South Carolina history, from colonial days to the present, emphasizing tools, costumes, household implements, agriculture and manufacturing. Next door is Timrod Park, with the Henry Timrod Shrine, a one-room schoolhouse in which the Confederate Poet Laureate taught.

Florence National Cemetery was established in 1865 for the interment of Union soldiers who had died in the nearby Florence Confederate Prison. There were about 2,800 buried at the time, all but 30 of them "unknown soldiers."

When Union troops occupied Beaufort and the nearby islands in 1861, they seized the property of families who had men serving the Confederacy, looted homes, and divided up plantations to give to the slaves. Many of the old mansions as well were given or sold to newly freed slaves, and few of the original owners ever recovered their property.

On the northern edge of the city is the Beaufort National Cemetery, established in 1863, containing graves of federal troops, whose bodies were brought here from Florida and Georgia as well as South Carolina.

The John Mark Verdier House in Beaufort, at 801 Bay St., is an Adam-style residence built in the late 1790's by one of the town's leading merchants. The Marquis de Lafayette was entertained here in 1825, and the house was used as headquarters of the Union forces at the end of the Civil War.

### Hilton Head Island

A semi-tropical paradise for modern pleasure-seekers, this island was the site of several Civil War activities. Fort Walker and Fort Mitchel were two important bastions. Fort Walker was part of the Confederate coastal defense, and was captured by the largest seaborne force in U.S. history—until that time—when 13,000 Union troops invaded in 1862. Hilton Head, held by the North until the end of the war, was the chief staging area for the federal blockade of Southern ports.

Fort Mitchel was constructed by the Union troops in order to guard Seabrook Landing, the chief supply center for coaling federal steamships and for other heavy supplies. Several cannon of the period remain at Fort Mitchel.

### Rivers Bridge State Park

Confederate earthern breastworks and an interpretative center tell the story of an important Civil War battle fought here. There are nature trails, a playground, swimming, camping and picnic facilities. The park is located seven miles southwest of Ehrhardt off SC 64, about 12 miles east of US 301.

### The Jefferson Davis Trail

This historic route, the only one of its kind in America, retraces the flight of the President of the Confederacy through South Carolina after the fall of Richmond in 1865, and the surrender of Lee's forces at Appomattox Courthouse in April of that year.

The route winds through the small towns, farmland, forests and rolling hills of the Piedmont area, far from the coastal plains, where Sherman's forces occupied every strategic point. Much of the countryside through which Jefferson Davis traveled has changed so little since the 19th century that the traveler gets the feeling of a trip through time as well as space. Towns along the route are large enough to provide rooms and meals, yet small enough to retain the old-fashioned air of Southern hospitality.

Once well-marked, the route now suffers from a dearth of signs, many of which have been stolen by unmannerly people or vandals. When you do find a sign, you'll know it by the letters "CS".

### A Bit of Background

During the night of April 2, 1865, the Confederate government evacuated Richmond, Virginia, when defense became impossible. General Lee surrendered his command at Appomattox on April 9, leaving President Jefferson Davis and his cabinet no recourse but to flee southward. By April 26, they reached South Carolina, and from then until May 3, traversed the state, being hospitably received by the people at every step. Local records tell of the staff being greeted with offerings of flowers, fresh strawberries and every form of help desired. The Piedmont area not having been devastated by war, President Davis and his group were well taken care of. Davis still refused to believe the Confederate cause was hopeless, but his generals finally persuaded him to accept the facts. At a Council of War held in Abbeville on May 2, it was decided to abandon any other course of action save that of affording the president's escape across the Mississippi, and, it was hoped, eventual flight to England via Mexico.

The party began to disperse after leaving Abbeville, with Davis and a small escort traveling south into Georgia. One week later, early in the morning of May 10, Davis and his companions were captured by federal troops near Irwinville, Georgia.

Wherever possible, the main route follows the nearest existing highways to Davis's route, but this has not always been possible either because documentation cannot be substantiated, or because local traditions conflict, or because Davis's party often took round-about ways to evade a party of Stoneman's Raiders, who were pursuing them all the way. The main trail nonetheless seldom deviates more than a few miles from the actual route. (Also note the side trips, which can be of special interest.)

## The Trail Begins

The trail enters South Carolina on US 21. Follow this highway about 2 miles, then turn left on US 21 (Business) about 1.8 miles to the home (c. 1805) of Col. A. B. Springs, where Davis spent the night of April 26.

Continue on US 21 (Business) about 2.5 miles to Fort Mill, where you can see monuments to Confederate heroes and "faithful slaves" in the park near the business district.

From Fort Mill, follow SC 160 north. At the edge of town is the home of Wm. Elliott White (c. 1830), where part of the Confederate Cabinet spent the night of April 26. The next day, the Cabinet's last meeting was held on the lawn (historic marker). The house is not open to the public, however.

Proceed another half mile and turn left on US 21. After crossing the Catawba River, look for the Nation Ford historical marker on your left, noting the crossing of Davis and his party here. Return to the main trail. US 21 (Business) and turn left, proceeding about 0.8 miles to Rock Hill, where Davis's route probably took him close to the present Winthrop College campus, then west on a road corresponding to present SC 5.

Leave Rock Hill on SC 274. At the edge of town is the Ebenezer Presbyterian Church, in whose cemetery can be seen the graves of several Confederate veterans.

Continue on SC 274 to Newport, then on SC 161 about 7.2 miles to York, where President Davis spent the night of April 27 in the townhouse of Dr. J. Rufus Bratton. Nearby is the building once known as the Rose Hotel, where Confederate Secretary of War Breckinridge spoke.

Leave York on SC 49 south through Lockhart, then go about 2.3 miles to SC 105, where you should turn right, proceeding about 1.9 miles to Robat. From here, continue about 6.8 miles on SC 105 to Pinckneyville. Jefferson Davis crossed the Broad River here. All that remains of this once-flourishing village are the jail, the store, and one lonely grave.

Return to SC 49, turn right and proceed to Union. (Davis and his party spent the night of April 28 somewhere between York and Union.) There are many antebellum residences here, including Judge Dawkins's 1845 home, which housed state papers and records when Sherman's advance on Columbia looked inevitable. A most important site is the home of Gen. William Wallace, where President Davis was entertained on April 29. Also see the Thomas B. Jeter home (he was Governor of South Carolina in 1880), the old jail (1823), and the Episcopal Church (1859).

Leave Union on SC 49 south. President Davis's route from Union to Joanna is not definitely established, so our path now follows the most modern road. According to tradition, however, Davis spent the night of April 29 in the J. R. R. Giles home, located somewhere between Union and Cross Keys (present location unknown). About 10.9 miles south of Union is Cross Keys House (1812), where Davis is said to have eaten his lunch on April 30.

A side trip from here to Padgett's Creek Baptist Church may be of interest. Turn left on S44–18 and proceed about 1.8 miles to the church (1844). Here Sen. William H. Gist (later Governor) spoke at an 1851 secession meeting. There are Confederate graves in the cemetery. Continue about 3.4 miles to S44–63 and turn left. Gist Cemetery is about 1.5 miles on the left. Continue about 1 mile to Rose Hill State Park, once part of a large cotton plantation. The present park includes the mansion (1828), outbuildings, and 44 acres of land, owned by Gist, signer of the Ordinance of Secession and governor from 1858 to 1860.

Return to Cross Keys House and turn left on S44–22, the main trail. It is about 4.2 miles to Enoree River, where a modern highway bridge crosses at the site of Jone's Ford, the probable site of Davis's crossing. The county road number changes to S30–98 across the river. Proceed on it about 6.5 miles to SC 56, where the main trail turns left.

Follow SC 56 about 2.2 miles to Clinton, where you should locate US 76. Take this highway west about 6 miles to Laurens, where Andrew Johnson, the president who succeeded Abraham Lincoln, once operated a tailor shop. Other places of note here include the Court House (1835), Episcopal Church (1846), Octagon House (c. 1850), the home of William D. Simpson (governor, 1879–1880), and the home of Robert A. Cooper (governor 1918–22).

Return to the main trail in Clinton and leave town on US 76, heading south. It is about 5 miles to Joanna, known as Martin's Depot when Davis passed through on the afternoon of April 30. (The town was later named Goldville.) From Joanna, find SC 66 and turn left, going about 8.6 miles to the Riser Brick House. There is a widely held local tradition that Davis crossed the Enoree River east of here and followed a road corresponding to present SC 66 on his way to Martin's Depot.

Return to the main trail in Joanna, turn left and follow SC 66 for about 2.7 miles, where the main trail continues straight ahead on SC 56 for about 1.1 miles.

At this point, the main trail picks up on S30–38 (left). Proceed 1.7 miles to the Lafayette Young House, where Davis spent the night of April 30.

Continue on the main trail, S 30–38, to the Griffin Williams House, where, on the morning of May 1, Davis joined others in his party who had spent the night in this mansion.

The main trail turns right on S30–30. Next is Col. John D. Williams's home, built by slaves in 1861, about 0.6 miles on the right. Continue through Cross Hill, where the main trail becomes SC 72.

Continuing on SC 72, you cross the river near Puckett's Ferry, the river crossing of Jefferson Davis, located near the bridge. Travel about 2.7 miles to Coronaca, where the trail turns right on SC 246 for about 8.5 miles to Cokesbury.

Jefferson Davis spent the night of May 1 in Cokesbury at the Thomas Gary House. Mrs. Gary was the mother of Confederate Gen. M. W. Gary. Continue on SC 246 about 1.4 miles to Hodges, where you turn right on SC 185 for 4.4 miles, at which point the main trail follows SC 203 for about 6.6 miles to Abbeville.

### The Last Hours

In this historic town, the main trail turns left on S1–2, heading for the business district. The Burt-Stark House here is the highlight of the trail. Here Jefferson Davis spent the night of May 2, and here the Council of War on the same day decided the Confederate cause was hopeless, and their only remaining objective was the safe escape of the president.

Davis left town on SC 28 south, then SC 72, and finally SC 823 to Mt. Carmel. At the intersection of SC 81 and S33–91 here, Jefferson Davis proceeded southwest where, just before Bordeaux, the main trail branches off from SC 81 onto S33–7 to Hickory Knob State Park, site of Fort Charlotte Plantation. This is very close to US 378, which crosses the Savannah River into Georgia, and is the end of the trail.

# PRACTICAL INFORMATION FOR SOUTH CAROLINA

 **FACTS AND FIGURES.** Columbia, located in the geographical center of the state, is the capital. Population of the state is about 2,746,000. The official state tree, the palmetto, has earned for the state its designation as the "Palmetto State." The state bird is the Carolina wren; the state flower, the yellow jessamine; the state stone, blue granite. The state animal is the white-tail deer, and the state fish is the striped bass. *Animus opibusque parati* ("Prepared in spirit and resources") and *Dum spiro spereo* ("While I breathe, I hope") are the state mottos.

 **HOW TO GET THERE.** *By air:* Charleston and Columbia may be reached by direct flights of Delta, Eastern, Piedmont and Southern from out of the state. In addition, National flies into Charleston. There are direct flights to Greenville/Spartanburg on Eastern, Piedmont and Southern; to Florence and Myrtle Beach on Piedmont. Southern Airways flies into Greenwood.

*By car:* Main routes coming into South Carolina include I-95, a multilane divided highway from Savannah, Georgia, into Hardeeville and continuing through the state and into North Carolina; I-20 from the Augusta, Georgia, area is also a main access to South Carolina; I-85, another multilane highway, brings visitors into South Carolina from the northern part of Georgia. Main routes into the state from North Carolina include I-85, I-77 from Charlotte, N. C.; I.-26 from Hendersonville; and I-95 from Lumberton into Dillon. US 17, a shoreline route, follows along from North Carolina through South Carolina and into Georgia. US 301 is another well-traveled route in and out of the state.

*By bus:* Trailways, Greyhound, Jefferson Lines, Inc., and Southeastern Stages, Inc. all go into South Carolina.

*By train:* Amtrak goes into Charleston and Columbia; Southern Railways into Greenville, Clemson and Spartanburg.

 **HOW TO GET AROUND.** *By air:* You can travel by air within the state on Delta, Piedmont, Southern and Commuter airlines.

*By car:* I-95, I-20, I-26 and I-85 crisscross within the state. US 17, which runs along the shoreline, and US 301, an inland route, are also good. US 123, 321, 52, 78, 378 and State 72 are also in this category.

*Car rental:* Rental service is available at the Charleston and Columbia airports. There are several rental firms operating in Orangeburg and Sumter.

*By bus:* Greyhound, Trailways, Jefferson Lines, Inc., and Southern Stages, Inc., have service within the state.

 **TOURIST INFORMATION.** To obtain detailed information about South Carolina write: South Carolina Department of Parks, Recreation and Tourism, P. O. Box 1358, Columbia 29202; or South Carolina Travel Council, 1002 Calhoun St., Columbia 29201. For information on South Carolina's two national forests, write South Carolina Wildlife and Marine Services Dept., Dutch Plaza, Bldg. D, Columbia 29202. To obtain information on the Grand Strand write: Greater Myrtle Beach Chamber of Commerce, P.O. Box 2115, Myrtle Beach 29577. Santee-Cooper Country, P.O. Box 12, Santee 29142, will supply information on the Santee-Cooper Lakes. The Hilton Head Island Chamber of Commerce, P.O. Drawer 5647,

Hilton Head Island 29928, will send you complete information on what the island offers. Complete hunting and fishing information and regulations may be obtained from the South Carolina Wildlife and Marine Resources Department, Division of Game, P.O. Box 167, Columbia 29202. Charleston Trident Chamber of Commerce, P.O. Box 975, Charleston 29402 will advise you on deep-sea fishing and charter boats.

 **SEASONAL EVENTS.** Much of South Carolina's history and tradition is relived through the many and varied festivals and events held throughout the state. Tours of historic homes and events such as the Annual Foothills Arts and Crafts Guild Festival return the modern-day South Carolinian to the days when craftsmen used pegs instead of nails and country music was the only kind to be heard. South Carolina is also a home of such modern-day attractions as the Southern 500 Stock Car Race.

Among the regularly held events in South Carolina are:

*January: January Jamboree,* Myrtle Beach and the Grand Strand. Golf tournaments and awards, *historic and garden tours,* special sales, golf films, entertainment and package activity at hotels and motels. *Annual Georgetown Camellia Show,* Georgetown. Thousands of blooms are on display from many of the surrounding plantations, as well as from the entire state, North Carolina and Georgia.

*February:* Charleston's famous gardens—*Cypress* and *Magnolia* (open Feb. 15 to May 1)—join *Middleton Place Gardens and Plantation Stableyards* (open all year) for spring garden tours. All three gardens are famous for their colorful profusion of camellias and azaleas and for fine old live oak and cypress trees. Magnolia and Middleton Place are on State 61; Cypress on US 52.

*March: Candlelight Tour of Historic Houses,* Charleston, mid-Mar. Several private homes and gardens open only on this one day. *Annual Canadian-American Days,* Myrtle Beach and the Grand Strand. Folk Music Festival, parade, beach games, cruises, kids' days at amusement parks, *historic tours,* teenage parties, square dance, daily news from Canada, antique show, golf tournaments and awards, fishing, band concerts, tours of the Air Force Base, historic garden and industrial tours and a musical stage show. *Charleston Festival of Houses,* Mar. to Apr. Afternoon and candlelight walking tours are offered. Magnificent private gardens and charming historic private homes are on display in this most historic city. The event is one of the highlights of touring the state's beautiful Low Country gardens in the spring.

*July: Mountain Rest Hillbilly Day,* Mountain Rest Community. This tiny community comes alive with the pageantry of city slickers gone country: square dancing, clogging, greased pig chases and hootenanny. The twang of real hillbilly music sets the background for the enjoyment of mountain victuals served atop the beautiful Blue Ridge Mountain.

*August: Annual Foothills Arts and Crafts Festival,* on the square in Pendleton. Exhibits, booths, artists at work in various media, crafts, demonstrations, etc.

 **STATE PARKS.** Thirty-four state parks enhance the state with campgrounds, well-stocked lakes, nature trails and picnic tables. The parks are open all year during daylight hours. Concessions generally close Labor Day and reopen May.

Parks and locations are: *Aiken,* 16 mi. E of Aiken off US 78; *Andrew Jackson,* 8 mi. N of Lancaster on US 521; *Baker Creek,* 3 mi. SW of McCormick on US 378; *Barnwell,* 7 mi. NE of Barnwell on State 3; *Charles*

*Towne Landing,* on SC 171 between US 17 and I–26 near Charleston; *Cheraw,* 4 mi. SW of Cheraw on US 1; *Chester,* 3 mi. SW of Chester on State 72; *Colleton Wayside,* 11 mi. N. of Walterboro on US 15; *Croft,* 3 mi. SE of Spartanburg off State 56; *Edisto Beach,* 50 mi. SE of Charleston on State 174; *Givhans Ferry,* 16 mi. W of Summerville on State 61; *Greenwood,* 17 mi. E. of Greenwood on State 702; *Hunting Island,* 16 mi. E. of Beaufort on US 21; *Hamilton Branch,* 15 mi. SE of McCormick off US 221; *Hickory Knob,* 8 mi. SW of McCormick off US 378; *Huntington Beach,* 3 mi. S of Murrells Inlet on US 17; *Kings Mountain,* 12 mi. NW of York on State 161; *Lee,* 7 mi. E of Bishopville off US 15; *Little Pee Dee,* 11 mi. SE of Dillon off State 57; *Myrtle Beach,* 3 mi. S of Myrtle Beach on US 17; *N. R. Goodale,* 2 mi. N of Camden off US 1; *Oconee,* 12 mi. NW of Walhalla off Rte. 28; *Paris Mountain,* 9 mi. N of Greenville off US 25; *Pleasant Ridge,* 22 mi. NW of Greenville off US 25; *Poinsett,* 18 mi. SW of Sumter off State 261; *Rivers Bridge,* 7 mi. SW of Ehrhardt off State 64; *Sadlers Creek,* 13 mi. SW of Anderson off US 29; *Santee,* 3 mi. NW of Santee off US 301; *Sesquicentennial,* 13 mi. NE of Columbia on US 1; *Table Rock,* 16 mi. N of Pickens off State 11; *Rose Hill,* 9 mi. SW of Union off US 176; *Old Dorchester,* 6 mi. S of Summerville on State 642.

 **CAMPING OUT.** South Carolina's commercial campgrounds and state parks are available from the mountains to the sea, offering to the camper the crisp air of the Blue Ridge Mountains or a quiet seaside beach. Camping fees at all parks reasonable. Obtain permit from Park Superintendent before setting up camp. No advance reservations. One week maximum stay. For complete listing, write for booklet, "Mountains, Beaches, Lakes, and Other Places to Camp in South Carolina," South Carolina Dept. of Parks, Recreation and Tourism, Box 113, Edgar A. Brown Building Columbia, South Carolina 29201.

All commercial campgrounds provide electrical and water hookups, showers and toilet facilities. Added attractions such as swimming and fishing are offered at the following campgrounds: *Lake Hartwell KOA Kampgrounds,* Rte. 3, Anderson; *Crystal Lake CG,* Box 379, Rte. 1, Chapin; *Charleston's Kampgrounds of America,* P. O. Box 1105, Charleston; *Wagon Wheel CG,* Dillon, 6 mi. N on US 301; *Buckhorn Ranch Family CG,* on I–95, 22 mi. S of Florence; *Rocks Pond CG,* Eutawville; *Lake Murray Family CG,* State 1, Gilbert; *Lake Pines KOA Kampground,* Hardeeville, 2 mi. No. on US 17; *Big Boo Family CG,* Rte. 3, Box 433, Moncks Corner; *Apache Family CG,* Star Rte. 2, Myrtle Beach; *Lake Arrowhead CG,* Star Rte. 2, Myrtle Beach; *Lakewood Family CG,* US 17 S, Myrtle Beach; *Pirateland Family CG,* US 17 S, Myrtle Beach; *Sherwood Forest CG,* US 17 N, Myrtle Beach; *Birch Canoe Family CG,* Myrtle Beach, US 17 & 5th Aves.; *Holiday Inn Trav-L-Park,* Myrtle Beach, 9 mi. No off US 17; *Ocean Lakes Family CG,* Myrtle Beach, 5 mi. S. on US 17 at intersection of Rte. 375; *Pebble Beach Family CG,* Myrtle Beach, on Rte. 73 (S. Ocean Blvd.); *Ponderosa Family CG,* Myrtle Beach, 10 mi. N on US 17; *Springmaid Family CG,* Myrtle Beach, S. Ocean Blvd.; *Riverside Family CG,* N Myrtle Beach, 2 mi. off US 17 on Little River Neck Rd.; *Sweetwater Lake CG,* 3½ mi. from I–26, just off US 21 near Orangeburg and St. Matthews (exit I–26 onto Rte. 22, proceed 2 mi. turn right onto Sweetwater Rd. and follow signs). *Harry's Fish Camp and CG,* Pineville, off Rte. 45; *Holiday Inn Trav-L-Park of Santee-Lake Marion,* Box 520, Sumter; *Shawnee CG,* P.O. Box 137, Santee; *Santee-Lake KOA Kampgrounds,* Rte. 3, Box 84, Summerton; *Woodland Park CG,* York, 8 mi. W on Rte. 5.

Camping areas and trailer stopovers are maintained also at the Francis Marion National Forest.

**TRAILER TIPS.** The following trailer parks have hookup facilities for travel trailers: *Pine Acres Mobile Home Park*, Aiken, 1 mi. N on US 1; *Nightfall Motel and Trailer Park*, Bamberg, 1 mi. N on US 301; *The Windmill*, Bamberg, 12 mi. S on US 301 at jct. of State 64; *Rainbow Trailer Court*, 5020 Rivers Ave., 11 mi. NW on US 52, Charleston; *Johnson's Trailer Park*, 106 New St., 1 mi. N on US 301 and US 76, Florence; *Lockhaven Camper's Court*, 7 mi. S on I–95 at Interchange of State 403, Florence; *Munnerlyn's Trailer Park*, Rte. 4, 3 mi. N on US 301, Florence; *Rainbow Mobile Home Estates*, 3 mi. N on US 29, Greenville; *Varsity Village Trailer Court*, 3 mi. N off US 29, Greenville; *Bobby's Overnite CG*, Manning, Intersection of I–95 and US 301; *Fairway Trailer Park*, 1 mi. S on US 301, Manning; *Twin Barns Trailor park*, 1 mi. S on US 321, North; *Pine-View Mobile Home Park*, 10 mi. N on US 501, Myrtle Beach; *Carolina Wren Motel and Trailer Park*, 2 mi. N on US 301, Orangeburg; *Kimbrell's Trailer Park*, 1223 Cherry Rd., on US 21, Rock Hill; *Moore Mobile Manor*, 160 Oakwood Dr., Intersection of I–26 and US 378, West Columbia.

 **MUSEUMS AND GALLERIES.** *Beaufort: Beaufort Museum.* Craven St. *Charleston: Charleston Museum*, 121 Rutledge Ave. The oldest municipal museum in the United States houses exhibits of pre-Columbian Indian weapons and artifacts and South Carolina history and culture. *Old Slave Mart Museum and Galleries*, 6 Chalmers St. Numerous artifacts of Black life and history. *Hunley Museum*, 50 Broad St. Exhibits of Confederate and Naval history with the focal point a replica of the Confederate States Submarine, *Hunley*, which was the first submarine to sink a surface vessel. *City Hall Council Chamber*, corner of Broad & Meeting Sts. Portraits of many important leaders, including George Washington. *Old Powder Museum*, 79 Cumberland St. Built about 1713 near the city's outer wall, the museum is made of bricks cemented with oyster shell mortar. Mon. to Fri. Closed Sept. Small admission charge. *Charles Towne Landing Exposition*, 1500 Old Town Rd. An exciting 300-acre exhibition park located on the site of the first permanent settlement in South Carolina. Features movies, exhibits and an Animal Forest with species indigenous to South Carolina in 1670 displayed in their natural habitat. Daily. *The Confederate Museum*, 188 Meeting St., a military museum. Tues. to Sat. from mid-Mar. to mid-Oct. Closed Sun., Mon., from mid-Oct. to mid-May. *Citadel Archives Museum*, The Citadel, a military museum. *South Carolina Historical Society*, 100 Meeting St.

*Clemson: Fort Hill* (Home of John C. Calhoun), Clemson University. *Hanover House*, Clemson University. Closed Mon.

*Columbia: Columbia Museum of Art and Science*, 1112 Bull Street. Here silver, miniatures, jewelry, pottery, and furniture from the historic heritage of Columbia and South Carolina are permanently displayed. Also exhibits of the sciences, natural history, art and history. Open Tues. to Sat. *Midlands Exposition Center, South Carolina State Historical Museum*, 1615 Blanding St. A general museum housed in 1820 Hampton-Preston mansion. *South Carolina Confederate Relic Room and Museum*, World War Memorial Bldg., Sumter at Pendleton. A history museum open Mon. to Fri.; by appointment only on Sat. Check for closing dates.

*Florence: Florence Museum*, 558 Spruce St. A general museum, but with many South Carolina history exhibits, including costumes of the War Between the States period. Free. *Georgetown: The Rice Museum*, Front & Screven Sts. A history museum housed in the Old Market Bldg. (1835), located on the site of the Old Market. Free. *Spartanburg: Spartanburg County Regional Museum*, 501 Otis Blvd. Free.

**HISTORIC SITES.** Charleston, site of the first settlement and where the "first shot" of the War Between the States was fired, is rich in historical sites. Its many and varied historic sites are listed in brochures which may be obtained from the Charleston Trident Chamber of Commerce, P.O. Box 975, Charleston 29402. *Fort Sumter National Monument,* in Charleston Harbor, may be reached by tour boats from Municipal Marina throughout the year. Trips per day vary. The monument is open daily.

Many historic churches may be seen in Charleston: *First Baptist Church,* 61–65 Church St., the oldest Baptist congregation in South Carolina, the present church begun in 1819. *St. Michael's Episcopal Church,* S.E. corner of Broad & Meeting Sts. The first service was held Feb. 1, 1761. Its bells have crossed the Atlantic Ocean five times. George Washington and Marquis de Lafayette both worshipped here when visiting Charleston. *French Huguenot Church,* S.E. corner of Church & Queen Sts., site of three successive Huguenot Churches. The present edifice, begun in 1844, was designed by Edward Brickell White. Only Huguenot church in America adhering exactly to the liturgy of the French Protestant Church. *St. Philip's Protestant Episcopal Church,* Church St., north of Queen. The present building was begun in 1835. In its two cemeteries lie many distinguished South Carolinians including John C. Calhoun. *St. John's Lutheran Church,* 10–12 Archdale St., one block west of King.

Historic homes open to the public in Charleston are: *Nathaniel Russell House,* 51 Meeting St. *Joseph Manigault House,* 350 Meeting St. May 2 to Feb. 28, Tues, to Sun. Mar. to Apr. daily. *Heyward-Washington House,* 87 Church St. Open year round. The *Arch Building* was constructed in the early 1800's and used as a "public house" for wagon masters and their helpers coming through Charleston.

Columbia, the capital and the geographical center of the state, offers the visitor much to see and enjoy. Stop at the State House, recognized as "one of the notable buildings of the world," and enter through the north entrance at the corner of Main and Gervais Sts. Bronze stars mark spots where shells from Sherman's army struck during occupation of the city in 1865. It's open weekdays and Sat. Just across from the State House, on Sumter St., is Trinity Episcopal Church, built in 1864. In the churchyard near the famous old "Governor's Oak" are graves of five South Carolina governors and other prominent citizens. And just down a few blocks on Sumter Street, you can enter the noted "Horseshoe" of the University of South Carolina.

Other historic points of interest include: *First Baptist Church,* 1306 Hampton St., built in 1859. The first Secession Convention met here on Dec. 17, 1860, but was moved to Charleston due to a smallpox epidemic. *Robert Mills Historic House and Park,* a restoration. This showplace of national architectural significance was designed by the famous Washington Monument architect, Robert Mills. The mansion was built in 1823 for the merchant prince Ainsley Hall. Closed Mon.

**SPECIAL INTEREST TOURS.** *Trails:* Retrace the flight of the President of the Confederacy, Jefferson Davis, through South Carolina after the fall of Richmond in 1865. The *Jefferson Davis Trail* winds through small towns, farmland, forests and rolling hills removed from interstate travel. Much of the countryside on this Trail has changed so little since the nineteenth century that the visitor feels like he is going back through time.

Along the route the visitor will see "CS" signs keyed to a printed guide with special points of interest marked with numbered signs. (**Note!** Many signs have been stolen, so refer to the "Jefferson Davis Trail" description earlier in this chapter for details.) Guide and sign numbers start at the northern border of South Carolina, where Jefferson Davis entered above Fort Mill.

Another tour which is distinctively signed is the *George Washington Trail*. When President Washington visited South Carolina in 1791, he followed the old King's Highway down the East Coast. This route is marked as the Coastal Section of the George Washington Trail from the South Carolina Welcome Center near Little River on US 17 to Savannah, where the President crossed over into Georgia. The Central Section of the Trail follows the route the President followed when he returned to South Carolina at the present town of North August. The Washington Trail is clearly marked with distinctive "Washington Coach" signs.

To obtain brochures which show the routings of both the Jefferson Davis Trail and the George Washington Trail write: South Carolina Department of Parks, Recreation and Tourism, Box 71, Room 29, Columbia 29202.

*Georgetown* has tours of *Plantations and town houses* sponsored by the Women of Prince George, Winyah Episcopal Church. These annual tours are held in the second week of April. The plantations and houses, many over a hundred years old, are privately owned and are open to the public only at this time each year. Tours take a different route daily, showing plantations along the Black, Pee Dee, Santee, and Waccamaw rivers. Plantations dating back to land grants from King George II retain names of ancestral homes of the founders from England and Scotland. At some, original slave quarters are still intact, and vestiges of the once powerful rice-planting industry are in evidence. Rice was the chief means of support for many years in thousands of coastal areas. Indigo culture, too, had a brief span of prosperity. Several plantation homes are maintained, in whole or in part, in the style of antebellum hospitality and luxurious living. Histories of the houses and maps showing the routes for the day are provided. Tours are not conducted, and visitors provide their own transportation. Only small buses can go on the tours because of many low-hanging oak limbs. *Hopsewee Plantation*, 12 mi. S on US 17. Open Mon., Wed., Thurs. and Fri. Closed holidays.

Churches, the parishes of which were established more than two hundred years ago, are also open to visitors. Visitors have an opportunity to see many beautiful pieces of silver used in church services for decades. Box lunches and tickets are on sale at the parish house, Highmarket St.

*Greenwood: Annual Greenwood County Historical Homes Tour* (usually in April) is sponsored by the Greenwood County Chamber of Commerce, 404 Main St., Greenwood, S.C. 29646.

*Charleston: Boone Hall Plantation*, on US 17, 8 mi. N of the city. Small admission charge. This old mansion, flanked by formal gardens, is 2½ stories high and has a spiral stairway, 18 rooms and a four-column facade. The property was originally a 17,000-acre plantation, and is now a 738-acre cattle and vegetable farm. "Slave Street," with nine original servants' cabins, is nearby. Open year-round.

Also near Charleston is *Magnolia Plantation & Gardens*, Route 4, also open year-round.

*Middleton Place*, outside Charleston, is open year-round. It has one of America's outstanding landscaped gardens, the first established in the colonies. Lush foliage and magnificent plantings give way to walkways that line the shaded banks of the Ashley River. Black and white swans float serenely on reflecting pools and the restored mansion evokes an air of great luxury. In a recreated stableyard, youngsters can ride mule-drawn wagons, see hens nesting and cows being milked. The animals are gentle and roam freely, to be petted and fed.

The *Island Queen Historical River Tour* is a marvelous way to enjoy the history and legends of the old plantations located along the banks of the Waccamaw and Pee Dee Rivers. The three-hour cruises leave from Wacca Wache Marina, about 15 miles south of Myrtle Beach, 2 miles west of US 17 beyond Murrells Inlet. In summer at 10 and 2, plus dinner cruises to the Bucksport Marina restaurant. Cost about $5 for adults. Phone ahead in spring and fall for schedule; reservations at all times are essential.

*Brookgreen Gardens,* an outdoor museum on the site of four old rice plantations, are full of sculpture, rice fields, and centuries-old live oaks. Many of the 350 sculptures are 19th-century. South of Myrtle Beach on US 17.

 **DRINKING LAWS.** Mixed drinks may be purchased in licensed restaurants, hotels and motels. Liquor is served in a miniature bottle, which the purchaser may mix or have mixed according to his taste. Liquor is sold by the bottle in state-licensed package stores. Hours of operation are from 9 A.M.-7 P.M. No sales on Sundays, election days, New Year's Day, July 4, Thanksgiving and Christmas. Wine and beer are available in most restaurants, or may be purchased in grocery stores. Minimum age is 18 for beer and wine, 21 for liquor.

 **HOTELS AND MOTELS.** Traditional Southern hospitality is the one ingredient common to all the hotels and motels in South Carolina. The facilities range from the modestly designed, which cater to the traveling man, to the lush and ornate, which cater to regional and national conventions.

Accommodations are listed according to their category. Based on double occupancy, price categories and ranges are as follows: *Deluxe:* $41–64; *Expensive:* $26–40; *Moderate:* $16–25; and *Inexpensive:* $10–15. For a more complete explanation of hotel and motel categories see *Facts at Your Fingertips* at the front of this volume.

## CHARLESTON

**BATTERY CARRIAGE HOUSE.** *Deluxe.* 20 S. Battery. Four-story mansion on famous Battery Row of beautiful houses in Old Charleston. Built in 1845.

**MILLS HYATT HOUSE.** *Deluxe.* Spank in the center of Charleston, and built on the site of the famous Mills House Hotel (1853), this modern version boasts real antiques in its public rooms, reproductions in the bedrooms. Swimming pool on the roof. Meeting and Queen streets.

**SWORDGATE INN.** *Deluxe.* Try to stay here if you can, but reserve well in advance, because this early 1800's house in the heart of Charleston's historic district has only 5 guest rooms. Breakfast on the patio in good weather, with grits and scones dripping with butter and honey. Superb service by the owners, who live in. 111 Tradd Street. (South Carolina's most famous ironsmith, Christopher Werener, who designed the gates of this house, also made a cast-iron palmetto tree, which can be seen on the capitol grounds in Columbia. The palmetto, the official state tree, is so realistic that birds build their nests in the fronds in springtime.)

**Holiday Inn–Riverview.** *Expensive.* Entertainment, dining room, pool.

**Dorchester Motor Lodge.** *Moderate.* 4½ mi. W on I–26 at Dorchester Ave.

Large. Very comfortable rooms, some with kitchens. Restaurant, coffee shop, pool. Golf privileges.

**Jack Tar Francis Marion Hotel.** *Moderate.* King & Calhoun Sts. Coffee shop, restaurant.

## COLUMBIA

**Best Western Host of America.** *Expensive.* All the amenities. The Red Fox restaurant has a mellow old-fashioned decor.

**Carolina Inn.** *Expensive.* Pool, restaurant, some entertainment.

**Wade Hampton Hotel.** *Expensive.* Coffee shop, restaurants. Opposite capitol.

**Downtowner.** *Moderate.* Member of the chain. Nicely furnished rooms. Dining room, pool.

**Days Inn.** *Inexpensive.* I–26 and SC 215. *Tasty World* restaurant, pool. Near airport.

 **DINING OUT.** South Carolina's traditions include a reputation for good food, with its table fare varying over the distinctive geographical sections of the state. Menus vary from country ham and grits with red-eye gravy in the Up Country, to the renowned "she-crab soup" of Charleston. But throughout the state you'll find many restaurants serving good food at economical prices.

Restaurants are listed according to their category. The categories and price ranges for a complete dinner are as follows: *Expensive:* $8–$14; *Moderate:* $5–$8; *Inexpensive:* $3–$5. For a more complete explanation of restaurant categories see *Facts at Your Fingertips* at the front of this volume.

## CHARLESTON

Local specialties of South Carolina's "Low Country" include she-crab soup, shrimp creole, roast oysters and okra soup. Try them whenever you can find them.

**The Colony House.** *Expensive.* 35 Prioleau St. Specialty is Low Country dishes, seafood. Baked pompano is a favorite.

**Henry's.** *Moderate.* Market Street. Also specializes in Low Country dishes.

**Scarlet O'Hara.** *Moderate.* Floating restaurant at foot of Charlotte Street at the Cooper River. Fun decor, atmosphere. Steak and seafood.

**Swamp Fox Room.** *Moderate.* At the Francis Marion Hotel, King at Calhoun Sts. American cuisine surrounded by nostalgic decor.

## COLUMBIA

**Red Fox.** *Moderate to Expensive.* In Best Western Host Motel. Rustic atmosphere and home baking featured here. Ask for the local specialties, such as fried country ham.

### EDGEFIELD

**Plantation Hotel.** *Moderate.* The dining room of this establishment, owned and operated by the Mimms family, features South Carolinian specialties. You'll love the place.

### GREENVILLE

**The Pantry.** *Inexpensive.* Two locations. Regional favorite with country ham and Southern fried chicken, chops, and seafood.

### MYRTLE BEACH

**Sea Captain's House.** *Moderate.* Informal restaurant at the edge of the ocean. Own pastries. Specialties: grasshopper pie and seafood.

**Yardarm.** *Moderate.* Wide variety of seafood and steaks. Courteous, fast service.

**WHITE HERON.** *Inexpensive.* Authentic Colonial structure with fireplaces. Try the pecan pie. Closed Jan.

### ORANGEBURG

**BERRY'S ON-THE-HILL.** *Inexpensive.* Pleasant atmosphere. Specializes in mouthwatering Southern cooking. Baking on premises. Children's portions.

### PICKENS

**COLONIAL HOUSE.** *Inexpensive.* Wonderful home-type meals. Old-time boarding house style.

### WALTERBORO

**LAFAYETTE GRILLE.** *Inexpensive.* Plain food. Well known for their "plantation" relishes and preserves. (New York restaurants serve Walterboro artichoke relish, made from root artichokes.)

# TENNESSEE

## *Chattanooga and Stones River*

Tennessee was the last of the eleven southern states to join the Confederacy, because of the protests of the East Tennesseans. The state supplied 31,000 troops to the Union Army (mostly East Tennesseeans) and 115,000 men to the Confederate forces. An East Tennessean, Andrew Johnson, served as Lincoln's Vice President and succeeded him upon his assassination. Another native of the state was Confederate General Nathan Bedford Forrest, a cavalry genius who contributed the immortal "Get there firstest with the mostest" to military lore. After the war Forrest came home to help found the Ku Klux Klan at Pulaski, Tennessee, and become its first Imperial Wizard.

When Tennessee seceded on June 8, 1861, it marked the state's second rupture with the Union. In 1785 the area that is now Tennessee was part of North Carolina. The settlers appealed to the state government for help against frequent Indian attacks, and North Carolina responded by ceding the territory to the federal government. The indignant Tennesseeans thereupon proclaimed themselves the independent State of Franklin. Though it was never recognized by the Union, North Carolina or scarcely anyone else, Tennessee history records that the State of Franklin existed for about three years. Thereafter the area was included in the territory south of the Ohio, and in 1796 it was admitted to the Union as the sixteenth state.

South of Johnson City on US 411 and 11E is Jonesboro, oldest town in Tennessee (founded in 1779) where the free state of Franklin was organized. A twenty-one-year-old Andrew Jackson migrated here from North Carolina in 1788 to practice law for two years. Among the old buildings to see in this town is the Methodist Church, dating from 1845, at 215 W. Main Street.

## Davy Was Born Here

On US 11E, near the little town of Limestone, is Davy Crockett Birthplace Park. On five acres along the Nolichucky River, the cabin where Crockett was born in 1786 has been reconstructed, a building for tourist information built, and pleasant picnic grounds provided. The limestone marker dates from the mid-1880's. Greeneville, twenty-two miles southwest of Jonesboro, was the home of Andrew Johnson, who became President following Lincoln's assassination. The city, founded in 1783, was named for Nathanael Greene, a general in the American Revolutionary War.

In downtown Greeneville, the town's most noted citizen is honored with the Andrew Johnson National Historic Site, containing his modest tailor shop and home and his burial place. Johnson's political career saw him successively as alderman, congressman, governor, senator, vice president, president, and then senator again.

Murfreesboro was capital of Tennessee from 1819 to 1825. On North Mancy Avenue is Oaklands, one of the outstanding houses in Middle Tennessee. Built in three periods, it developed into a beautiful antebellum home. Prior to the Civil War, its guests included such personages as John Bell, presidential candidate against Lincoln in 1860, and Leonidas Polk, the bishop-general.

## Modern Memphis

Memphis, capital of the mid-South and one of the South's largest cities, is a progressive, forward-looking metropolis mindful of the past. A visitor senses the contrast when he stands amid the Civil War relics in Confederate Park and looks at the downtown skyscrapers.

Maryville was a pioneer town. Sam Houston attended Maryville Academy (now Maryville College) here. En route to Knoxville, off US 129, you can visit the restored Sam Houston Schoolhouse, six miles northeast of Maryville. Houston, who taught at the school from spring until fall of 1812, later served as congressman from Tennessee and as the state's governor before moving on to Oklahoma and Texas.

Knoxville, on the Tennessee River, dates from 1786 and was named in honor of Henry Knox, Secretary of War from 1785 to 1794. Its first settlers were traders. Knoxville in its early days was distinguished for its lively and colorful goings-on instead of its drawing-room charm.

### Antebellum Mansions

East Tennessee, mostly an area of small farms, was, in general, loyal to the Union. The siege of Knoxville in 1863 was an unsuccessful Confederate attempt to dislodge Union troops stationed there. After the war many of these Northern men returned to Knoxville to settle.

Confederate Memorial Hall, 3148 Kingston Pike, an antebellum mansion which served as Gen. Longstreet's headquarters during the siege of Knoxville, was restored and is now maintained as a museum by the United Daughters of the Confederacy. It contains a collection of Civil War relics.

### Chattanooga

Because of its strategic location, Chattanooga was an important prize in the Civil War; three battles were fought nearby, at Chickamauga Creek, Lookout Mountain, and Missionary Ridge. The eventual victory of Union forces in November 1863 provided Sherman with a supply base for his Atlanta campaign.

South of the city, in Georgia, is the Chickamauga and Chattanooga National Military Park. Its nine separate parts include Point Park on Lookout Mountain, Signal Point on Signal Mountain, Missionary Ridge, Orchard Knob. Park Headquarters are just below Chattanooga in North Georgia, site of one of America's bloodiest battles—Chickamauga (34,500 casualties in 3 days). Two thousand markers and monuments commemorate the men who died in these battles.

### Civil War Battlegrounds

Chattanooga has a variety of attractions to offer the visitor. The movie *The Great Locomotive Chase* documented the role the locomotive *General* played in local Civil War history. Captain James J. Andrews, with twenty-one other Federal raiders, managed to seize the train near Marietta, Georgia, and move north along the track toward Chattanooga, destroying track and bridges as they went, while another Confederate engine, the *Yonah,* was gaining on them all the while. Andrews' raiders attempted to escape in the woods near the Tennessee line but all were captured. One of the nation's largest National Cemeteries is located in the Center of Chattanooga (US 11 and US 64). Captain Andrews is buried here, as are the other heroes of the "Chase." The *General* is on display in Union Station Concourse at 124 West Ninth Street.

The city is the home of the University of Tennessee at Chattanooga on McCallie Avenue, founded in 1886 as the U.S. Grant University.

The top of Lookout Mountain, that "rock rising to a point," can be reached on what may well be the world's steepest passenger railroad, overcoming a seventy-two per cent grade as it approaches the top.

You can also drive up Lookout Mountain via Lookout Mountain Road or Ochs Highway, reaching an elevation of 2,225 feet, some 1,700 feet above the city. The view is spectacular. It was here that the Battle Above the Clouds was fought in 1863.

Point Park, atop Lookout Mountain, offers a magnificent view of the Tennessee River's Moccasin Bend and the city below. The Ochs Memorial Museum and Observatory are located here.

Opposite the park, the Lookout Mountain Museum contains Civil War items, Indian relics, and dioramas. Nearby, Cravens House, built in 1856 was the center of the 'Battle Above the Clouds.' Most of it was destroyed; the present reconstruction was built on the original foundations.

"Confederama" is an unusual diversion located at the foot of Lookout Mountain, at 3742 Tennessee Avenue. It is an attempt to show the Chattanooga Campaign, using miniature soldiers on a scaled-down battleground, with music and narration.

Nine miles north of the city, on US 127, is Signal Mountain, another high point giving a majestic view. Below is the Tennessee River, running through the "Grand Canyon" of the Tennessee. The mountain was used by the Confederates for signaling.

### Grant at Chattanooga

Rosecrans' army, having started out offensively, was now shut up in Chattanooga, as Bragg took up positions on Lookout Mountain and Missionary Ridge. The Union commander accepted investment and thus surrendered his freedom of action. Burnside, at Knoxville, was too far away to render immediate aid. There were no strong Confederate units north of Chattanooga, but Rosecrans' line of communications was cut away. The Nashville and Chattanooga Railroad, instead of running directly into the city, reached the river at Stevenson, crossed at Bridgeport southwest of Chattanooga, and ran through Confederate territory into town. River steamers could get to within only eight miles of Chattanooga; beyond, the Tennessee River was swift and narrow. Supplies therefore came over the mountains in wagons, but starting September 30 Confederate cavalry under Maj. Gen. Joseph Wheeler, one of Bragg's cavalry corps commanders, raided as far north as Murfreesboro. Though heavily and effectively opposed in his effort to tear up the railroad, he managed to destroy many precious Union supply wagons. With the mountain roads breaking down under the heavy traffic in wet weather, rations within Chattanooga ran short. Men went hungry, and horses, and mules began to die of starvation. Rosecrans prepared to reopen his line of communications by means of an overland route to the west. But this route was dominated by Confederate troops on Raccoon and Lookout Mountains. Additional troops to clear these strongpoints were required if the Army of the Cumberland was to survive.

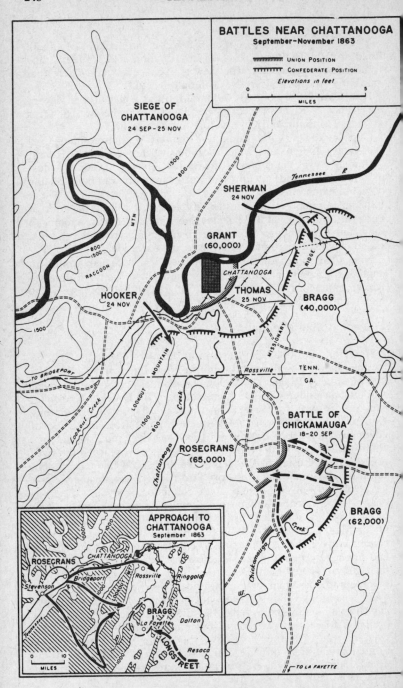

**BATTLES NEAR CHATTANOOGA**
September–November 1863

Union Position
Confederate Position
*Elevations in feet*

0     MILES     5

**SIEGE OF CHATTANOOGA**
24 SEP–25 NOV

*Tennessee R.*

**SHERMAN**
24 NOV

**GRANT**
(60,000)

*Chattanooga*

**HOOKER**
24 NOV

**THOMAS**
25 NOV

**BRAGG**
(40,000)

MISSIONARY RIDGE

*Rossville*    TENN.
        GA.

TO BRIDGEPORT

LOOKOUT Mountain

Lookout Creek

Chattanooga Creek

**BATTLE OF CHICKAMAUGA**
18–20 SEP

**ROSECRANS**
(65,000)

*Chickamauga Creek*

**BRAGG**
(62,000)

TO LA FAYETTE

**APPROACH TO CHATTANOOGA**
September 1863

**ROSECRANS**

*CHATTANOOGA*

*Bridgeport*

*Rossville*   *Ringgold*

*Stevenson*

*Tennessee R.*

**BRAGG**

*La Fayette*   *Dalton*

**LONGSTREET**

*Resaca*

0     MILES     10

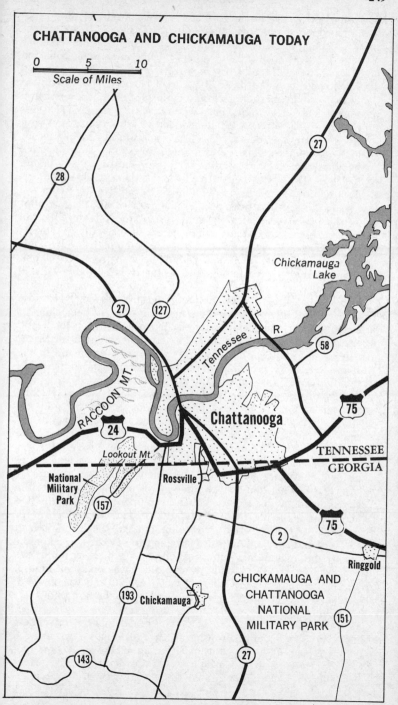

CHATTANOOGA AND CHICKAMAUGA TODAY

0     5     10
Scale of Miles

Washington finally awoke to the fact that an entire Union army was trapped in Chattanooga and in danger of capture. In a midnight council meeting on September 23, the President met with Secretary Stanton, General Halleck, and others to determine what could be done. As General Meade was not then active in the east, they decided to detach two corps, or about 20,000 men, from the Army of the Potomac and send them by rail to Tennessee under the command of General Hooker, who had been without active command since his relief in June. The forces selected included 10 artillery batteries with over 3,000 mules and horses. The 1,157-mile journey involved four changes of trains, owing to differing gauges and lack of track connections, and eclipsed all other such troop movements by rail up to that time. The troops began to entrain at Manassas Junction and Bealton Station, Virginia, on September 25 and five days later the first trains arrived at Bridgeport, Alabama. Not all of the troops made such good time—for the majority of the infantry the trip consumed about nine days. And movement of the artillery, horses, mules and baggage was somewhat slower. Combined with a water-borne movement of 17,000 men under Sherman from Mississippi, the reinforcement of the besieged Rosecrans was a triumph of skill and planning.

Chickamauga had caused Stanton and his associates to lose confidence in Rosecrans. For some time Lincoln had been dubious about Rosecrans, who, he said, acted "like a duck hit on the head" after Chickamauga, but he did not immediately choose a successor. Finally, about mid-October, he decided to unify command in the west and to vest it in General Grant, who still commanded the Army of the Tennessee. In October Stanton met Grant in Louisville and gave him orders which allowed him some discretion in selecting subordinates. Grant was appointed commander of the Military Division of the Mississippi, which embraced the Departments and Armies of the Ohio, the Cumberland, and the Tennessee, and included the vast area from the Alleghenies to the Mississippi River north of Banks' Department of the Gulf. Thomas replaced Rosecrans, and Sherman was appointed to command Grant's old army.

Now that Hooker had arrived, the line of communications, or the "cracker line" to the troops, could be reopened. Rosecrans had actually shaped the plan, and all that was needed was combat troops to execute it. On October 26 Hooker crossed the Tennessee at Bridgeport and attacked eastward. Within two days he had taken the spurs of the mountains, other Union troops had captured two important river crossings, and the supply line was open once more. Men, equipment, and food moved via riverboat and wagon road, bypassing Confederate strongpoints, to reinforce the besieged Army of the Cumberland.

In early November Bragg weakened his besieging army by sending Longstreet's force against Burnside at Knoxville. This move reduced Confederate strength to about 40,000 at about the same time that Sherman arrived with two army corps from Memphis. The troops immediately at hand under Grant—Thomas's Army of the Cumberland, two corps of Sherman's Army of the Tennessee, and two corps under Hooker from the Army of the Potomac—now numbered about 60,000. Grant characteristically decided to resume the offensive with his entire force.

The Confederates had held their dominant position for so long that they seemed to look on all of the Federals in Chattanooga as their ultimate prisoners. One day Grant went out to inspect the Union lines and he reached a point where Union and Confederate picket posts were not far apart. Not only did his own troops turn out the guard, but a smart set of Confederates came swarming out, formed a neat military rank, snapped to attention, and presented arms. Grant returned the salute and rode away. But plans were already afoot to divest the Confederates of some of their cockiness.

Grant planned to hit the ends of the confederates' line at once. Hooker would strike at Lookout Mountain, and Sherman moving his army upstream across the river from Chattanooga, and crossing over by pontoons, would hit the upper end of Missionary Ridge. While they were breaking the Confederate flanks, Thomas' men could make limited attacks on the center, and the Army of the Cumberland's soldiers, already nursing a bruised ego for the rout at Chickamauga, realized that in the eyes of the commanding general they were second-class troops.

Hooker took Lookout Mountain on November 24. On the same day Sherman crossed the Tennessee at the mouth of Chickamauga Creek and gained positions on the north end of Missionary Ridge. The next day his attacks bogged down as he attempted to drive southward along the Ridge. To help Sherman, Grant directed the Army of the Cumberland to take the rifle pits at the foot of the west slope of Missionary Ridge. These rifle pits were the first of three lines of Confederate trenches. Thomas' troops rushed forward, seized the pits, and then, having a score to settle with the Confederates positioned above them, took control of this phase of the battle. Coming under fire from the pits above and in front of them, the Federals simply kept on going. When Grant observed that movement he muttered that someone was going to sweat for it if the charge ended in disaster. But Thomas's troops drove all the way to the top, and in the afternoon Hooker swept the southern end of the ridge. The Federals then had the unusual experience of seeing a Confederate army disintegrate into precipitate retreat and beckoned to their Northern comrades: "My God! Come and see them run!" Grant pursued Bragg the next day, but one Confederate division skillfully halted the pursuit while Bragg retired into Georgia to regroup.

The battles around Chattanooga ended in one of the most complete Union victories of the war. Bragg's army was defeated, men and matériel captured, and the Confederates driven south. The mountainous defense line which the Confederates had hoped to hold had been pierced; the rail center of Chattanooga was permanently in Union hands; and the rich, food-producing eastern Tennessee section was lost to the Confederacy. Relief had come at last for the

Union sympathizers in eastern Tennessee. With Chattanooga secured as a base, the way was open for an invasion of the lower South.

## The Twin Rivers Campaign

Students of the Civil War often concentrate their study upon the cockpit of the war in the east—Virginia. The rival capitals lay only a hundred miles apart and the country between them was fought over for four years. But it was the Union armies west of the Appalachians that struck the death knell of the Confederacy.

These Union forces in late 1861 were organized into two separate commands. Brig. Gen. Don Carlos Buell commanded some 45,000 men from a headquarters at Louisville, Kentucky, while Maj. Gen. Henry W. Halleck with headquarters at St. Louis, Missouri, had 91,000 under his command. These troops were generally raw, undisciplined western volunteers. Logistical matters and training facilities were undeveloped and as Halleck once wrote in disgust to his superior in Washington, "affairs here are in complete chaos."

Affairs were no better among Confederate authorities farther south. Facing Buell and Halleck were 43,000 scattered and ill-equipped Confederate troops under General Albert Sidney Johnston. Charged with defending a line which stretched for more than 500 miles from western Virginia to the border of Kansas, Johnston's forces mostly lay east of the Mississippi River. They occupied a system of forts and camps from Cumberland Gap in western Virginia through Bowling Green, Kentucky, to Columbus, Kentucky, on the Mississippi. Rivers and railroads provided Johnston with most of his interior lines of communications since most of the roads were virtually impassable in winter. To protect a lateral railroad where it crossed two rivers in Tennessee and yet respect Kentucky's neutrality, the Confederates had built Fort Henry on the Tennessee River and Fort Donelson on the Cumberland River just south of the boundary between the two states. On the other hand, hampering the Confederate build-up were southern governors whose states' rights doctrine led them to believe that defense of their respective states had higher priority than pushing forward the needed men and munitions to a Confederate commander, Johnston, at the front.

At the beginning of 1862, Halleck and Buell were supposed to be co-operating with each other but had yet to do so effectively. On his own, Buell moved in mid-January to give token response to Lincoln's desire to help the Unionists in east Tennessee. One of his subordinates succeeded in breaching the Confederate defense line in eastern Kentucky in a local action near Mill Springs, but Buell failed to exploit the victory.

In Halleck's department, Brig. Gen. Ulysses S. Grant, at the time an inconspicuous district commander at Cairo, Illinois, had meanwhile proposed a river expedition up the Tennessee to take Fort Henry. After some hesitance and in spite of the absence of assurance of support from Buell, Halleck approved a plan for a joint Army-Navy expedition. On January 30, 1862, he directed 15,000 men under Grant, supported by armored gunboats and river craft of the U.S. Navy under Flag Officer Andrew H. Foote, to "take and hold Fort Henry." The actions of subordinate commanders were at last prodding the Union war machine to move.

## Capture of Forts Henry and Donelson

Grant landed his troops below Fort Henry and together with Foote's naval force moved against the Confederate position on February 6. At the Federals' approach the Confederate commander sent most of his men to Fort Donelson. Muddy roads delayed the Union Army's advance, but Foote's seven gunboats plunged ahead and in a short fire fight induced the defenders of Fort Henry to surrender. Indeed, the Confederates had lowered their colors before Grant's infantry could reach the action. The Tennessee River now lay open to Foote's gunboats all the way to northern Alabama.

General Grant was no rhetorician. Sparing with words, he never bombarded his troops with Napoleonic manifestos as McClellan did. After the capture of Fort Henry he simply telegraphed the somewhat surprised Halleck: "I shall take and destroy Fort Donelson on the 8th and return to Fort Henry." But inclement weather delayed the Federal movement until February 12. Then river craft carried some of the troops by water around to Fort Donelson. The rest of the troops moved overland under sunny skies and unseasonably mild temperatures. The springlike weather caused the youthful soldiers to litter the roadside with overcoats, blankets, and tents.

But winter once more descended upon Grant's forces (soon to swell to nearly 27,000 men) as they invested Fort Donelson. Johnston, sure that the fall of this fort would jeopardize his entrenched camp at Bowling Green, hurried three generals and 12,000 reinforcements to Fort Donelson and then retired toward Nashville with 14,000 men. Even without reinforcements, Fort Donelson was a strong position. The main earthwork stood 100 feet above the river and with its outlying system of rifle pits embraced an area of 100 acres. The whole Confederate position occupied less than a square mile. Grant and Foote first attempted to reduce it by naval bombardment, which had succeeded at Fort Henry. But this time the Confederate defenders handled the gunboats so roughly that they withdrew. Grant then prepared for a long siege, although the bitter cold weather and lack of assault training among his troops caused him to have some reservations.

The Confederates, sensing they were caught in a trap, essayed a sortie on February 15, and swept one of Grant's divisions off the field. But divided Confederate command, not lack of determination or valor on the part of the fighting men, led to ultimate defeat of the attack. The three Confederate commanders could not agree upon the next move, and at a critical moment, Grant ordered counterattacks all along the line. By the end of the day Union troops had captured a portion of the Confederate outer works. Now surrounded by Union forces that outnumbered them almost two to one, the Confederate leaders decided they were in a hopeless situation. In a scene resembling *opéra bouffe,* Brig. Gen. John B. Floyd, who had been Buchanan's Secretary of War and feared execution as a traitor, passed the command to Brig. Gen. Gideon Pillow. Pillow passed the command immediately to Brig. Gen. Simon B. Buckner, who asked Grant, an old friend, for terms. Soon afterward Grant sent his famous message: "No terms except unconditional and immediate surrender can be accepted. I propose to move immediately upon your works."

Some Confederates escaped with Floyd and Pillow, and Col. Nathan Bedford Forrest led his cavalry through frozen backwaters to safety. But the bulk of the garrison "from 12,000 to 15,000 prisoners . . . also 20,000 stand of arms, 48 pieces of artillery, 17 heavy guns, from 2,000 to 4,000 horses, and large quantities of commissary stores" fell into Federal hands.

Poor leadership, violation of the principle of unity of command, and too strict adherence to position defense had cost the South the key to the gateway of the Confederacy in the west. The loss of the two forts dealt the Confederacy a blow from which it never fully recovered. Johnston had to abandon Kentucky and most of middle and west Tennessee. The vital industrial and transportation center of Nashville soon fell to Buell's advancing army. Foreign governments took special notice of the defeats. For the North the victories were its first good news of the war. They set the strategic pattern for further advance into the Confederacy. In Grant the people had a new hero and he was quickly dubbed "Unconditional Surrender" Grant.

Fort Donelson National Military Park and Cemetery is one mile west of Dover. The national military park contains the well-preserved fort and earthworks, as well as the Dover Tavern in which the surrender occurred. The Visitor Center presents a 15-minute theater program and also houses a museum. During the summer there is a living history program with demonstrations of cannon and musket firing.

## Confederate Counterattack at Shiloh

As department commander, Halleck naturally received much credit for the Union victories. President Lincoln decided to unify command of all the western armies, and on March 11 Halleck received the command. Halleck, nicknamed "Old Brains," was well known as a master of the theory and literature of war. Lincoln's decision gave him jurisdiction over four armies—Buell's Army of the Ohio, Grant's Army of the Tennessee, Maj. Gen. Samuel Curtis' Army of the Southwest in Missouri and Arkansas, and Maj. Gen. John Pope's Army of the Mississippi. While Pope, in co-operation with Foote's naval forces, successfully attacked New Madrid and Island No. 10 on the Mississippi River, Halleck decided to concentrate Grant's and Buell's armies and move against Johnston at Corinth in northern Mississippi. Grant and Buell were to meet at Shiloh (Pittsburg Landing) near Savannah on the Tennessee River. Well aware of the Federal movements, Johnston decided to attack Grant before Buell could join him. The Confederate army, 40,000 strong, marched out of Corinth on the afternoon of April 3. Muddy roads and faulty staff co-ordination made a shambles of Confederate march discipline. Mixed up commands, artillery and wagons bogged down in the mud, and green troops who insisted upon shooting their rifles at every passing rabbit threatened to abort the whole expedition. Not until late in the afternoon of April 5 did Johnston's army complete the 22-mile march to its attack point. Then the Confederate leader postponed his attack until the next morning and the delay proved costly.

Grant's forces were encamped in a rather loose battle line and apparently anticipated no attack. The position at Shiloh itself was not good, for the army was pocketed by the river at its back and a creek on each flank. Because the army was on an offensive mission, it had not entrenched. Grant has often been criticized for this omission, but entrenchment was not common at that stage of the war. The fact that the principle of security was disregarded is inescapable. Very little patrolling had been carried out, and the Federals were unaware that a Confederate army of 40,000 men was spending the night of April 5 just two miles away. The victories at Forts Henry and Donelson had apparently produced overconfidence in Grant's army, which like Johnston's, was only partly trained. Even Grant reflected this feeling, for he had established his headquarters at Savannah, nine miles downstream.

Johnston's men burst out of the woods early on April 6, so early that Union soldiers turned out into their company streets from their tents to fight. Some fled to the safety of the landing, but most of the regiments fought stubbornly and yielded ground slowly. One particular knot of Federals rallied along an old sunken road, named the Hornet's Nest by Confederates because of the stinging shot and shell they had to face there. Although this obstacle disrupted Johnston's timetable of attack, by afternoon the Confederates had attained local success elsewhere all along the line. At the same time the melee of battle badly disorganized the attackers. Johnston's attack formation had been awkward from the beginning. He had formed his three corps into one column with each corps deployed with divisions in line so that each corps stretched across the whole battlefront, one behind the other. Such a formation could be effectively controlled neither by army nor corps commanders.

Then, almost at the moment of victory, Johnston himself was mortally wounded while leading a local assault. General Beauregard, Johnston's successor, suspended the attack for the day and attempted to straighten out and reorganize his command. As the day ended, Grant's sixth division, which had lost its way while marching to the battlefield, reached Shiloh along with advance elements of Buell's army.

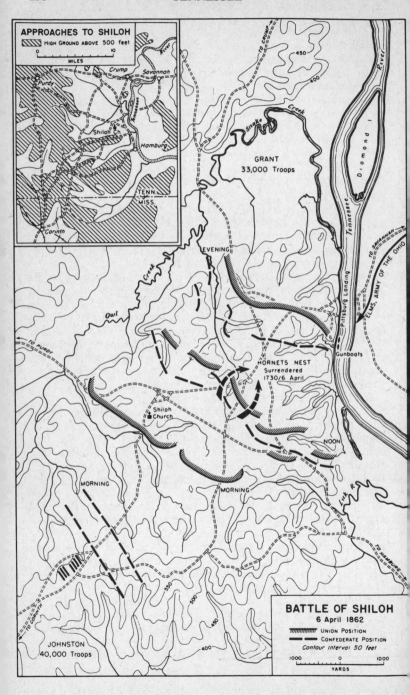

APPROACHES TO SHILOH

High Ground Above 500 feet

MILES

Purdy

Crump

Savannah

Shiloh Ch.

Hamburg

Tennessee River

TENN.
MISS.

Corinth

TO CRUMP

450

400

Snake

Creek

GRANT
33,000 Troops

Diamond I.

Tennessee River

TO SAVANNAH

EVENING

Owl

Creek

Pittsburg Landing

ELMS, ARMY OF THE OHIO

TO PURDY

HORNETS NEST
Surrendered
1730/6 April

Gunboats

Shiloh
Church

NOON

MORNING

MORNING

Lick R.

TO HAMBURG

JOHNSTON
40,000 Troops

550

500

450

400

TO CORINTH

**BATTLE OF SHILOH**
6 April 1862

UNION POSITION
CONFEDERATE POSITION
Contour Interval 50 feet

1000　　0　　1000

YARDS

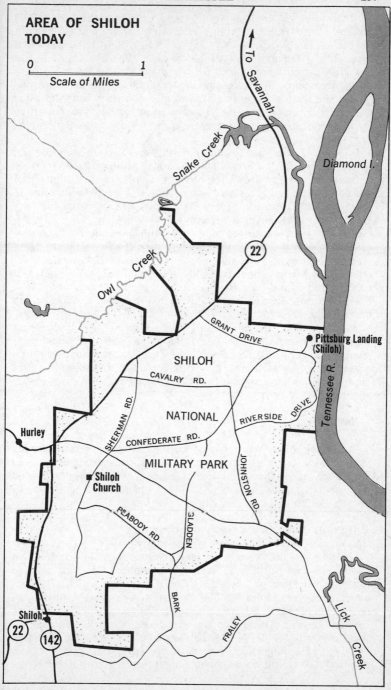

AREA OF SHILOH
TODAY

0            1
Scale of Miles

To Savannah

Snake Creek

Diamond I.

Owl   Creek

22

GRANT DRIVE

Pittsburg Landing
(Shiloh)

SHILOH

CAVALRY RD.

Tennessee R.

SHERMAN RD.

NATIONAL

RIVERSIDE DRIVE

Hurley

CONFEDERATE RD.

MILITARY PARK

Shiloh
Church

JOHNSTON RD.

PEABODY RD.

3LADDEN

BARK

Shiloh

22

142

FRALEY

Lick Creek

Next morning Grant counterattacked to regain the lost ground and the Confederates withdrew to Corinth. There was no pursuit. Shiloh was the bloodiest battle fought in North America up to that time. Of 63,000 Federals, 13,000 were casualties. The Confederates lost 11,000. Fortunate indeed for the Federals had been Lincoln's decision to unify the command under Halleck, for this act had guaranteed Buell's presence and prevented Johnston from defeating the Union armies separately. Grant came in for much denunciation for being surprised, but President Lincoln loyally sustained him. "I can't spare this man; he fights."

On US 64 is the little town of Crump, where a five-mile side trip south on State 22 leads to Shiloh National Military Park. Markers indicate important sites. The Visitor Center has exhibits and presents a film, and provides a leaflet for a self-guided auto tour. In the National Cemetery here 3,700 soldiers from both sides are buried, two-thirds of them unidentified.

Halleck was a master of military maxims, but he had failed to concentrate all his forces immediately for a final defeat of Beauregard. As it was, Pope and Foote took Island No. 10 in April, opening the Mississippi as far as Memphis. Halleck, taking personal command of Grant's and Buell's forces, then ponderously advanced toward Corinth. Remembering Shiloh, he proceeded cautiously, and it was May 30 before he reached his objective. Beauregard had already evacuated the town. Meanwhile Capt. David G. Farragut with a naval force and Maj. Gen. Benjamin F. Butler's land units cracked the gulf coast fortifications of the Mississippi and captured New Orleans. By mid-1862, only strongholds at Vicksburg and Port Hudson on the Mississippi blocked complete Federal control of that vital river.

## Nashville

In 1862 Nashville was renamed Fort Johnson, a stockade having been built around it when Union forces occupied the city. In December, 1864, the Confederates under General John B. Hood atempted to regain the city; they were unsuccessful, and Hood's army broke up.

### Thomas Protects the Nashville Base

Sherman, as the western theater commander, did not learn of Nashville's fate until he reached Savannah. He had planned Nashville's defense well enough by sending his IV and XXII Corps under Maj. Gen. John M. Schofield to screen Hood's northward move from Florence, Alabama. Schofield was to allow Thomas some time to assemble 50,000 men and strengthen Nashville. The aggressive Hood with his 30,000 men had lost a golden opportunity to trap Schofield at Spring Hill, Tennessee, on November 29, 1864. Unopposed, the Union troops made a night march across Hood's front to escape capture. Bitterly disappointed, Hood overtook Schofield the next day at Franklin.

Grant's continental timetable could have at this point been upset by Hood. Booty at Nashville might carry Hood to the Ohio or allow him to concentrate with Lee before Richmond. But Franklin turned into one of the Confederacy's most tragic battles. It commenced about 3:30 P.M. on November 30 and ended at dusk as Hood threw 18,000 of his veterans against a solidly entrenched force of Federals. Like Pickett's charge at Gettysburg, Hood's frontal assault gained nothing. He lost over 6,000 men, including 13 general officers. At nightfall Schofield brought his troops in behind Thomas' defenses at Nashville.

Hood was in a precarious position. He had been far weaker than Thomas to begin with; the battle of Franklin had further depleted his army; and, even worse, his men had lost confidence in their commander. The Federals in Nashville were securely emplaced in a city which they had been occupying for three years. Hood could do little more than encamp on high ground a few miles south of Nashville and wait. He could not storm the city; his force was too small to lay siege; to sidestep and go north was an open invitation to Thomas to attack his flank and rear; and to retreat meant disintegration of his army. He could only watch Thomas' moves.

Thomas, the Rock of Chickamauga, belonged to the last bootlace school of soldiering. In comparison with Grant and Sherman, he was slow; but he was also thorough. He had gathered and trained men and horses and was prepared to attack Hood on December 10, but an ice storm the day before made movement impossible. Grant and his superiors in Washington fretted at the delay, and the General in Chief actually started west to remove Thomas. But on December 15 Thomas struck like a sledgehammer in an attack that militarily students have regarded as virtually faultless.

Thomas' tactical plan was a masterly, co-ordinated attack. His heavily weighted main effort drove against Hood's left flank while a secondary attack aimed simultaneously at Hood's right. Thomas provided an adequate reserve and used cavalry to screen his flank and extend the envelopment of the enemy left. Hood, on the other hand, was overextended and his thin line was concave to the enemy, denying him the advantage of interior lines. Hood's reserve was inadequate, and his cavalry was absent on a minor mission.

The two-day battle proceeded according to Thomas' plan as the Federals fixed Hood's right while slashing savagely around the Confederate left flank. They broke Hood's first line on December 15, forcing the southerners to retire to a new line two miles to the rear. The Federals repeated their maneuver on the 16th, and by nightfall the three-sided battle had disintegrated into a rout of Hood's army. Broken and defeated, it streamed southward, protected from hotly pursuing Union cavalry only by the intrepid rearguard action of Forrest's horsemen. The shattered Army of the Tennessee reached Tupelo, Mississippi, on January 10, 1865. It no

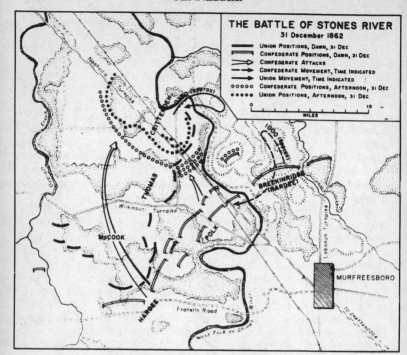

THE BATTLE OF STONES RIVER
31 December 1862

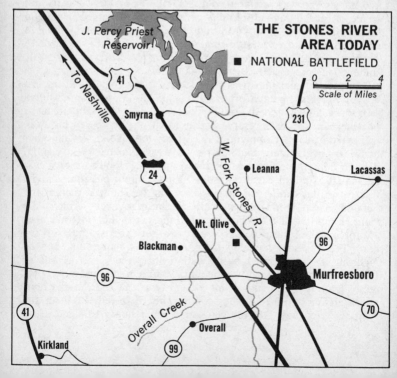

THE STONES RIVER AREA TODAY
■ NATIONAL BATTLEFIELD

longer existed as an effective fighting force; Hood was relieved of command and his scattered units were assigned to other areas of combat. The decisive battle of Nashville had eliminated one of the two great armies of the Confederacy from a shrinking chessboard.

### Stones River

Leaving Nashville on US 41, driving southeast, the first town you reach is Smyrna. Turn left on State 104 and go east one mile to reach the Sam Davis Home, a historic site honoring the nineteen-year-old Confederate hero. A Confederate scout, he was captured by Union forces and hanged as a spy for refusing to betray the Union man who had given him information. This was his boyhood home. His body is buried here.

Farther south on US 41, about thirty miles out of Nashville, is the Stones River National Battlefield, covering 324 acres. This was the scene of the Battle of Stones River, which took place from December 31, 1862, to January 2, 1863, resulting in high casualties on both sides without giving either a real victory. The graves or markers of over 6,000 Union soldiers are in the twenty-acre cemetery.

By Christmas Bragg was back in middle Tennessee, battered but still anxious to recoup his losses by recapturing Nashville. Buell had been dilatory in pursuing Bragg after Perryville and had been replaced in command of the Army of the Ohio (now restyled the Army of the Cumberland) by Maj. Gen. William S. Rosecrans. In spite of urgent and even threatening letters from the War Department, the new commander would not move against Bragg until he had collected abundant supplies at Nashville. Then he would be independent of the railroad line from Nashville to Louisville, a line of communications continually cut by Confederate cavalry.

On December 26 Rosecrans finally marched south from Nashville. Poorly screened by Union cavalry, his three columns in turn knew little about Confederate concentrations near Murfreesboro, thirty miles southeast of the Tennessee capital. Here Bragg had taken a strong position astride Stones River on the direct route to Chattanooga and proposed to fight it out. Rosecrans moved into line opposite Bragg on the evening of December 30. Both army commanders proceeded to develop identical battle plans—each designed to envelop the opponent's right flank. Bragg's objective was to drive Rosecrans off his communications line with Nashville and pin him against the river. Rosecrans' plan had the same objective in reverse, that of pinning the Confederates against the stream. Victory would probably belong to the commander who struck first and hard.

Insufficient Federal security and Rosecrans' failure to insure that the pivotal units in his attack plan were also properly posted to thwart Confederate counterattacks resulted in Confederate seizure of the initiative as the battle of Stones River opened on December 31. At dawn, Maj. Gen. William J. Hardee's corps with large cavalry support began the drive on the Federal right. Undeceived by their opponent's device of extra campfires to feign a longer battle line, Confederate attacking columns simply pushed farther around the Union flank and promptly rolled the defenders back. Applying the principles of mass and surprise to achieve rapid success, Bragg's battle plan forced Rosecrans to modify his own. The Union leader pulled back his left flank division, which had jumped off to attack Maj. Gen. John C. Breckinridge's Confederate units north of Stones River. While Sheridan's division, as at Perryville, provided stubborn resistance to General Polk's corps in the center, Hardee's units continued their drive, which by noon saw the Union battle line bent back against the Nashville pike. Meanwhile the Confederate cavalry had wrought havoc among Rosecrans' rear area elements. As was typical of many Civil War battles the attacking columns of Polk and Hardee became badly intermingled. Their men began to tire, and by afternoon repeated Confederate assaults against the constricted Union line along the Nashville pike had bogged down.

That night Rosecrans held a council of war. Some of the subordinate commanders wanted to retreat. Rosecrans and two of his corps commanders. Maj. Gen. Thomas L. Crittenden and Maj. Gen. George H. Thomas, vetoed the scheme. Brigades were then returned to their proper divisions, stragglers rounded up, and various other adjustments made in the Federal position. New Year's Day, 1863, dawned quiet and little action occurred that day.

The sunrise of January 2 revealed Rosecrans still in position. Bragg directed Breckinridge to attack the Union left wing, once more thrown across Stones River on the north. But massed Union artillery shattered the assaults and counterattacking Federals drove Breckinridge's men back to their line of departure. The armies remained stationary on January 3 but Bragg finally withdrew from the battlefield that evening, permitting victory to slip from his grasp. Tactically a draw, Stones River so badly mangled the Army of the Cumberland that it would be immobilized for six months. Yet, more than most other battles of the war, Stones River was a conflict between the wills of the opposing army leaders. Rosecrans, supported by Thomas and others, would not admit himself beaten and in the end won a victory of sorts.

The great Confederate counteroffensives of 1862 had failed in the west, yet Chattanooga, the key to east Tennessee and Georgia, remained in southern hands. Farther west Federal forces had penetrated only slightly into northern Mississippi. The war was simply on dead center in the west at the end of the year.

## PRACTICAL INFORMATION FOR TENNESSEE

 **FACTS AND FIGURES.** The state derives its name from *Tenassee,* the ancient capital of the Cherokee Indians. Its nickname is the Volunteer State. The iris is the state flower; the tulip poplar, the state tree; the mockingbird, the state bird. "Agriculture and Commerce" is the state motto. "My Homeland Tennessee" is the state song.

Nashville, population 469,000, is the state capital. The state population (1975 est.) is 4,136,000.

**HOW TO GET THERE.** *By air:* To Memphis and Nashville there are direct flights on Allegheny, American, Braniff, Delta, Eastern, Piedmont and Southern. In addition, Ozark has direct flights to Nashville; Frontier, Texas International and United to Memphis. Knoxville may be reached on direct flights of American, Delta, Piedmont and United; Chattanooga on Delta, Eastern and Southern; Tri-City Airport on Piedmont, Southern and United; Clarksville on Ozark; and Jackson on Southern.

From Canada, Nashville may be reached on direct flights of American out of Toronto; connecting flights of Nordair and Allegheny out of Montreal and Hamilton. Memphis may be reached on connecting flights of Nordair and Allegheny out of Montreal; connecting flights of United and Delta out of Toronto.

*By car:* There are a number of interstate highways to bring the visitor into the state. I–65 runs from Alabama through Tennessee into Kentucky. I–55 comes from Mississippi into Memphis and out of Tennessee into Arkansas. I–40 comes in from Arkansas to Memphis, through Nashville and Knoxville and into North Carolina. I–81 comes in from Bristol, Virginia, to Bristol, Tennessee, and on to Knoxville, I–24 comes from Georgia up to Nashville. I–75 from Georgia to Chattanooga, up to Knoxville and into Kentucky.

*By bus:* There is good service into the state: Greyhound and Trailways; ABC Coach Lines, Arrow Coach Lines, Crown Transit Lines, Inc., Great Southern Coaches, Inc., Gulf Transport Co., Illini-Swallow Lines, Inc., Indiana Motor Bus Co., Jefferson Lines, Mid-Continent Coaches, Inc. Oklahoma Transport Co., Short Way Lines, Southeastern Stages, Inc., Southwestern Transit Co., Inc., Sunnyland Stages, T.N.M. & O. Coaches, Inc., and Wells Bus Line.

*By train:* Amtrak trains come in from Chicago, Indianapolis, Louisville and Bowling Green.

*By boat:* The *Delta Queen* has added a Nashville side trip to its Cincinnati/New Orleans cruises.

**HOW TO GET AROUND.** *By air:* Allegheny, American, Braniff, Delta, Ozark, Piedmont, Southern and United serve cities within the state. *By car:* Tennessee has interstate highways criss-crossing within the state to make traveling by car a breeze. I–40 runs from Memphis through the middle of the state into North Carolina; I–65 divides the state and runs north and south; I–24, I–75 and I–81 complete the picture. US 51, 70, 79, 64, 45, 231, 431, 41, 27, 11 and 11W & 11E help visitors tour the state conveniently. Before the energy shortage, the speed limit on interstates was 75.

*Car rental:* Avis or Hertz cars may be rented in Chattanooga, Kingsport, Knoxville, Memphis and Nashville. In addition, Hertz has rental offices in Bristol, Jackson, Johnson City, Oak Ridge and Smyrna.

*By bus:* Greyhound and Trailways, as well as ABC Coach Lines, Brooks, Continental 5-Star, Great Southern Coaches, Gulf Transport Co., Illini-Swallow Lines, Inc., Jefferson Lines, Inc., Oklahoma Transport Co., Short Way Lines, Southeastern Stages, Inc. and Tri-State Bus Lines, Inc. serve some cities within the state.

*By boat:* For an unusual carefree vacation, consider renting a houseboat and cruise the beautiful Great Lakes of Tennessee at your own pace. Boats accommodate 6 to 8 persons and may be rented by the day or week. Contact:

Hixson Recreation Rentals, 4815 Glenmar Circle, Chattanooga 37416, for further information.

 **TOURIST INFORMATION.** For information and pamphlets write to Division of Tourism, Room 1028, Andrew Jackson Bldg., Nashville 37219. Eight Welcome Centers, conveniently located on the interstate highways entering Tennessee, are in operation 24 hours a day. Information about area attractions may be obtained, rest rooms and free pamphlets are available to visitors. For complete information on facilities at any of the 26 state parks, write the Tennessee Department of Conservation, Division of State Parks, 2611 West End Ave., Nashville 37203.

Public Information Office, Tennessee Department of Transportation, 106 Highway Building, Nashville 37219; Tennessee Dept. of Conservation, Division of Tourist Promotion, 2611 West End Ave., Nashville 37203; Public Relations Department, Tennessee Game & Fish Commission, Ellington Agricultural Center, Nashville 37220; Tennessee Historical Commission, Room 422, State Library and Archives Building, Nashville 37202; and U.S. Corps of Engineers, P.O. Box 1070, Nashville 37202, are helpful addresses for the visitor to obtain information on many aspects of Tennessee's activities.

 **SEASONAL EVENTS.** March: *The Tennessee Pilgrimage* is arranged by the Association for the Preservation of Tennessee Antiquities. Tours of historic Tennessee homes and other sites are featured in various Tennessee cities, 3rd. wk.

April: *Ramp Festival,* Cosby, paying tribute to this rare member of the onion family; public *Fish fry,* Paris, billed as the world's largest. Tours of beautiful homes and gardens, concerts, antique shows and art exhibits are seen at the *Dogwood Arts Festival,* Knoxville.

May: *Cotton Carnival,* Memphis, 2nd wk. *Strawberry Festival,* Humboldt, with horseshows, parades, beauty contests, street dances and band contests. All held during the 1st wk. *Strawberry Festival,* Dayton. *Old Timers Day,* Dickson, is the highlight on the last Sat. Local people wear old costumes and ride in old buggies and wagons in parades.

 **STATE PARKS.** Tennessee's state parks are among the nation's finest. There are 26 in operation. Accommodations range from campsites to suites in modern, motel-type inns at up to $30 a day. Furnished housekeeping cabins are available at weekly rates in 11 parks. There are swimming, boating, fishing, and one park, *Henry Harton,* near Lewisburg, has an 18-hole golf course. Many of the parks overlook lakes and have sandy beaches. All parks are wildlife refuges. Playing fields include tennis courts, baseball diamonds, and softball and badminton places. Hiking trails, bridle paths and horses are available at some. There are excellent restaurants and dining rooms, and convenient picnic places. The parks are popular, so reservations for overnight accommodations should be made well in advance.

*Nathan Bedford Forrest State Park* commemorates the spot where the Confederate general set up hidden artillery in 1864 and destroyed the Union base and warships on the opposite shore of the Tennessee River. The park contains a museum. Located northeast of Camden.

**TRAILER TIPS.** Nineteen of Tennessee's state parks have tent camping areas. Six have hookups for trailers. Camp sites are obtained on a first-come, first-served basis. For full information write Division of Tourism, Room 1028, Andrew Jackson Bldg., Nashville 37219. In several parks cabins are available from mid-May to mid-Sept. Rentals are mostly by the week and reservations should be made at the park of your choice.

Excellent camping and trailer facilities also are available in the Cherokee National Forest and the Great Smoky Mountains National Park in East Tennessee, the Tennessee Valley Authority's Land Between the Lakes recreation area in West Tennessee, and the Cumberland Gap National Historical Park in Northeast Tennessee.

**MUSEUMS.** Athens: *McMinn County Chapter East Tennessee Historical Society.* Court House. Open to visitors by appointment only.

Benton: *Old Fort Marr,* an historic building (1814). Guided tours daily.

Harrogate: *Lincoln Memorial University* has a history museum with exhibits on Abraham Lincoln and the Civil War. Free. Closed Thurs., mid.-Aug. to mid-Sept. and holidays.

Nashville: *American Association for State and Local History,* 1315 Eighth Ave., South Nashville, a regional history museum. Closed Sat., Sun., national holidays. *Tennessee State Museum,* 301 Capitol Blvd., a general museum is closed Mon., national holidays. *Travellers' Rest Museum House,* 1125 Chickering Park Dr., is a general museum located in the 1790 home of Judge John Overton. Closed Dec. 25, Jan. 1.

**SPECIAL INTEREST MUSEUMS.** Chattanooga: *Houston Antique Museum,* 201 High St. Closed Sat. and holidays. It houses a collection of 15,000 pitchers, china, copper and gold luster, as well as rare porcelains and furniture. *Hall of Presidents Wax Museum.* Foot of Lookout Mt., open daily from June to Labor Day. During Apr.-, May, wknds only. *Tennessee Valley Railroad Museum,* No. Chamberlain Ave., at the foot of historic Missionary Ridge, open wknds. *Lookout Mountain Museum,* in Point Park on Lookout Mountain. Excellent Indian exhibits as well as armor and weapons from the Civil War.

Gatlinburg: *American Historical Wax Museum,* on US 441.

**HISTORIC SITES.** Because of its geographical location, Tennessee was a Civil War battleground as well as one of the more important states in the westward movement of the pioneers. The names of Crockett and Boone echo through the rich history of the state.

Chattanooga: Lookout Mountain: *Cravens Terrace,* an 1856 Civil War home, is open Tues. to Sun., holidays. Closed mid-Dec. to mid-Feb.

Columbia: *The Athenaeum,* built in the 1830s, served as headquarters for Union generals Negley and Schofield; it has been restored.

Dover: *Fort Donelson National Military Park,* off US 79, has a military museum with many items from the Civil War. Open daily. Closed Dec. 25.

Franklin: *Carter House,* 1140 Columbia Ave., was the Union command post during the Battle of Franklin. Fully restored, the house is furnished with fine period furniture, and there is a basement museum housing uniforms, flags, guns, maps and other memorabilia. Guided tours daily. *Battle-O-Rama,* 1143 Columbia Ave., is a multimedia recreation of the conflict.

Greeneville: *Andrew Johnson National Historic Site,* Depot St., is open to the public, and contains his family homestead, grave and monument, and the tailor shop where he plied his trade before entering politics.

Johnson City: *Tipton-Haynes Living Historical Farm,* Erwin Hwy. 19W. Historic buildings are open to the public: Tipton and Haynes house, Slave Quarter, Haynes Law Office. Closed national holidays.

Jonesboro: *Tennessee's oldest town,* still one of the most historic and picturesque communities in the South, has many buildings of note. On US 411, 8 mi. W of Johnson City.

Kingsport: *1803 Netherland Inn* and *1820 Exchange Place* are open to the public.

Knoxville: *Confederate Memorial Hall "Bleak House",* 3148 Kingston Pike, is open daily. *Craighead-Jackson House,* 1000 State St. Closed Mon., Dec. 25; Thanksgiving. *General James White's* home (1786) and *White's Fort* which is restored. Closed Dec. 25. *Ramsey House,* Thorngrove Pike, is open Apr. to Oct.

Monteagle: The Archives of the *University of the South* contain some rare material pertaining to the history of the Confederacy. Open by appointment only.

Murfreesboro: Union General Duffield surrendered Murfreesboro to Confederate General Forrest at *Oaklands,* a 19th-century mansion which had served as Duffield's headquarters. Now restored and furnished in period style. *Stones River National Battlefield* contains the oldest Civil War monument (1863) and a national cemetery. Self-guided tours, museum, living history demonstrations.

Nashville: *Belle Meade Mansion,* the "Queen of Tennessee Plantations," on Leake Ave. off US 70 (Harding Road). Interesting to enthusiasts for antebellum architecture, historians, and lovers of thoroughbred horses.

Shiloh: *Shiloh Military Park,* site of one of the crucial battles of the war, contains markers and monuments to the fallen of both sides, and many of the original emplacements are still clearly marked for the visitor.

Smyrna: The *Sam Davis Home* has been called "the most beautiful shrine to a private soldier in the U.S." Davis, a Confederate soldier, was executed by Union forces as a spy after being captured behind their lines and refusing to reveal any information to his captors. His boyhood home has been restored and contains some of the original furniture. On the grounds are a smokehouse, slave cabins, and the family cemetery where Davis is buried.

**TOURS.** *By car:* Drive through scenic, historic 300 acres at *Reflection Riding* in Chattanooga. Historic details are noted; nature trails give the visitor relaxed enjoyment.

*By bus: WSM Scenic Tours,* a 3-hr. bus tour of historic and cultural Nashville.

*By boat:* The *Memphis Queen Line Riverboats,* Riverside Dr., foot of Monroe, provides visitors with a lovely 1½-hr. cruise on the Mississippi River. The *Delta Queen* paddlewheeler has cruises for a weekend or longer on the Mississippi from Spring to late Fall, departing from Memphis. Contact Greene Line Steamer Cruises for details. *Julia Belle Swain Steamboat,* at Chattanooga, has 1½-hour sight-seeing trips Sat., Sun., holidays. An entertaining historic narration is given on the sightseeing trips. *The Border Star,* departing from the foot of Market St., Knoxville, takes her passengers on a 1½-hour cruise on the Tennessee River. An informative narrative is included. The 250-passenger modern paddlewheeler operates most of the year. A boat ride on the Cumberland River in the 86-foot paddlewheeler *Belle Carol* can be had by visitors to Nashville. Departs from 1 Ave. N., near Fort Nashborough May-Oct.

**DRINKING LAWS.** Beer is sold in all counties; hard liquor may be purchased in liquor stores in the counties of Shelby (Memphis), Davidson (Nashville), Hamilton (Chattanooga), Knox (Knoxville), Maury (Columbia), Williamson (Franklin), Lake (Tiptonville), and Dyer (Dyersburg). Stores are open 8 A.M. to 11 P.M.; closed on Sun. Liquor by-the-drink is illegal, except in the municipalities of Knoxville, Chattanooga and Oak Ridge. Minimum age is 18.

**HOTELS AND MOTELS** in Tennessee run the full range from the oldest establishments in many of the downtown urban areas to the slick-looking motels along the major highways. As headquarters for the gigantic *Holiday Inn* chain, Memphis has ten of those establishments alone!

Listings are in order of price category. Based on double occupancy in peak season, without meals, price categories and ranges are as follows: *Expensive:* $22–$45; *Moderate:* $16–$22; *Inexpensive:* $8 $16. For a more complete explanation of hotel and motel categories see *Facts at Your Fingertips* at the front of this volume.

## CHATTANOOGA

**CHOO-CHOO HILTON INN.** *Expensive.* S. Market St., in Terminal Station. New, double-story motor inn in a restored 1905 train station. Many suites available in renovated Victorian sleeper cars. Luxury accommodations in turn-of-the-century atmosphere. Restaurants, lounge with entertainment; shops. Heated pool (indoor).

**Sheraton Inn.** *Expensive.* Two locations: 407 Chestnut St., 6710 Ringgold Rd. Restaurants, lounges, pools.

**King's Lodge.** *Moderate.* 2400 West Side Drive. Large motor inn. Pool, restaurant.

**Mark Inn (Best Western).** *Moderate.* 6650 Ringgold Rd. Three-story motel. Restaurant, pool, poolside service.

**Shamrock Motel.** *Inexpensive.* 5659 Brainerd Rd. Free coffee, pool, playground, restaurant adjoining.

## ELIZABETHTON

**Camara Inn.** *Expensive.* Pleasant rooms, some with refrigerators. Restaurant, pool.

## GATLINBURG

**Cox's Gateway Court.** *Expensive.* Lovely landscaped grounds. Accommodations in either motel or cottage units. Restaurant nearby. Heated pool. Lower winter rates.

**GATLINBURG INN.** *Expensive.* 755 Parkway. Rms tastefully decorated in Colonial decor. Suites available. Heated pool, play area. Tennis.

**Laurelwood Motel.** *Moderate.* Comfortable rooms. Complimentary coffee. Restaurant nearby. Heated pool, play area. Picnic area. Closed Nov. to Mar.

## KNOXVILLE

**Hyatt Regency-Knoxville.** *Expensive.* 500 Hill Ave. SE. A 12-story hotel with lovely rooms. Restaurant, lounge with entertainment, coffee shop. Heated pool.

**University Travel Inn.** *Moderate.* 1700 Clinch Ave. Spacious, nicely furnished rooms. Dining room, pool.

**Scottish Inn.** *Inexpensive.* Two locations; Walker Springs Rd. at I–40; northeast at jct. I–40 and Asheville Hwy. Pools, cafes.

## MEMPHIS

**Sheraton.** *Expensive.* Two locations: Airport, 2411 Winchester Rd.; Skyport, Memphis Airport. Restaurants, lounges with entertainment, heated pools.

**Pilot House Motor Inn.** *Moderate.* 100 Front St. Cafe, pool.

**Lamplighter Motor Inn.** *Inexpensive.* 667 S. Bellevue Rd. Complimentary coffee.

## MURFREESBORO

**Holiday Inn.** *Expensive.* Restaurant, heated pool.

**Quality Inn.** *Moderate.* Restaurant, pool.

**Days Inn.** *Inexpensive.* Restaurant, pool.

## NASHVILLE

**Hilton Inn Central.** *Expensive.* 211 North 1st St. Restaurant, coffee shop.

**Howard Johnson's.** *Expensive.* Two locations: 2401 Brick Church Pike, 6834 Charlotte Pike. Restaurants, pools.

**Days Inn.** *Moderate.* Four Locations: I–65 and Trinity Lane; I–40 and Bell Road; I–24 and Murfreesboro Rd.; I–40 and Old Hickory Rd.

**Scottish Inn.** *Inexpensive.* Two locations: I–40 and Briley Pkway.; 970 Murfreesboro Rd. Pleasant rooms. Pool, restaurant.

 **DINING OUT** in Tennessee often means fresh Tennessee River catfish or such country specialties as ham with red-eye gravy (sometimes made in Tennessee with coffee instead of water). Accompanying the meal may be hush puppies or home-baked biscuits, and desserts can include such Tennessee delights as pecan pie, blueberry pie, or fruit cobbler.

Restaurants are listed according to their price category. Categories and ranges for a complete dinner are as follows: *Expensive:* $9 and up; *Moderate:* $5-$9; *Inexpensive:* $2-$5. For a more complete explanation of restaurant categories see *Facts at Your Fingertips* at the front of this volume.

## CHATTANOOGA

**Town and Country.** *Moderate.* 110 N. Market St. Leisurely dining is the order of the day, with emphasis on quality service and delicious sirloins. Salad bar.

**S & W Cafeteria.** *Inexpensive.* 824 Broad St. This modern cafeteria with a Victorian motif is one of those places where frills have been eliminated in favor of an abundance of good food at reasonable prices.

## GATLINBURG

**Pioneer Inn.** *Expensive.* Novel decor. Situated to provide dining on the river. Steaks, roast beef, chicken and flaming shishkebab.

**Open Hearth.** *Moderate.* Pleasant, friendly dining room with steak as specialty.

## KNOXVILLE

**Regas Restaurant.** *Expensive.* 318 N. Gay St. Informal service and excellent food. Superb seafood, strawberry shortcake.

**Rathskeller.** *Moderate.* 4509½ Kingston Pike. Reminiscent of old Heidelberg, with 3 dining rooms in which to enjoy well-prepared beef, seafood and other specialties.

**Britling Cafeterias.** *Inexpensive.* There are three of these quality cafeterias with good food: 3134 N. Thomas St.; 20 Poplar Highland Plaza; 4550 Poplar Ave. Neat, clean and inviting.

## MEMPHIS

**CLARK STATION.** *Expensive.* 5100 Poplar Ave. Rich in railroad folklore, guests may dine in the "Memphis Special" or other replicas of plush dining cars at the turn of the century. Entertainment.

**FOUR FLAMES.** *Expensive.* 1085 Poplar Ave. Enjoy superb dining in a charming antebellum house. American, Continental cuisine. Steak, seafood (New Orleans-style) are specialties here. Lounge with entertainment. Jacket and tie a must.

**JUSTINES.** *Expensive.* 919 Coward Pl. at East St. A superb restoration of an old mansion, on attractive grounds, is the setting for excellent French cuisine. In the summer, terrace dining. Reservations recommended.

## NASHVILLE

**Mario's.** *Expensive.* 1915 West End Ave. Continental menu, bar, elegant decor. Italian dishes a specialty.

# TEXAS

## *Where the South Meets the West*

### by
### DEAN BOSWELL

*Dean Boswell is a Dallas newspaper and public relations writer. He was a wartime correspondent in Africa and Italy for the Army newspaper* Stars and Stripes.

The War for Southern Independence left few physical scars in Texas, but Reconstruction laid her waste economically while maiming her politically. Texas was restored to the Union in 1872, though Texans did not regain control of their own government until 1877. The war and its aftermath left a heritage of sorrow and mistrust that has yet to be entirely forgotten. And, as a result of the war, Texans acquired yet another identity: as well as Americans and Texans, they were now also former Southerners. In recent decades, especially with the flourishing of their western regions, Texans have come increasingly to identify with the Southwest. But their Southern heritage goes deep; for every school named after Sam Houston, there is one bearing the name of Robert E. Lee, and marble Confederate warriors stare unseeing across the lawns of many a Texas courthouse.

Many Texans served in Hood's Brigade under Gen. John Bell

Hood during the Civil War as the Kentucky native gained fame as a brigade and division commander, battled Gen. William T. Sherman at Atlanta and held commands in conflicts at Franklin and Nashville.

Hood, a graduate of the U.S. Military Academy, made his home in Texas and Louisiana after the war, and Fort Hood, a major military installation in central Texas, bears his name. The fort spreads over nearly 400 square miles and is home for the 111 U.S. Army Corps. 1st Cavalry Division, 2nd Armored Division, 13th Corps Support Command, 6th Cavalry Brigade and lesser units. The fort, with a civilian and military population of over 70,000, is located in the city of Killeen, off I–35. The Hood's Texas Brigade Association holds an annual reunion in mid-April at Hillsboro, north on I–35 where routes from Dallas and Forth Worth meet.

Gen. Albert Sidney Johnston fought with Texas in its war for independence from Mexico, and when the Republic of Texas was organized, functioned as Secretary of War from 1838 to 1840. A native of Kentucky, he was graduated from the U.S. Military Academy at the age of 23. In the struggle between the states, forces commanded by Johnston encountered those of Union Gen. Ulysses S. Grant in the fighting at Shiloh. With victory almost within his grasp, the general was fatally wounded. A school in Dallas bears the general's name. His body is interred in the State Cemetery at Austin.

Twenty-nine miles south of Fort Worth on Texas 171 lies Hillsboro with its courthouse dating from 1889. Visitors have likened it to a cathedral, denounced it as a monstrosity, and expressed lots of opinions in between. You'll understand the controversy when you see the building. Also in Hillsboro is the Confederate Research Center and Gun Museum. There are books, maps, letters and pictures at the Center and the gun collection has a companion display of edged weapons. Both attractions are on the Hill Junior College campus.

## Dallas

Thirty-six concrete headstones, formed in two rows and bearing the names of Confederate officers and soldiers, occupy a special plot in Greenwood Association Cemetery, 3020 Oak Grove. A 20-foot high marker in the center of the plot is topped by a life-size statue of an officer in uniform. Cemetery officials say there are more Confederate veterans buried in other locations and family plots, including Gen. Cabell. (The Dallas Federal Building is named for a descendant of the general.)

The cemetery itself bears a Texas Historical Commission marker as having been part of a Republic of Texas land grant given for service at the Battle of San Jacinto. The Greenwood Cemetery Association assumed operation of the grounds in 1896, according to the marker.

In Pioneer Cemetery (1848), alongside the Dallas Convention Center, another statue honors men who fought for the South. In Lee

Park, 3511 N. Hall at Turle Creek Blvd., there is an impressive statue of General Robert E. Lee.

Some restored homes and structures, with furnishings of Civil War times, have been assembled in City Park, a few blocks from the Convention Center.

## Northeast Texas

If you're traveling southeast from Dallas on US 175, you might want to visit Milner's Gristmill in Poynor and pick up some recipes printed on the mill's antique printing press. "Antique" will be a good theme-word for the region you're entering, the green, lush woodlands of northeast Texas. Four National Forests range the region which, in both wildlife and American heritage, is really the western flank of the Old South. Tyler, northeast of Poynor on Texas 155, was the site of a huge POW compound during the Civil War. The ambience couldn't be more different now—Tyler is famous for roses and rosebushes. The Goodman-LeGrand House, 624 N. Broadway, has a collection of old medical and dental instruments as well as fine furnishings that recall the antebellum era when Gallatin Smith had the mansion built. If you travel north on US 271, then go about sixty miles east on I–20, you'll reach the historic town of Jefferson. Jefferson has a population of under 3,500 but thirty of its buildings are registered historic sites. The town was a prominent outpost on the Big Cypress River, navigable in the 1830s by steamboat from New Orleans.

Your exploration can start off at the four-story Historical Society Museum in the Federal Building. The documents and articles exhibited give a general overview of Jefferson's early years. Then take a stroll around the town: The Manse, headquarters for preservation activities in town, is the oldest structure still standing. The Excelsior Hotel, still in business, offers mementoes of the Gilded Age, when statesmen and celebrities stopped over. During the summertime the Cypress Queen, replica of a 19th-century paddle-wheel steamboat, begins narrated cruises on the river.

Architecturally the equal of any Old West building in the State is the Ginocchi Hotel in nearby Marshall. It too was a gathering point for prominent residents and visitors. The hotel is now open as a museum.

During the 1861–65 period, Marshall, following the fall of Vicksburg, was the western capital of the Confederacy, and also was the capital of Missouri when that state's governor set up an exile government.

General's Row, where several Confederate generals made their homes, is a Marshall showplace today, along with over 100 buildings and residences going back at least a century. Tour maps are available at the Chamber of Commerce.

Mexican-American history takes a Civil War twist involving Goliad, for here in 1829 was born Ignacio Zaragoza, who grew up to be a general in the Mexican army. In 1862, the last year of his life, he commanded the army that forced the French to retreat to the sea after they had penetrated deep into the interior of Mexico. The French campaign was instigated by the French emperor Louis Napoleon who sought a foothold on American soil and was prepared, upon gaining it, to help supply the Confederates in the American Civil War. The South (which included Texas) was thus denied vital aid through the exploits of Zaragoza, the son of Goliad, Texas (where his victory is celebrated every May 5th).

## Austin

The best place to start a Civil War-related walking tour of Austin is the state capitol building. The capitol was constructed in 1888 out of Texas red granite taken from Granite Mountain near Marble Falls. The dome is seven feet higher than the national capitol. The Archives and Library Building, just east, has historic relics and documents of Texas under six flags. At 11th and Brazos, south of the capitol, is the Old Land Office Building, now the location of museums operated by the Daughters of the Confederacy and the Daughters of the Texas Republic.

If intrigue grips you, a visit to Longhorn Cavern, sixty miles northwest of Austin, via Texas 71 and US 281 to Park Road 4, is a must. Now a State Park and designated Natural Landmark, the cavern is the world's third largest, and its two miles of wonders charm tourists the year around. But, during the 1860s conflict, gun powder was surreptitiously turned out there 130 feet underground! Civil War items are among the displays in the cavern museum.

Some ruins of Fort Croghan, established in 1849 and hub for the later town of Burnet (where some stone and log buildings have been restored, housing guns and frontier relics), attract visitors from Memorial Day through Labor Day. Fort and town can be reached by driving north on US 281 from the cavern and east on Texas 29. From Austin, US 183 shoots forty miles or so to Texas 29 and the fort and Burnet. Inks Lake State Park, in the area, is a popular camping site.

## Sabine Pass Battle

By most military standards, the Confederate-Union Battle of Sabine Pass would hardly be worth a mention. But it did mark one of the few Texas invasion attempts by the Union, and even today, visitors can stand at the foot of a magnificent monument to the Stars and Bars hero of that encounter and draw upon their own imaginations as to how it all happened.

Sabine Pass is a city of less than 2,000 people, lying south of Beaumont and Port Arthur and hardly a good jump from the Gulf. Gen. Sam Houston himself helped map the city in 1836. The pass allows access between Texas and Louisiana to Port Arthur.

It was here on Sept. 9, 1863, that U.S. Navy gunboats attempted to secure the landing of an invasion force of 5,000 men. The objective was control of southeast Texas in addition to supporting the port blockades already established.

But the landing was not to be. Reports say that Lt. Richard Dowling, commanding a defending force of less than fifty men armed with half a dozen cannon, knocked out three gunboats and stopped the thrust.

In Sabine Pass Battleground State Historical Park, a lifesize bronze likeness of Lt. Dowling stands on guard atop a base of pink granite bearing appropriate recounting of the incredible victory. Take US 69, 287 from Beaumont to Port Arthur and Texas 87 to Sabine Pass.

Galveston was an important city when the 1860s brought Civil War. Some say it was the most important city in the state. Certainly the federal government had recognized this, and had built three structures at Pelican Split, across the channel from the city with plans to fortify them.

When Texas seceded, the Confederacy occupied the structures, placed some earth defenses and mounted several guns. At the port, a sidewheeler of an independent line was converted into a "warship" and named the *General Rusk,* while a schooner underwent similar modification. Both were active, supplementing Confederate garrisons in the city.

But Galveston was captured in 1862 when a federal fleet gained the harbor after firing on the city and Confederate forces and much of the population withdrew. This condition existed for some three months until Confederate Gen. J.B. Margruder lead a combined water and rail attack which regained the city. Scars from Union cannon are still to be seen on many buildings along The Strand.

An adobe replica of Fort Bliss stands on the U.S. Army Air Defense center near El Paso. Fort Bliss was originally established in 1848 to protect settlers from Indian raids and to assert U.S. authority over lands acquired from Mexico during the Mexican War. During the Civil War, it was the local headquarters for the Confederate Army. Later, the fort supplied the armies that battled Geronimo.

## PRACTICAL INFORMATION FOR TEXAS

**TEXAS FACTS AND FIGURES.** Texas takes its name from *Tejas,* the Spanish name for the Hasinai Indians. The state's nickname is "Lone Star State." The bluebonnet is the state flower, the pecan the state tree, the mockingbird the state bird. "Friendship" is the state motto. "Texas, Our Texas" is the state song.

Austin is the state capital. The state population is estimated at 11,196,730.
Texas lost its proud claim to "Biggest state in the union" when Alaska acquired statehood, but it remains a state worthy of superlatives—and not loath to apply them. It is a land of wide-open spaces, vast cattle ranches, proud and boastful citizens, and great mineral wealth. It leads the nation in production of oil, natural gas, sulphur, and livestock. It is also a booming industrial center, site of several major federal military and scientific installations, and a major agricultural producer, with cotton the leading crop. The

vast Texas land mass stretches from the flat coastal plain on the Gulf of Mexico, up through the rolling prairie of the Central Lowland, to the flat plains of the Panhandle, reaching rugged mountains in the far west. The climate varies by region; the west is dry, the east, humid; summers are hot, with mild winters in the south, cold in the north. The Gulf Coast is occasionally struck by hurricanes, and tornadoes, hailstorms, and floods are not uncommon in much of the state.

**HOT TO GET THERE.** *By car:* Major roads up from Mexico, from east to west are #40 to McAllen (via Reynosa), #85 to Laredo (via Nuevo Laredo), #57 to Eagle Pass (via Piedras) and #45 to El Paso (via Ciudad Juarez). From Arizona, take I–10 to southern Texas. From the Roswell, N.M., area, use US 285 toward San Antonio, US 60 toward Amarillo. The traveler from Santa Fe or Albuquerque heads east on I–40 to Amarillo, then jags SE on US 287 for the center of the state. From Denver, pick up US 287 in Lamar, Colo. If you're entering Texas from the north, US 83 crosses western Kansas and the Oklahoma panhandle, then goes through Perryton, Childress, Abilene, passes between San Angelo and Austin, then heads for Mexico via Uvalde and Laredo. I–35, from Wichita and Oklahoma City, checks into Texas at Gainesville and goes on by Dallas-Fort Worth, Waco, Temple, Austin and San Antonio. US 181 continues to Corpus Christi. Besides I–35, routes into Dallas include I–30 from Little Rock, Arkansas (via Texarkana), and I–20 from Shreveport, La. (via Marshall). The Dallas-Houston-Galveston link is I–45. I–10 reaches Houston from southern Louisiana.

*By air:* Dallas-Forth Worth Region Airport and Houston Intercontinental Airport are the state's giants. Also, Love Field Airport in Dallas and Hobby Airport in Houston have some commercial schedules.

Other Texas cities boasting major carrier service include Abilene, Amarillo, Austin, Beaumont, Brownsville and Valley points, Corpus Christi, El Paso, Lubbock, Midland-Odessa and San Antonio. Texas can count some 1,300 landing facilities of all kinds spreading over the state. So, come on, Texans will find you a place to land.

*By bus:* Coast-to-coast service by *Trailways* and *Greyhound* is routed too far north to serve any Texas city directly except Amarillo. But the *Greyhound* express schedule includes a Tulsa-Oklahoma City-Dallas-Austin-San Antonio-Laredo run while Trailways' "Rebel Route" includes Shreveport, La., and the Texas stations at Longview, Tyler, Dallas and El Paso. These are just examples of the many itineraries that reach into every corner of the Lone Star State. Regional bus companies serving Texas include *T.N.M. & O.*, *Oklahoma Transportation* and the twin outfits, *Kerrville* and *Painter Bus Cos.*

*By train:* Three passenger trains serve Texas. Amtrak's InterAmerican runs a tri-weekly schedule between Chicago and Laredo at the Mexico border. Texas stops include Texarkana, Marshall, Longview, Dallas, Fort Worth, Cleburne, McGregor, Temple, Taylor, Austin, San Marcos, San Antonio and Laredo. The line's Lone Star operates daily from Chicago, entering Texas at Gainesville with stops at Fort Worth, Cleburne, McGregor, Temple, Brenham, Rosenberg and terminating in Houston. The Sunset Limited originates in New Orleans and runs tri-weekly to Beaumont, Houston, Rosenberg, San Antonio, Del Rio, Sanderson, Alpine and El Paso, and continues to Los Angeles.

**HOW TO GET AROUND.** *By air:* Competition is literally wing-to-wing and a leading contributor to the state's economy. *American Airlines* serves Dallas-Fort Worth, El Paso, Houston and San Antonio; *Braniff*

*International* flies from Dallas-Fort Worth to Amarillo, Austin, Brownsville, Corpus Christi, El Paso, Houston, Lubbock and San Antonio; *Continental Airlines* serves Austin, Dallas-Fort Worth, El Paso, Houston, Lubbock, Midland-Odessa, San Antonio and Wichita Falls; *Davis Airlines*—Dallas-Fort Worth to College Station, and from Houston to College Station; *Rio Airways* —Dallas-Fort Worth to Fort Hood-Killeen, Temple, Waco and Wichita Falls; *Southwest Airlines*—Dallas Love Field to Houston's Hobby Airport with 18 daily flights, Austin, Corpus Christi, El Paso, Harlingen, Lubbock, Midland-Odessa and San Antonio; *Texas International*—Dallas-Fort Worth, Abilene, Amarillo, Austin, Beaumont-Port Arthur, Corpus Christi, Harlingen, Houston, Laredo, Longview, Lubbock, Midland-Odessa, San Antonio, San Angelo, Texarkana, Tyler, Waco, Wichita Falls; *Metro Airlines*—Dallas-Fort Worth to Clear Lake City, Greenville, Houston, Longview-Gladewater, Lufkin, Nacogdoches and Tyler.

*By bus: Greyhound Lines* and *Continental Trailways* serve the major sections of the state. In addition, nearly 30 other lines provide intercity service on regular schedules. In all, some 1,100 cities and towns are on bus routes. Some of the regional operators are *Sun-Set Stages,* between Abilene and San Angelo; *Jordan,* between Texarkana and Paris on an interstate basis only; *Texas Electric* between Dallas and Waco; *Southwestern Transit,* between Fort Hood and Temple; *Arrow,* Abilene to Austin or Waco; *Central Texas Bus Lines, Inc.,* to Galveston; and Tyler by *Texas Bus Lines* via Houston and Beaumont.

*By car:* If time allows, your visit to Texas should be a fun thing. The Texas Highway Department maintains 70,000 miles of highways—and they are beauties—that will get you directly between points, usually bypassing cities. These are multilaned, usually divided, with flowers and shrubs in the center if the divider is earthen, or else planted along the right-of-way. But if you prefer to explore, there are ten *Texas Trails* branching off major highways and offering roundtrip adventures off the traffic-beaten paths.

**TOURIST INFORMATION.** Simply because of distance, a visit or vacation in Texas is in itself a challenge. The Texas Highway Department maintains attractive, friendly, modern tourist bureau stations at Amarillo, Anthony, Austin (in the state capitol), Denison, Gainesville, Langtry, Laredo, Orange, Texarkana, Waskom and Wichita Falls. These provide maps and information about roads, camper and trailer regulations, the latest weather and the location of state-maintained roadside rest areas, state parks and camp sites.

If you like to plan in advance, write Texas Tourist Development Agency, Box 12008, Dept. DB, Austin, Texas 78711. They will send you, free of charge, detailed colorful material about vacationing in Texas.

**SEASONAL EVENTS.** The first Monday in January is the time for Trades Days at Canton, fifty miles southeast of Dallas on I–20, and at Weatherford, twenty-five miles west of Fort Worth on US 180. Both events have been held monthly for over one hundred years. Visitors will find just about everything imaginable for sale. Canton actually opens its sale on the weekend preceding First Monday.

In East Texas, motorists follow marked trails to enjoy the beauty of azaleas in Tyler, pink and white dogwood in Palestine and Athens, and crimson clover, Indian paintbrush and redbud in the watermelon-growing town of Mineola. Woodville, near the Big Thicket, celebrates the blossoming dogwood with a week's special welcome to tourists. History buffs pilgrimage to

Jefferson in late April-early May to tour the ante-bellum homes, see Jay Gould's private railroad car, and marvel at the ageless Excelsior House.

Marshall, hub of government and a supply center for Civil War activity, harnesses up for Stagecoach Days in mid-April. There are rides for visitors.

Also in May, the outdoor historical musical, "The Lone Star," begins a summer run (through Sept. 2) with performances nightly, except Monday, at Mary Moody Northern amphitheater in Galveston Island State Park.

In beautiful Palo Duro Canyon, the historical drama, "Texas," runs June 20 through August 25 with performances Monday through Saturday nights. In fifteen years, nearly 1,500,000 people have acclaimed this outdoor amphitheater showing.

Columbus, where Stephen F. Austin colonists settled in 1823, stages a Magnolia Homes Tour in late May, and adds antique and art shows, sidewalk dining and a "marquee drama." Lockhart, south of Austin on US 183 and near the scene of an 1840 Indian battle, puts together a Chisholm Trail Roundup and cornbread cook-off.

July is the month for old settler reunions, fireworks and more rodeos. Decatur, an 1880s stop on the Butterfield stage route, turns out for a reunion that had its start as a gathering of Confederate supporters. Hico, US 281, is close to the century mark with its reunion program.

Fairfield, on US 75 off I-40, the Freestone County Fair (August) brings 10,000 visitors to a town of 2,500 population. The whole thing started with Confederate reunions.

In October, the Confederate Air Force (mostly manned by former World War II pilots who have restored fighting planes and bombers of the period) take to the air at Harlingen for their annual show. The State Fair of Texas runs in Dallas and visitors with an historical bent will want to see the Hall of State centering the fairgrounds.

 **CAMPING OUT.** Camping is permitted in most of the 80 state parks, some 200 public campgrounds, and the four national forests. Texas also counts over 130 public lakes and reservoirs, and many of these are open to campers. Additionally, there are numerous commercial campgrounds. Campers and travelers can acquire free packets of information at any Highway Department Tourist Bureau immediately upon entering the state or by writing the State Department of Highways and Public Transportation, Travel & Information Division, P.O. Box 5064, Austin, Texas 78763.

 **TRAILER TIPS.** Just because Texas is so big (roughly eight hundred miles from north to south and from east to west), the traveler might be well advised to consider how many miles he can travel, where he wants to go and how much time he has available. The Travel and Information Division of the Parks and Wildlife Department, both at Austin, will gladly, and without charge, furnish specific information for the individual traveler. Upon entering the state, the traveler may find a stop at a Texas Tourist Bureau helpful.

Kampgrounds of America (KOA), lists over 35 locations in Texas, some serving other closeby towns or special attractions. Facilities vary, but their slogan is "If it's KOA, it's A-OK." Texas KOA Owners Association, 6805 Guadalupe St., Austin, Texas 78752 lists these locations: Abilene, Amarillo, Arlington/Six Flags, Austin, Brownsville, Columbus, Cotulla, Crocket, Dalhart, Dallas, El Paso, Fort Worth/Weatherford, Fredericksburg, Galveston/Freeport, Greenville/Caddo Mills, Houston, Junction, Kingsville, Lake Corpus Christi/Mathis, Lake Livingston/Bridgeport, Lake Sam Rayburn, Lubbock, Madisonville, McAllen/Edinburgh/Pharr, Midland/

Odessa, Mt. Pleasant, Orange/Beaumont/Port Arthur, Rockport, San Angelo, San Antonio, Tyler, Van Horn, Waco/West, Wichita Falls/Burkburnett, Belton/Temple/Killen.

**MUSEUMS AND GALLERIES.** As a rule, most museums are open Mon. through Fri., and afternoons Sat. and Sun. Admission, if any, is small. *The Jefferson Historical Museum* in Jefferson is housed in a three-story, gabled building on which construction was started in 1888 and which served for years as the post office and federal court. The Jefferson Historical Society acquired the property in 1965 and operates the museum. Displays are arranged in the basement and three above-ground floors. Attractions include Civil War artifacts, Republic of Texas documents, papers of Sam Houston, a 200-year-old cloth loom, a primitive kitchen, Caddo Indian relics, antique furniture and a children's room, clothing and toys.

**HISTORIC SITES.** The *home of Jim Hogg,* governor of Texas in the 1890s, is a park and shrine near Quitman, county seat of Wood County, north off US 80 at Mineola. An *Old Settlers' Reunion* is held there annually in August. Area is expanding as a recreational and residential point. The *Governor Hogg Shrine* offers restrooms, picnicking area, and a museum. The *Jim Hogg Historical Park* is located at Rusk in Cherokee County, more than fifty miles south on US 69. Lake Quitman provides a trailer park offering boathouse rentals. Reservation required.

The *Varner-Hogg Plantation* at West Columbia was given to the state by Miss Ima Hogg, daughter of Texas' first native governor, with an endowment to perpetuate an appreciation of the simple, industrious, and sometimes elegant life of the early settlers of Texas. The colonial period and the early days of the Republic of Texas are reflected in its furnishings and documents.

The plantation takes its name from the first grantee of the land and the last purchaser of the property before its gift to the state. James Stephen Hogg acquired the plantation about 1901 and made it his country home until his death in 1906.

Best records indicate that the present plantation house was built about 1835. The First Congress of the Republic of Texas assembled there on Oct. 3, 1836. Two houses were used, one for the Senate, and one for the House of Representatives. They were surrounded by giant live oak trees. One, especially noted for its size and triple trunk, became known as "Independence Oak."

The Plantation House is open to visitors. It is designated a State Historic Park. Admission.

**DRINKING LAWS.** Sale of beer and low alcohol-content wine, and distilled spirits and strong wine in the 254 counties, and even within precincts, may be determined by local option vote. Bottle sales of liquor and strong wines, even in the so-called "wet" areas, is legal only from package stores, which are open from 10 A.M. to 9 P.M. except Sunday. In these areas, liquor by the drink and beer may be purchased at taverns and restaurants if the owner is licensed; separate licenses are required. Sale hours are from 7 A.M. to midnight, except Saturday, when the deadline is 1 A.M. Sunday. Special "after hours" licenses, permitting sales to 2 A.M., may be obtained by tavern and restaurant owners for an additional fee.

Drive-in groceries and food stands in the same wet areas can sell beer and low-content wine from 7 A.M. to midnight and from 12 noon to midnight

Sunday, except that by local option, sales at such establishments may be limited to off-premise consumption. Inside the state, motorists can legally transport a quart of whiskey or one case of beer in their car. Most of the major counties and leading cities are "wet," while the small populated counties are dry. Legal age for purchase of beer or liquor is 18.

 **HOTELS AND MOTELS** outside the major metropolitan areas run the entire range from the deluxe hotel of the big cities to the Wild West atmosphere of the *7-A Ranch;* from plain motels along the lesser highways to magnificent Spanish-style motor inns. The traveler can soak up history in the high-ceilinged rooms of Austin's Driskill Hotel—opened Christmas Day, 1885—or relish the 1850s atmosphere of the Excelsior House in Jefferson, where Presidents Grant and Hayes were among the famous guests.

Cost figures generally are for a double room for two and average as follows: *Deluxe* $30 and up, *Expensive* $22-$30, *Moderate* $19-$22, and *Inexpensive* $12-$19.

## AUSTIN

**THE DRISKILL HOTEL.** *Expensive.* 117 E. 7th. A gathering place for Austin residents and state office-holders and legislators for most of the years since 1886. Original section of the hotel now joined by new section with shops and additional rooms. Tea room, ballroom, dining room. Maximillian Room represents the past.

## BEORNE

**OLD KENDALL INN.** *Inexpensive.* Nothing fancy here—just simple basic accommodations, very low prices and a friendly staff. Old stagecoach stop, built in 1859, boasting handhoned limestone walls 18 inches thick and a guest list including Robert E. Lee. Air conditioned, private baths. On I-10, 30 miles northwest of San Antonio.

## CALDWELL

**THE SURREY INN.** *Moderate.* Modern motel featuring antique furniture and Old West atmosphere. Near site of earlier predecessor on Old San Antonio Road, now Texas 21.

## CASTROVILLE

**THE LANDMARK INN.** *Inexpensive.* Small inn dating from 1846 recently acquired as historic site by Texas Parks and Wildlife Commission. On banks of Medina River with 1854 grist mill and other old buildings on grounds. Some fine antique furniture. Air conditioned but no TV or private baths.

## CORPUS CHRISTI

**Downtowner Motor Inn.** *Moderate.* Conveniently located near business district with views of the Gulf. Pool, restaurant.

## JEFFERSON

**THE EXCELSIOR HOUSE.** *Moderate.* Small, gracious hotel dating from the 1850's. Lavishly restored. Each room furnished with authentic antiques. U.S. Grant was a guest. On US 59, north of Marshall.

## MARSHALL

**GINOCCHIO HOTEL.** *Moderate.* Across the tracks from the Texas & Pacific Depot. Curly pine, used in much of the hotel construction, came from Louisiana. Hotel open for tours. Excellent food served. On US 80 in East Texas.

## NACOGDOCHES

**HALFWAY HOUSE.** *Moderate.* An inn, still in remarkable repair, where many notables of the Civil War period stopped. Take Texas 21 some twenty miles east.

**FREDONIA INN.** *Inexpensive.* Downtown, filled with history.

## NEW BRAUNFELS

**PRINCE SOLMS INN.** *Moderate.* Built in 1899, restored to early elegance and charm. Nine rooms, no telephones, no television. On I–35 and Texas 46.

## PALESTINE

An old hotel is being restored here, but no more information is available at presstime. On US 79, 287.

## SALADO

**THE STAGECOACH INN.** *Expensive.* Historic stopping place of the Old Chisholm Trail once providing lodging for such figures as Sam Houston, Generals Lee and Custer, and a string of badmen including the notorious James brothers. Restored in the '40s, inn now is one of the Southwest's most luxurious, with dining rms., oak-sheltered patio, pool, music, putting green, and playground. No pets. Opposite the Central Texas Area Museum, relics and antiques.

## SAN ANTONIO

**MENGER HOTEL.** *Expensive.* One of Texas' most historic structures carefully restored. Guest list has included Lillie Langtry, Sarah Bernhardt, Robert E. Lee, U.S. Grant and Sam Houston. Teddy Roosevelt recruited Rough Riders in the Menger bar. Excellent restaurant. Pool.

 **DINING OUT.** With modern highways tending to skirt many of the smaller cities and towns, good off-highway franchise operations, often of special building design for easy recognition by the traveler, offer American menus in comfortable, air-conditioned surroundings. Restrooms are convenient. Yet, it's often fun to drive into town and get a townsman's recommendation: maybe a family operation where food is good and plentiful. If Mexican food is your dish, you will find Dallas-based El Chico and El Fenix restaurants dotted about the state.

Restaurant price categories are as follows: *Deluxe* $12.50 and up, *Expensive* $10-$12.50, *Moderate* $6-$10, and *Inexpensive* under $5. These prices are for hors d'oeuvres or soup, entree, and dessert. Not included are drinks, tax and tips. For a more complete explanation of restaurant categories refer to *Facts at Your Fingertips.*

## ABILENE

**BUFFALO GAP STEAK HOUSE.** *Moderate.* Nice atmosphere, good food. Specializes in Mexican and American dishes.

## AMARILLO

**Rhett Butler's.** *Moderate.* 2805 W. 15th. The decor is not much in the way of Southern charm, and certainly the place doesn't go back to Rhett's day, but you can't beat a name like this!

## AUSTIN

**GREEN PASTURES.** *Expensive.* A favorite with Austinites, convention visitors and vacationers, at 811 W. Live Oak, established in 1888. Old South charm exudes from this two-story white frame home, where the menu for the day is written on a blackboard.

**SHOLZ GARTEN.** *Moderate.* 1607 San Jacinto. An historical marker cites the original owner for Civil War participation. The German-style food is excellent, and there is an outdoor beer garden, popular in summer with university students and statehouse people.

**THE INN IN BRUSHY CREEK.** Historic old frontier home dating from 1830's, and listed on the National Register of historic sites. Continental and American menu.

## CALDWELL

**SURREY INN.** *Moderate.* Upholds the tradition for good food handed down from an 1840s predecessor. On Texas 21, 26.

## DALLAS

**BRENT'S PLACE.** *Expensive.* In Old City Park, south of downtown, operates in a restored early-period building moved to the park as part of a recreation of a pioneer town. Excellent luncheon served weekdays by members of the Dallas County Heritage Society.

**VICTORIA STATION.** *Moderate.* The Quadrangle at 2910 North. Railroad theme restaurant with very interesting atmosphere recreated in old boxcars and a caboose. Specializes in steaks and prime rib.

## HOUSTON

**OLD SAN FRANCISCO STEAK HOUSE.** *Moderate.* 8611 Westheimer. Good steak house with atmosphere of the 1890's.

## LIVINGSTON

**INN OF THE 12 CLANS.** *Moderate.* On the Alabama-Coushatta Indian Reservation off Route 3. Native-owned restaurant in working Indian village. American and Indian food. No liquor. During summer, pre-dinner Indian show at sundown.

## JEFFERSON

**RIVERBOAT RESTAURANT.** *Moderate.* Riverboat warehouse, built 1852. Casual, informal restaurant known for its good food.

## MARSHALL

**GINOCCHIO HOTEL AND RESTAURANT** carries on the reputation of an earlier-day operation. The menu is a newspaper with the front page devoted to news events of the hotel founding and the wounding of Maurice Barrymore, actor and patriarch of the Barrymores. Luncheon, dinner served. On US 59, 80.

## NEW BRAUNFELS

**Krause's Cafe.** *Moderate.* has a reputation of half a century for outstanding breakfasts. I–35, Texas 46.

## ROUND ROCK

**INN AT BRUSH CREEK.** *Expensive.* Operates in an 1850s residence, and has built a following for exceptional continental cuisine. Decor is close to Old South charm. On I–35, northeast of Austin.

## SALADO

**THE STAGECOACH INN.** *Expensive.* Lavishly restored old stagecoach stop known in the area for its fine food. No menu—daily selection of well-prepared entrees.

## SAN ANTONIO

**LA LOUISIANE.** *Deluxe.* 2632 Broadway. Expensive French restaurant specializing in New Orleans-style dishes. Superb cuisine and service.

## TEMPLE

**LITTLE RIVER MERCANTILE.** *Moderate.* Established 1911, was this area's only general store. Furnishings retained in changeover to restaurant (the old cast iron stove now is a serving point for soup) and quality of food brings diners from as far as Austin. Seven miles east of I–35 on FM 436.

## WAXAHACHIE

**DURHAM HOUSE.** *Expensive.* Turn-of-the-century residence with antiques. Candlelight dining. Open weekends. Reservations required.

## WOODVILLE

**THE PICKET HOUSE.** *Moderate.* In Heritage Garden Village, serves luncheons daily, family style, and is famed for chicken and dumplings, a daily special. On US 90 at US 67, 287.

# VIRGINIA

## Major Battleground of War

### by
### PARKE ROUSE, JR.

*Parke Rouse, Jr., a lifelong Virginian, is director of the Jamestown-Yorktown Foundation at Jamestown and a well-known author and historian.*

When Virginia voted on April 17, 1861, to secede from the Union, it doomed itself to become a major battleground of a war between North and South. It had not long to wait. On May 27, farmers living at Newport News Point, at the junction of Hampton Roads and the James River, saw troop-laden vessels approach their shore. The Yankees had come! The peaceful farmlands of Virginia would be red with blood before peace finally came at Appomattox four years later.

The actual area of combat was defined after the Confederate States moved their capital from Montgomery, Alabama, to Richmond. The focus of the conflict was to be from Washington, capital of a Union of 22 million people, across the Potomac to Richmond, capital of a Confederacy of nine million. From the beginning, the odds for the South were slim.

As the potential cutting edge of the Confederacy, Virginia hoped for a lightning war. Like other Southerners, Virginians had inordinate faith in the skill at arms of the South's outdoorsmen. Like South Carolina's Wade Hampton, they thought "Southern hotheaded dash, reckless gallantry, spirit of adventure" would overwhelm the North. Only a few realists like Robert E. Lee understood what adverse odds the South faced.

Lee, who had declined the Army's offer of command of Union forces, resigned his federal commission to become commander of Virginia's forces. "Trusting in almighty God, an approving conscience, and the aid of my fellow citizens," he said, "I devote myself to the service of my native State, in whose behalf alone will I ever again draw my sword."

Unfortunately, Lee's sentiments were shared chiefly by eastern Virginians. In the trans-Appalachian northwest counties, slavery and secession were anathema. At a meeting in Wheeling a few months later, western Virginia in turn "seceded" from Virginia and sought protection of the Federal government. Thus the proud Old Dominion lost one-third of her territory and citizens.

After the pro-Unionist Wheeling Convention of 1861–62, the mountainous regions beyond the Appalachians were enemy country.

Once Jefferson Davis and his Confederate cabinet were installed in Richmond in 1861, the Confederates hoped to carry the war to the North in blitzkrieg fashion. However, Lincoln and his generals had other ideas. They saw the South's weak navy as an invitation to invade Virginia by sea and then to march swiftly up the peninsula to Richmond, supported by Federal gunboats in the James and York. The result was George B. McClellan's peninsula campaign of 1861–62, which was defeated at last by Lee's defense of Richmond in the Seven Days' Battles of June, 1862.

The South's earliest offensive began in 1861 with victory at Bull Run, only thirty miles southwest of Washington. So well defended was the District of Columbia, however, that the Confederacy aimed its further efforts at Maryland and Pennsylvania instead. In northern Virginia and Maryland there were many displays of "Southern hotheaded dash," and "reckless gallantry," but after the bloody debacle of Gettysburg in 1863, the South's hopes for early victory died.

One of the most brilliant Confederate efforts was the Valley Campaign, led by Stonewall Jackson in 1862. An instructor at Virginia Military Institute when the war broke out, Jackson became Lee's best commander until mortally wounded by his own men at Chancellorsville. Other able Virginia soldiers were Joseph E. Johnston, Jeb Stuart, Richard S. Ewell, John S. Mosby, Ambrose P. Hill, Turner Ashby, Daniel H. Hill, Jubal Early, and William Mahone.

Union naval superiority in Virginia's waters was challenged at Hampton Roads in 1862 by the Confederate ironclad *Virginia*, (originally the federal frigate *Merrimack*), which battled the Union's *Monitor* to a standoff while spectators watched from Norfolk, Hampton, and Newport News. Neither ship seriously damaged the other, but the battle introduced the age of armored ships to the world.

Like the Revolution, the Civil War reached its climax in Virginia. After a succession of hapless Union commanders, Lincoln in 1864 named Ulysses S. Grant, who at first suffered heavy losses in the Wilderness Campaign in Fredericksburg and Spotsylvania County in May and June, 1864. Grant then moved more successfully against Lee at Petersburg, an important railhead and supply center.

Grant's siege and destruction of food supplies led at last to Lee's evacuation of Petersburg and Richmond in April 1865. The Confederate government fled across the James to Danville and on to Greensboro, N.C., before it finally dissolved. Pursued by Grant to Appomattox Courthouse, Lee surrendered his exhausted army on April 9, 1865. Other Confederate capitulations followed, and Jefferson Davis was captured in Georgia and brought back to Fort Monroe as a prisoner of war.

After a five-year military occupation called Reconstruction, Virginia in 1870 was readmitted to the Union. Though its ex-Confederates swore allegiance, their pride in the "lost cause" and in Lee, Jackson, Stuart, and other commanders remained very much alive. A Confederate Memorial Society was organized in Richmond, and a Confederate Memorial Day was observed at cemeteries and churches each May. Camps of Confederate veterans held frequent reunions in tented towns at Richmond and other Southern cities. Civil War battlegrounds became national parks in Fredericksburg, Petersburg, Appomattox, and elsewhere. Houses associated with the Confederacy were preserved in Richmond and Danville, and a Confederate Museum was created.

Two Civil War sites—Libby Prison in Richmond and the McLean House, where Lee surrendered—were dismantled and moved from Virginia to World's Fairs. However, the McLean House was later returned to its Appomattox site, where it stands today. In Richmond, heroic statues were placed along Monument Avenue to honor Lee, Jackson, Stuart, Davis, and Commodore Matthew Fontaine Maury, who served the Confederate Navy. Other monuments arose elsewhere, placed in counties and cities to honor their Confederate dead. Newport News reconstructed a series of dams and trenches built by Confederates in 1861 to deter General McClellan's progress up the peninsula.

Visitors in search of Civil War records and reminders will find a wealth of them in all these places as well as in the Virginia State Library and at the Fredericksburg and Petersburg battlefields. Although a century has dimmed our memories of America's greatest tragedy, its combatants are enshrined on the battleground named Virginia.

## Major Civil War Sites in Virginia

To follow the Civil War in Virginia, you should start at Hampton on the peninsula, where McClellan in 1861 launched his drive

towards Richmond. Then, following the war in roughly chronologi-
cal order, you should drive west up the peninsula to Richmond,
proceed thence to Fredericksburg and Alexandria, and then turn
westward to Winchester. After following the Valley of Virginia in a
southwesterly direction to Lexington, turn to Southside Virginia and
Hopewell, Petersburg, Sayler's Creek, and finally to Appomattox.

At Hampton is Fort Monroe, the Federal "dagger at the heart of
the Confederacy," which was a Union threat throughout the war.
There is located the commandant's house which President Lincoln
visited early in the war, the quarters occupied many years earlier by
Capt. Robert E. Lee and his family, and the Casemate Museum of
the fort and its history. Nearby is the casemate cell which Jefferson
Davis occupied for two years, after his capture in May 1865, while
awaiting trial for treason. He was released without trial in 1867.

Near the Hampton–Newport News shoreline in Hampton Roads is
the site of the battle of the ironclads *Monitor* and *Virginia* (formerly
*Merrimack)* in 1862. The site, offshore from Hampton Roads
Avenue, is marked by a permanent visual display. Near the battle
site in Hampton Roads is the island once fortified by the Union as
Fort Wool, now touched by the new Hampton Roads Bridge-
Tunnel. On the outskirts of Hampton is Big Bethel, where the first
engagement between Federal and Confederate troops occurred in
the spring of 1861.

At nearby Newport News is the Mariners Museum containing
numerous paintings, models, and displays of the Civil War at sea.
Extending laterally across the peninsula from the James to the York
near Hampton–Newport News is a series of defense lines built by
Confederates in 1861–62 under Gen. John B. Magruder, designed to
halt Federal progress up the peninsula. Dam No. 1 is a part of the
Newport News City Park, on Virginia route 143 at the western end
of Newport News. Confederate gun positions and Union trenches
are still visible. The parks Visitor Center contains maps.

East of Williamsburg, adjoining the Fort Magruder Quality Inn,
on Route 60, are the remains of the Confederates' principal
Williamsburg defense, Fort Magruder. On the campus of the College
of William and Mary, you may visit the Wren Building, which served
as Federal headquarters in Williamsburg in 1862–63, until it was
accidentally burned by Federal occupants. It was rebuilt about 1900
with a Federal appropriation of $64,000.

At Berkeley Plantation, 25 miles west of Williamsburg on the
James River, was the headquarters of General McClellan during part
of the Peninsula Campaign. There Lincoln reviewed some of "Little
Mac's" 100,000 troops in 1862, and there the bugle call known as
"taps," "evening retreat," or "lights out" was first played during the
occupation of the area by Gen. Daniel Butterfield in 1862. Though
privately owned, the house is open to the public. Nearby is Shirley, a
Carter family plantation and erstwhile home of Anne Carter, who
married Lighthorse Harry Lee and became the mother of Robert E.
Lee. The privately owned house is also open to the public.

East of Richmond, near Berkeley and Shirley, lie the fields of the

Seven Days' Battles, fought in June 1862. Here Confederate troops commanded first by Gen. Joseph E. Johnston and, after his injury, by Robert E. Lee, finally turned back the Union's massive peninsula campaign assault on Richmond, capital of the Confederacy. These battlefields are administered as Richmond National Battlefield Park, whose visitor center is at Chimborazo Hill in Richmond, open 9 to 5 daily. The visitor may drive the 57-mile Battlefield Route: first by Route 156 to Mechanicsville, thence to Route 5 near the James River and westward to Richmond's Church Hill; and thence on Interstate 95 to Drewry's Bluff.

## The Peninsular Campaign

As the year 1862 began in the eastern theater, plans prepared in Washington were aimed at the capture of Richmond rather than destruction of the army commanded by Joseph E. Johnston, now a full general. Precise methods for reaching the Confederate capital differed. President Lincoln favored an overland advance which would always keep an army between the Confederates and Washington. McClellan agreed at first, then changed his views in favor of a waterborne move by the Army of the Potomac to Urbana on the Rappahannock. From there he could drive to Richmond before Johnston could retire from the Manassas area to intercept him. The Washington fortifications, an elaborate system of earthen forts and battery emplacements then in advanced stages of construction, would adequately protect the capital while the field army was away. Johnston, however, rendered this plan obsolete; he withdrew from Manassas to Fredericksburg, halfway between the two capitals and astride McClellan's prospective route of advance. Early in March McClellan moved his army out to the deserted Confederate camps around Manassas to give his troops some field experience. While he was in the field President Lincoln relieved him as General in Chief, doubtless on the ground that he could not command one army in the field and at the same time supervise the operations of all the armies of the United States. Lincoln did not appoint a successor. For a time he and Stanton took over personal direction of the Army, with the advice of a newly constituted Army board consisting of the elderly Maj. Gen. Ethan A. Hitchcock and the chiefs of the War Department bureaus.

When events overtook the Urbana scheme, McClellan began to advocate a seaborne move to Fort Monroe, Virginia (at the tip of the peninsula formed by the York and James Rivers), to be followed by an overland advance up the peninsula. If the troops moved fast, he maintained, they could cover the seventy-five miles to Richmond before Johnston could concentrate his forces to stop them. This plan had promise, for it utilized Federal control of the seas and a useful base of operations at Fort Monroe and there were fewer rivers to cross than by the overland route. Successful neutralization of the *Merrimac* by the *Monitor* on March 9 had eliminated any naval threat to supply and communications lines, but the absence of good

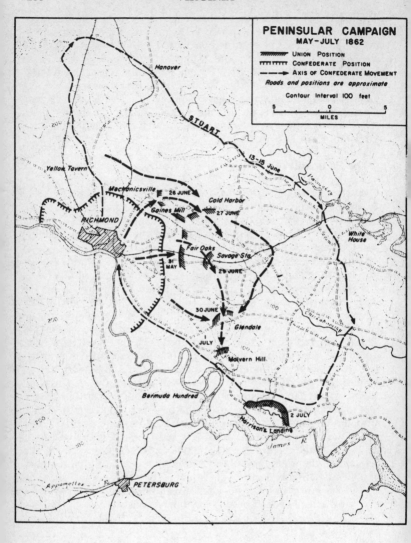

PENINSULAR CAMPAIGN
MAY–JULY 1862

Union Position
Confederate Position
Axis of Confederate Movement
Roads and positions are approximate

Contour Interval 100 feet

MILES

roads and the difficult terrain of the peninsula offered drawbacks to the plan. Lincoln approved it, providing McClellan would leave behind the number of men that his corps commanders considered adequate to insure the safety of Washington. McClellan gave the President his assurances, but failed to take Lincoln into his confidence by pointing out that he considered the Federal troops in the Shenandoah Valley to be covering Washington. In listing the forces he had left behind, he counted some men twice and included several units in Pennsylvania not under his command.

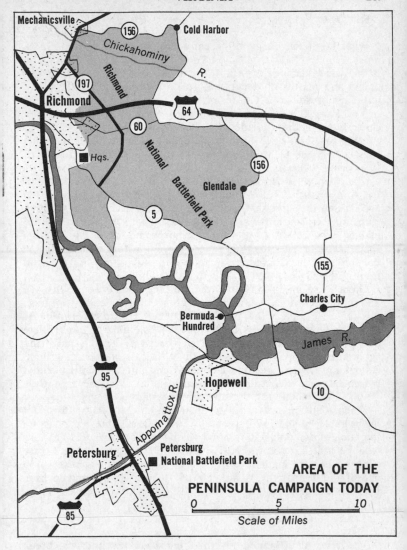

AREA OF THE
PENINSULA CAMPAIGN TODAY

0            5            10
Scale of Miles

Embarkation began in mid-March, and by April 4 advance elements had moved out of Fort Monroe against Yorktown. The day before, however, the commander of the Washington defenses reported that he had insufficient forces to protect the city. In addition, Stonewall Jackson had become active in the Shenandoah Valley. Lincoln thereupon told Stanton to detain one of the two corps which were awaiting embarkation at Alexandria. Stanton held back McDowell's corps, numbering 30,000 men, seriously affecting McClellan's plans.

### Fair Oaks

When McClellan reached the peninsula in early April he found a force of ten to fifteen thousand Confederates under Maj. Gen. John B. Magruder barring his path to Richmond. Magruder, a student of drama and master of deception, so dazzled him that McClellan, instead of brushing the Confederates aside, spent a month in a siege of Yorktown. But Johnston, who wanted to fight the decisive action closer to Richmond, decided to withdraw slowly up the peninsula. At Williamsburg, on May 5, McClellan's advance elements made contact with the Confederate rear guard under Maj. Gen. James Longstreet, who successfully delayed the Federal advance. McClellan then pursued in leisurely fashion. By May 25, two corps of the Army of the Potomac had turned southwest toward Richmond and crossed the sluggish Chickahominy River. The remaining three corps were on the north side of the stream with the expectation of making contact with McDowell, who would come down from Fredericksburg. Men of the two corps south of the river could see the spires of the Confederate capital, but Johnston's army was in front of them. *(see Map)*

Drenching rains on May 30 raised the Chickahominy to flood stage and seriously divided McClellan's army. Johnston decided to grasp this chance to defeat the Federals in detail. He struck on May 31 near Fair Oaks. His plans called for his whole force to concentrate against the isolated corps south of the river, but his staff and subordinate commanders were not up to the task of executing them. Assaulting columns became confused, and attacks were delivered piecemeal. The Federals, after some initial reverses, held their ground and bloodily repulsed the Confederates.

When Johnston suffered a severe wound at Fair Oaks, President Davis replaced him with General Lee. Lee for his part had no intention of defending Richmond passively. The city's fortifications would enable him to protect Richmond with a relatively small force while he used the main body of his army offensively in an attempt to cut off and destroy the Army of the Potomac. He ordered Jackson back from the Shenandoah Valley with all possible speed.

### The Seven Days' Battles

McClellan had planned to utilize his superior artillery to break through the Richmond defenses, but Lee struck the Federal Army before it could resume the advance. Lee's dispositions for the Battle of Mechanicsville on June 26 present a good illustration of the principles of mass and economy of force. On the north side of the Chickahominy, he concentrated 65,000 men to oppose Brig. Gen. Fitz-John Porter's V Corps of 30,000. Only 25,000 were left before Richmond to contain the remainder of the Union Army. When Lee attacked, the timing and co-ordination were off; Jackson of all people was slow and the V Corps defended stoutly during the day. McClellan thereupon withdrew the V Corps southeast to a stronger position at Gaines' Mill. Porter's men constructed light barricades and made ready. Lee massed 57,000 men and assaulted 34,000 Federals on June 27. The fighting was severe but numbers told, and the Federal line broke. Darkness fell before Lee could exploit his advantage, and McClellan took the opportunity to regroup Porter's men with the main army south of the Chickahominy.

At this point McClellan yielded the initiative to Lee. With his line of communications cut to White House—his supply base on the York River—and with the James River open to the U.S. Navy, the Union commander decided to shift his base to Harrison's Landing on the south side of the peninsula. His rear areas had been particularly shaky since Confederate cavalry under Brig. Gen. J. E. B. Stuart had ridden completely around the Federal Army in a daring raid in early June. The intricate retreat to the James, which involved 90,000 men, the artillery train, 3,100 wagons, and 2,500 head of cattle, began on the night of June 27 and was accomplished by using two roads. Lee tried to hinder the movement but was held off by Federal rear guards at Savage Station on June 29 and at Frayser's Farm (Glendale) on the last day of the month.

By the first day of July McClellan had concentrated the Army of the Potomac on a commanding plateau at Malvern Hill, northwest of Harrison's Landing. The location was strong, with clear fields of fire to the front and the flanks secured by streams. Massed artillery could sweep all approaches and gunboats on the river were ready to provide fire support. The Confederates would have to attack by passing through broken and wooded terrain, traversing swampy ground, and ascending the hill. At first Lee felt McClellan's position was too strong to assault. Then, at 3 P.M. on July 1, when a shifting of Federal troops deceived him into thinking there was a general withdrawal, he changed his mind and attacked. Again staff work and control were poor. The assaults, which were all frontal, were delivered piecemeal by only part of the army against Union artillery, massed hub to hub, and supporting infantry. The Confederate formations were shattered because Lee failed to carry out the principle of mass. On the following day, the Army of the Potomac fell back to Harrison's Landing and dug in. After reconnoitering McClellan's position, Lee ordered his exhausted men back to the Richmond lines for rest and reorganization.

The Peninsular Campaign cost the Federal Army some 15,849 men killed, wounded, and missing. The Confederates, who had done most of the attacking, lost 20,614. Improvement in the training and discipline of the two armies since the disorganized fight at Bull Run was notable. Also significant was the fact that higher commanders had not yet thoroughly mastered their jobs. Except in McClellan's defensive action at Malvern Hill, which was largely conducted by his corps commanders, neither side had been able to bring an entire army into co-ordinated action.

## Richmond

Surviving in Richmond are many sites of the 1861–65 conflict: the Virginia Capital, which was the seat of the Confederate government from 1861–1865; the "White House of the Confederacy," where President Jefferson Davis lived from 1861 to 1865; Lee's wartime residence at 707 East Franklin Street; St. Paul's Episcopal Church, where Davis was attending Sunday worship when Lee sent word of his impending evacuation of Petersburg; the onetime site of Libby Prison on Libby Hill, overlooking the James; and Chimborazo Park, wartime site of the Confederates' Chimborazo Hospital and a center of Civil War activity.

Also in Richmond are the Confederate Museum, adjoining the "White House of the Confederacy"; Hollywood Cemetery, where Jefferson Davis and other prominent Confederates are buried; Battle Abbey, headquarters of the Virginia Historical Society with its famous Hoffbauer murals of the war; the United Daughters of the Confederacy National Headquarters; the Valentine Museum with its mementos of the Civil War and model of the recumbent statue of Lee; and various outdoor monuments, including the Confederate Soldiers' and Sailors' Monument on Libby Hill, the A. P. Hill statue on Chamberlayne Avenue, and statues of Lee, Jackson, Stuart, Davis, and Maury on Monument Avenue.

Richmond has several excellent libraries of Civil War records, prints, and photographs.

## Lee Cornered at Richmond

On the morning of May 4, 1864, Meade and Sherman moved out to execute Grant's grand strategy. The combat strength of the Army of the Potomac, slimmed down from seven unwieldy corps, consisted of three infantry corps of 25,000 rifles each and a cavalry corps. Commanding the 12,000-man cavalry corps was Maj. Gen. Philip H. Sheridan, an energetic leader brought east by Grant on Halleck's recommendation. Meade again dispersed his cavalry, using troopers as messengers, pickets, and train guards, but young Sheridan, after considerable argument, eventually succeeded in concentrating all of his sabers as a separate combat arm. Grant reorganized Burnside's IX Corps of 20,000 infantrymen, held it as a strategic reserve for a time, and then assigned the IX Corps to Meade's army. Lee's army, now 70,000 strong, was also organized into a cavalry and three infantry corps.

Grant and Lee were at the height of their careers and this was their first contest of wills. Having the initiative, Grant crossed the Rapidan and decided to go by Lee's right, rather than his left. *(see Map)* First, Grant wanted to rid himself of the need to use an insecure railroad, with limited capacity back to Alexandria, Virginia. Second, he wanted to end the Army of the Potomac's dependence on a train of 4,000 wagons; the Army's mobility was hobbled by having to care for 60,000 animals. Finally, Grant wanted to use the advantages of Virginia's tidewater rivers and base his depots on the Chesapeake Bay. He was willing to accept the risk inherent in moving obliquely across Lee's front in northern Virginia.

With little room for maneuver, Grant was forced to advance

through the Wilderness, where Hooker had come to grief the year before. As the army column halted near Chancellorsville to allow the wagon trains to pass the Rapidan, on May 5 Lee struck at Meade's right flank. Grant and Meade swung their corps into line and hit hard. The fighting in the battle of the Wilderness consisting of assault, defense, and counterattack, was close and desperate in tangled woods and thickets. Artillery could not be brought to bear. The dry woods caught fire and some of the wounded died miserably in the flame and smoke. On May 6 Lee attacked again. Longstreet's I Corps, arriving late in battle but as always in perfect march order, drove the Federals back. Longstreet himself received a severe neck wound, inflicted in error by his own men, that took him out of action until October 1864. Lee, at a decisive moment in the battle, his fighting blood aroused to a white heat, attempted to lead an assault in person; but men of the Texas brigade with whom Lee was riding persuaded the southern leader to go to the rear and direct the battle as their Army commander. On May 7 neither side renewed the battle.

Now came the critical test of Grant's execution of strategy. He had been worsted, though not really beaten, by Lee, a greater antagonist than Bragg, Joseph E. Johnston, and Pemberton. After an encounter with Lee, each of the former Army of the Potomac commanders, McClellan, Burnside, and Hooker, had retired north of the Rappahannock River and postponed any further clashes with that great tactician. But Grant was of a different breed. He calmly ordered his lead corps to move south toward Spotsylvania as rapidly as possible to get around Lee's flank and interpose the Army of the Potomac between Lee and Richmond.

Lee detected Grant's march and, using roads generally parallel to Grant's, also raced toward the key road junction at Spotsylvania. J. E. B. Stuart's cavalry harassed and slowed Grant; Lee arrived first and quickly built strong earth-and-log trenches over commanding ground which covered the roads leading to Richmond. In this crossroads race, Sheridan's cavalry would have been useful, but Meade had dissipated the cavalry corps' strength by deploying two divisions of horse to guard his already well-protected trains. Sheridan and Meade argued once again over the use of cavalry, and the General in Chief backed Sheridan, allowing him now to concentrate his cavalry arm. Grant gave Sheridan a free hand in order to stop Stuart's raids. Leading his corps southward in a long ride toward Richmond, its objective a decisive charge against Stuart, Sheridan did the job. He fought a running series of engagements that culminated in a victory at Yellow Tavern, in which the gallant Stuart was mortally wounded. The South was already short of horses and mules, and Sheridan's 16-day raid ended forever the offensive power of Lee's mounted arm.

For four days beginning May 9 Meade struck repeatedly at Lee's roadblock at Spotsylvania but was beaten back. Twice the Federals broke through the trenches and divided Lee's army, but in each case the attackers became disorganized. Supporting infantry did not or

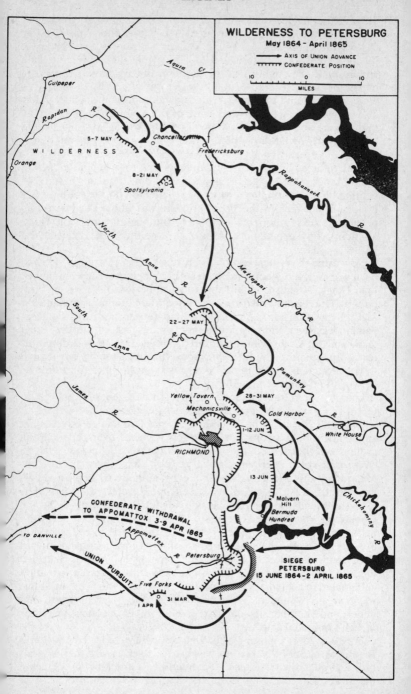

WILDERNESS TO PETERSBURG
May 1864 - April 1865

Axis of Union Advance
Confederate Position

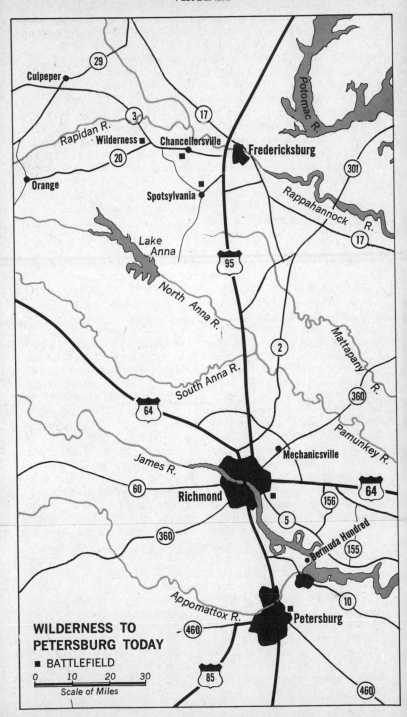

## WILDERNESS TO PETERSBURG TODAY

■ BATTLEFIELD

0    10    20    30
Scale of Miles

could not close in, and Confederate counterattacks were delivered with such ferocity that the breakthroughs could be neither exploited nor held. On the morning of the 11th, Grant wrote Halleck: "I propose to fight it out on this line if it takes all summer." On May 20, having decided the entrenchments were too strong to capture, Grant sideslipped south again, still trying to envelop Lee's right flank.

With smaller numbers, Lee skillfully avoided Grant's trap and refused to leave entrenched positions and be destroyed in open battle. Lee retired to the North Anna River and dug in. Grant then continued to move south, to his left, in a daring and difficult tactical maneuver. Butler had meanwhile advanced up the peninsula toward Richmond, but Beauregard outmaneuvered him in May and bottled up Butler's men at Bermuda Hundred between the James and Appomattox Rivers. Eventually Butler and Banks, who did not take Mobile, were removed from command for their failure to carry out their assignments in the grand strategy.

Lee easily made his way into the Richmond defenses with his right flank on the Chickahominy and his center at Cold Harbor, the site of the Gaines' Mill action in 1862. The front extended for eight miles. On June 3 Grant assaulted Lee's center at Cold Harbor. Though bravely executed, the attack was badly planned. The Confederates repulsed it with gory efficiency, and Grant later regretted that he had ever made the attempt. Cold Harbor climaxed a month of heavy fighting in which Grant's forces had casualties totaling about 55,000 as against about 32,000 for those of Lee. After Cold Harbor, Grant executed a brilliant maneuver in the face of the enemy. All Union corps were on the north bank of the deep, wide James by June 14 and crossed over a 2,100-foot ponton bridge, the longest up to that time in modern history. Having established a new and modern base depot at City Point, complete with a railroad line to the front, Grant on June 18, 1864, undertook siege operations at Petersburg below Richmond, an effort which continued into the next year.

After forty-four days of continuous fighting, Lee was fixed finally in position warfare, a war of trenches and sieges, conducted ironically enough by two masters of mobile warfare. Mortars were used extensively, and heavy siege guns were brought up on railway cars. Grant still sought to get around Lee's right and hold against Lee's left to prevent him from shortening his line and achieving a higher degree of concentration. When Lee moved his lines to counter Grant, the two commanders were, in effect, maneuvering their fortifications.

Now that Lee was firmly entrenched in front of Grant, and could spare some men, he decided to ease the pressure with one of his perennial raids up the Shenandoah Valley toward Washington. Confederate Maj. Gen. Jubal A. Early's corps in early July advanced against Maj. Gen. David Hunter, who had replaced Sigel. Hunter, upon receiving confused orders from Halleck, retired up the valley. When he reached the Potomac, he turned west into the safety of the Appalachians and uncovered Washington. Early saw his chance and drove through Maryland. Delayed by a Union force on

July 9 near Frederick, he reached the northern outskirts of Washington on July 11 and skirmished briskly in the vicinity of Fort Stevens. Abraham Lincoln and Quartermaster General Meigs were interested spectators. At City Point, Grant had received the news of Early's raid calmly. Using his interior waterway, he embarked the men of his VI Corps for the capital, where they landed on the 11th. When Early realized he was engaging troops from the Army of the Potomac, he managed to escape the next day.

Grant decided that Early had eluded the Union's superior forces because they had not been under a single commander. He abolished four separate departments and formed them into one, embracing Washington, western Maryland, and the Shenandoah Valley. In August, Sheridan was put in command with orders to follow Early to the death. Sheridan spent the remainder of the year in the valley, employing and co-ordinating his infantry, cavalry, and artillery in a manner that has won the admiration of military students ever since. He met and defeated Early at Winchester and Fisher's Hill in September and shattered him at Cedar Creek in October. To stop further raids and prevent Lee from feeding his army on the crops of that fertile region, Sheridan devastated the Shenandoah Valley.

### Fredericksburg

Fifty miles north of Richmond lies Fredericksburg, which vies with Richmond and Petersburg in Civil War importance in Virginia. Located halfway between Richmond and Washington, it was a frequent target for both sides in the bitter war years. No other city was so embattled. From Marye's Heights in Fredericksburg, Lee's army in December 1862 repelled some of the war's bloodiest attacks by Burnside's Federal troops. Fierce fighting also raged nearby in the battles of Chancellorsville, the Wilderness, and Spotsylvania Court House. This is the Virginia of the war's "Bloody Angle."

Fredericksburg's Civil War interpretation is centered at Fredericksburg National Battlefield Park, which has artifacts, a diorama of the battles, and an audiovisual program. Guided tours are offered in summer. Fredericksburg National Cemetery, where 15,000 Federal soldiers lie buried, is near the Park's Visitor Center. Tours of the battlefield may be made at will or by renting for $2.50 a tape player which directs you through the park.

Near Fredericksburg is Chatham Plantation, the onetime Fitzhugh mansion known in the Civil War as the Lacy house. Several rooms are open to the public from 9 to 5 daily. Also in town is the Fredericksburg Historic Museum, with a room devoted to the Civil War.

### Fiasco at Fredericksburg

After Antietam both armies returned to face each other in Virginia, Lee situated near Culpeper and McClellan at Warrenton. But McClellan's slowness, his failure to accomplish more at Anti-

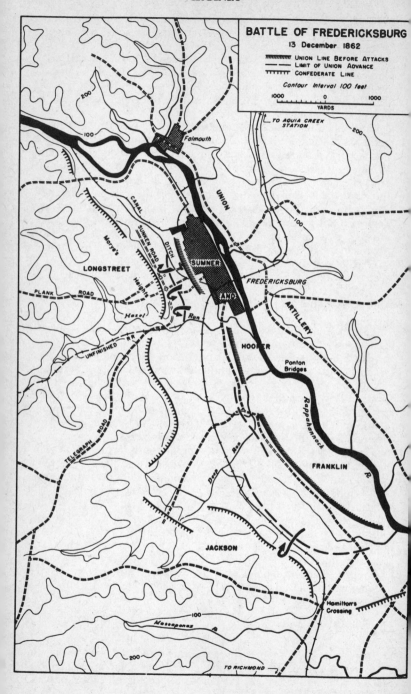

### BATTLE OF FREDERICKSBURG
13 December 1862

| | UNION LINE BEFORE ATTACKS |
| | LIMIT OF UNION ADVANCE |
| | CONFEDERATE LINE |

Contour Interval 100 feet

1000  0  1000
YARDS

TO AQUIA CREEK STATION

Falmouth

UNION

CANAL

SUNKEN ROAD

DITCH

Morye's

LONGSTREET

Marye's Heights

SUMNER

FREDERICKSBURG

PLANK ROAD

Hazel

Run

ARTILLERY

UNFINISHED RR

HOOKER

Ponton Bridges

TELEGRAPH ROAD

Deep Run

Rappahannock R.

FRANKLIN

JACKSON

Hamilton's Crossing

Massaponax R.

TO RICHMOND

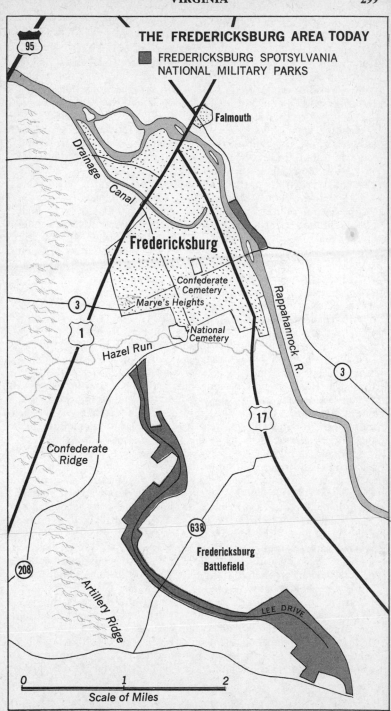

THE FREDERICKSBURG AREA TODAY

☐ FREDERICKSBURG SPOTSYLVANIA NATIONAL MILITARY PARKS

Falmouth

Drainage Canal

Fredericksburg

Confederate Cemetery

Marye's Heights

National Cemetery

Rappahannock R.

Hazel Run

Confederate Ridge

Fredericksburg Battlefield

Artillery Ridge

LEE DRIVE

95

3

1

3

17

208

638

0      1      2

Scale of Miles

etam, and perhaps his rather arrogant habit of offering gratuitous political advice to his superiors, coupled with the intense anti-McClellan views of the joint Congressional Committee on the Conduct of the War, convinced Lincoln that he could retain him in command no longer. On November 7, 1862, Lincoln replaced him with Burnside, who had won distinction in operations that gained control of ports on the North Carolina coast and who had led the IX Corps at Antietam. Burnside accepted the post with reluctance.

Burnside decided to march rapidly to Fredericksburg and then advance along the railroad line to Richmond before Lee could intercept him. *(see Map)* Such a move by the army—now 120,000 strong—would cut Lee off from his main base. Burnside's advance elements reached the north bank of the Rappahannock on November 17, well ahead of Lee. But a series of minor failures delayed the completion of ponton bridges, and Lee moved his army to high ground on the south side of the river before the Federal forces could cross. Lee's situation resembled McClellan's position at Malvern Hill which had proved the folly of frontal assaults against combined artillery and infantry strongpoints. But Burnside thought the sheer weight of numbers could smash through the Confederates.

To achieve greater ease of tactical control, Burnside had created three headquarters higher than corps—the Right, Center, and Left Grand Divisions under Maj. Gens. Edwin V. Sumner, Joseph Hooker, and William B. Franklin, respectively—with two corps plus cavalry assigned to each grand division. Burnside originally planned to make the main thrust by Center and Left Grand Divisions against Jackson's positions on a long, low-wooded ridge southeast of the town. The Right Grand Division would cross three ponton bridges at Fredericksburg and attack Marye's Heights, a steep eminence about one mile from the river where Longstreet's men were posted. On the morning of December 13, he weakened the attack on the left, feeling that under cover of 147 heavy siege and field guns on the heights on the Union side of the river much could be achieved by a better-balanced attack along the whole line.

Burnside's engineers had begun laying the bridges as early as December 11. But harassment from Confederate sharpshooters complicated the operation, and it was not until the next day that all the assault units were over the river. After an artillery duel on the morning of the 13th, fog lifted to reveal dense Union columns moving forward to the attack. Part of the Left Grand Division, finding a weakness in Jackson's line, drove in to seize the ridge, but as Burnside had weakened this part of the assault the Federals were not able to hold against Confederate counterattacks. On the right, the troops had to cross a mile of open ground to reach Marye's Heights, traverse a drainage canal, and face a fusillade of fire from the infamous sunken road and stone wall behind which Longstreet had placed four ranks of riflemen. In a series of assaults the Union soldiers pushed to the stone wall but no farther. As a demonstration of valor the effort was exemplary; as a demonstration of tactical skill it was tragic. Lee, observing the shattered attackers, commented: "It is well that war is so terrible—we should grow too fond of it."

The Army of the Potomac lost 12,000 men at Fredericksburg while the Army of Northern Virginia suffered only 5,300 casualties. Burnside planned to renew the attack on the following day and Jackson, whose enthusiasm in battle sometimes approached the point of frenzy, suggested that the Confederates strip off their clothes for better identification and strike the Army of the Potomac in a night attack. But Lee knew of Burnside's plans from a captured order and vetoed the scheme. When the Federal corps commanders talked Burnside out of renewing the attack, both armies settled into winter quarters facing each other across the Rappahannock. Fredericksburg, a disastrous defeat, was otherwise noteworthy for the U.S. Army in that the telegraph first saw extensive battlefield use, linking headquarters with forward batteries during the action—a forerunner of twentieth century battlefield communications.

## Chancellorsville

At Chancellorsville, west of Fredericksburg, is another battlefield preserved by the Park Service. The Visitor Center here contains exhibits and a slide program. Battlefield tours may be made on your own or with the aid of a rented tape guide. A monument near the battlefield marks the site where Stonewall Jackson was wounded.

At Wilderness Battlefield near Chancellorsville is an exhibit center, which serves as the starting point of a self-guided tour. Signs and markers point out principal sites.

Near Fredericksburg and the Wilderness is Spotsylvania Battlefield, where visitors may tour with the aid of markers and printed instructions. The highlight of the tour is the "Bloody Angle," which was the scene of desperate hand-to-hand combat between Union and Confederacy in 1864. During summer months, a National Park Service historian is available at Spotsylvania to answer visitors' questions.

## Hooker Crosses the Rappahannock

After the battle of Fredericksburg (December 13, 1862), Burnside's Army of the Potomac went into winter quarters on the north bank of the Rappahannock, while the main body of Lee's Army of Northern Virginia held Fredericksburg and guarded the railway line to Richmond. During January, Burnside's subordinates intrigued against him and went out of channels to present their grievances to Congress and the President. When Burnside heard of this development, he asked that either he or most of the subordinate general officers be removed. The President accepted the first alternative, and on January 25, 1863, replaced Burnside with Maj. Gen. Joseph Hooker. The new commander had won the sobriquet of "Fighting Joe" for his intrepid reputation as a division and corps commander.

He was highly favored in Washington, but in appointing him the President took the occasion to write a fatherly letter in which he warned the general against rashness and overambition, reproached him for plotting against Burnside, and concluded by asking for victories.

Under Hooker's able administration, discipline and training improved. Morale, which had fallen after Fredericksburg, rose as Hooker regularized the furlough system and improved the flow of rations and other supplies to his front-line troops. Abolishing Burnside's grand divisions Hooker returned to the orthodox corps. of which he had seven, each numbering about 15,000 men. One of Hooker's most effective innovations was the introduction of distinctive corps and division insignia. He also took a long step toward improving the cavalry arm of the army, which up to this time had been assigned many diverse duties and was split up into small detachments. Hooker regarded cavalry as a combat arm of full stature, and he concentrated his units into a cavalry corps of three divisions under Brig. Gen. George Stoneman. On the other hand Hooker made a costly mistake in decentralizing tactical control of his artillery to his corps commanders. As a result Union artillery would not be properly massed in the coming action at Chancellorsville.

Hooker had no intention of repeating Burnside's tragic frontal assault at Fredericksburg. With a strength approaching 134,000 men, Hooker planned a double envelopment which would place strong Union forces on each of Lee's flanks. *(see Map)* He ordered three of his infantry corps to move secretly up the Rappahannock and ford the stream, while two more corps, having conspicuously remained opposite Fredericksburg, were to strike across the old battlefield there. Two more corps were in reserve. The cavalry corps, less one division which was to screen the move up river, was to raid far behind Lee's rear to divert him. Hooker's plan was superb; his execution faulty. The three corps moved quickly up the river and by the end of April had crossed and advanced to the principal road junction of Chancellorsville. They were now in the so-called "Wilderness," a low, flat, confusing area of scrub timber and narrow dirt roads in which movement and visibility were extremely limited. Maj. Gen. John Sedgwick crossed the Rappahannock at Fredericksburg on the 29th, and the two remaining corps moved to within supporting distance of Hooker at Chancellorsville. So far everything had gone according to plan, except that Stoneman's diversion had failed to bother Lee. One of Stuart's brigades kept Stoneman under surveillance while the main body of cavalry shadowed Hooker so effectively that the southern commander knew every move made by the Union army. By the morning of April 30, Lee was aware of what was afoot and knew that he was threatened by double envelopment. Already Hooker was sending his columns eastward toward the back door to Fredericksburg. A less bold and resolute man than Lee would have retreated southward at once, and with such ample justification that only the captious would have found fault. But the southern general, his army numbering only 60,000, used the princi-

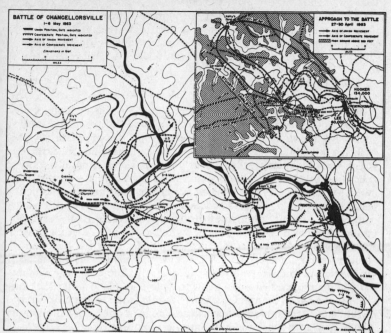

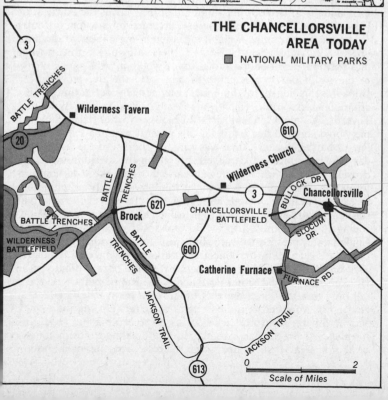

## THE CHANCELLORSVILLE AREA TODAY

☐ NATIONAL MILITARY PARKS

**Wilderness Tavern**

**Wilderness Church**

**Chancellorsville**

**Brock**

CHANCELLORSVILLE BATTLEFIELD

BULLOCK DR.

SLOCUM DR.

BATTLE TRENCHES

BATTLE TRENCHES

BATTLE TRENCHES

WILDERNESS BATTLEFIELD

**Catherine Furnace**

FURNACE RD.

JACKSON TRAIL

JACKSON TRAIL

3

20

610

621

600

613

3

0        2

Scale of Miles

ples of the offensive, maneuver, economy of force, and surprise to compensate for his inferior numbers. Instead of retreating, he left a part of his army to hold the heights at Fredericksburg and started west for Chancellorsville with the main body.

## Lee's Finest Battle

When Lee began to move, Hooker simply lost his courage. Over protests of his corps commanders, he ordered the troops back into defensive positions around Chancellorsville. The Federals established a line in the forest, felled trees for an abatis, and constructed earth-and-log breastworks. Their position faced generally south, anchored on the Rappahannock on the east; but in the west it was weak, unsupported, and hanging in the air. Lee brought his main body up and on May 1 made contact with Hooker's strong left. That day Stuart's cavalry discovered Hooker's vulnerable right flank and promptly reported the intelligence to Lee. Conferring that night with Stonewall Jackson, Lee made another bold decision. Facing an army much greater than his own, he decided to divide his forces and further envelop the envelopers. Accordingly, Lee committed about 17,000 men against Hooker's left to hold it in place while Jackson with some 26,000 men made a wide 15-mile swing to get beyond the right flank. At first glance Lee's decision might appear a violation of the principles of mass and concentration, but while Lee's two forces were initially separated their common objective was the Army of the Potomac, and their ultimate routes converged on a common center.

Jackson's force, in a 10-mile-long column, moved out at daybreak of May 2, marching southwest first, then swinging northwest to get into position. The Federals noted that something was happening off to the south but were unable to penetrate the defensive screen; Hooker soon began to think Lee was actually retreating. In late afternoon Jackson turned onto the Orange turnpike near Wilderness Tavern. This move put him west of Hooker's right flank, and since the woods thinned out a little at this point it was possible to form a line of battle. Because time was running short and the hour of the day was late, Jackson deployed in column of divisions, with each division formed with brigades abreast, the same kind of confusing formation Johnston had used at Shiloh. Shortly after 5 P.M. Jackson's leading division, shrieking the "rebel yell" and driving startled rabbits and deer before it, came charging out of the woods, rolling up Maj. Gen. Oliver O. Howard's XI Corps in wild rout. The Confederates pressed forward; but fresh Union troops, disorganization of his own men, and oncoming darkness stymied the impatient Jackson. While searching for a road that would permit him to cut off Hooker from United States Ford across the Rappahannock, Jackson fell prey to a mistaken ambush by his own men. The Confederate leader was wounded and died eight days later. During the night of May 2, Stuart, Jackson's successor as corps commander, re-formed his lines. Against Stuart's right, Hooker launched local counterattacks which at first gained some success, but the next morning withdrew his whole line. Once more Hooker yielded the initiative at the moment he had a strong force between Lee's two divided and weaker forces.

Stuart renewed the attack during the morning as Hooker pulled his line back. Hooker was knocked unconscious when a shell struck the pillar of the Chancellor house against which he was leaning. Until the end of the battle he was dazed and incapable of exercising effective command, but he did not relinquish it nor would the army's medical director declare him unfit. Meanwhile Sedgwick, who shortly after Jackson's attack had received orders to proceed through Fredericksburg to Chancellorsville, had assaulted Marye's Heights. He carried it about noon on May 3, but the next day Lee once more divided his command, leaving Stuart with 25,000 to guard Hooker, and moved himself with 21,000 to thwart Sedgwick. In a sharp action at Salem Church Lee forced the Federals off the road and northward over the Rappahannock. Lee now made ready for a full-scale assault against the Army of the Potomac huddled with its back against the river on May 6, but Hooker ordered retirement to the north bank before the attack. Confederate losses were approximately 13,000; Federal losses, 17,000. But Lee lost far more with the death of Jackson. Actually, Lee's brilliant and daring maneuvers had defeated only one man—Hooker—and in no other action of the war did moral superiority of one general over the other stand out so clearly as a decisive factor in battle. Chancellorsville exemplified Napoleon's maxim: "The General is the head, the whole of the army."

Hooker was a talented tactical commander with a good reputation. But in spite of Lincoln's injunction, "This time, put in all your men," he allowed nearly one-third of his army to stand idle during the heaviest fighting. Here again was a general who could effectively lead a body of troops under his own eyes but could not use maps and reports to evaluate and control situations that were beyond his range of vision. Hooker, not the Army of the Potomac, lost the battle of Chancellorsville. Yet for the victors, Chancellorsville was a hollow triumph. It was dazzling, a set piece for the instruction of students of the military art ever since, but it had been inconclusive, winning glory and little more. It left government and army on both sides with precisely the problems they had faced before the campaign began.

## Stonewall Jackson's Shrine

Not far from Interstate 95 south of Fredericksburg is the marked turnoff to the Jackson Shrine, marking the place where Stonewall Jackson died several days after he was wounded in 1863 at Chancellorsville, 30 miles away. The Guinea Station plantation outbuilding in which Jackson died has been preserved, its deathbed in place and its mantel clock still ticking away the time. The shrine is open daily from 9 to 5 in summer; from Friday through Tuesday in spring and fall; and from Saturday through Monday in winter.

A few miles west of Fredericksburg, along Virginia Route 3

through Chancellorsville and the Wilderness, is Salem Church, where an important battle was fought in May 1863. The church was used as a fortification during the engagement and afterwards briefly as a hospital. It is open to the public in summer and on some weekends in spring and fall.

Thirty miles east of the Jackson Shrine is Stratford Hall, the lordly plantation house near the Potomac where Robert E. Lee was born in 1807. Here visitors may see the room in which he was born. The house is furnished with much of the furniture which graced it in 1807, and it contains many reminders of the Confederate chieftain.

Further north, in Prince William County, is Manassas Battlefield, also preserved as a National Battlefield Park. Here, at the First Battle of Manassas in July 1861, Gen. Thomas J. Jackson won the nickname "Stonewall" and the opposing Union general, Irvin McDowell, was forced to reverse his march and retreat to Washington. In the Second Battle of Manassas, in August 1862, Federal forces under Gen. John Pope drove back the Confederates under Gen. James Longstreet. The two engagements are sometimes designated the battles of Bull Run.

### Manassas (Battle of Bull Run) *(1861)*

In the early summer of 1861 a partly trained 90-day militia, some almost untrained volunteers, and one newly organized battalion of Regulars—a total force of 50,000 Federals commanded by Brig. Gen. Irvin McDowell—defended the nation's capital. Thirty miles to the southwest, covering the rail and road hub at Manassas, Virginia, General Beauregard posted some 20,000 Confederates, to be joined by 2,000 more within a few days. To the left, on their defensive line along the Potomac, the Confederates stationed another 11,000 men under Brig. Gen. Joseph E. Johnston in the Shenandoah Valley town of Winchester. Opposing Johnston around Martinsburg, with the mission of keeping the Confederates in place, was Maj. Gen. Robert Patterson with 18,000 Federals. On the extreme right of the Confederate northern Virginia defense line was Col. Joseph B. Magruder's force, which had recently repulsed Maj. Gen. Benjamin F. Butler's Union troops at Big Bethel, Virginia, on 10 June, and forced them back into their sanctuary at Fort Monroe.

Big Bethel, the first large-scale meeting engagement of the Civil War, demonstrated that neither opponent was as yet well trained. The Confederates had started preparations earlier to protect northern Virginia and therefore might have had a slight edge on their opponents. General McDowell, only recently a major of Regulars, had less than three months to weld his three types of units—militia, volunteer, and Regular—into a single fighting force. He attempted to do too much himself, and there were few competent staff officers in the vicinity to help him. McDowell's largest tactical unit was a regiment until just before he marched out of Alexandria. Two to four brigades, plus a battery of Regular artillery—the best arm against raw infantry—formed a division. In all, thirteen brigades were organized into five divisions. McDowell parceled out his forty-nine guns among his brigade commanders, who in turn attached them to their regiments. His total force for the advance was 35,732 men, but of these one division of 5,752 men dropped off to guard roads to the rear.

McDowell's advance against Beauregard, on four parallel routes, was hastened by northern opinion, expressed in editorials and Congressional speeches, demanding immediate action. Scott warned Lincoln against undertaking the "On to Richmond" campaign until McDowell's troops had become disciplined units. But Lincoln, eager to use the 90-day militia before they departed, demanded an advance, being aware that the Confederates were also unseasoned and cherishing the belief that one defeat would force the South to quit. Scott, influenced by false intelligence that Beauregard would move immediately on Washington, acceded. Accordingly, McDowell's battle plan and preparations were expedited. The plan, accepted in late June, called for Butler and Patterson to prevent the Confederates facing them from reinforcing Beauregard, while McDowell advanced against Manassas to outflank the southern position. Scott called it a good plan on paper but knew Johnston was capable of frustrating it if given the chance. McDowell's success against the Confederate center depended upon a rapid 30-mile march, if 35,000 Federals were to keep 22,000 Confederates from being reinforced.

On July 16, 1861, the largest army ever assembled on the North American continent up to that time advanced slowly on both sides of the Warrenton pike toward Bull Run. McDowell's march orders were good, but the effect was ruined by one unwise caution to the brigade commanders: "It will not be pardonable in any commander . . . to come upon a battery or breastwork without a knowledge of its position." The caution recalled to McDowell's subordinates the currently sensationalized bugbear of the press of being fooled by "masked batteries," a term originating at Sumter where a certain battery was constructed, masked by a house which was demolished just before the guns opened fire. Accordingly, 35,000 men moved just five miles on the 17th. Next day the Federals occupied Centreville, some four miles east of Stone Bridge, which carried the Warrenton pike over Bull Run. (see Map)

Beauregard's advanced guards made no effort to delay the Federals, but fell back across the battle line, now extending some three miles along the west bank of Bull Run, which meandered from Stone Bridge southeast until it joined the Occoquan stream. The country was fairly rough, cut by streams, and thickly wooded. It presented formidable obstacles to attacking raw troops, but a fair shelter for equally raw troops on the defensive. On the 18th, while McDowell's main body waited at Centreville for the trains to close up, the leading division demonstrated against Beauregard's right around Mitchell's Ford. The Federal infantry retired after a sharp musketry fight, and a 45-minute artillery duel ensued. It was the first exchange of four standard types of artillery ammunition for all

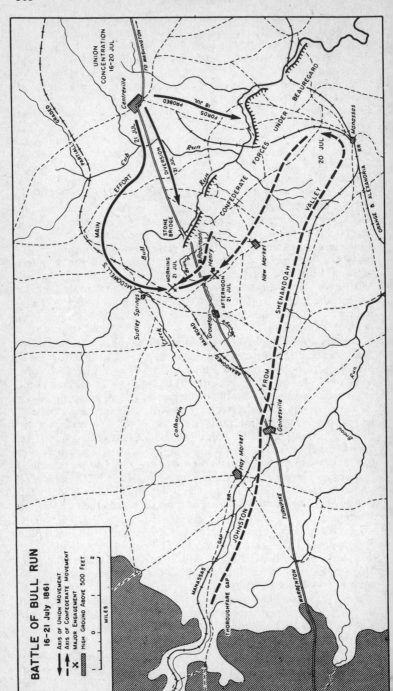

BATTLE OF BULL RUN
16-21 July 1861

—↓ Axis of Union Movement
━↓ Axis of Confederate Movement
X MAJOR ENGAGEMENT
▨ High Ground Above 500 Feet

MILES
1    0    1    2

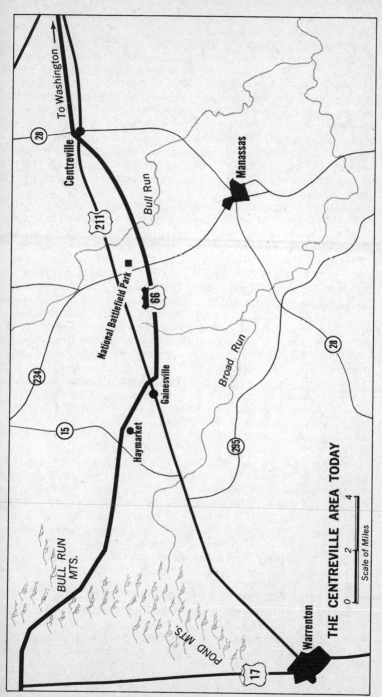

THE CENTREVILLE AREA TODAY

muzzle-loading guns, whether rifled or smoothbore. Solid shot, shell, spherical case or shrapnel, and canister from eight Federal guns firing 415 rounds were answered by seven Confederate pieces returning 310 rounds. Steadily withdrawing its guns, the oldest and best drilled unit of the South, the Washington Light Artillery of New Orleans, broke off the fight against well-trained U.S. Regular artillery. Both sides had used rifled artillery, which greatly increased the accuracy and gave a range more than double that of the smoothbores. Yet rifled guns never supplanted the new, easily loaded Napoleons. In the fight, defective Confederate ammunition fired from three new 3-inch iron rifles would not fly point foremost but tumbled and lost range against McDowell's gunners. That the error went undetected for days reveals the haste in which Davis had procured his ordnance.

Sure that his green troops could not flank the Confederate right, McDowell tarried two more fateful days before he attacked in force. Engineers reconnoitered for an undefended ford north of Stone Bridge. Finding no vedettes at the ford near Sudley Springs, McDowell decided to envelop the Confederate left on July 21 and destroy the Manassas Gap Railroad to keep Johnston from reinforcing the outnumbered Beauregard. The idea was excellent, but the timing was slow.

While McDowell frittered away four and a half days before he was ready to envelop in force, new tools of warfare swung the advantages of mobility, surprise, and mass at critical points toward Beauregard. On July 17 spies in Washington told of McDowell's departure from Alexandria. By electric telegraph Beauregard in turn alerted Richmond. Davis, also telegraphing, ordered commanders around Richmond, at Aquia Creek, and at Winchester to concentrate their available strength at Manassas. Johnston lost no time in deceiving Patterson by using Col. J. E. B. Stuart's cavalry as a screen and adroitly maneuvering his infantry away from the valley. Johnston selected the best overland routes for his artillery and cavalry marches and arranged for railroad officials to move his four infantry brigades. Brig. Gen. Thomas Jackson's lead brigade, accompanied by Johnston himself, covered fifty-seven miles in twenty-five hours by road and rail, reaching Beauregard on the 20th.

At daylight on the 21st, McDowell unmasked the first phase of his attack plan. Three brigades of Brig. Gen. Daniel Tyler's division appeared before Stone Bridge, and a huge 30-pounder Parrott rifle dragged into place by ten horses commenced a slow fire, directed by six cannoneers of the 2d U.S. Artillery. Five brigades in two divisions directly under McDowell's command meanwhile marched on an eight-mile circuitous route toward the undefended ford at Sudley Springs. McDowell's goal was the Confederate left rear and a chance to cut the railroad. At 9 A.M. a signal flag wigwag from the Henry house announced the point of the enveloping columns at Sudley's crossing, and the intelligence was immediately relayed to Beauregard and Johnston, who were three miles away on the Confederate right.

The first weight of the Federal attack fell against eleven Confederate companies and two guns. For an hour McDowell's regiments, firing one by one and moving forward cautiously in piecemeal fashion, tried to overrun Beauregard's left flank. The timid tactics gave Beauregard time to redeploy ten regiments across a three-mile front to form a second defensive line across the north face of the hill behind the Henry house. At 10:30 A.M., as the summer sun grew hotter, a portentous dust cloud, rising ten miles northwest of Manassas, heralded the arrival of Kirby Smith's brigade, the tail of Johnston's reinforcements from the Shenandoah Valley.

For two hours the roar of the battle swelled in volume. Federal musketry crashes and the thunder from the heavier pieces indicated that McDowell was now committing whole brigades, supported by four batteries of artillery. North of the Warrenton turnpike, the Confederate infantry began to lose its brigade cohesion and fall back in disorder. As Beauregard and Johnston rode to the sound of battle, some 10,000 Federals were punishing 7,000 Confederates in the vicinity of the Henry and Robinson houses. Johnston, though senior in command, turned the battle over to Beauregard and galloped off toward Manassas to direct the arrival of reinforcements. Brig. Gen. Barnard E. Bee's brigade was pushed back from its advanced position toward the flat-crested hill behind the Henry house, where Jackson's newly arrived brigade had formed. In rallying his routed troops, Bee shouted: "Look at Jackson's Brigade; it stands like a stone wall! Rally behind the Virginians!" (Out of these words came a nickname that Jackson would carry to his grave, and after his death in 1863 the Confederate War Department officially designated his unit the Stonewall Brigade.) Screened by a wooded area, three brigades regrouped behind Jackson's lines, and the rally became a great equalizer as McDowell's strength dissipated to 9,000 men, with no immediate infantry reserves in sight.

The cloud of dust moved closer to Manassas Junction, but McDowell ignored it and allowed a lull to settle over his front for almost two hours. At 2 P.M., having deployed two batteries of Regular artillery directly to his front around the Henry house with insufficient infantry protection, McDowell renewed the battle. By midafternoon the dust had blended sweaty uniforms into a common hue, and more and more cases of mistaken identity were confusing both sides in the smoke of the battle. Then, as part of the confusion came a fateful episode. To the right front of McDowell's exposed artillery, a line of advancing blue-clad infantry, the 33d Regiment, Virginia Volunteers suddenly appeared through the smoke. The Federal artillery commander ordered canister, but the chief artillery officer on McDowell's staff overruled the order, claiming that the oncoming blue uniforms belonged to friendly infantry arriving in support. The Virginians advanced to within seventy yards of the Federal guns, leveled their muskets, and let loose. The shock of their volley cut the artillery to shreds, and for the remainder of the day nine Federal guns stood silent, unserved, and helpless between the armies.

About 4 P.M., Beauregard, with two additional fresh brigades, advanced his entire line. Shorn of their artillery, the faltering Federal lines soon lost cohesion and began to pull back along the routes they knew; there was more and more confusion as they retired. East of Bull Run, Federal artillery, using Napoleon smoothbores in this initial pullback from the field, proved to the unsuspecting Confederate cavalry, using classic saber-charging tactics, that a determined line of artillerymen could reduce cavalry to dead and sprawling infantry in minutes.

As in so many battles of the Civil War yet to come, there was no organized pursuit in strength to cut the enemy to ribbons while he fled from the immediate area of the battlefield. At Bull Run the Federal withdrawal turned into a panic-stricken flight about 6:30 P.M., when Cub Run bridge, about a mile West of Centreville, was blocked by overturned wagons. Sunset would fall at 7:15 P.M., and President Davis, just arrived from Richmond, had two daylight hours to arrive at a decision for pursuit. In council with Johnston and Beauregard, Davis instructed the whole Confederate right to advance against the Centreville road, but apparently his orders were never delivered or Beauregard neglected to follow them. Davis thus lost a splendid opportunity for seeing in person whether the unused infantry and artillery on the right of his line could have made a concerted effort to destroy McDowell's fleeing forces. Logistically, Federal booty taken over the next two days by the Confederates would have sustained them for days in an advance against Washington.

Strategically, Bull Run was important to the Confederates only because the center of their Virginia defenses had held. Tactically, the action highlights many of the problems and deficiencies that were typical of the first year of the war. Bull Run was a clash between large, ill-trained bodies of recruits, who were slow in joining battle; masked batteries frightened commanders; plans called for maneuvering the enemy out of position, but attacks were frontal; security principles were disregarded; tactical intelligence was nil; and reconnaissance was poorly executed. Soldiers were overloaded for battle. Neither commander was able to employ his whole force effectively. Of McDowell's 35,000 men, only 18,000 crossed Bull Run and casualties among these, including the missing, numbered about 2,708. Beauregard, with 32,000 men, ordered only 18,000 into action and lost 1,982.

Both commanders rode along the front, often interfering in small unit actions. McDowell led his enveloping column instead of directing all his forces from the rear. Wisely, Johnston left the battlefield and went to the rear to hasten up his Shenandoah Valley reserves. Regiments were committed piecemeal. Infantry failed to protect exposed artillery. Artillery was parceled out under infantry command; only on the retreat was the Union senior artillery officer on the scene allowed to manage his guns. He saved 21 guns of the 49 that McDowell had. Beauregard's orders were oral, vague, and confusing. Some were delivered, others were never followed.

## Second Manassas *(1862)*

Failure of the Union forces to take Richmond quickly in the Peninsular Campaign forced President Lincoln to abandon the idea of exercising command over the Union armies in person. On July 11, 1862, he selected as new General in Chief Henry W. Halleck, who had won accclaim for the victories in the west. The President did not at once appoint a successor in the west, which was to suffer from divided command for a time. Lincoln wanted Halleck to direct the various Federal armies in close concert to take advantage of the North's superior strength. If all Federal armies co-ordinated their efforts, Lincoln reasoned, they could strike where the Confederacy was weak or force it to strengthen one army at the expense of another, and eventually they could wear the Confederacy down, destroy the various armies, and win the war.

Halleck turned out to be a disappointment. He never attempted to exercise field command or assume responsibility for strategic direction of the armies. But, acting more as military adviser to the President, he performed a valuable function by serving as a channel of communication between the Chief Executive and the field commanders. He adeptly translated the President's ideas into terms the generals could comprehend, and expressed the soldier's views in language that Mr. Lincoln could understand.

Shortly before Halleck's appointment, Lincoln also decided to consolidate the various Union forces in the Shenandoah Valley and other parts of western Virginia—some 45,000 men—under the victor at Island No. 10, Maj. Gen. John Pope. Pope immediately disenchanted his new command by pointing out that in the west the Federal armies were used to seeing the backs of their enemies. Pope's so-called Army of Virginia was ordered to divert pressure from McClellan on the peninsula. But Jackson had left the valley and Federal forces were scattered. On August 3, Halleck ordered McClellan to withdraw by water from the peninsula to Aquia Creek on the Potomac and to effect a speedy junction at Fredericksburg with Pope. Meanwhile Pope began posting the Army of Virginia along the Orange and Alexandria Railroad to the west of Fredericksburg.

Lee knew that his Army of Northern Virginia was in a dangerous position between Pope and McClellan, especially if the two were to unite. On July 13, he sent Jackson, with forces eventually totaling 24,000 men, to watch Pope. After an initial sparring action at Cedar Mountain on August 9, Jackson and Pope stood watching each other for nearly a week. Lee, knowing that McClellan was leaving Harrison's Landing, had departed Richmond with the remainder of the Army of Northern Virginia and joined Jackson at Gordonsville. The combined Confederate forces outnumbered Pope's, and Lee resolved to outflank and cut off the Army of Virginia before the whole of McClellan's force could be brought to bear.

A succession of captured orders enabled both Lee and Pope to learn the intentions of the other. Pope ascertained Lee's plan to trap him against the Rappahannock and withdrew to the north bank astride the railroad. Lee, learning that two corps from the Army of the Potomac would join Pope within days, acted quickly and boldly. He sent Jackson off on a wide turning movement through Thoroughfare Gap in the Bull Run Mountains around the northern flank of Pope's army and subsequently followed the same route with the divisions commanded by General Longstreet.

Pope took note of Jackson's move, but first assumed that it was pointed toward the Shenandoah Valley. Then Jackson, covering nearly sixty miles in two days, came in behind Pope at Manassas on August 26, destroyed his supply base there, and slipped away unmolested. Pope marched and counter-marched his forces for two days trying to find the elusive Confederates. At the same time the Union commander failed to take Lee's other forces into account. As a result he walked into Lee's trap on the site of the old battlefield of Manassas or Bull Run. Pope attacked Jackson, posted behind an abandoned railroad embankment, but again the attack consisted of a series of piecemeal frontal assaults which were repulsed with heavy casualties. By then Porter's V Corps from the Army of the Potomac had reached the field and was ordered to attack Jackson's right (south) flank. By this time also, Longstreet's column had burst through Thoroughfare Gap, and deploying on Jackson's right, it blocked Porter's move.

Next day, August 30, Pope renewed his attacks against Jackson, whom he thought to be retreating. Seizing the opportunity to catch the Federal columns in an exposed position, Lee sent Longstreet slashing along the Warrenton turnpike to hit Pope's flank. The Federal army soon retired from the field and Pope led it back to Washington, fighting an enveloping Confederate force at Chantilly on the way.

Lee, by great daring and rapid movement, and by virtue of having the Confederate forces unified under his command, had successfully defeated one formidable Union army in the presence of another even larger one. Halleck, as General in Chief, had not taken the field to co-ordinate Pope and McClellan, and Pope lost the campaign despite the advantage of interior lines.

President Lincoln, desiring to use McClellan's admitted talents for training and reorganizing the battered eastern armies, had become convinced that bitter personal feelings between McClellan and Pope prevented them from working effectively in the same theater. On September 5, Halleck, upon the President's order, dissolved the Army of Virginia and assigned its units to the Army of the Potomac. He sent Pope to a command in Minnesota. The Union authorities expected that McClellan would be able to devote several months to training and reorganization, but Lee dashed these hopes.

### Alexandria

The pre-Revolutionary city of Alexandria, the largest city in the northern Virginia area in which so many battles were fought, has many associations with Robert E. Lee. The city did not figure directly in the fighting, however, for when Virginia seceded in 1861, Federal troops took over Alexandria and held it for the duration. At Oronoco Street in Alexandria is the Fitzhugh-Lee House, where the young Robert E. Lee lived with his mother from age 4 until he entered West Point at 18. On Cameron Street is the house where Lee's father, Lighthorse Harry Lee, lived earlier. A third house, the Lee-Fendall House, at 429 North Washington Street, also has associations with Lighthorse Harry. Both the Fitzhugh-Lee and the Lee-Fendall houses are open to the public.

In a park on Braddock Road in Alexandria stands reconstructed Fort Ward, duplicating in a 40-acre area the Federal fort built there in the autumn of 1861, after the Confederate victory of First Manassas (Bull Run). It was named for Comdr. James Harmon Ward, first Union naval officer killed in the war. Fort Ward was one of 68 fortifications surrounding Alexandria to protect against Confederate attack. This City of Alexandria exhibit includes a museum of Civil War history and a reconstructed Civil War Officers' hut. It is open daily from 9 to 5.

Crowning the Potomac across from the District of Columbia is Arlington House, long the plantation of Lee's father-in-law, George Washington Parke Custis, and now part of Arlington National Cemetery. Lee proposed to Mary Randolph Custis there, and the Lees inherited the house from her father. The house is preserved as an exhibit and is open to the public.

One of the proudest chapters of the Confederacy's life was Stonewall Jackson's Valley Campaign of 1862. By means of rapid marches, Jackson attacked Federal troops under Gen. Irvin McDowell in a series of six engagements in the Valley of Virginia between March 23 and June 9, 1862, winning all but one. During the winter of 1862–63 Jackson's army headquartered in Winchester, and the house Jackson occupied there at 415 North Braddock Street is preserved and open to the public. Another Civil War site in Winchester is the erstwhile headquarters of Union Gen. Philip Sheridan, who wintered there in 1864–65 after his campaign through the Valley of Virginia. The house Sheridan occupied is now the Elks Club, at the intersection of Piccadilly and Braddock streets.

At Belle Grove, between Winchester and New Market, stands the historic Hite house which served as Gen. Philip Sheridan's headquarters in 1864. It is important as the objective of Sheridan's hectic 12-mile ride in 1864 when he learned, in Winchester, that Confederates under General Early were about to attack Sheridan's Union army at Belle Grove. Sheridan rushed up in time to win. Nearby, on Chester Street in Front Royal, is the Warren Rifles Confederate Museum which has memorabilia of Lee, Jackson, Davis, Mosby's Ranger, and Belle Boyd.

An important Civil War site is the New Market Battlefield Park, with its Hall of Valor, between Winchester and Lexington. Built with funds given by an alumnus of Virginia Military Institute to honor VMI cadets who fought at New Market in 1864, it preserves the battlefield and the Bushong House, which stood there in the war. The Hall of Valor has motion pictures and exhibits of the war in the Valley, with emphasis on Jackson's heroism (he taught at VMI before the war) and on the VMI cadets' combat, which ended in death for ten and injuries for 47.

New Market is one of the sites on a Valley of Virginia "Circle Tour" which was created for the Civil War Centennial of 1961. It provides markers and maps at eight Valley battle sites along US 11 and US 340 between Winchester and Lexington: Winchester, Cedar Creek, Fisher's Hill, Front Royal, Kernstown, Cross Keys, and Port Republic. Printed material about the tour is available at New Market.

## Jackson's Valley Campaign

While a small Confederate garrison at Yorktown made ready to delay McClellan, Johnston hurried his army to the peninsula. In Richmond, Confederate authorities had determined on a spectacularly bold diversion. Robert E. Lee, who had rapidly moved to the rank of general, had assumed the position of military adviser to Jefferson Davis on March 13, 1862. Charged with the conduct of operations of the Confederate armies under Davis' direction, Lee saw that any threat to Washington would cause progressive weakening of McClellan's advance against Richmond. He therefore ordered Jackson to begin a rapid campaign in the Shenandoah Valley close to the northern capital. The equivalent of three Federal divisions was sent to the valley to destroy Jackson. Lincoln and Stanton, using the telegraph and what military knowledge they had acquired, devised plans to bottle Jackson up and destroy him. But Federal forces in the valley were not under a locally unified command. They moved too slowly; one force did not obey orders strictly; and directives from Washington often neglected to take time, distance, or logistics into account. Also, in Stonewall Jackson, the Union troops were contending against one of the most outstanding field commanders America has ever produced. Jackson's philosophy of war was:

> Always mystify, mislead, and surprise the enemy, if possible; and when you strike and overcome him, never give up the pursuit as long as your men have strength to follow; for an army routed, if hotly pursued, becomes panic-stricken and can then be destroyed by half their number.

By mobility and maneuver, achieved by rapid marches, surprise, deception, and hard fighting, Jackson neutralized and defeated in detail Federal forces three times larger than his own. In a classic campaign between March 23 and June 9, 1962, he fought six battles: Kernstown, McDowell, Front Royal, Winchester, Cross Keys, and Port Republic. All but Kernstown were victories. His presence alone in the Shenandoah immobilized McDowell's corps by keeping these reinforcements from joining McClellan before Richmond.

## Lexington

The most interesting Civil War town in the Valley of Virginia is by all odds Lexington, where both Lee and Jackson lie buried. The recumbent statue of Lee in the chapel of Washington and Lee University is the most celebrated of all Confederate monuments, created by Edward Virginius Valentine in the 1890s to depict the great captain asleep in his tent in wartime. Lee Chapel museum preserves other Lee mementos as well as Lee's office as president of the school from 1865 to 1871. Lee and his family are buried in crypts beneath the chapel.

Jackson's grave is in the Lexington cemetery on Main Street, marked by a monument. Nearby are the residences of both Lee and Jackson on Washington Street, the former a part of the campus of Washington and Lee, and the latter open to the public as a museum; the VMI Chapel with its heroic painting of the cadets at New Market; and the VMI Museum with objects and exhibits of the war. The institute buildings, burned by General Hunter in his raid on Lexington in 1864 and later rebuilt, have associations with Commodore Matthew Fontaine Maury and many other Confederates besides Jackson.

An important Civil War artery in the struggle for control of Kentucky and Tennessee was the Wilderness Road, which since Revolutionary times had led from southwest Virginia westward through Cumberland Gap to the trans-Appalachian area. The historic mountain pass is now incorporated in Cumberland Gap National Historical Park, at a point where Virginia, Kentucky, and Tennessee meet. The pass was first held by the South, then captured by Union troops, who evacuated it three months later. Again it was captured by a Union army under Burnside in 1863, in whose hands it stayed until the end of the war. The Union's earth fort is one of 12 historic sites on a 12-stop tour of the 20,000 acre park. A guide map and literature are available in the Visitor Center, which included a museum. The park begins in the southwestern tip of Virginia, on US 58.

The final act of the Civil War tragedy in Virginia was fought out in the southside counties, south of the James River. At Hopewell on the James is Appomattox Manor, the Epes family plantation where Lincoln stayed to confer with Grant during the 1864–65 siege of Petersburg. It has been acquired by the Park Service to become part of the Petersburg National Battlefield exhibits.

Downtown Petersburg preserves its Civil War appearance more clearly than any other Virginia town. General information for travelers is dispensed at the city's Visitor Center at 400 E. Washington Street. The ten-month siege is graphically depicted in another Visitor Center at Petersburg National Battlefield Park, close to town and open daily from 8 to 5. Along the battlefield route visitors may listen to tape recordings of the battle and its incidents. In spring and summer, actors re-enact siege scenes of 1864–65. Recently opened in old Petersburg is the Siege Museum, housed in the former Exchange, to depict wartime life in the southside city. Also open in old Petersburg is Dodson's Tavern, onetime "select boarding-house" and favorite dining place of Lee's. An exhibit soon to be added is Centre Hill, the Petersburg mansion which became the headquarters of Petersburg's postwar Union commander.

The siege of Petersburg was the longest which any American city has ever endured, and its end on April 2, 1865, spelled doom for the Confederacy. Within the battlefield is the site of the Battle of the Crater, an heroic effort by Union soldiers to tunnel beneath Confederate lines and blow them up. However, the effect of the explosion was largely offset by the quick and heroic response of Confederate Gen. William Mahone, "hero of the Crater," who later became a postwar Virginia political leader.

On Crater Road near Petersburg is Old Blandford Episcopal Church, built in 1735 and restored in 1901 as a Confederate shrine. Thirty thousand Confederate victims of the siege are buried in its grounds. The church contains 15 original stained-glass windows executed about 1900 by Louis Comfort Tiffany and considered prime examples of art deco. In the church's Interpretation Center is a 17-minute recorded program on the lives of soldiers buried at Blandford. It is open daily from 9 to 5.

A few miles west of Petersburg is Sayler's Creek Battlefield Historical State Park, whose Hillsman House, once a Federal field hospital, provides information on the flight of Lee's army from Petersburg. Here occurred a battle between Lee and Grant on April 6, 1865, which developed as Lee's armies retreated west from Petersburg. At Sayler's Creek the exhausted Confederates lost 8,000 men and valuable supplies, hastening Lee's surrender. The park is open year-round from 9 to 5.

The final Civil War shrine in Virginia is Appomattox Courthouse, a few miles west of Sayler's Creek. Here Lee on April 9, 1865, surrendered to Grant, his former West Point schoolmate. The chief point of interest at this Park Service site is the McLean House, where the surrender took place. (The house was dismantled and moved to the 1876 World's Fair but later brought back.) Here also is the former Appomattox Courthouse, now a Visitor Center; Meeks General Store, once the village social center; Clover Hill Tavern, built in 1819 for stage travelers; and Surrender Triangle, where the Confederates lay down their arms after the April 9 surrender. It is open year-round, 8:30 to 5. (From mid-June through Labor Day, it is open 8:30 to 6.)

In addition to its many sites and battlefields, Virginia has an extensive network of state historical markers, many of which designate Civil War maneuvers and battles.

## PRACTICAL INFORMATION FOR VIRGINIA

**VIRGINIA FACTS AND FIGURES.** The state is named in honor of the Virgin Queen, Elizabeth I, of England. Because of the Colony's loyalty to the Crown, Charles II called it the Old Dominion. The first Constitution, adopted June 19, 1776, termed it the Commonwealth of Virginia. Chambers of Commerce have styled it the Mother of Presidents, for having had eight native sons in the White House; the Mother of States, because under the Royal Charter of 1609 Virginia's territory included the present states of Kentucky, Ohio, Indiana, Illinois, Wisconsin, West Virginia, and part of Minnesota; and the Mother of Statesmen for having produced such distinguished offspring as Chief Justice John Marshall, George Wythe, who taught John Marshall at the College of William and Mary, and orator Patrick Henry. The American dogwood is the state flower; the oyster, the state shell; the cardinal, the state bird; the foxhound, the state dog. *Sic Semper Tyrannis* ("Thus always to tyrants") is the state motto. "Carry Me Back to Old Virginia" is the state song. Lowest point: sea level, Atlantic Ocean. Highest point: 5,719 ft., Mt. Rogers, in Smyth and Grayson Counties, named for William Barton Rogers, state geographer and first president of the Massachusetts Institute of Technology. Speed limit: 55 mph, or as posted. Population is 4,825,000 (1972 est.). Richmond (pop. 249,621) is the capital.

**HOW TO GET THERE.** *By car:* I–95 parallels US 1 running north-south in the eastern portion of the state. I–95 passes through Washington, D.C., Richmond and Petersburg. I–81 parallels US 11 northeast-southwest in the western part of Virginia. I–64 is the major east-west route connecting Norfolk, Richmond, Charlottesville and Charleston, W. Va. The Chesapeake Bay Bridge Tunnel connects Cape Charles and Norfolk on US 13.

*By air:* Washington, D.C., Roanoke, Richmond and Norfolk are the busiest airports in the state and are served by numerous airlines. *Piedmont Airlines* also serves Greenbrier, Charlottesville, Lynchburg and Danville.

*By train: Amtrak* has trains to Washington, D.C., Norfolk, Charlottesville, along with stops at smaller towns. The *Southern Railway* stops at Washington, D.C., Charlottesville, Danville and towns in between.

*By bus: Greyhound* and *Trailways* are the largest interstate carriers in Virginia. The state is also served by *Hudson Bus, Short Way* and *Gray Coach,* among others.

**HOW TO GET AROUND.** *By car:* The traveler encounters tolls over the Chesapeake Bay Bridge-Tunnel (car and passengers $5.25, with a combination ticket including the Hampton Roads Bridge-Tunnel at $5.75). Regular fare for the Hampton Roads Bridge-Tunnel is $1.25. The Greys Point-Whitestone Bridge across the Rappahannock River to the Northern Neck charges car and passengers 75¢. US 17 and 258 carry the tourist across the 4.5-mile James River Bridge for 90¢. The Coleman Bridge at Yorktown (State 17) costs 75¢. Fare for the Norfolk-Portsmouth Tunnels is 40¢. The Virginia Beach-Norfolk Expressway charges 25¢. The Richmond-Petersburg Turnpike collects 95¢ for the full route. Finally, the Jamestown Ferry from Jamestown to Scotland in Surry County charges 80¢ one way and $1 for the round trip. It is one of the pleasantest rides in the Commonwealth and offers a fine view of the shore where the first settlers landed.

*By bus: Greyhound* and *Trailways* offer a variety of excursion tours in addition to their regular scheduled trips. *Gray Line* of Washington offers tours in northern Virginia and the Shenandoah Valley.

**TOURIST INFORMATION.** The Virginia State Travel Service is located at 6 North Sixth St., Richmond, Virginia 23219. Tel. (804) 774-4484. The Travel Service also maintains offices at 11 Rockefeller Plaza, New

York City (212) 245-3080; and in Washington at 900 17th St., NW (202) 293-5350.

 **SEASONAL EVENTS.** *August:* The Virginia Highlands Arts and Crafts Festival takes place in Abingdon during the first two weeks. Along with the craft exhibits there are plays, demonstrations and classes. An Old Fiddlers Convention is held at Galax near the Blue Ridge Parkway. The Jousting Tournament at Natural Chimneys is the oldest continuous sporting event in America.

*October:* Many of the homes in the Waterford area have been preserved much as they were in the 18th and 19th centuries and are open for tours during the Waterford Homes Tour and Craft Exhibit. The Highland County Fall Foliage Festival celebrates the beauty of the upland hardwood trees. For details write the Chamber of Commerce in Monterey.

*December:* The Christmas Walk in Historic Alexandria takes place in the first days of the month. Christmas in Williamsburg, beginning on the 19th, tries to recapture the spirit of Colonial Christmas.

 **CAMPING OUT.** Camping is permitted at all state parks from April 1 to December 1, except designated natural areas and historic parks. To reserve a campsite or cabin the Virginia State Parks use the Ticketron reservation system. Reservations may be made at any Ticketron office or by mail to Ticketron, Box 62284, Virginia Beach, Va., 23462. There is a charge of $1.50 for each reservation. The Division of Parks, 1201 State Office Building, Richmond 23219, administers the parks and publishes a pamphlet entitled "Open Up!" which describes each park and the facilities offered.

There are camping facilities at the following Parks: *Blue Ridge Parkway, Shenandoah National Park, Prince William Forest Park, George Washington National Forest,* and *Jefferson National Forest.*

 **TRAILER TIPS.** There are more than 300 commercial and 38 publicly owned campgrounds in Virginia. All have dumping stations and all except Longwood at Kerr Reservoir have flush toilets. Almost all have hot showers. Water and electric hookups are available at Natural Chimneys, Breaks Interstate and Gatewood Lake. *Camping in Virginia,* available from the Virginia State Travel Service, 6 North Sixth St., Richmond 23219, has a complete list of commercial and public campgrounds and trailer parks.

  **MUSEUMS AND GALLERIES.** *Richmond: Valentine Museum* reflects the history of Richmond and the life of its people. Source material for a vivid, accurate picture includes more than 20,000 photographs and the third largest costume department in the United States. Open Tues.–Sun.

*White House of the Confederacy* was built in 1817 and occupied by Jefferson Davis during the Civil War. The relics of both the battlefields and the home front give a graphic picture of the war. Open daily.

*Newport News: The Mariners Museum* is superb and ranks with the Peabody Museum in Salem, Mass., and the Whaling Museum at New Bedford. It displays figureheads, boats, ropework, marinescapes, ceramics, nautical and lighthouse equipment. An absorbing show for children. Open daily.

*Big Stone Gap: Southwest Virginia State Museum* contains exhibits tracing the region's history from frontier days to contemporary times. Closed Mon.

**DRINKING LAWS.** In 1968, the state's General Assembly approved liquor-by-the-drink, the most radical change in the Alcoholic Beverage Control laws since their inception in 1934. The provisions permit "qualified establishments," meaning bona fide restaurants, not saloons, to serve mixed alcoholic beverages, subject to local option. Liberalizing of ABC laws apparently has caused no significant changes in the Commonwealth's cultural and social scene. Licensed establishments may serve mixed alcoholic beverages until 2 A.M.; most close at 1 A.M. or earlier. There are 250 ABC stores selling liquor by the package and 9,000 establishments selling beer and wine. Minimum age 21; 18 for beer.

**HOTELS AND MOTELS** in Virginia span a wide range. Generally, accommodations west of the Blue Ridge are less expensive than those in the Piedmont and Tidewater areas. A competitive thrust, now extending along the East Coast to Texas, originated in Virginia with Econo-Travel Motor Hotels. There are more than 40 in that economical chain spread through Virginia.

Williamsburg offers a variety of prices for lodging. The Williamsburg Chamber of Commerce, for instance, will furnish visitors with an approved list of private homes offering rooms at quite moderate prices.

The price categories in this section, for double occupancy, will average as follows: *Deluxe* $35 and up, *Expensive* $25 to $35, *Moderate* $15 to $25, and *Inexpensive* below $15. For a more complete description of these categories see the Hotels and Motels section of *Facts At Your Fingertips*.

## ABINGDON

**MARTHA WASHINGTON INN.** *Inexpensive.* 150 W. Main St. Set back off the main street and opposite the Barter Theatre, this is an old-fashioned inn with a broad veranda. The rooms are furnished with antiques, including four-posters. the buffets in the spacious dining room are famous. Parlors are comfortable, home-like.

## ALEXANDRIA

**Old Town Holiday Inn.** *Deluxe.* 480 King St. Colonial-style luxury hotel in heart of restored area. Indoor pool.

**Best Western Olde Colony.** *Expensive.* First & N. Washington Sts. 18 blks. N of I–95 exits I–E, I–N. Pool. Free continental breakfasts.

**Crystal City Marriott Hotel.** *Expensive.* 1999 Jeff Davis Highway. (US Rt. 1), ZIP 22202.

**The Guest Quarters.** *Expensive.* 100 S. Reynolds St. One- and two-bedroom suites with equipped kitchens. Hotel services.

**Ramada Inn, Old Town.** *Expensive.* 901 N. Fairfax St. Modern high-rise hotel overlooking the Potomac.

**Travelers Motel.** *Moderate.* 5916 Richmond Hwy.

## APPOMATTOX

**Lee-Grant Motel.** *Inexpensive.* RFD 4, US 460. Children and dogs are welcome and there are facilities for entertainment.

**Traveler's Inn.** *Inexpensive.* US 460 near State 24. Attractive, clean rooms.

## BEDFORD

**Peaks of Otter Lodge.** *Expsni.* Blue Ridge Parkway at State 43 above Bedford, at the foot of Flat Top and Sharp Top mountains. Surrounded by national forest, rustic but comfortable. Delicious country-style cooking. Open April–Nov.

## CHARLOTTESVILLE

**Boar's Head Inn.** *Expensive.* 1 mi. W of bypass on US 250. Spendidly designed country inn exudes hill-country charm. Heated pool, trout fishing, tennis, sauna. Old Mill Room has gourmet dishes, including rack of lamb, beef Chateaubriand.

**Best Western Cavalier Inn.** *Moderate.* Intersection of US 29 and 250. Near the Univ. of Va. Pool, Polynesian Room.

**Best Western Mt. Vernon Motel.** *Moderate.* Jct. US 29 and 250 bypass. Quiet, high above the road, overlooking mountains. Fine restaurant. Protected area at rear for pets.

**Holiday Inn–North.** *Moderate.* US 29 & 250 bypass. Convenient to city, one of a complex of excellent accommodations at highway junction.

## DOSWELL

**Best Western Kings Quarters.** *Moderate.* I–95 & Rt. 30. Lodging at Kings Dominion theme park. Low commercial rates off season.

## FREDERICKSBURG

**Ramada Inn.** *Expensive.* I–95 & Rt. 3. Pool and restaurant.

**Sheraton Motor Inn.** *Expensive.* State 3 at I–95. Attractive rooms, balconies or patios. Pool, wading pool, tennis, golf.

**Holiday Inn–South.** *Moderate.* US 1 & I–95. Heated pool, wading pool, kennel. Golf privileges.

**Thunderbird Motor Inn.** *Moderate.* I–95 & Rt. 3E. (2205 Plank Rd.) Restaurant, pool.

## FRONT ROYAL

**Quality Inn.** *Expensive.* On Rt. 522 bypass. Good dining room in addition to usual facilities.

**Shenandoah Motel.** *Moderate.* US 340, 522 & State 55, N of Front Royal.

Excellent family hotel in wooded hills, near northern end of Skyline Dr., Washington, D.C.

## HAMPTON

**Chamberlain.** *Moderate.* Off I–64 to Fort Monroe. Modernized, well-maintained hotel on the waterfront at Hampton Roads. Watch the world's ships glide by. Spacious rooms, terraces. Adjacent to Fort Monroe.

**Strawberry Banks Motor Hotel.** *Moderate.* Adjoining Hampton Roads Bridge Tunnel, on shoreline not far from site of *Monitor-Merrimack* battle.

## HOT SPRINGS

**Cascades Inn.** *Deluxe.* (Up to $56 for dbl. rm.) 3 mi. S of Hot Springs. The Homestead's slightly less expensive relation. Guests at Cascades may use the Homestead's resort facilities.

**Homestead.** *Deluxe.* (Price of double room up to $100 daily.) Rt. 220, Warm Spring Valley. One of America's great resorts. High ceilings, enormous rooms exquisitely furnished. Sports in season: skiing, skeet shooting, fishing in stocked trout stream, tennis, horseback riding, carriage drives along woodland roads, golfing on three 18-hole courses. Dance orchestra and movies every night.

## LEXINGTON

**Holiday Inn.** *Moderate.* Routes I–64 and I–81 at US 11.

**Howard Johnson.** *Moderate.* Routes I–64 and I–81 at US 11.

**Keydet-General Motel.** *Moderate.* US 60 west. Splendid mountain panorama, comfortable surroundings.

**Lexington Motel.** *Moderate.* US 11A & US 11. Within easy distance of Washington and Lee University, VMI and the George Marshall Reserach Library.

## LURAY

**Luray Caverns Motels.** *Moderate.* Motels on US Rt. 211 north and south, both near Luray Caverns.

**Mimslyn Motor Inn.** *Moderate.* W. Main St. A gracious inn used by local residents for entertaining. Pool, rec. rm. Small pets on leash.

## MANASSAS

**Olde Towne Inn Motor Lodge.** *Moderate.* On State 28, Center & Main Sts. Dining room, pool.

## MARION

**Holiday Inn.** *Moderate.* Exit 17 off I–81, Jct. of US 11 east.

**Ramada Inn.** *Moderate.* Exit 17 off I–81, Jct. of US 11 east.

## NATURAL BRIDGE

**Natural Bridge Hotel and Motor Inn.** *Moderate.* On US 11 at the famed natural wonder. Gracious, modern hotel has replaced classic structure which burned. The bridge is still there.

## NEW MARKET

**Quality Inn.** *Moderate.* I–81 at exit 67.

**Shenvallee Lodge.** *Moderate.* I–81 exit 67. Golf and other resort facilities.

## NEWPORT NEWS

**King James Motor Hotel.** *Moderate.* James River Bridge Circle and Jefferson Ave. All hotel services. Handy to Mariner's Museum.

## NORFOLK

**Omni International Hotel.** *Expensive.* 777 Waterfront Drive. Norfolk's newest showplace. First class in every respect.

**Quality Inn–Lake Wright.** *Moderate.* On US 13 at 6280 Northampton Blvd. ½ mile E of Jct. I–64: 6 mi. S of Chesapeake Bay Bridge-Tunnel. Pool. Playground. Tennis. Airport transportation.

## PETERSBURG

**Best Western America House Motor Inn.** *Moderate.* 405 E. Washington St. Comfortable, colorful. Traditional decor.

**Holiday Inn.** *Moderate.* I–95 at Washington St., at exit 3.

**Ramada Inn.** *Moderate.* I–95 Exit 3. Pool restaurant, 1 mile from Ft. Lee.

## RICHMOND

**Hotel John Marshall.** *Expensive.* Franklin & 5th Sts. Located within a half block of Richmond department stores and shops.

**Richmond Hyatt House.** *Expensive.* W. Broad at I–64. A fine new hotel; indoor and outdoor pools.

**HOTEL JEFFERSON.** *Moderate.* Jefferson & Main Sts. The grand dame of Richmond hostelries has been modernized to include such amenities as ample parking and yet retains its Victorian elegance.

**Econo-Travel Motor Hotels.** *Inexpensive.* 3 locations: 5408 Williamsburg Rd. at Byrd Airport entrance; 6523 Midlothian Turnpike; and I–95 at Willis Rd. exit.

## ROANOKE

**ROANOKE HOTEL.** *Expensive.* Wells Ave. & Williamson Rd. A handsome, rambling structure in Old English decor set on high, spacious, landscaped grounds within easy walking distance of the center of downtown. Heated indoor pool.

**Econo-Travel Motor Hotels.** *Inexpensive.* 6221 Thirlane Ave. (I–581 & Peters Creek Rd.), and at 3816 Franklin Rd. (Intersection US 220 & Rt. 419 across from Tanglewood Mall.)

## WINCHESTER

**Best Western Lee-Jackson Motor Inn.** *Moderate.* East on Rt. 50. Exit 80 from I–81. Pool, restaurant.

**The Elms Motel.** *Moderate.* S on US 11. Pool, dining room.

## YORKTOWN

**Duke of York Motel.** *Moderate.* Yorktown waterfront at Ballard Street.

**Traveler's Motel.** *Inexpensive.* 3 mi. S of Yorktown on US 17, 20 minutes from Williamsburg.

**Yorktown Motor Lodge.** *Inexpensive.* 3 mi. S on US 17. Offers room service, room phones, and a pool. Restaurant adj. Excellent lodgings.

 **DINING OUT** in Virginia can be as varied as the state's geography. US 460, from Petersburg to Suffolk, runs through peanut-and-ham country in Southside Virginia. It's as if the traveler is passing a smorgasbord all the way. On the coast, around Norfolk, Newport News, Northern Neck, and Eastern Shore, fresh seafood abounds. On the Peninsula, Colonial Williamsburg's seven dining facilities set an unflagging standard. The urban areas of Richmond and northern Virginia stimulate fine cuisine. In unpretentious places in southwest Virginia, old-style Southern cooking is at its best— and at its best, it's unbeatable. Restaurant price categories are as follows: *Deluxe* $9–$12.50, *Expensive* $6.50–$9, *Moderate* $4–$6.50, *Inexpensive* under $4.

## ALEXANDRIA

**GADSBY'S TAVERN.** *Expensive.* 130 N. Royal St. Historic restored tavern of the Colonial period. Seafood and Southern specialties.

## BIG STONE GAP

**Terminal Cafe.** *Inexpensive.* E. 5th St. just off US 23. Table cloths, home-style cooking (chicken and dumplings, country fried steak and gravy, country ham) at amazingly low prices. Open 7 A.M. to 10 P.M.

## CHARLOTTESVILLE

**MICHIE TAVERN.** *Inexpensive.* Rte. 53, ½ mile below Jefferson's Monticello. Rustic structure was operated by Patrick Henry's father. One basic, tasty menu: Colonial fried chicken, black-eyed peas, stewed tomatoes, cornbread and biscuits, choice of 4 salads. Dining room open 11 A.M. to 3 P.M. every day except Christmas, New Year's Day.

## CLARKSVILLE

**Roberts Restaurant.** *Moderate.* Virginia Ave. at 2nd St. on US 58, specializing in fried chicken, country ham, steak. Offers children's plates. Closed Dec. 24–25.

## HANOVER

**HANOVER TAVERN.** *Moderate.* Rt. 301. Dining and dinner theater in historic stagecoach stop that catered to colonial leaders. Country dinners featured.

## LEESBURG

**LAUREL BRIGADE INN.** *Expensive.* Rt. 7. Southern specialties. Parts of Inn date from 1766. Also modest rooms at low prices.

## McLEAN

**EVANS FARM INN.** *Moderate.* 1696 Chain Bridge Road, State 123. Ample servings of Southern cooking.

## MIDDLEBURG

**RED FOX TAVERN.** *Expensive.* US 50, in the middle of the hunt country, a haunt for those who ride to the hounds. Restored building (c. 1728). Open weekdays 8 A.M. to 8:30 P.M.; Sun., 8 A.M. to 7:30. Closed Mon.

## SMITHFIELD

**Smithfield Inn.** *Moderate.* 112 Main St. Southern cooking featuring, of course, Smithfield ham and fried chicken. Homemade pies and cobblers. Lunch and dinner.

## WOODBRIDGE

**LAZY SUSAN INN.** *Moderate.* I–95 Woodbridge exit. Antique fire engines outside delight children. Lazy Susans on each table offer home-made jams. Salad bar features 15 items. Closed Mon.

# WASHINGTON, D.C.

## *The Cockpit of the Union*

### by
### KATHARINE D. WALKER

*Mrs. Walker is co-author with her husband of* The Walker Washington Guide.

With the beginning of the Civil War, Washington became the nerve center of the Northern war effort and the goal of the Confederate armies. Its streets swarmed with politicians, soldiers, camp followers and fugitives.

By late June of 1861 over 50,000 volunteers were stationed in and around the capital. On July 21 of that year, many of the troops stationed in the District set off toward Manassas and the creek called Bull Run. Residents of Washington could hear the rumble of the cannons thirty miles away. Congressmen and their wives set out in carriages to picnic near the scene of the battle "to watch the Union triumph." They returned in a panic, followed at dawn on the 22nd by exhausted soldiers struggling back to the city on foot. Carts filled with wounded men jolted through the streets. People turned their houses into nursing homes and the government commandeered buildings. (Later battles were to fill half the federal office buildings with the wounded.) The newly organized Sanitary Commission rushed supplies to hastily improvised hospitals, women volunteered as nurses, and grisly amputations were performed by Army surgeons.

Between the first battle of Bull Run and the end of the war, thousands of soldiers died of wounds, dysentery and typhoid fever in military hospitals within sight of the Capitol. In the passageways of the huge Patent Office Building (now the National Collection of Fine Arts), wounded men lay side by side in passageways between glass cases filled with miniature models of inventions. They lay in the halls of the Capitol, in churches and at the Insane Asylum. At night the dead were carried in carts to Oak Hill Cemetery in Georgetown (to this day a spot of tranquil beauty), Mt. Olivet Cemetery, or Arlington Cemetery. Dedicated in June 1864, Arlington Cemetery became the final resting place for both Confederate and Union soldiers. Visitors to Arlington House today may view the home of General Robert E. Lee and the many Civil War graves on the hills to the south of the Mansion.

Washington was threatened repeatedly by direct assault and by encirclement. By 1862 forty-eight forts ringed the District. In the summer of 1864 General Jubal Early and a force of 19,000 Confederate soldiers marched through Silver Spring, Maryland, and drove to Fort Stevens, just five miles above Boundary Street. Union forces held and repulsed the Confederates, but a small national cemetery on the spot today shows how deep was the penetration.

Present-day visitors to the city may have a hard time envisioning war-time Washington. Cattle pens and a slaughter house were set up on the Washington Monument grounds. (The monument itself was a mere stub rising above the tidal marshes that surrounded it.) Foggy Bottom, the area now occupied by the Kennedy Center and the Watergate Hotel, was filled with corrals for 30,000 horses and mules. The unfinished Corcoran Gallery of Art (now the Renwick Gallery) was commandeered by Quartermaster General Montgomery C. Meigs for his headquarters. From Giesboro Point, now part of the Air Force's Bolling Field, over 21,000 tons of forage were shipped monthly to the Army of the Potomac. Across the Mall, railroad tracks had been laid, and more than 30,000 loaded cars carried supplies to the Army in northern Virginia. The smells, due to lack of sanitation, were appalling. The hotels did a land office business, with five hundred new arrivals a day not unusual. Contractors, men seeking special favors, men and women seeking wounded relatives poured into the city.

As the war progressed, skyrocketing price and inflation gripped Washington. Killings were made in real estate, and saddlers, blacksmiths, suppliers of mattresses and bedsteads, tailors and stationers were enriched by the demand for their goods and services. Common laborers, people on salaries, and families whose income had derived from the South or the hire of their slaves faced real financial hardships.

Joseph Henry, the first great American scientist after Benjamin

Franklin and the first secretary of the Smithsonian Institution, contributed his knowledge of gases, meteorology and wind currents by helping the aeronauts of the Army observation balloon corps. As one of Lincoln's chief technical advisers during the war, he maintained his offices in the original Smithsonian building, the Red Castle on the Mall, still a Washington landmark. The Army Medical Library and Museum had their start from the records and statistics compiled by officers of the Medical Corps. Today both the Medical Library in Bethesda, Maryland and the Medical Museum on the grounds of Walter Reed Army Hospital are open to the public.

### Statues and Monuments

The Capitol today bears little resemblance to the building whose basement served as an Army bakery during the war years. In the Rotunda, the Massachusetts Eighth Regiment was encamped. The 19½-foot-high statue of *Freedom* by Thomas Crawford was erected atop the newly completed iron dome on December, 1863, in the hope that the ceremony would provide inspiration for dispirited Union troops. The plaster mold of *Freedom* was prepared in Italy, shipped to the United States, and cast in bronze in Bladensburg, Maryland, ironically, by slave labor. Visitors to the Rotunda today will note with interest the standing figure of Lincoln sculpted by Vinnie Ream Hoxie, a talented 17-year-old girl who was invited by President Lincoln to come to his White House office to model his portrait in clay. For five months she worked on the portrait, finishing it on the afternoon of April 14, 1865, just a few hours before Lincoln left for Ford's Theatre. Two years later Congress awarded her a $10,000 contract for the memorial you see in the Capitol. This was the first art contract awarded to a woman by the Federal government, and it caused a national uproar. The monument to Admiral David Farragut—"Damn the torpedoes! Full speed ahead!"—was commissioned by the Admiral's widow and graces Farragut Square. It was the first monument erected in Washington to a naval war hero.

The importance of the Civil War in the life of the city is obvious today in the great number of memorials, mostly bronze statues of Union generals on horseback. Thomas Circle, Logan Circle, Scott Circle, and many other small parks, each has its equestrian statue (generally with pigeons upon it). Less imposing and rarely seen by tourists is the statue of a life-size Lincoln in Lincoln Park, East Capitol and 11th Streets N.E., bidding a slave rise to freedom. Known as the *Emancipation Monument,* it was erected by the Western Sanitary Commission of St. Louis from funds contributed by emancipated slaves.

The Pension Building at 4th and F Streets N.W. was designed by Lincoln's quartermaster general, Meigs, in 1882, and was inspired by the sixteenth century Palazzo Farnese in Rome. It was to be used to disburse pensions to Civil War veterans. The frieze running continuously around the building is 3 feet high and 1,200 feet long, and depicts naval, infantry, cavalry, artillery and medical units on active duty. Not far away, at the foot of Capitol Hill at the east end of the Mall, is the Grant Memorial, amongst the most important sculptures in the city. The sculptor, Henry Merwin Shrady, took 20 years to complete the memorial, which includes a centrally-located equestrian statue of General Grant astride his charger "Cincinnatus," with two sculpture groups of military figures at each end of the 252-foot-long marble platform. The sculptor died two weeks before the dedication of the monument on April 27, 1922, the centennial of Grant's birth.

Although Washington may have mixed feelings about these various generals and their memorials, there is a very special feeling, one shared by the rest of the country, about the Civil War president, whose determination and wisdom and compassion is a bequest. The long shadow of Abraham Lincoln would remain even without the magnificent memorial erected in his memory.

Visiting the Lincoln Memorial is to many the greatest emotional experience of visiting the city. It was brilliantly conceived, built and located. Neither a tomb nor a shrine in the religious sense, it is considered by many to be the most eloquently moving memorial erected in memory of any man. Its architect was Henry Bacon.

In the massive statue by Daniel Chester French, Lincoln is seated looking out over the city's great Mall, past the spire of the Washington Monument and the long reflecting pools to the Capitol building, two miles away.

The Lincoln Memorial attracts almost as many visitors at night as in the daytime. Whenever it is open, you will find visitors, from many lands and of many ages, reading the words of two of his greatest speeches carved on the walls of the chamber, the Gettysburg Address and the Second Inaugural Address.

Carved above the statue itself are the words:

"In this temple, as in the hearts of the people for whom he saved the Union, the memory of Abraham Lincoln is enshrined forever."

About the Lincoln Memorial, Roger Angell wrote of the "tired, infinitely distant eyes" of Lincoln and of the "great hands" and of "the soft light falling through the marble ceiling." A good time to visit the Memorial is at night when it is floodlighted. After enjoying the view toward the Capitol, walk along the portico toward the Potomac River and Arlington Memorial Bridge. In a direct line you will see Arlington House, formerly the Custis-Lee Mansion, the plantation home of Robert E. Lee. Directly below the hilltop home is the eternal flame, visible at night, marking the grave of President Kennedy.

## PRACTICAL INFORMATION FOR WASHINGTON D.C.

**TOURIST INFORMATION SERVICES.** Contact the Washington Area Convention and Visitors Association, 1129 20th St., N.W., Washington, D.C. 20036 (tel. (202) 857-5500) for pamphlets and brochures on hotels, motels and sightseeing here and in the environs.

Visitors arriving by train will find comprehensive visitors information at the National Visitor Center located in Union Station, Massachusetts and Delaware Aves.; open 7 days a week from 9:30 to 5:30. Facilities include Traveler's Aid, the National Book Store, a fast food restaurant, language assistance by telephone for international visitors, and a Gift Shop with native American handicrafts. The Metro subway and the Tourmobile both serve the Center.

Foreign visitors may receive help from IVIS, the International Visitors Information Service, 801 19th St., N.W. (tel. (202) 872-8747), just a few blocks from the White House. Open from 9 to 5, Monday through Friday, IVIS distributes free maps in foreign languages and a few multilingual brochures. IVIS also maintains a Language Bank and serves as the Washington coordinator of the Americans-at-Home program.

At the Gateway Tour Center, 4th and E Sts., S.W. (tel. (202) USA-0000) visitors arriving by car may park their car for the day and use a free shuttle to the Mall where the Tourmobile stops. Other facilities at the Center include an official information center, a cafeteria, gift shop, Wax Museum, and a film. Open 7 days a week.

The Public Visitors Center, a Ralph Nader organization, provides tourists with calendars and information on what is going on in Washington, with emphasis on Congressional hearings and meetings open to the public. Located at 1200 15th St., N.W. (tel. (202) 659-9053) the Center will arrange walking tours of Capitol Hill for a small fee.

Detailed information on movies, theater, sports and cultural events is carried in the *Washington Post's* "Weekend" supplement on Friday, and the *Washington Star's* Sunday "Calendar."

Especially helpful is the *Washingtonian* magazine, published monthly ($1.75) and available at newsstands. In its "Where and When" section may be found all you want to know about current happenings in the capital.

 **THE SEASONS.** If you are free to plan your trip at any time of year, consider the advantages of visiting Washington in fall or winter. With the first crocus, buses from Keokuk to Kalamazoo disgorge their loads of eager high school students, and this state of affairs continues until early June. Summer brings family groups, long lines, hot weather, and a wealth of things to do. With Labor Day, the natives return and the city gets back to normal. Washington's fall is justifiably famous, with day after day of mild, sunny weather often lasting well into November. Winters are passable, with few snowy or bitterly cold days.

Memorial Day at Arlington National Cemetery is marked by special services at the Amphitheater. The President (or his representative) lays a wreath at the Tomb of the Unknowns, and each grave in the cemetery is decorated by a flag placed there by volunteer groups.

*July 4.* Spectacular display of fireworks erupts on the grounds of the Washington Monument.

 **MUSEUMS AND GALLERIES.** *National Collection of Fine Arts and National Portrait Gallery. 8th and G Sts., N.W. 628-4422.* Open daily 10 A.M.-5:30 P.M. Free. This handsome edifice was once the Old Patent Office Building, served as a barracks, hospital and morgue during the Civil War, and was saved by Congress from the wrecker's ball a few years ago for eventual use as a downtown parking lot! Built in 1837, the building was designed by the famous architect, Robert Mills, whose Washington Monument and Treasury Building are better known. The Lincoln Gallery on the third floor was the scene of Lincoln's Second Inaugural Ball. Especially noteworthy are the 445 paintings of George Catlin's Indian Gallery, the "Art: U.S.A." collection of S.C. Johnson and Son, Inc., and the always outstanding special exhibits. Lunch is served at the cafeteria, Patent Pending, and may be eaten out-of-doors in the warm weather in the stunning inner courtyard. You may ride (free) a red London double-decker bus which shuttles back and forth between these museums and the National Museum of History and Technology, 14th St. and Constitution Ave., N.W.

*Truxton-Decatur Naval Museum.* 1610 H. St., N.W. 783-2573. Open every day, 10:30 A.M.-4 P.M.; closed Mon. Exhibits on naval history; prints, models and paintings. Free.

*National Archives.* 8th St. and Constitution Ave., N.W. Open Mon.-Sat., 9 A.M. to 10 P.M.; Sun. and holidays, 1 P.M. to 10 P.M. 523-3000. The Declaration of Independence, the Constitution, and the Bill of Rights handsomely displayed. You are welcome to trace your roots here. Use entrance at 7th St. and Pennsylvania Ave., N.W. Here are stored some of the collection of over 5,000 of Mathew Brady's photographs taken during the Civil War.

*Smithsonian Institution.* Jefferson Dr. betw. 9th and 12th Sts., S.W. Open daily 10 A.M. TO 5:30 P.M., Labor Day to Apr. 1; 10 A.M. to 9 P.M., Apr. 1 to Labor Day. This red castle on the Mall houses the administrative offices of the Smithsonian. Near the entrance is the tomb of James Smithson, an Englishman, who in his 1826 will provided that his entire fortune of $541,379 should go to America to found an Institution bearing his name. 628-4422.

*Museum of History and Technology.* Betw. 12th and 14th Sts., N.W., on Constitution Ave. Imposing new building containing gowns of First Ladies, The Star Spangled Banner, famous inventions, early automobiles, locomotives, stamps; cultural and technological development of the United States from Colonial times. Cafeteria (lunch served Sept. through Mar.; lunch and dinner, Apr. through Aug.).

*Museum of Natural History.* 10th St. and Constitution Ave., N.W. Hall of Dinosaurs, Hall of Gems (see the Hope Diamond).

*Renwick Gallery.* 17th St. and Pennsylvania Ave., N.W. Near White House. Victorian building filled with Americana. This was Washington's first art gallery. A gift to the city by William Wilson Corcoran, the building was unfinished when the Civil War broke out. Montgomery Meigs, Lincoln's Quartermaster General, used it for his headuqarters.

A final suggestion would be a visit to *Ford's Theatre,* 511 10th St., N.W., open daily 9 A.M.-5 P.M., to see the restored playhouse where John Wilkes Booth shot President Lincoln on April 14, 1865. (During the season live performances are given evenings and some afternoons; hours for visiting theater restricted.) The *Lincoln Museum* exhibits material relevant to Lincoln's life and presidency. Across the street at the *Petersen House,* 516 10th St., N.W. (open same hours), you will see the small bedroom where Lincoln died. Lincoln admirers will want to visit the New York Avenue Presbyterian Church, 1313 New York Ave., N.W., sometimes referred to as *"The Lincoln Church."*

**TOURS.** The tour's the thing for the more than 50 sightseeing companies whose concern is the patronage of Washington's 20 million annual visitors. The larger companies, *D.C. Transit, Gray Line, White House and Blue Line,* amongst others, will pick you up at your hotel or motel 30 minutes before the scheduled time of your tour's departure, and return you without extra charge.

Half-day tours include a drive around downtown Washington, and viewing from the outside the principal monuments and Government buildings. An all-day tour might in addition include Alexandria, Mount Vernon, and Arlington Cemetery. If your group contains about forty members (a full bus) consider the advantages of a custom-made tour with museum-trained guides. Write in advance to National Fine Arts Association, 5402 Duval Dr.,Washington, D.C. 20016.

Information on the highly recommended Landmark Service Tourmobiles is presented under *How to Get Around*.

**STAGE AND REVUES.** Theaters are usually open during the entire year. However, it is wise to check the schedule of performances in a newspaper or by phone, as some productions are held over longer or are closed earlier than previously planned.

*Ford's Theatre,* 511 10th St., N.W., has been restored to the way it appeared the night Lincoln was shot in the Presidential box, April 14, 1865. Plays with family appeal are emphasized. Check for summer opening.

**DRINKING LAWS.** Liquor is sold in package stores from 10 A.M. to 9 P.M., Mon. to Fri., until midnight on Saturday, never on Sunday. In restaurants it is served from 8 A.M. to 2 A.M., Mon. to Thurs.; 8 A.M. to 3 A.M., Fri. and Sat.; 10 A.M. to 2 A.M., Sunday. The legal drinking age is 18 for beer and wine; 21 for hard liquor. Proof of age in the form of a driver's license is usually required. Beer may be bought in grocery stores.

**HINTS FOR THE HANDICAPPED.** *Access Washington: A Guide to Metropolitan Washington for the Physically Disabled* may be obtained free of charge by writing to the District of Columbia Society for Crippled Children, 2800 13th Street. N.W., Washington, D.C. 20009, or by calling AD 2-2342. The Handicapped Visitor Services Booth at the National Visitors Center in Union Station, 50 Massachusetts Ave., N.E., is open 7 days a week.

**HOTELS AND MOTELS.** With more than 20 million visitors to Washington each year, tourism has become the capital's principal industry. Even with new facilities opening each month, particularly in the suburbs of Maryland and Virginia, demand for hotel space often exceeds space available. Be sure to write or phone in advance for confirmed reservations.

Downtown in the District of Columbia is where the majority of hotels are located. Some of them were built many years ago and show the signs of old age, but many are undergoing face-lifts. For this reason it is difficult to rate some of the accommodations, as they will vary considerably from room to room. In this motor age, many will prefer staying at a motel, usually found in the suburbs, though a few have been built in the downtown area. Motels have been listed at all the major approaches to the city—the south through Alexandria, Virginia, the west through Fairfax, Falls Church and Arlington, Virginia, the north through Bethesda and Silver Spring, and the northeast from the Baltimore-Washington expressway. None of the motels listed is more than 35 minutes by car from downtown Washington.

Double-occupancy lodgings in Washington are categorized as follows: *Deluxe* $60 and higher; *Expensive* $50-$60; *Moderate* $40-$50; *Inexpensive,* under $30.

**Hay-Adams.** *Deluxe.* 16th and H Sts., N.W. 20006. Has the finest location of all—overlooking Lafayette Park and the White House. An older hotel of quiet distinction, with a paneled lobby, dignified Tudor dining room and well-appointed rooms. Visit the President Adams Room; piano bar.

**Sheraton Carlton.** *Deluxe.* 16th and K St., N.W. An elegant old hotel recently restored to its original gracious atmosphere.

**Georgetown Inn.** *Expensive.* 1310 Wisconsin Ave., N.W. Southern charm, beautifully appointed rooms and good restaurants. In the heart of Georgetown's busiest street.

**Jefferson.** *Expensive.* 1200 16th St., N.W. An older, well-established hotel not far from the White House. Smallish, semi-residential, with European atmosphere. Lacks some amenities.

**Mayflower.** *Expensive.* 1127 Connecticut Ave., N.W. A Washington landmark in downtown area.

**The Gralyn.** *Moderate.* 1745 N St., N.W. A small (34-room) inn on a pretty, tree-lined street near Dupont Circle. Lots of atmosphere and charm; some rooms without bath. A converted 4-story house which once served as the Persian Embassy.

**Hotel Washington.** *Moderate.* 15th and Pennsylvania Ave., N.W. One of the city's older, large hotels with good restaurants and an incomparable location near White House; every parade passes here. Roof garden in summer with fine view of lighted monuments at night.

 **DINING OUT** in Washington can be as educational as it is fun. In the past few years the number of fine restaurants has increased tremendously, with an ever-growing variety of cuisines serving authentic dishes from Europe, Asia and Latin America. There is good dining-out for the "steak and chops" types, or the more experimental visitor who would prefer to try Indian or Middle-Eastern food. Whatever your taste in food, whether your purse is fat or lean, *bon appetit.*

For mid-priced dinners on each menu, the following categories apply: *Deluxe* $15-$20, *Expensive* $10-$15, *Moderate* $8-$10, and *Inexpensive* under $6. Prices are for a complete dinner including soup, entreé and dessert.

**1789.** *Deluxe.* This English-style cottage is nestled among the row houses of Georgetown. The house is divided into several distinctive dining areas, each decorated with Civil War prints and posters, and our favorite is the room with the fireplace. The establishment has recently received a new wave of publicity from its use as one of the locations in the film "The Exorcist." The French dishes are beautifully prepared and elegantly served. 1226 36th Street N.W.

**EVANS FARM INN.** *Expensive.* The seven mile drive to McLean, Va. is well worth the trip. Distinctively American dishes, such as Plantation Chicken, roast duckling, Spoon Bread, and many others are served by waiters in colonial costumes. 1696 Chain Bridge Road (McClean, Va.).

**W. H. BONE CO., INC.** *Expensive.* 401 M St., S.W. The only true Southern restaurant in the city. Ribs, Southern fried chicken and even chittlins. Music; open late.

**JOUR ET NUIT.** *Moderate.* 1204 30th St., N.W. In this delightful old Georgetown house, good French foods are served. Especially pleasant in summer.

**LA CHAUMIERE.** *Moderate.* 2813 M St., N.W. A restaurant with the charm of a rustic country inn; robust French food.

**NATHAN'S.** *Moderate.* 3150 M St., N.W. The dining room behind the bar serves some of the best Northern Italian food in town. Lots of "old Georgetown" atmosphere.

**Old Europe.** *Moderate.* 2434 Wisconsin Ave., N.W. This somewhat schmaltzy restaurant has all the old German favorites including Wiener Schnitzel, sauerbraten, and wursts. First rate German wines.

**Piccadilly.** *Moderate.* 5510 Connecticut Ave., N.W. A pleasant neighborhood restaurant offering traditional dishes from the British Isles. Outdoor cafe in summer.

**IRON GATE INN.** *Inexpensive.* 1734 N St., N.W. Middle Eastern cuisine in a restaurant with notable ancestry: a stable. On a quiet street off Dupont Plaza. Eat in a small courtyard under a grape arbor in summer.

**OLD EBBIT GRILL.** *Inexpensive.* 1427 F St., N.W. A real saloon that's been at this same location since before the Civil War. Good food. Open for lunch and late dinner (fine for after the theater). In heart of downtown.

**Patent Pending.** *Inexpensive.* In National Collection of Fine Arts and National Portrait Gallery Building. Sightseers appreciate this unusual cafeteria and the opportunity to eat in the courtyard in the warm weather.

**Au Pied Du Cochon.** *Inexpensive.* 1329 Wisconsin Ave., N.W. Lots of activity in this French bistro with a limited, but filling, menu.

# WEST VIRGINIA

## Born of the Civil War

### by
### JUSTIN H. FAHERTY

*Mr. Faherty is a former executive of the St. Louis* Globe-Democrat, *the New York* Herald Tribune, *and the Bergen (N.J.)* Record. *He has written for newspapers on all 50 of the United States.*

When the Civil War started, the state of Virginia extended from the Potomac River, Chesapeake Bay, and the Atlantic Ocean, northward and westward to the Ohio River and to the borders of Pennsylvania, Ohio, and a long stretch of Kentucky. It was great in size, a leader in historic enterprise, and a place of singular beauty.

Sweeping diagonally across the midriff of the state are the Allegheny Mountains. Eighty years before the Civil War, the people west of these mountains wanted to separate from the state. Their reasons included the facts that the trade interest of the two sections differed, the taxes levied by the eastern-controlled government were considered unfair, and political injustices were felt to have been imposed by the eastern majority. Beyond this, there was a difference in temperament—a new kind of thinking, a different breed of men had grown up in the western mountains. They were bold and adventurous, and as rugged and fierce as the terrain in which they lived.

West Virginia played a prominent part in the Civil War. John Brown, leading a band of 22 men, attempted to take Harper's Ferry in 1859, but was captured two days later by Robert E. Lee, then a colonel in the U.S. Army.

The first land battle of the war was fought in West Virginia on June 3, 1861, when Gen. George McClellan, leading a force out of Ohio, defeated a Confederate unit at Philippi. A month later McClellan's Union forces again defeated the Confederates at Rich Mountain and Carrick's Ford. These victories assuaged the humiliating loss at Bull Run and led to McClellan's appointment as leader of the Army of the Potomac.

During the summer of 1861, Union troops fought their way up the Kanawha River, on foot and by boat, and established a base at Gauley Bridge. Battles here and at Carnifex Ferry, assured U.S. control of the western portion of Virginia. Skirmishes continued throughout the war. Romney was the scene of 56 minor battles, Keyser changed hands 14 times.

The new state of West Virginia was created during the war, in 1863, with boundary projections running north to Wheeling and northwest to Harper's Ferry. Visits to the major sites and points of interest associated with the war will supply valuable material for the Civil War buff.

A good place to begin a tour is Harper's Ferry. It is the easternmost town in the state and is situated on US 340 in the clawlike appendage at the north of the panhandle. The town has old stone and brick houses and narrow streets; it is in the process of being restored to the way it looked in 1859 when John Brown's raiders seized the arsenal and demonstrated their antipathy to slavery. Those captured, including Brown, were hanged. Harper's Ferry is now a National Historical Park, with a Visitor Center open from March through November. John Brown's Civil War Showcase and the John Brown Wax Museum are open year-round. On a nearby hillside stands the mansion of the founder of the town, Robert Harper, and beyond it are the ruins of St. John's Episcopal Church, with trees growing up through the nave.

The area around Harper's Ferry is extraordinarily beautiful—Thomas Jefferson was one of its most ardent admirers—and from a vantage point above the town the Potomac and Shenandoah rivers can be seen flowing together near the place where Virginia, Maryland, and West Virginia meet. Contact the Appalachian Trail Conference in Harper's Ferry for hiking information. Another point of interest in the town is the Harper's Ferry Cavern, with two levels, two waterfalls, and two lakes, one of which is bridged.

Charles Town, eight miles to the southwest, was named after Charles Washington, George's brother. Charles Town is noted for its thoroughbred horseracing and stately mansions. It was here that John Brown was tried for treason. Two miles west of town are the ruins of St. George's Chapel, where George Washington worshipped. Charles Town has its Mountain Heritage Arts and Crafts Festival in June and an Annual House and Garden Tour in the spring. South of Charles Town is Bunker Hill, where Morgan Morgan built the first permanent home in what is now West Virginia.

Organ Cave, one of the largest in the United States, was discovered in 1704. It was visited by Jefferson in 1778 and was used by Robert E. Lee as a refuge during the Civil War.

To the east of Clarksburg on US 50s Grafton, where West Virginia's only National Cemetery is located. Bailey Brown, the first Union soldier to be killed in the Civil War, is buried there.

## PRACTICAL INFORMATION FOR WEST VIRGINIA

**WEST VIRGINIA FACTS AND FIGURES.** The state takes its name from Virginia, of which it was a part until the Civil War, when West Virginians sided with the North and broke away from the mother state. It was the 35th state to enter the Union, joining on June 30, 1863. Its nicknames are *Mountain State* and *Panhandle State*. The state flower is the *Rhododendron maximum* (big laurel); tree, sugar maple; bird, the cardinal; animal, the black bear. The state motto is *Montani Semper Liberi* ("Mountaineers are always free").

Charleston is the state capital. The average altitude is 1,500 feet, higher than any other state east of the Mississippi. The Allegheny Mountains, part of the Appalachian chain, stretch the length of the state and are the oldest in the world. This is the most mountainous state in the East and its landscape is deeply folded where swift rivers have cut valleys and canyons between the hills. The climate is moderate—not too cold in winter, not too hot in summer—but this is the rainiest of the Middle Atlantic states.

**HOW TO GET AROUND.** *By car:* Wheeling, in the northern panhandle, is on I–70 between Washington, Pennsylvania and Martins Ferry, Ohio. I–79 runs north-south from Pittsburgh through Morgantown and Clarksburg, with traffic flowing into I–64 and I–77 at Charleston. I–64 carries traffic east-west from Huntington to White Sulphur Springs (portions are not yet completed). I–77 carries traffic from Parkersburg southeast through East Mountain tunnel at Bluefield. From Charleston to Princeton for the present it is incorporated into the West Virginia Turnpike running between Bluefield and Charleston. I–81 will take you to Martinsburg in the eastern panhandle.

*By air:* There are regularly scheduled flights to Charleston, Morgantown, Elkins, White Sulphur Springs, Beckley, Princeton, Huntington, and Parkersburg. *Piedmont, Allegheny* and *United* are the carriers.

*By bus: Trailways, Greyhound, Black and White,* and *Short Way* are the major carriers in West Virginia. Charleston and Huntington are the busiest depots.

*By train:* Amtrak has service to Charleston, Huntington, Harpers Ferry, Martinsburg and Cumberland, Maryland, on the border of the West Virginia's eastern panhandle.

**TOURIST INFORMATION.** For maps, calendars of events, or any questions, you might write the Office of Economic and Community Development, State Capitol, Charleston 25305. The phone number is (304) 348-2286, or the toll-free number east of the Rockies, 1-800-624-9110.

**STATE PARKS.** West Virginia has 34 state parks. Accommodations for visitors include lodges at some parks and deluxe, standard, economy and rustic cabins. All the cabins have refrigerators and stoves but "rustic" cabins do not have running water. Deluxe cabins have heat, others have fireplaces. Reservations for all must be made in advance. For lodges, write directly to lodge offices. For cabins, write to *Division of Parks and Recreation* of the West Virginia Natural Resources Department in Charleston. You can call toll free from Indiana, Ohio, Kentucky, Pennsylvania, western New York, Maryland, Virginia, New Jersey, Delaware, North Carolina, South Carolina, and Washington, D.C.; the number is 1-800-624-8632. West Virginia residents call 1-800-642-9058.

**STATE FORESTS.** West Virginia has nine state forests. All offer scenic views, hunting and fishing. Four forests have cabins: *Cabwaylingo,* near Williamson, 13 standard; *Greenbrier,* near White Sulphur Springs, 12 standard; *Kumbrabow,* near Webster Springs, 5 rustic; *Seneca,* near Hillsboro, 7 rustic. Tent and trailer camping is permitted at all except *Calvin W. Price,* which adjoins *Watago State Park.* Winter sports (ice skating and skiing) are offered at *Coopers Rock,* near Morgantown. Visitors may rent horses near *Greenbrier. Camp Creek* has the best stocked trout stream in its area, near Princeton. Pre-Revolutionary ruins of iron furnaces and a powder mill may be seen at *Coopers Rock.* Featured at *Kanawha* are outstanding wildflower exhibitions in backwoods atmosphere, and many migratory birds may be seen. *Panther* is rich in legends of the panthers which roamed this forest 135 years ago, and it is said their howls still echo with the wind.

**HOTELS AND MOTELS** in West Virginia run the gamut from elegant resorts with spacious grounds and superb service to small, family-owned establishments which take great pride in providing the comforts and wholesome home cooking.

The price categories in this section, for double occupancy, will average as follows: *Deluxe* $30 and up, *Expensive* $20-30, *Moderate* $15-$20 and *Inexpensive* below $15.

## BECKLEY

**Ramada Inn.** *Deluxe.*

**Best Western Motor Lodge, Holiday Inn, Honey in the Rock Inn,** all *Expensive.*

**Charles House,** *Moderate.*

## CLARKSBURG

**Sheraton.** *Expensive.* 151 W. Main St. Six stories with an elevator, heated pool, coffee shop, restaurant, doctor on call, direct-dial phones. Pets OK.

**Stonewall Jackson Hotel.** *Moderate.* 215 S. 3rd St. Coffee shop, restaurant and room phones in a large, well-maintained establishment.

**Colonial Court.** *Inexpensive.* E on US 50. A small, pleasant motel with a café within a mile.

**Towne House.** *Inexpensive.* A 2-story motel with room phones, café, color TV in lobby and a baby sitter list. Pets OK.

## LEWISBURG

**Antebellum, General Lewis Hotel, Fort Savannah Inn, Old Colony Inn, Sunset Terrace Motel,** all *Moderate,*

## MARTINSBURG

**Holiday Inn,** *Moderate.*

**Motel 81, Wheatland Motel, Windewald Motel,** all *Inexpensive.*

## ROMNEY

**Manorland Post,** *Moderate.*

## WHITE SULPHUR SPRINGS

**The Greenbriar,** old and gracious, *Deluxe.*

**Old White, Colonial Court,** both *Moderate.*

 **DINING OUT** in West Virginia might mean an opportunity to enjoy delicious country-style ham (salt or sugar-cured), Southern specialties like grits or hush puppies, or such staples as steaks, seafood or fried chicken. Decor ranges from very simple in the establishments found along the highway, to the more elaborate dining rooms of the posh resorts.

Restaurant price categories are as follows: *Expensive* $6.00 and up, *Moderate* $4-$5.99, *Inexpensive* below $4.00. These prices are for hors d'ouevres or soup, entree and dessert. Not included are drinks, tax and tips. In order to serve liquor in West Virginia a restaurant must have a club license; those restaurants listed which do have a club license are so indicated.

Restaurants, other than hotel and motel, are in Civil War areas:

**BECKLEY.** *Moderate.* The Char

**LEWISBURG.** *Moderate.* Gen. Lewis Dining Room (ante-bellum).

# INDEX